Christina,
You have
the ability to
change the
world with
your voice.
please use it!
Bessonn Aglowbyo

CHANGE AGENTS

The World's Leading Experts Reveal Their Secrets for Successfully Changing the Status Quo To...
...Help Their Clients Lead BETTER Lives and Run BETTER Businesses

CELEBRITY PRESS®
Winter Park, Florida

CONTENTS

CHAPTER 1

YOU ARE A GENIUS

BY BRIAN TRACY

Your ability to adapt quickly to change and challenge largely determines your success in life and business. As Charles Darwin said, "Survival goes not to the strongest or most intelligent creature, but to the one most adaptable to change."

The good news is that there is no problem you cannot solve, no obstacle you cannot overcome, and no goal that you cannot achieve by unleashing and harnessing the powers of your mind. Fully 95% of the population has the capacity to function at exceptional, even genius levels, and this means you.

Research at the Stanford Brain Institute indicates that the average person uses not 10% of their mental abilities, as has long been thought, but closer to 2%, and in many cases, only 1% of their ability to think.

In his book, *Frames of Mind*, Dr. Howard Garner of Harvard demonstrates that you have seven different kinds of intelligence that you use all the time. However, only two of these intelligences — verbal and mathematical — are ever tested in school.

YOU ARE A NATURAL GENIUS

Einstein said, "Every child is born a genius." The fact is that you are probably a genius, right now, and you don't even know it. If you are like most people, the very idea of having the ability to function at genius levels is something you have probably never considered. Even if you have come up with some great ideas in the past, you have probably dismissed them quickly as being lucky events, or flukes that don't really disprove the facts that you only have average intelligence.

Let's do an experiment. When scientists come up with a bright idea, they engage in an exercise called "Hypothesis Testing." What this means is that they create a statement that is *opposite* to their new idea, and then attempt to prove that statement. If they are unable to prove that the opposite is true, it proves, by extension, that their original idea is correct.

For example, in the early days of research into subsonic and supersonic jet travel, the hypothesis was that no plane could travel faster than the speed of sound without disintegrating in the air. So the engineers and scientists went to work to disprove this hypothesis, which they did, when Chuck Jaeger broke the sound barrier for the first time at a test site in California.

ASSUME THAT YOU ARE A GENIUS

For our purposes, let us assume that you are a genius. The hypothesis you can test is that "You are *not* a genius." In an attempt to disprove this negative hypothesis, you will start thinking and acting like a genius. And I promise you this; when you begin to talk, think and behave the way that people of exceptional intelligence do, you will begin to get the same results. You may even surprise yourself. At the very least, you will unleash a flood of creative ideas that you can use to solve your problems, overcome your obstacles and achieve your goals.

The human brain has approximately 100 billion cells, each of these cells connected and interconnected with as many as 20,000 other cells. The possible combinations of thoughts and ideas in your brain are the number "1" with eight pages of zeros after it. This means, according to brain expert Tony Buzan, that your brain has more possible thought combinations than the number of all the atoms in the known universe.

To all intents and purposes, your creative capacity is infinite. There are no limits on what you can accomplish with your mind, except for those limits you impose on yourself as the result of using ineffective methods of thinking and analysis.

UNLEASH YOUR IMAGINATION

Einstein also said that, "Imagination is more important than intelligence." You know that there is usually a very close association between intelligence and creativity. However, intelligence is not simply a matter of IQ. IQ only tests verbal and mathematical abilities. You also have physical intelligence, emotional intelligence, interpersonal intelligence, musical intelligence, intuitive intelligence, intrapersonal intelligence, and visual-spatial intelligence, plus entrepreneurial intelligence, perhaps the highest paid intelligence of all.

Intelligence is not simply a matter of IQ. Instead, it is a way of *acting*. If you act intelligently, you are smart. If you act stupidly, you are stupid, irrespective of your IQ or your grades in school.

If you agree with this, that a person who acts intelligently is intelligent, then what, by definition, is an intelligent way of acting? The answer is simple. You are acting intelligently when you are doing something that is moving you toward a goal that is important to you. You are acting stupidly when you are doing anything that is moving you away from one of your own self-selected goals.

MOVE TOWARD YOUR GOALS

The only measure of an intelligent or creative act is whether or not it is helping or hurting you, based on your own definition of what it is you really want in life.

A person who wants to be healthy and fit, but eats junk foods and refuses to exercise, is a person who is acting stupidly, even if he graduated from Harvard or Yale. A person who has clear written goals and who works on them every day, making progress bit by bit, is acting with the highest intelligence, irrespective of his or her educational or social background.

The Law of Use says that, "If you don't use it, you lose it." Your creativity is like a muscle. The more you use it, the stronger it becomes. The less you use it, on the other hand, the weaker it becomes. But the good news is that it is always there, and you can begin building it up at any time by flexing it and straining it and using it in a variety of different ways.

CREATIVITY DEFINED

There are two definitions of creativity that I particularly like. The first is by Mike Vance, who said that, "Creativity is the creation of the new and the rearranging of the old in a new way."

Whenever you find a new, better or different way of accomplishing a task or goal, and you implement it, you are flexing your creative powers and making them stronger.

Carl Albrecht says that, "Creativity is any new, novel or imaginative way to improve some aspect of the human condition."

Your ability to find new, better, faster, easier ways to accomplish tasks for yourself and others, is the true measure of your creative capacity. Ideas are the keys to the future. Every change in your life will begin when your mind collides with a new idea of some kind. The more new ideas your mind collides with, the more likely it is that you will come across the right idea, at the right time, in the right situation, to achieve the right result that may enable you to jump ahead five or ten years in your life and career.

BOMBARD YOUR MIND WITH IDEAS

Creative people are those who are always organizing and reorganizing their lives so that they are continually bombarded by stimuli. They associate with intelligent people who have ideas and insights that are different from theirs. They ask a lot of questions and listen carefully to the answers. They remain open, fluid, and flexible, recognizing that change is accelerating at a greater rate than we have ever seen and almost everything we know is becoming obsolete faster than ever before. It is only those with new ideas and insights that will be masters of the future, rather than victims.

Creative people continually read different magazines, newsletters and books. They are on a lifelong search for that idea or insight that they can use at a particular moment in time to leap forward. They listen to audio programs in their car and they watch educational videos. They attend conferences and association meetings. They register for seminars, sit down in front and take careful notes.

They ask questions of the instructors and they make a point of meeting other intelligent, creative people who also attend these events. They know that one good idea is all you need to start a fortune.

Many times, your life will be changed by a casual remark by a passing stranger. He or she will tell you about a book, an article, an invention, or a breakthrough that has occurred somewhere else. That piece of information may be all that you need to turn a situation to your advantage.

WINNING A NOBEL PRIZE

When the researchers at the IBM labs in Geneva were frustrated in their search for the secrets to superconductivity, they decided to take a couple of days off and change their mental spaces. One of them went home to his family and then went out golfing. The other, an unmarried scientist, went down to the library at the IBM labs and began leafing through recent publications at random. He came across a publication of the French Institute of Ceramic Science, which contained an article on a new form of ceramic product that allowed items to pass across its surface without creating friction. His mind almost exploded. He saw that this breakthrough in ceramics was exactly what they had been looking for to solve the puzzle of superconductivity.

He went back to the laboratory, called his friend, and together they completed the superconductivity project. The very next year they were jointly awarded the Nobel Prize in physics for one of the most important scientific breakthroughs in the world at that time.

THERE IS NO PROBLEM YOU CAN'T SOLVE

You are a genius. Whenever you are confronted with a problem or difficulty of any kind, affirm to yourself, over and over, "I'm a genius! I'm a genius! I'm a genius!"

When you pass this command from your conscious mind to your subconscious mind, and you say it to yourself with enthusiasm, your subconscious mind will accept these words as instructions, and go to work to release creative ideas. These ideas will pop to the surface of your conscious mind exactly when you need them.

In addition, when your subconscious mind is properly programmed and activated with powerful commands, your superconscious mind will kick into action as well. You will begin to attract into your life all kinds of insights and ideas that will help you to solve your problems and achieve your goals.

THREE SPURS TO CREATIVE THINKING

The three main stimuli to creative thinking are: intensely desired goals, clearly worded questions, and pressing problems.

The word imagination comes from the word "image." When you have a clear mental image or vision, or visualization, of your goal, of exactly what it is you want to accomplish, and what it will look like when it is achieved, you stimulate your creative mind to release a steady flow of ideas to help you achieve that goal.

Most people who are unhappy in life have no goals. The very act of sitting down and writing out a list of goals will change your perspective completely. When you take your list of goals, organize it by priority and then make written plans to achieve your most important goals, your mind will start to sparkle with ideas that will help you. Your negativity and pessimism will vanish. You will experience a surge of energy and enthusiasm, and you will want to get up and get going immediately on whatever it is you have written down.

When you ask precisely worded questions that stimulate thought, you will find yourself coming up with great ideas and performing at higher levels of creativity than you had imagined possible.

When you have pressing problems, clearly defined and articulated, you will start to see all kinds of ways to solve those problems and remove those obstacles that stand in your way.

Just as you build physical muscles by pumping iron in the gym, you build mental muscles by pumping mental iron. Mental iron consists of clear goals, pressing problems, and well-worded questions. The more of them you have, the smarter and more creative you become.

Remember, all creativity is aimed at improvement. Creativity has very little to do with writing prize-winning novels, painting pictures or producing music. It is a simple, every day function of your mind that everyone has, but which few people use.

PROVE THAT YOU ARE A GENIUS

We said earlier that we are going to be testing the hypothesis that you are *not* a genius, so that we can prove that you really *are* a genius. Geniuses throughout the ages have been found to possess three special characteristics.

First, all geniuses seem to have developed the ability to *concentrate* single mindedly on one question, problem or goal at a time, and to exclude all other diversions or distractions. The more intensely you concentrate your thoughts and attention, and the more intensely you are emotionally involved with a problem or goal, the more likely it is that your mind will respond with the kind of creative ideas that you need. And the good news is that concentration comes from practicing the process of concentrating whenever you have something you want to accomplish.

One of the best ways to develop this habit of concentration is to define your goal or problem clearly, in writing, at the top of a piece of paper. Then, write down every single detail that you can think of that pertains to that goal or problem. Write every fact, figure and piece of information that you have. The more you write, the more likely it is that you will come up with exactly the idea that you need to solve the problem or difficulty that is currently holding you back.

APPROACH PROBLEMS SYSTEMATICALLY

The second quality of geniuses is that they have developed a *systematic* approach to solving problems. Usually, they write the problem clearly on paper in advance. Accurate problem definition leads to a solution in 50% of cases. Most of the time, when you have a problem or series of problems that is causing you worry or concern, it is because you have not yet sat down and clearly defined exactly what the problem is.

One of the key parts of approaching your problems or goals systematically is validating the information that you have. As the humorist Josh Billings once wrote, "The trouble with most folks isn't their ignorance. It's knowin' so many things that ain't so."

There are enormous numbers of things that you think you "know" about your life and situation that are simply not true. One of the best ways to manage your creativity is to carefully check and double-check your facts and figures, to be sure that they are accurate.

KEEP AN OPEN MIND

The third characteristic of a genius is that *they invariably have open minds*. They are curious, friendly, and even playful. They refuse to jump to conclusions or to cut off any line of thinking or train of thought. They continually ask questions, especially, "What if?"

"What if?" questioning is one of the hallmarks of developing and managing your creativity. For example, what if everything that you are doing in your current job or situation to achieve your goal or to solve your major problem was completely wrong? What if there was a better way? What if you were operating on the basis of false information or wrong assumptions? What if what you were attempting to do was actually impossible and that is why you are having such problems with it?

CHALLENGE YOUR ASSUMPTIONS

I have known many people who have been in bad jobs. They were constantly coming up with ideas to make their jobs more acceptable. Finally, they realized that the boss was always going to be negative, the company was always going to be bureaucratic and the marketplace was always going to be ruthless. So instead of trying to find a solution to their current job, they changed jobs and turned out later to be very happy and much better paid. Could this apply to you?

Many companies try hard, hard, hard to bring a product to market and to achieve a certain level of sales success. In many cases, it is an exercise in futility because the market has changed, the competitor's product is better or cheaper, and the company lacks the resources or the abilities to achieve a position of market dominance. Could this apply to your business?

The more you do of what you're doing, the more you'll get of what you've got. Managing your creativity requires that you continually dig deep into yourself and generate more, newer, better, faster, cheaper, different ideas that you can use to improve the important parts of your life.

Seven Qualities of the Creative Thinker

There are seven qualities of the creative thinker. When you practice one or more of these qualities, you begin to prove to yourself that you are truly a genius, and you simultaneously disprove the negative hypothesis.

The first quality is that creative thinkers are intensely *curious*. They are always asking questions. Very much like children do, they ask questions like "Why?" frequently.

Then they ask: "Why not?", "Why can't we do it?", "Even if it hasn't been done before, can it be done now?"

When Federal Express developed their initial business plan they were told by countless experts that they would fail. They were told that if there was a market for overnight mail delivery, there would *already* be a service offering it. Since there was no service offering overnight mail delivery, there could not possibly be a market. Today, Federal Express is a multibillion-dollar company and all the initial founders are extremely wealthy men. And it was all because they asked, "Why not?"

PRACTICE ZERO BASED THINKING

The second quality of creative thinkers is that they practice "Zero-Based Thinking" all the time. They continually ask themselves, "If I weren't doing what I'm doing today, knowing what I now know, would I do the same thing?"

And if the answer is no, they cut their losses, discontinue what they are doing, and start doing something else. It is absolutely amazing how many people persist in doing something that they wouldn't even get into if they had the chance to do it over again. And they still wonder why they are making so little progress.

BE WILLING TO CHANGE

The third quality of creative thinkers is that they have a willingness to change. They recognize that in a world such as ours, the unwillingness or inability to change is fatal. They prefer to be in charge of their lives rather than being caught up in the flash flood of change that is inevitable and unavoidable.

The words of the truly flexible person, the person who is willing to change, are simply, "I changed my mind."

According to researchers, fully 70% of the decisions you make turn out to be wrong in the long run. This means that you must be willing to change your mind and try something else most of the time. Mental flexibility is the most important quality that you will need for success in the 21st century.

ADMIT WHEN YOU ARE WRONG

The fourth quality of highly creative people is their willingness to admit when they are wrong. Fully 80% of people burn up most of their mental and emotional energy refusing to admit that they made a wrong decision. Don't let this happen to you. Truly intelligent, highly creative people are open minded, fluid, flexible and willing to both change their mind, and admit that they are wrong when their earlier decisions turn out to be incorrect.

ADMIT YOUR IGNORANCE

The fifth quality is that highly creative people can say, "I don't know." They recognize that it is impossible for anyone to know everything about anything, and it is very likely that almost everyone is wrong to some extent, no matter what they are doing. So when someone asks them a particular question that they don't know the answer to, they admit it early and often. They simply say, "I don't know." And if necessary they go about finding the answer.

Here's an important point. No matter what problems you have there is someone, somewhere, who has had the same problem, has already solved the problem, and is using the solution today. One of the smartest and most creative things you can do is to find someone else, somewhere, who is already implementing the solution successfully and then copy him or her.

The smartest person is not necessarily the person who comes up with the idea. It may be just a lucky flash of insight. The smartest person is the one who copies the idea first. And it is often the person to recognize the value of a new idea that makes a fortune from the idea, while the originator makes little or nothing.

FOCUS ON YOUR GOALS

The sixth quality of creative people is that they are intensely goal-oriented. They know exactly what they want. They have it written down very clearly. They visualize it on a regular basis. They imagine what their goal would look like if it were a reality today. And the more they visualize and imagine their goal as a reality, the more creative they become and the faster they move toward achieving it.

CONTROL YOUR EGO

The seventh quality of highly creative people is that they have less ego involvement in being right. They are more concerned with what's right rather than who's right. They are willing to accept ideas from any source to achieve a goal, overcome an obstacle, or solve a problem.

GENERATE MORE IDEAS

The most important part of managing your creativity is your ability to generate ideas. And the greater the quantity of ideas that you generate, the greater the quality your ideas will be. The more ideas you have, the more likely you are to have the right idea at the right time.

But generating ideas is only 1% of the equation. As Thomas Edison once wrote, "Genius is one percent inspiration and 99 percent perspiration." Your ability to come up with an idea, to test it and validate it, and then to implement it and execute it in your life to achieve results, is the true mark of genius.

Every single time you originate a new idea, write it down, make a plan for its implementation, and then take action, you are behaving like a genius. And the more you manage your creativity in this way, the smarter you will become. And the smarter you become, the more you will achieve in every area of your life. Your future will become unlimited.

About Brian

Brian Tracy is Chairman and CEO of Brian Tracy International, a company specializing in the training and development of individuals and organizations. Brian's goal is to help people achieve their personal and business goals faster and easier than they ever imagined.

Brian Tracy has consulted for more than 1,000 companies and addressed more than 5,000,000 people in 5,000 talks and seminars throughout the US, Canada and 55 other countries worldwide. As a Keynote speaker and seminar leader, he addresses more than 250,000 people each year.

For more information on Brian Tracy programs, go to: www.briantracy.com

CHAPTER 2

THE MAVERICK WAY OF CREATING IMPACT AND GIVING ~~BACK~~ FORWARD

BY YANIK SILVER

Ok I admit I was wrong…

I used to say "Give Back" was one of the key concepts of the Maverick Entrepreneurs philosophy. (Hell, it says so right here on the cover of the first version of my best-selling 34 Rules for Maverick Entrepreneurs book. "Make More Money, Have More Fun and Give More Back").

I've now realized this isn't quite right.

With my background as a copywriter, I'm pretty careful about most of the words I choose. It's your words (and even your internal dialogue) that have a tremendous impact on how you think, feel and behave. By saying the words 'giving back' this implies entrepreneurs, like us, have taken something.

Let's think about that for a second…

I assert that entrepreneurs and businesses can only succeed by providing and delivering value. Period. End of story. It's simply a universal law. In fact, one of my core values in my very first journal said, *"I get rich by enriching others 10x – 100x what they pay me in return."* There's no other way that it could possibly occur because, in the long run, the marketplace is always self-correcting.

The notion of 'giving back' seems to echo an undeserving indebtedness or even guilt for success. Should you begrudge entrepreneurs like Steve Jobs, Richard Branson or Bill Gates for their wealth?

Absolutely not.

Each one of them created immense value exponentially in proportion to what they've received. (And that's not counting the thousands of jobs, additional utility, new startups piggybacking on their success, etc.)

My friend and mega mansion builder/real estate artist/philanthropist, Frank McKinney, sums it up with a saying he told our Maverick1000 group in Haiti, ***"We have to be careful not to weaken the strong in order to strengthen the weak."***

At our core, entrepreneurs are simply growth-oriented innovators and value creators. They almost can't help themselves. Take Bill Gates for instance. Aside from his impact on micro-computing, his greatest contribution going forward will be around the Gates Foundation eradicating disease and driving new educational initiatives.

And he's not alone. Other billionaires are not content to just "give back". **They're giving forward by applying entrepreneurial talent, energy and capital to solve some of the biggest issues facing the globe.** But you don't have to be at the level of a Gates or Branson to make a difference. Today, a group of 21st century maverick entrepreneurs are leading the way to change the way business is played and even the rules by which we keep score.

Who says it's only about one measurement on your P&L?

BUSINESS CAN BECOME ONE OF THE BIGGEST LEVERS FOR GOOD – WHILE ACTUALLY BEING GOOD FOR BUSINESS.

Look at TOMS shoes. Yes, they've been the poster child for creative impact with their "Buy One, Give One" initiatives but it's for good reason. They've created a powerful (and profitable) business model tied directly into doing something that will have a significant impact. And the best part is their customers, retail partners and vendors want to help spread that story driving increased sales.

I love looking at businesses that are doing something that matters tied in with the causes they support in a real, genuine and authentic way. In many cases, you can create a way to automatically give and support causes important to you – creating a win/win/win for everybody.

Your business can actually flourish because incoming research is proving customers are favorably disposed to doing business with you if there's an added bonus of philanthropy "baked" in. In fact, I've directly seen results of split tests with one of our Maverick1000 members showing a 10% increase in sales because $50 from every sale went to a charity featured. Not only do they sell more products, but also the cause involved gets additional support and exposure.

Nearly all the successful people I know give. There's a special kind of satisfaction that comes from helping and serving others. Entrepreneurs are some of the most generous and giving individuals I've been fortunate enough to associate with.

THE MAVERICK METHOD OF GIVING

A lot of people talk about how they want to donate some huge sum of money to a charity or their church, but then never get around to it because they feel like they don't have enough right now or it's not the right time. Frankly, I think it's because it is not a systematic, regimented giving plan. If you would have told me a few years ago – I'd regularly be giving $10k, $15k, $20k+ checks to charities – I would have thought you were crazy because I could use that extra money myself for something. But when it becomes just a way you operate it's much easier to start writing those checks with big zeros behind them. My dad thinks I'm nuts when I told him how much I donate, but I'm more than pleased with my decision.

WHERE I FOUND THIS

One of the first times I heard about this was from the late Foster Hibbard, who worked with Napoleon Hill. Foster talked about setting up a "giving account" and a "wealth account." The set-up was simple. You would take a fixed percentage of all money that comes in to you (i.e. 5%, 10%, etc.) and put that amount into both accounts each time you received it. I only do monthly – but this follows the "pay yourself first" philosophy of getting rich also. So each month 5% gets paid off the top no matter what to myself (for investments and buying assets not toys), and 5% gets paid to a charity of my choice. (Dan Kennedy worked with Foster Hibbard and has a great distillation of this and his own wealth building philosophy in his book *"No BS Wealth Attraction for Entrepreneurs."*)

Fact is, I could see significant jumps in my own income once I started this 5% charitable giving. Some of the wealthiest and most successful people of all-time had discovered this secret. It's been said that Rockefeller walked around everyday with a roll of dimes and gave them away. Carnegie was one of the biggest philanthropists building public libraries. Many people talk about the 'filthy rich' or how 'greedy' rich people are – I've found just the opposite. Most of the truly wealthy and successful individuals are some of the biggest & most generous contributors around.

I FIRMLY BELIEVE YOU CANNOT OUT-GIVE THE UNIVERSE.

If that statement is true than anything you give out comes back to you in kind multiple times. Meaning from a pragmatic standpoint, you could look at this really as a return on "charitable investment." But that's almost too logical. There's an incredible feeling from knowing one check you wrote sustained an entire village of entrepreneurial upstarts – like when we donate to Village Enterprise (**villageef.org**). Or when you get a handwritten note from one of the charities you support talking about how surprised they were to get a $15,000 check out of the blue and what that kind of help means to their program.

Personally, I do due diligence on the charity I'm going to support for that particular month, and then I write the check without expectation of what is going to happen with the money.

TIME, TALENT & TREASURE

One of our Maverick members has a saying that I love and that's, "You can give time, talent or treasure." So perhaps if you're short on finances, give some of your time or talent away. Quite frankly, for years now we pretty much only donated money (treasure) since that's what I had the most abundance of. Today with the Young Entrepreneur sessions, we run on Maverick trips and virtual mentorship where we have the opportunity to actively engage and give forward. Previously, I would donate to a lot of different charitable organizations, but now I'm pretty much focused on my passion around young entrepreneurship only.

Authentic Altruism or 'Quick-dry' Charity Make-Over?

(http://www.internetlifestyle.com/blog/philanthropy/authentic-altruism-quickdry-charity-makeover/)

It's been incredible to see so many new companies and products adding charitable components to what they're doing or even go all the way and back that into their 'DNA' as a socially conscious but still capitalistic company. I love it!

Sometimes though you wonder if companies might be doing this just for the PR value and not really for authentic reasons that resonate with their brand, their customers or the owners. For instance, I recently came across a campaign for Kentucky Fried Chicken to donate 50 cents for every pink bucket of chicken they sell.

Hmmm….

While I'm all for breast cancer research and help (my Mom died from breast and ovarian cancer) but I don't see the connection. And I'm not the only one, I've seen some snarky blog posts about how KFC is trying to use this do-good campaign to gloss over the fact fried chicken could lead to obesity and heart disease. It just doesn't fit the KFC brand and I cannot see customers really getting behind this in a genuine way. Plus, they are already seeing some negative backlash for their "good corporate deed".

If you're going to use your business to promote or support a cause there should be a personal reason. Case in point, a recent rose wine I just had produced by former Olympian Peggy Fleming is called "Victories." Peggy went through a fight with breast cancer and now for every bottle purchased a significant portion goes to breast cancer causes. I like the way this is authentic plus it really ties into the product itself, a rose, since pink has become the color for breast cancer awareness.

Here's another interesting example that fits the product personality - Elivse and Kreese make high-end luxury goods out of discarded fire hose and other recycled material. *Yup, I said fire hose!*

They've also used waste coffee sacks, scrap sail cloth, used air traffic control flight strips, parachute silk and all sorts of other industrial waste. They donate 50% of their profits back to Firehouse Brigade charities and that fits perfectly with their brand and actual product. It's a beautiful congruent element that once again gets customers talking.

Personally, I've incorporated my adventurous personality into many different fundraisers including one for Virgin Unite. Me and my buddies, Mike Filsaime and Rob Olic, joined up to do a "Fall-a-Thon" where our goal was to raise $1 per every foot we fell out of the sky. (Oh…did I mention it was from 30,000 feet – the cruising altitude of a jet?)

So the big questions to ask yourself are:

- What causes matter to you and to your customers?
- What is the personality of my product, service or company?
- How does what we do help create zealots to spread our message?

Entrepreneurs are the lifeblood of growth, adding value and solving many of the problems we're encountering on a local or global level.

This trend is exciting to me because it's part of our Maverick philosophy and I see more and more businesses getting involved in ventures and projects that have 'goodness' tied to them. Look at Pepsi's RefreshEverything.com campaign, where they give away millions of dollars for ideas that have significant impact.

On the bigger corporate side, here's a recent one from Canadian credit union Servus. The campaign was called "Feel Good Ripple." They pledged $200,000 CDN in $10 increments for people to do good and pass it along. FeelGoodRipple.ca

I have a shirt I wear that asks you to do "a random kindness" each time you wear it. I like the notion of your clothing 'reminding' you about giving values

BEING PART OF SOMETHING BIGGER

Groups are mobilized around a common mission or feeling like they're part of something bigger than themselves. You can harness this for your business and create brand zealots spreading your message.

One company that really does this well is FEED. They started with a simple concept – buy one bag = feeding 1 child for a year in a developing country. Boom! Simple idea combined with an outwardly physical symbol (the bag) and you've got a winning combination.

Their idea was simple but profound. Create a fashionable bag that people would want and that also feeds X amount of children per year – hence the name FEED Bag. The only problem was the UN is not an entrepreneurial venture. From small beginnings just a few years ago – they've raised millions to feed tens of thousands of children.

Now the big lesson. Feed Bag is actually a for-profit enterprise with a social conscious. I love the idea of creating something (that's wanted) with a by-product for good, i.e., buy a fashionable bag and feed "x" number of children. There is no guilt involved like many charities play on, however, there is strong psychology at work. The bag is very prominently printed with the words FEED on it and it gives the user a feel-good story to tell others. Plus anyone else who knows what the bag stands for will recognize the person as having a social conscious. Win-win.

Blake Mycoksie founder of TOMS shoes, has a similar model. You buy one pair of shoes and one pair of shoes goes to a child in need. It's tangible and easy to understand. Once again a 'wanted' product with a charitable by-product. I see this as one of the most innovative charity models. We saw this a bit with the one laptop per child program, but I don't think that was that big of a hit because not too many people wanted the laptop for themselves or their children. The Feed Bag and TOMS shoes are "cool" and that's part of having switched-on fans – they have to believe they are part of something cool!

SMALL GIVING = BIG RESULTS

Taylor Conroy's story of how he raised $10k in less than 3 hours to build a school. (http://destroynormalblog.com/we-built-a-school-in-3-hours)

I love the concept he put out there – it was simply getting 33 people to donate $3.33/day for 3 months to create that $10k donation. It really makes you think about the impact a small group of committed individuals can have with small change found in their pocket. Check it out and watch the video.

WHY DOING GOOD IS GOOD FOR YOUR BOTTOM LINE TOO

This is really exciting! I've got some more empirical proof that you make more when you give more.

Check out this case study from Maverick1000 member, Brett Fogle.

Brett was launching a new Forex trading course and he had decided to split test this certificate on his sales page, ForexMastery.com. They tested with the certificate and without, and with it raised the conversion 10%. Now this was a $2,000 product they released and sold several hundred copies. The 10% bump helped them write a $40,000.00 charity check to a group that builds houses for the poorest of the poor in Haiti. Very exciting because that 10% bump also represented tens of thousands in additional sales that wouldn't have happened without this certificate.

I've always believed one entrepreneur can change the world…now let's see what happens when we stand together to create a transformative catalyst for what matters most.

About Yanik

Yanik Silver has successfully bootstrapped eight different product and service ideas hitting the million-dollar sales mark from scratch without funding, taking on debt or even having a real business plan.

His story and businesses have been featured in Fox Business News, TIME.com, *USA Today,* SmartMoney.com, *MSN Money,* Conde Naste's Portfolio.com, Entrepreneur.com, *WIRED Magazine,* WORTH.com, *The Boston Globe, The Wall Street Journal,* and many others.

Yanik is the author of several best-selling entrepreneurial books and tools including *Instant Sales Letters®*, *34 Rules for Maverick Entrepreneurs* and *Maverick Startup.* He is the founder of the Underground Online Seminar®, 3% Forward and Maverick1000, a private group of game-changing entrepreneurs, out to change the way business is played.

He is passionate about catalyzing and connecting innovative 21st century entrepreneurs to co-create new business breakthroughs, enhance their happiness and provide greater meaning and impact through their ventures.

Yanik leads small groups of high impact entrepreneurs on re-energizing epic experiences with business icons such as Jesse James, Tony Hsieh, Tony Hawk, Tim Ferriss and John Paul DeJoria. Whether that's blasting 80 mph through the Baja, experiencing a Zero-gravity flight, flying MiG jets in Russia, going on an African Safari, scuba diving in between tectonic plates in Iceland or helping create self-sustaining villages in Haiti and private brainstorming sessions with Sir Richard Branson on his private island.

He calls Potomac, Maryland home with his wife, Missy, and 2 mini-Mavericks in the making, Zack and Zoe.

CHAPTER 3

LIFE IS ADAPTATION

BY DR. STEVEN SPERLING

Pain can be a powerful motivation for change. Frustration is too. One of the most humbling experiences in life comes when you realize that you don't have all the answers and you have to ask for help. This help can come in many forms: Guidance from a spiritual advisor, mentor or trusted friend. Sometimes it comes in the form of inspiration seemingly given in answer to thoughts put out into the universe. The practice of meditation and quiet contemplation can make these inspirations occur on a much more regular basis. Time spent in this way can yield many flashes of insight into complex problems that otherwise seem unfathomable.

We live in an ever-changing world and we need to be able to adapt as change occurs. This process of adaptation can create pain and frustration but this often precedes change, and allows a person or organization to function at a much higher level. A key part of this is being able to guide or direct the change in a positive way. Part of this is being able to control and guide our thoughts because our thoughts precede action and action precedes behavior. Or as the following quote from William Arthur Ward states, "our words reveal our thoughts; our manners mirror our self-esteem; our actions reflect our character; our habits predict the future." If we think in the right way, we will behave in the right way. How then do we go about thinking in the right way?

I have found after much wasted time and effort, that one of the most efficient ways to go about this is to ask for the help of a mentor or coach. I am by nature stubborn and like to do things my own way. When the pain and frustration of not getting the results I want becomes great enough even I can become open to change. I have learned through trial and error what many people just seem to know by their own nature, that is, that the experience and strength of the many is superior to the experience and strength of just me. I have been fortunate through the years to be able to have access to many various experts and people I could look up to. Many of my early athletic coaches were such people. They would help me improve not only my athletic performance but also my performance in life. They were good role models and I wanted to be like them. I even went so far as to become a coach myself at an introductory level. I thought maybe I could share some of my experience with young people. In fact, I thought I had life pretty much figured out, and that they would listen to me if they knew how fortunate they were to have someone who had read more than one coaching book. I share the following story to illustrate just how wrong that attitude was.

Several years ago, my son's youth soccer team needed a coach so I volunteered. I had just completed reading two books, so of course I knew what I was doing. I was eager to try some of the new ideas. Anyone who has been around soccer knows about the tryouts. They give you a sheet to grade each player on their talents (or lack of). There are different columns for kicking, passing and probable position. Then there is a draft where coaches choose their team members. As the draft progressed I was running out of guys to pick. It was my last draft choice and there were three kids left. I quickly checked my evaluation sheets. There was one kid named Brian and two other boys with loud mouthed parents. In the comments block beside Brian's name I had written: lacks talent, uncoordinated... I chose Brian.

We began our practices and I was feeling really good about myself for trying many of the ideas I had read about. After a few practices it became clear Brian had not read the same books; in fact it was clear he had never played the game before. He didn't know the positions and he couldn't run, pass or kick. Other than that he was just fine. I became frustrated at how much extra time I had to spend with Brian on the simplest of skills. I was impatient and not making any progress trying to help him get any better.

I remember coming home and venting to my wife:

- In other towns these kids of been playing soccer since they were six years old. What kind of parent sends their kid out to play soccer for the first time at age 12?
- Don't they know they are setting this kid up for failure?
- Why didn't someone teach him at least to kick and pass a little before they sent him out there?
- I'm going to have a chat with his parents as soon as I have the opportunity.

When practice ended the next night all the players were picked up on time ... except for Brian. We waited around for a long 20 minutes. I tried to appear busy shuffling the roster. I tried to ask Brian about school and his friends but he wasn't into small talk. This kid was beginning to make me feel uncomfortable. By the time Brian's mom arrived, I was pretty ticked off. As she walked toward the field, I thought, "Here is my chance. I need to let her know my concerns." But she immediately launched into an apology about how she gotten tied up at work, caught in traffic, etc... I was about to ask her why the boy's father hadn't properly prepared him when she abruptly stopped talking, sent Brian to the car and said the following: "Coach, I need to tell you something. This team has been the best thing to happen to Brian in a long time. See last year Brian's dad was killed by a drunk driver. He took it real hard and has hardly spoken to anyone for the last several months. I was walking by the park and rec a few weeks ago and saw the sign for registration. I thought it would be good for him to get out of the house and make some friends. Since joining your team he actually comes home from practice happy. He talks to me at home about all the things you are teaching him. I want to thank you for the impact you are having on my son. This team is just what he needed."

All of the sudden I didn't feel very good. My stomach began to be a little queasy and I felt all the blood rising to my face in embarrassment. The only brilliant response I could come up with was mumbling: "It's my pleasure. He's a good kid." When my mind began to function again I came up with one more thought. I am utterly ashamed of myself. Who was I to presume to know anything about this boy's situation? Who was I to pass judgment on him or his family? I went home and thought long and hard about it.

At the next practice I increased my efforts to help Brian and spent extra time after practice on the simple fundamentals... kicking and passing. As the season progressed so did Brian's talent and enthusiasm. We were fortunate enough to make it into the playoffs and Brian made an incredible effort to help us win the game. Brian won more than the game that day. He won the respect and admiration of his teammates. More importantly, he increased his own self-respect and for probably the first time, saw himself as the winner he truly was.

That experience with Brian and his mom taught me a lot. I decided then to make a pledge to myself. I have used it with those I teach, with those I coach, and with the people that I treat at my dental office:

1) I will not pass judgment on any person without knowing their background.
2) I will meet every player/Person exactly where he is physically, mentally, and emotionally and will do everything in my power to help him improve himself as a player and a person.
3) I will give every patient/Player entrusted to my care my best effort every day no matter how I feel at that time. They all deserve it.

In my dental office we try to do things the same way. We try to develop good team players and instill values into them much as we do the players on any team. We like to surround ourselves with good people not only because it creates a positive work environment, but it's just fun to be around positive people. We all spend so much precious time at our place of work; why not make it as pleasant as possible by creating a winning team.

The importance of creating a winning team cannot be emphasized enough. I cannot accomplish as much as "we" can. "We" can do what "I" cannot do. We can create a positive environment where all can flourish. We can support each other through life's inevitable difficulties. We can feed off each other's energy and enthusiasm.

Just like any team needs a good coach, in the business world any team needs a good leader. The team will thrive when it has good leadership. People need and want a leader. It is the vision of the leader and the values of the leader that determines the values of the team. We have a set of core values in our group that affects every decision that we make. These are values like loyalty, courtesy, respect, integrity, going the extra mile, and putting the needs of the patient first. We use these values in things as diverse as hiring the right people to choosing which vendors we will be working with. These values define who we are and help us to stay on course and headed in the right direction.

There have been times in the past however, when we have managed to get off purpose. I remember one particularly trying time several years ago when we were going through a rough spot. There were conflicts everywhere we turned. We had personnel conflicts, time conflicts and space conflicts. We were literally heading down a path that I wasn't sure we could ever recover from. My frustration level was extremely high and I remember thinking that certainly one day I was going to be the last one out the door to turn off the lights and that would be it, we would be done. As it happened, that low point preceded great changes in our office, which have continued to this day. Some difficult decisions had to be made and actions taken, but since that time we have been able to add multiple employees, space and equipment. We have expanded our circle of influence dramatically. It was difficult at the time to see that, once again, the pain and frustration preceded a change to a higher level. The systems necessary to function at a higher level could not evolve until the need arose. "When the student is ready, the teacher will appear."

At our meetings we talk about concepts that help us serve People. We talk about things like, "if you do things in the right way, you will succeed." The right way is to give someone greater value in service than what they give you in money. We need to be clear with the value we bring to the marketplace. If you know that what you do has value, then what you are doing is really solving problems, it is changing lives, it is making someone feel better.

Our job is to help people make decisions and then give them a compelling reason to do it now. There are literally hundreds of people whose lives I have helped change in a very positive way, who at the time I met them, if I didn't give them a reason to do it now, would've never done it and they would've missed out on that opportunity. There should be no back off on this if you understand the value you bring to the marketplace. If the people don't make a decision and take action, then I have not helped them. If I give a talk and the people do nothing, then it was a waste of time. If I give a talk and they do something, then that is productive. That is a good use of my time, I am kind of living up to my potential and I am having an impact on the person's life.

Earl Nightingale defined success as "a progressive realization of a worthy ideal." One of the ways to measure our progress toward success is to periodically set new goals and review them on a regular basis. It is extremely important that these goals be written down and have a timeline associated with them. I have been influenced in setting goals by some of the most recognized people in the field of helping people reach their true potential; people like Brian Tracy, Anthony Robbins and Wayne Dyer. But just as important as it is to listen to these experts, it is also important to listen to the influential people in one's own life; People like your spouse, your family or your clergy; People on a local level like Lorne Grosso, our local high school hockey coach.

By the time this is printed, Lorne will have received the John Mariucci Award in Naples, Florida. This national award is given by the American Hockey Coaches Association to a secondary school coach who best exemplifies the spirit, dedication and enthusiasm of legendary University of Minnesota hockey coach John Mariucci. Lorne has coached for 47 seasons with 662 victories at the same high school. He knows a bit about winning. His time coaching and teaching hundreds of young men on his teams about life through sports is a passion for him. I never played for Lorne, but was fortunate to have him as a teacher and his passion for teaching kids about values for living was just as evident in the classroom. He instilled in us enthusiasm for learning and concepts like doing what you say you will do, personal integrity and going the extra mile. He used humor to get his point across and he gave us the tools to grow into responsible, productive adults. I credit him as much as the more well known experts in the field of human potential for any small success I have achieved so far.

If you want to "Win friends and influence people," read Dale Carnegie. If you want to become a better person and change lives, spend five minutes talking to Lorne.

About Dr. Steve

Steve Sperling DDS is a practicing Dentist in Rochester, Minnesota. He is co-owner of a group practice with two locations and six dentists. In his free time, he enjoys tennis, skiing, biking and training for the upcoming Tough Mudder obstacle course with his sons. He and his wife have an interest in mission work, specifically using their talents in the dental field, and have travelled to many countries with various groups for mission trips. He recently returned from a mission trip in rural Tanzania, which ended with a successful climb to the top of Mt. Kilimanjaro. Other interests include diving, soaring, fishing and finding balance in a life filled with competing opportunities.

His favorite quote is:

The master in the art of living makes little distinction between his work and his play, his labor and his leisure, his mind and his body, his information and his recreation, his love and his religion. He hardly knows which is which. He simply pursues his vision of excellence at whatever he does, leaving others to decide if he is working or playing. To him, he is always doing both.

~ Francoise Chateaubriand

CHAPTER 4

THE HARD ROAD PAYS

BY ADAM KOCH

Necessity is the mother of invention; cliché, I know. Losing a job can be just what you need to get you to the place you need to be. My wife and I had just adopted our daughter and moved to a new city to start my career as an apartment manager for a number of apartment communities. This was my first real job after graduating from Texas A&M the previous year. I was doing a great job too! That is at least what I thought until, as I like to proclaim, they "fired my rear." The owners of the business decided they could pay two people for what they had been paying me. They graciously gave me 2 full weeks to depart the apartment they furnished us to live. Now the questions began to circle around me. What am I going to do? Where are we going to live? How am I going to provide for my new family? I learned that I have some very good friends and family. With their help and definitely the grace of God, we made it through the next many months.

I discovered something soon after about myself that changed my life forever. While I was not sure what I would do next, one thing was crystal clear—I knew that I would never work for someone else again; I never wanted to be at the mercy of somebody's subjective view of the job I was doing. I was going to be the boss. Thankfully, I was able to take some time to figure out what my next career move should be.

I investigated businesses that were low capital and easy entry, so I was looking at financial markets when I happened upon an ad for insurance agents. The ad made no pretense; you work hard and in a year or two, you can actually afford a peanut butter and jelly sandwich twice a week. You make it to three years, you can even add the crunchy peanut butter. OK, maybe I exaggerate a bit...but not by much. This did not sound like some sort of "get rich scheme" but exactly like what I was looking for. My efforts would be rewarded; my failures would be my own. Soon after, I was selling insurance with a national insurance company as an agent. I learned quickly that I actually really like insurance. A topic that would make my very patient wife's eyes literally glaze over and unprompted yawns to occur.

So, where are we now? To put it simply, we are commercial mavericks in a personal lines world. Last year my office wrote more commercial insurance policies in the state of Texas than the next 4 agencies combined for Farmers Insurance.

We are not an insurance mill to just simply churn out polices with no regard to quality. Our philosophy is to educate every client, to be sure they know what protection insurance does and does not afford them and their business. We have taken this concept, run with it and intend to expand it even further. I have found that many of my competitors prefer to write personal policies because they are the easy road with a quicker close. Commercial insurance tends to take a great deal longer to close from start to finish and require a great deal more industry knowledge. Experience tells us that the hard road pays when you follow the signs.

#1. EDUCATE YOURSELF

Become an expert in specific markets or businesses and realize that you do not have to service them all. Once you learn one market, it is easy to apply what you have learned to the next one. The more you have a mind for it, the easier it becomes to see those gaps in coverages for each business and each type of policy.

In any business, being the expert in your field differentiates you from your competition. Instead of starting out "scattershot" and trying several different fields, which I have done, it can be more beneficial to build and develop one industry and gain credibility there before moving on to the next. The scattershot approach requires a bigger learning curve than concentration in a single area at a time. It can also be a huge drain on marketing dollars.

Create a plan of attack. Where will you go? How will you meet your customer's needs? Each time I write a policy for a contractor, I know that for his success he may need certificates of insurance from me on an ongoing basis. Garnering business in that industry will necessitate that an insurance office have the staff to accommodate the need for those certificates, and the right systems in place to track the certificate holders and policy endorsements. Therefore, make sure infrastructure is in place to know how to do it and to meet the client needs effectively.

Certain industries require specific endorsements; an agent needs to know what those endorsements mean and which carriers write them. Do your homework and plan accordingly. In the beginning, before we invested in software specific to the project, we had a team member who dedicated more than 50% of her day processing certificates of insurance for clients. For some clients, it would literally take two and a half weeks each year to print the certificates required at policy renewal time. Granted, that was in the midst of her other duties, but still a huge waste of human resources. Now that we have the right processes and infrastructure in place, this same task takes 5 minutes or less. An educated agent will not overlook their infrastructure.

We routinely deal with people who have brand new businesses or who have never had insurance before. About 50% of our new business comes from people who have no idea what they need when asking about insurance. Therefore, after educating ourselves, our next job is to educate the clients.

#2. EDUCATE YOUR CLIENTS

Do not rely on commissions. Rely on the satisfaction of selling the right policies for the right reasons. Take premium out of the discussion. As has been said in many different ways by many different people, price is the issue only when value is a mystery. In insurance, and other businesses to be sure, when you prove your value and help the client's business grow, your business will grow in turn.

When I approach a potential client, one of the first things I inquire about is what they are looking for in an insurance policy. That can be a rather loaded question, so be ready for a wide range of answers. The most common answer is, "I'm looking for the cheapest premium" or "I just want enough coverage for the contract I am trying to get." Both of those answers generally mean I will have to work awfully hard to show the value of the policy. Some of these clients I can educate, many I cannot. I do not spend a majority of my time with that type of client. Spend your time on those that are receptive. The result is a book of business made up of clients that actually want to have an insurance policy with you instead of those that have it just because they are required to.

Educating your clients creates an opportunity to contact them more frequently as well. A business, or an agent, that does not keep in close contact with its clients might miss opportunities.

#3. KEEP IN CONTACT

Contact your clients. It's that simple. Call them, email them, and send them letters in the mail. Tell them what you do. Keep in constant contact with your clients. As you grow, this can be a rather daunting task, but it is worth putting systems in place to automate as much of this as possible. Let me ask, how frustrating would it be to find out a long time business client you are visiting for the first time in a year just started a worker's compensation policy, a $2,000,000 key man life policy and set up their business 401(k) a week earlier. How more frustrating would it be if they said, "Well I would have come to you, but I didn't know you provided those services." Yeah, it was pretty frustrating. Let them know what you do and then tell them again and again and again. The constant communication also instills a sense of familiarity and trust. It's hard to develop a relationship with anyone if you rarely talk to them.

#4. BE AN ADVISOR, NOT A SALESPERSON

One of the reasons that I love to work with new businesses is because I get to be there to build their business with them from the ground up. New business clients often do not know what they need, and frequently do not understand the insurance industry at all. This presents the opportunity to be a teacher to the client and make that client an informed purchaser.

Discuss a client's goals for his business and his plans for growth. This information is useful in advising the client about products that will grow with the business or make that business more marketable. Sometimes, the advisor talks a client through bouts of shortsightedness that might adversely affect his business.

Devotion to becoming an advisor and not a salesperson sometimes means losing a quick sale; it reflects quality not quantity. This can be a hard road for some agents or businesses that are used to the faster-paced world of: sign-the-contract-and-move-on-to –the-next-client. Doing it right is not necessarily easy.

Often a client and I end up discussing everything BUT insurance. We relate and develop a relationship, because I know and share some of the pitfalls that befell our business when we first opened. I am not an accountant, but I can share with my client what happens when you do not have one. I can tell them about co-mingling funds and not knowing you were doing it. I can tell them about the nightmares of preparing your own business taxes, etc. The hard road to building our insurance business is paved with lessons learned about doing things right and not always doing it in the most cost- effective way.

I educate clients that insurance is not an evil thing. It protects your business, not just for the one job that you are working on. I teach them to look at their insurance as an opportunity cost, not an expense and suggest to them that they can now leverage this policy to obtain more business, most especially for contractors. Essentially, educate the client to see their insurance as a *marketing* expense rather than a general business expense. I educate the client that his job, as is mine, is to be the Ambassador and CEO of his business and that he needs to think bigger than the average small business owner. Through this approach, the salesperson becomes a trusted advisor and part of the inner circle for life. It is incumbent upon the advisor to be ethical at all times in this process, never knowingly advising a client to purchase or to do something that will compromise his business or erase their trust in you.

#5. BE ETHICAL AND GROW STRONG

While growing up in a very modest singlewide mobile home with VERY limited means, I learned the most important lesson of my life: take care of what you have. Having "new" all the time was not a possibility, nor was it necessary. Inherent in any business should be the value of people and things. Seek quality and not quantity. Value your customers, instead of mistakenly thinking you can easily replace them.

The most successful businesses embrace the hard and ethical road. If you press the easy button, you do not learn the correct lessons from the things around you. Determining the correct clients to pursue and not faltering until earning their business requires hard work. The key to transitioning lead generation—fliers, doors knocked on, business cards handed out and Internet advertising—to clients is numbers. Developing a large lead list then personally approaching every prospect is challenging, but the numbers speak for themselves. Harder still is turning down business from customers who are not a good match for your company, like the clients who base their decisions strictly on price. Have the integrity to leave those clients to your competition. Additionally, there is a trickle of personal lines policies originating from business clients; do not neglect them. Instead, hire the personnel to harvest the additional business from your existing client base.

#6. PLACE THE RIGHT PERSON IN THE RIGHT JOB

Nothing kills the inner workings of your business faster than an employee who is not happy and successful in his job. This is the one bad apple adage at work. Placing an emphasis on matching an employee's personality with the position in which they work holds the biggest key to their success and the success of your business. Placing a sales- minded individual into a paper-pushing desk job creates a frustrated employee who underperforms. Give that same employee the freedom to drum up business creatively, and you have business spreading like wildfire.

Hiring a warm body to fill a seat can be very tempting when your business is on an upswing and you are anxious to keep up momentum. Beware. Spend the time to find the right personality for each job. When hiring a salesperson, try to convince them not to take the job. If they fight for the job and win you over, you will know they are naturally sales-driven and are "hungry" enough to work for the business.

People can be weird about insurance. Potential clients will try to avoid insurance agents because of the industry's "bad name." A prospect once told me that she did not want to talk to me about changing her automobile policy because she would then have to walk all the way to her car to change out the insurance card in her vehicle! Sure, overcoming objections is awful but so was being fired from the property management job I held. Choosing to be a maverick in an already under-appreciated industry might seem like masochism, but the hard road pays. In the words of Robert Frost, "I took the one less traveled by, and that has made all the difference."

About Adam

Adam Koch began his journey as an insurance agency owner with Farmers Insurance in 2004. Since that time he has learned many valuable lessons on how not to run an agency. Thankfully, for the sake of his family, he also learned from those mistakes and figured out a way to do it right. Adam has consistently proven that he has a fondness for helping new and existing small businesses do it right as well, at least as far as insurance is concerned. Among his peers he is considered an expert in the field of commercial insurance for small businesses and has been recognized as a top-producing agent many times by Farmers Insurance. More importantly, he is considered an expert among his clients as they put their trust in him to offer solutions to protect their business and personal assets correctly.

Adam has assembled and leads a team of experienced professionals to provide practical solutions to small business owners that can help them safeguard their future. With the wide array of options in their portfolio, he and his team work diligently with each client to create a customized insurance program to help them achieve their objectives. Additionally, he will pursue every viable alternative to ensure he can present the client with cost-effective, yet adequate coverage for their property, in the event of significant losses due to unexpected occurrences.

Adam Koch earned his BS in Economics from Texas A&M and remains a passionate Aggie football fan. He lives just north of Houston with his wife and two children and two rather useless dogs. He is a worship leader at the church he attends.

If you would like to know more about Adam Koch, or his award winning agency, visit: www.kochig.com or call: 866-491-3651.

CHAPTER 5

A TALE OF POSITIVE PERSONAL TRANSFORMATION — How Positive Inner Growth Leads To Positive Outer Growth

BY BALA G. GOPURALA, MD

Be the change that you wish to see in the world.
~ Mahatma Gandhi

More people are going to have personal success and live longer than ever before in history. Your question is how to be one of them. In the pages ahead I'm going to show you how. Imagine you purchased a powerful and an expensive computer. You paid about $6,500 with all the bells and whistles of technology. It does not, however, have an operator manual or any assistance with it. How could you have the best experience with it in such a situation? Of course you would at least need an operator manual. Similarly, how would you like to have an operator manual to your life, a manual of "conscious awareness" and a direction called "vision for your life?" This is exactly what this chapter will address.

CHANGE AND GROWTH

I came to understand through my life experiences and 20 years of medical practice, that many are walking around without proper knowledge and awareness of optimal health and personal growth. As a result, we are having a suboptimal experience with our mind, physical body and environment. We constantly seek success outside ourselves. We tend to seek a pill as an answer to most of our emotional, physical and social issues. I myself was in the same automatic daily rut of routine life, and then I read *Maximum Achievement* by Brian Tracy, and a study by Jack Canfield and Paul Scheele called *Effortless Success*. I also took a course on *7 Habits of Highly Effective People* by Stephen Covey. This information has certainly influenced me. I made a personal decision that I wanted to be the "captain of my soul" and I wanted to consciously direct my life where I wanted it to go. I was tired of complaining and looking outside myself for success. I began to read, listen to, and associate with people who are successful. I began to see through the lens of "life's big picture." This change may not happen all of a sudden, as it certainly didn't in my case. It is a process. We need to learn to be patient with ourselves.

BEGINNING

My life began in one of the world's largest democracies, India. I am the oldest of three siblings. I have a brother and sister. My parents were in public service as educators and philanthropists. They both believed deeply in democracy. My father was involved in Gandhi's nonviolence movement for Indian democracy. My parents operated three elementary and middle schools which served underprivileged children. They provided shelter, food, and education. My parents and grandparents had a tremendous influence on my life. My grandfather was a physician and mayor of the city. He led the community by example.

From the very beginning of my life, I was exposed to the concept of "be the change that you wish to see in the world." I went to one of my parents' schools. My parents and grandparents were role models. My mother was the headmistress of the school. I clearly remember how she operated the weekly mentorship session. Children from different religious backgrounds brought their Gita, Bible, and Koran. Everyone would take a turn and read. She moderated discussions and synthesized these teachings as bits of wisdom that connected us. On many occasions she said to students, "If you have to choose between being right and being kind, always choose to be kind."

THE AMERICAN DREAM

Somewhere along my journey, I caught the American Dream. After completing medical school and some additional training, I came to the world's most powerful democracy, America. I visited the University of Alabama at Birmingham as a scientist-physician. By virtue of my scholarly work I was invited to obtain permanent residency, and now I am a US citizen. I completed the medical board exams, residency, and fellowships in medicine, hematology and oncology. Because of my experience in medicine and because of the problems we are facing in the health industry, I have become deeply interested in optimal health, human potential, and personal growth. The term "health industry" is a misnomer. We could just as well refer to it as the "sickness industry," focusing on disease rather than proactively working on health.

PERSONAL TRANSFORMATION

As I continuously grow in my transformation, I also influence other people along the way, first starting from my home. My seven-year-old daughter recently observed on a family trip, "Dad, you be the example and brother and I will follow you." My eight-year-old agreed, "Yes, Dad, we will follow you." I also influence my wonderful and supportive wife. I can identify principles that have changed my life. These are time-tested principles and many studies have proved their worth and integrity. As my mother said, "Some principles are universal, they unify humanity, and they work in every society." They have worked in my life, and they should work in yours. You have to study them and work at them.

PERSONAL VISION

On one long-call night, I saw Mr. R, a 25 year-old male college student in the ER because he used cocaine his friend gave him the night before his final exam. He had a heart attack and left-sided stroke and was on a ventilator for several weeks. Defying medical understanding, miraculously, he recovered. This incident resulted in a setback of many years of valuable time in his life. However, he has since changed and has gotten a new vision for his life with encouragement from his family.

Now he has completed business school and has a successful career. The question I asked myself is, "Do I have to have a life catastrophe to get an awareness of personal vision or can I be proactive with my life?" Helen Keller said, "Having no vision is worse than not having eye sight." The following information lists my one-page vision statement that has worked well for me and the people under my care.

Complete mental well-being

- Emotional
- Interests
- Spirituality

Complete physical well-being

- Optimal nutrition
- Optimal activity/exercise

Complete social well-being

- Relationships
- Spouse
- Children, grandchildren
- Friends
- Family
- Coworkers
- Area of work
- Finance
- Legacy

OPTIMAL HEALTH

Mr. D, a forty-six-year-old busy executive, was admitted into the hospital with chest pain, and he had a heart attack. He was the CEO of a small-company of 50 employees and had high work-related stress. He was the father of 3 children. He smoked two packs of cigarettes a day, constantly on the go, grabbing fast food. He said, "Doc, I have not had time to get a physical in the last ten years." Further testing showed he had a 70% occlusion of a major heart blood supply, hypertension, increased lipids, and diabetes mellitus, Type 2. Mr. D changed his lifestyle. In the next six months, he lost 30 pounds and showed improvement in his health. He realized he needed to be in a proactive meaningful action mode, rather than a reactive response mode.

In 1946, the representatives from 61 countries at the World Health Organization defined 'Health' as a state of complete physical, mental, and social well-being and not merely the absence of disease or infirmity. After this definition entered into force on 7 April 1948, it has not been amended. This means we look at health as a whole and not as one single aspect of a person. Mr. D. clearly understood this and made a vision for his life as described earlier. He took charge of what went into his mind as well as into his mouth. Subsequent annual physical examinations and tests were consistently excellent for his age.

GRATITUDE

I came to understand the attitude of gratitude is key to personal fulfillment. I maintain a daily gratitude journal. First thing in the morning, I write all the things I am grateful for in life. This puts me in a proactive state for the day. Robert Emmons and his colleagues, in a series of studies, has demonstrated that people who maintain gratitude have fewer health problems, get more sleep, feel more refreshed in the morning, are more proactive, and even experience fewer heart attacks. Oprah Winfrey says writing a gratitude journal is the single most important thing she has done in her life for the last 16 years. Many of Deepak Chopra's teachings focus on cultivating gratitude. He explains we can become more grateful by taking a walk in the neighborhood, around the office, or in nature. He advises us to pay attention to the senses – including seeing, hearing, smelling, tasting, and touching. Being present in the moment and acknowledging life's blessings will improve our mood.

DAILY READING

I came with the mentality of reading only for the examinations. However, I started to realize the joy and personal growth that come with reading after I committed myself to daily reading. By reading books, I started to understand my emotions and myself. It made me think who I really am and what makes life more meaningful. I understood I can either obtain the knowledge and experience with my personal time and energy, or I can learn from mistakes of wise people through the association of books, teaching or mentorship. I learned about the Book-of-the-

Month Club from Oprah Winfrey and how reading books has changed her life. I voraciously read health and personal development books. I clearly understood what kind of person I become is dependent upon what kind of books I read, who I associate with, and how I internalize and act on the positive life-changing experiences. Learning from the mistakes of others is quite inexpensive and easy. Certainly reading leads to personal transformation.

PERSONAL CHOICE

Mrs. V. was a 45-year-old female with pelvic pain and was seen in the ER, found to have infection and got treated. She also had an abnormal Pap smear and was urged to follow-up with her regular doctor on three different occasions. However, three years later she was brought back to the ER by her family with symptoms of stage IV cervical cancer that had spread to her lungs. She said she made the choice of ignoring the prior advice with the hope that it was not a serious problem. Unfortunately, her cancer did not respond to the therapy and three months later she passed away. This was a heart-rending and frustrating moment in practicing medicine. Cervical cancer is a very treatable and even curable illness, provided one makes the right choice of prompt care. Psychologist and Nobel Prize winner, Daniel Kahneman, in his work on the way people make their decisions, describes ease with which we draw the conclusions without much analysis. He calls this tendency 'what you see is all there is.' Every choice we make has influence on our lives. Even no choice is also a choice of no choice.

Family: After I came to the US, I was adopted into an American family. I took care of Mama Sparks, an 80-year-old with Dementia. I truly experienced how her children worked together and took care of her until she passed away four years later. It was a graceful experience looking back, but not at the time. I learned Mama Sparks, who was married for 65 years to her husband, lived a wonderful life. More than one-half of my medical practice consists of people 65 or older. It is interesting to find one half to two thirds of them have been in a committed relationship for over 30 years. I am always interested to find out the health effects in these long-term commitments. Then I read Robert G Wood's publication in 2007 from the Office of Assistant Secretary for Planning and Evaluation, Office of Human Services Policy, US Department of Health, that summarizes the effect of marital status on several of the positive health outcomes of parents as well as their children in the United States. These benefits include increased healthcare access and use through retaining health insurance status from the other spouse after a major life event. The report also describes decreased depression, improved physical health, and longevity in the couples. There is an inter-generational health effect in that the children of these parents have better physical health in adulthood and increased longevity. Preserving a family unit is an important element for personal success.

FAITH

I learned that faith is a very important aspect of a person's life. Faith is an antidote for failure. Fear, doubt and worry rob our faith and keep us from moving forward. A growing body of research shows people who practice religious faith have positive health benefits, including prevention of illness or better coping and recovery when they fall ill. Dr. Harold G. Koenig, professor of psychiatry and behavioral sciences at Duke University Medical Center, has shown improvement of long lists of these medical conditions including cancer to cardiac surgery in people with religious faith. How do we develop faith? Faith is choice. One can literally think and talk oneself into faith just as one can think and talk oneself into fear, doubt and worry. Without faith a person is powerless. Napoleon Hill said faith is the 'eternal elixir', which gives life's power and action to the impulse of thought. So faith is a glue that binds and molds our lives.

PEACE OF MIND

I learned through my personal study that peace of mind is the unifying essential goal of a person's life. It shook me when Brian Tracy exposed me to the concept: " You can only be successful as a person to the degree to which you can achieve your own happiness, your own contentment, your own sense of personal well being – in short, your own peace of mind." Initially it was difficult for me to understand that I am responsible for my own peace of mind. As I internalized this very important principle, I understood I could not give away what I do not have. Where do I find peace of mind? What conditions will get me there? Or how do I get there? I found out systematic elimination of or at least minimizing negative emotions like, fear, anger, guilt, doubt, and resentment will automatically result in peace of mind. This is worth thinking about.

I have had several opportunities to interact with people who are at the end of their life. I have developed close relationships in taking care of them over a long period of time. I often asked the questions: Is there anything you would have liked to see more of in your life? Is there anything you wished you had done that you didn't? Everyone of them said they would have planned their life better. They would have spent more time with family. They all said they would have made peace of mind a priority.

ACTION EXERCISE

Ask yourself the same questions I asked my people. Also think about what you would do differently if you had to start your life today. How would you define your optimal health? Consider for the next twenty-four hours, be aware of what goes into your mind as well as your mouth.

About Dr. BalaG

Bala G. Gopurala, MD, M.Sc., (DrBalaG) is a physician, American Board of Internal Medicine, Double Board Certified Medical Oncologist, a Best-Selling Author and a Golden Quill Award Nominee from the National Academy of Best-Selling Authors. He has combined 20 years of medical practice and has taken care of more than ten thousand patients. He was a National Institute of Health Research Fellow. He was involved in HIV and Cancer Research.

Dr. BalaG has received numerous awards including Research Scholar Award, Resident of the Year Award, Outstanding Young Investigator Award, Outstanding Physician Award, and Outstanding Community Health Service Award. He served on numerous committees including international mentor, interdisciplinary medical council, improving quality, care, education and service for the patients. He was also inducted into the International Who's Who of Professionals. He has been selected as one of America's top Oncologists. He is a lifelong learner. He has a fulfilling medical practice in Shelby County, Alabama.

As an insider he is observing changes in the medical industry, and he clearly brings into his daily practice the wisdom of the old adage "an ounce of prevention is worth a pound of cure." He approaches every person comprehensively, as a whole individual in the context of presenting illness. This approach has truly helped patients alleviate their suffering and regain true "Health" as defined by the World Health Organization. He inspires and empowers people to the highest Awareness of Optimal Health. He regularly gives lectures, conducts workshops and seminars on Optimal Health, Personal Development and Human Potential. He is happily married and has two children.

Dr. BalaG is a leadership consultant as well as executive health and wellness advisor. He helps leaders to enjoy optimal health and embrace personal development. He developed a skill-based training system to help individuals and corporations to improve personal health thereby transforming healthcare from cost to investment. This system has changed the equation of healthcare perceived as an asset rather than a liability and this also increased productivity and employee morale. He is currently involved in writing a book on Optimal Health and Personal Growth.

His teachings have a common sense health approaches to daily complex issues, thereby helping people to think outside of the box. This helps the person as well as the entire family, as he or she understands and takes responsibility for health and personal growth. He has a unique and effective way of delivering information and influencing people to take responsibility for life. He is easily approachable and gets along well with his clients and helps them see the big picture and at the same time focus on the important details that are vital to life's health decisions. Dr. BalaG brings a unique set of medical training, research and a depth of understanding of the importance of personal growth and transformation in helping his clients to succeed. Outside of work, he spends time with his family. His interests include reading, swimming, table tennis and nature exploration.

You can reach Dr. BalaG at: www.DrBalaG.com for further information or call: 1-866-466-1244 for a consultation.

CHAPTER 6

TRANSFORMATIONAL WORK: Becoming Change Agents Through Our Professional Lives

BY LEIGH STEINBERG

Most of you reading this chapter regularly watch a favorite sport on TV. Whether it's baseball, basketball, football, hockey, soccer or another collegiate or pro sport, you tune in to cheer for your favorite team - or maybe just to witness the amazing feats of a superior player.

When you watch those games, you probably just see them as a pleasant diversion that will take you away from your troubles for a few hours. When I watch them, however, I see one of the most powerful platforms available to affect needed progress in our society.

That's because I've been lucky enough to combine two of my most powerful passions – sports and creating positive change – into one incredibly gratifying career. As one of the country's leading sports agents, I not only advocated for the best deals for my player-clients, I also advocated to them to get involved and make a difference – however they could.

That may surprise you. After all, the name of this book is *Change Agents* – and few associate that concept with my profession. The only thing the average person thinks a sports agent wants to change is the amount in his bank account – to make it higher and higher. We're supposed to be ruthless, cutthroat characters who have to "show the money" to our clients. Anyway, that's the media stereotype of my profession.

Of course, I suppose I contributed my bit to that stereotype, as I served as a consultant for the HBO original series, *Arli$$*, as well as the Technical Consultant for such sports-themed films as *Any Given Sunday*, starring Al Pacino, *For the Love of the Game*, starring Kevin Costner and, perhaps most famously, *Jerry Maguire*, starring Tom Cruise.

That last film portrayed a sports agent that quantifies conscience – even if it took him awhile to find it.

I've always had a conscience, especially when it came to creating positive social change for the world – and, in that respect, I've always aspired to be a "Change Agent." Yes, sports – and any industry, for that matter – can make a positive difference to our society – if the individuals involved make a commitment to combining their work with a higher vision.

I actually view that as an obligation – and I would hope everyone does.

BECOMING A CHANGE AGENT

Where did that feeling of obligation come from – and why have I always carried it with me?

There's a very simple answer to that question – my parents. When you're the son of a teacher and a librarian, you can't help but feel some responsibility to serve the public good. My father, more specifically, raised me to retain two core values throughout my life. One was to treasure relationships – especially family. And the second was that I should always attempt to make a positive difference in the world and help those who can't help themselves. He used to say, " There is no they, the they is you."

There was a corollary to that second value that has also stayed with me – and that was not blaming other people for your problems or a sticky situation you may find yourself in. There's no point in muttering to yourself, "Well, *they* did this to me..." or "*They* need to fix this for me..." The vast majority of times, there is no "*they*" to blame.

Because "they," in fact, is *you.*

It's up to each and every one of us to step up and take care of our own lives and deal with the consequences of our own actions. And also to do what you can for those who *truly* need outside assistance in their own lives.

I've written elsewhere about how I sort of stumbled into becoming a sports agent. I was a grad counselor in an undergrad dorm at UC Berkeley, working my way through law school, when the school moved the freshman football team into my dorm. Steve Bartkowski was a star member of that football team – and, in 1975, he was the very first player picked in the very first round of the NFL draft by the Atlanta Falcons. Just as I was choosing from various legal career options, Steve asked me to represent him in contract negotiations.

That was the beginning for me - not just of my success as a sports agent, but also to my dedication to becoming a true "Change Agent." As I mentioned, my thought, from the very start, was to motivate my athlete-clients to create positive change and target problems in society through their influential position in our American society.

THE THOUGHT POWER OF SPORTS

Why did I consider pro sports to be the right venue for tackling social issues? Because sports occupies a unique high-profile position in this country – and the position carries with it a certain responsibility.

There were weeks during the 2012-2013 NFL season where the top five Nielsen-rated television shows were prime time football games. That's right – the top *five*, all football. Of course, you would think that twenty-two guys on the gridiron could easily beat *Two and a Half Men,* not to mention *Two Broke Girls* - but every other show as well? And occupying the top five slots? That's an incredible achievement - and the culmination of a trend that's been snowballing over the past few decades.

When I began as a sports agent, it was also the beginning of a major expansion of media; cable and satellite television, satellite radio, the additional of literally hundreds of channels in both TV and radio, along with the explosion of Internet sports sites, has given the average fan thousands of choices and more sports content and analysis than ever before in history.

Is it any wonder that the athletes with the highest profiles are transformed into larger-than-life heroes?

Many men and increasing numbers of women grow up loving sports, playing sports and aspiring to be collegiate or pro athletes. Realistically, only a tiny percentage will make that giant leap – and that leaves millions with an incredible passion for sports that can only be fulfilled by following those who did make it to the pros.

I believe it's useless to argue, as my friend Charles Barkley once did, that only parents should be role models, not athletes. In an ideal world, that would be true. But the reality of family life is that there are a high percentage of single parent families that are specifically missing fathers. Filling that void in many kids' lives? The ubiquitous presences of athletes on larger-than-life huge HD screens into every young person's living room.

Sports have a profound impact on millions in this country, young and old, and there was never a moment I didn't understand that and want to use that impact for good.

CREATING ALL-STAR INITIATIVES

Beginning with my first signing, I made it clear to the athletes I worked with that they had the capacity to trigger imitative behavior for young people – and that was a power that needed to be directed correctly.

That's why I asked them to retrace their roots to their high school and collegiate communities, as well as their current professional ones, in order to set up charities in these locales. That would give them the opportunity to be role models for great values, as well as give themselves a sense of real self-respect and worthwhile achievement beyond what they did on the field. By establishing a scholarship fund or helping a church charity or even retrofitting the athletic equipment for a local high school, they could make a statement that a community can pitch in together and solve whatever problems might be holding them back.

At the collegiate level, a number of my player-clients ended up creating scholarship programs – programs funded by enough money to spawn an amount of interest that alone would pay for actual awarded scholarships for years to come.

For example, Edgerrin James, a running back for the Indianapolis Colts at the time, donated $350,000 back to his alma mater, the University of

Miami, for that kind of scholarship program. Troy Aikman, Dallas Cowboy quarterback, and Eric Karros, Los Angeles Dodgers first baseman, both endowed scholarships at UCLA. Kerry Collins, NY Giants quarterback did the same for Penn State, and Drew Bledsoe, New England Patriots quarterback, at Washington State University.

At the pro level, I challenged each of my athletes to find a cause they felt strongly about supporting – or a negative condition they felt passionate about wanting to change. And so we established foundations in cities across the country that had advisory boards containing the leading area political, community and business leaders, as resources for those charities. The star power of the athlete leading each of these foundations gave them the kind of credibility and profile that attracted these kinds of influential figures.

NFL great, Running Back Warrick Dunn set up a "Homes for the Holidays" program, which assisted single mothers with ownership of the first homes they would ever have. His foundation made the down payments to enable these moms to make this big move – and also brought Home Depot on board to help fix up those homes. This program dramatically changed these women's lives. Similarly, NFL Hall of Famer Steve Young funded the Forever Young Foundation, which to this day helps children in the San Francisco area facing significant physical, emotional, and financial challenges.

In total, the athletes I worked with have been able to raise over 700 million dollars for these causes. That kind of financial support works wonders, of course, but I still believe that the messaging these athletes are capable of delivering is even more important than the money they can contribute.

For example, my client Lennox Lewis, the last undisputed world heavyweight-boxing champ did a PSA (Public Service Announcement) in which he said real men don't hit women. That did more to impact young rebellious adolescent attitudes towards domestic violence than dozens of lectures from authority figures could ever have done.

Similarly, two other clients at the time, boxer Oscar De La Hoya and Steve Young did a PSA that said, "Prejudice is Foul Play." Again, young people tune out messages from most adults. They may not listen to a teacher or a parent – but a tough macho fighter or a top NFL quarterback can permeate the perceptual screen that kids create to tune out those kinds of pro-social messages.

BATTLING THE BIGGER ISSUES

There are more systematic problems in our society that, of course, require much more than an athlete's participation to solve.

In the wake of the tragic Oklahoma City bombing of a federal building which claimed 168 lives, carried out by a domestic terrorist ring, I became concerned that skinheads and hate groups were on the rise. I went to the Anti-Defamation League of B'nai Brith, headed by the amazing Abe Foxman, and proposed that I fund a training program, which they ended up calling the Steinberg Leadership Institute, in order to help young leaders take on this fight against hate.

In America's thirty largest cities, from New York to Miami, Chicago to Houston, Seattle to San Diego, young doctors, lawyers and teachers received a year of training on how to spot these kinds of hate groups and use that information to help local law enforcement officials track them down. They were also taught how to go to local school districts and promote ethnic tolerance. I'm proud to say we trained thousands of young leaders with this program.

Here in Orange County, where I live and work, I created a program with the Human Relations Commission that brought together middle school and high school students from every ethnic background and put them together for a week in a special summer camp, where they received leadership training and learned to appreciate everyone else's cultural heritage, as opposed to being afraid of those who were different and sticking to harmful stereotypes that promote divisiveness. Those students were encouraged to stay in touch as they went on to college in order to become a vanguard against hate.

Hate is a poison in our society that we may never be able to fully eliminate – but there is another issue that I'm deeply concerned about that is a far greater threat to us all: Climate change. The groundbreaking scientist Galileo, in his time, spent his life under house arrest. His crime? Asserting the world was round instead of flat and that the earth was, in fact, not the center of the universe. Similarly, the easily-grasped truth of global warming is routinely denied by many in pivotal political positions.

Ice caps have melted, oceans have risen, and what once were aberrational weather patterns are becoming commonplace. The world has not reacted rapidly enough to something that could kill off our entire species, which has a remarkable ability to ignore the plain-as-day peril that grows with each passing day.

I don't want to be one of the first generation in the history of this country to hand down a degraded quality of life to our kids. That's why we've proposed the creation of a program called The Sporting Green Alliance, in which we would aggregate sustainable technologies in wind, solar, recycling, resurfacing and water to take to stadiums, arenas and practice fields at the high school, collegiate and professional level.

The goal would be to drop carbon emissions as well as energy costs and transform those venues into educational platforms - so that the hundreds of millions of fans that attend games in this country can actually see a waterless urinal, a solar panel or some other green technology they might not otherwise be exposed to. That will help the people of this country understand that these innovations are practical *right now* to incorporate into their own homes and businesses.

What this would do is put sports in the forefront of perhaps our most important societal challenge - combatting climate change, saving the planet and, ultimately, saving ourselves.

As you can see, I believe sports still has an awesome potential to be a Change Agent for us all. My challenge to you is – how can you be a Change Agent in your specific business?

When you make a difference in the world through your work, you gain a passion that takes whatever your profession might be to a higher level of satisfaction. It becomes more than your work – it becomes your life's work. And it also gives everyone around you a greater degree of motivation and fulfillment than they would experience by simply aspiring to add more digits to their bank account balances.

When we can agree on what needs to be done to create a better world and make concrete plans to get it done, that breeds results we can all feel good about. More importantly, it empowers a quality future for generations to come. When it comes to that goal, it's been "game on" for me from the beginning. And I sincerely hope it's a team you'll consider playing with.

About Leigh

Leigh Steinberg, the world's first "super agent," founded his sports law practice in 1975 when he negotiated a then-record contract for the first overall pick in the NFL draft Steve Bartkowski. Since then, Leigh has solidified his name as one of the premiere player representatives in all of sports, and specifically the NFL where he represented a record eight different number-one NFL draft picks, over 60 first round draft picks, and consistently negotiated record-breaking contracts. His past clients include NFL stars and hall of famers Troy Aikman, Steve Young, Warren Moon, Drew Bledsoe, Ben Roethlisberger, Thurman Thomas, Eric Dickerson, Derrick Thomas, Edgerrin James, Jevon Kearse, and Bruce Smith, boxing legends Lennox Lewis and Oscar De La Hoya, and a plethora of NBA, MLB, and Olympic athletes. In all, Leigh has negotiated over a billion dollars in NFL contracts, and over two billion dollars in athlete contract and endorsement deals.

Driven by the philosophy that professional athletes possess the cultural influence to reach the masses and have a significant social impact, Leigh has helped his clients to become valuable members of their communities and to be models for imitative behavior. Specifically, Leigh has helped his clients develop over a hundred charitable foundations, which have raised over $700 million for innumerable causes. Leigh challenges his players to find a cause which they feel passionate about and fight for it. For example, Rolf Benirschke's "Kicks for Critters" helped fund protection of endangered species and Warrick Dunn's "Homes for the Holidays" gives single parents the opportunity to own a home for the first time in their lives.

Leigh created the Steinberg Leadership Program with the Human Relations Commission of Orange County to give leadership and tolerance training to high school and middle school leaders in a series of one-week camps.

Leigh has been named Man of the Year over a dozen times by a diverse group of organizations that include the March of Dimes, Cedars Sinai, the Southern California Boy Scouts, the Orange County and Los Angeles Human Relations Commissions, the Orange County and Los Angeles divisions of the Anti-Defamation League. Leigh has been awarded the "Keys to the City" of four cities: San Francisco, CA, Memphis, TN, Jacksonville, FL, Concord, CA and Indianapolis, IN.

An accomplished speaker, Steinberg has traveled the world addressing topics ranging from sports and entertainment, to political and economic issues. In 1992, Steinberg helped lead a successful campaign to prevent the San Francisco Giants baseball club from relocating to Florida. For his efforts, then San Francisco Mayor Frank Jordan honored him by declaring "Leigh Steinberg Day" in the city of SF soon after.

In 1994, then Oakland Mayor Elihu Harris utilized Steinberg as a consultant in his successful bid to prevent the Oakland Athletics baseball club from relocating to Sacramento or San Jose.

Steinberg has been active in pursuits to attract a new football franchise to locate in Los Angeles.

Leigh wrote a best-selling book in 1998, *Winning with Integrity,* providing readers insight on how to improve their life through non-confrontational negotiating. Leigh also just finished writing his autobiography, which is scheduled to be published in February 2014.

CHAPTER 7

GETTING IN THE POCKET: Launching Your Business' Mobile App and Website

BY DAMON COCKREL

Apple introduced the iPhone in June of 2007 and the entire world changed. Other data-capable phones had come before it, but with the iPhone, the cellphone became the smartphone. Apple had created an easy-to-use, handheld computer that put more processing power in your pocket than there was in the computers aboard the Apollo 11 spacecraft. As ground-breaking as that was, more important than the technology, was the affect it had on people. Apple showed us that the power of the smartphone wasn't in its specifications or capabilities, but in the relationships that people developed with it.

IT'S THAT PERSONAL?

75 percent of Americans bring their phones to the bathroom.
(Source: CBS News, 2012)

The smartphone is absolutely the most personal and intimate electronic device a person owns. This pocket-sized unit directly reflects who we are, our interests and our priorities. It's an extension of our personality. Visit any Apple store and you will quickly see that every iPhone is the same when it comes out of the box, but within moments it becomes as unique and individual as a fingerprint. After setting up email, adding a few contacts, choosing ringtones and wallpaper, adding a designer case and other accessories, that phone becomes "mine."

The "Why" of Mobile Strategy

It's this intimacy that allows a smartphone to become the primary, personal computing and lifestyle device for most owners. People use them to play games, access social networks, consume entertainment such as music and movies, and manage email. Most importantly, they use their smartphones to shop; making business owners around the world rejoice.

Mobile consumers make shopping lists, research product features, check product availability and compare prices. They find store locations, look for coupons, deals and make online purchases of goods and services. In fact, the Monetate Ecommerce Quarterly (EQ4 2012) reports that "Mobile" now drives 20% of e-commerce traffic. Are you getting your share?

When speaking with business owners about mobile websites or apps, it still amazes me to hear comments like; "An app would be a waste of money for us. We're a local, small business. We wouldn't have any need for that. Besides, our customers don't really use apps and we've already got a great website." Look, the big boys have already figured out how important it is to have a mobile strategy. Don't believe me? Let's play a game.

Pick an industry, or better yet, take your own industry. Now, take out your smartphone. Go to the iTunes App Store, Google Play or whatever app marketplace your device has. Search for apps using the keywords a customer would use to find information about the industry you've chosen. Look at the results. It should come as no surprise that the major players in that industry already have mobile apps in place. You should too. They didn't decide to do this arbitrarily. I'm telling you, you want a piece of that action.

GETTING IN THE POCKET: YOUR MOBILE WEBSITE

There is a common path that mobile customers follow to choose a business to patronize. It begins with a search -- usually on Google, who completely dominates the mobile search space. They type keywords into the search engine and receive a list of results. Since smartphones contain GPS chips, local businesses actually have an advantage. Those that are closest to the mobile customer's current location will generally place higher in the search results.

Now, go back to your phone. Open your search engine and search using the same keywords you used earlier when we were looking for apps. Select a business from your search results and open that link. More likely than not, you've now just entered something I call "zoom-and-scroll hell."

Most business have invested a great deal of time and money in the development of wonderful websites. They are full of features, information and images that truly showcase the firm, making it easy for customers to find exactly what they need...from a desktop or laptop computer. That same website, when viewed on a mobile device, can become an absolute nightmare, especially on a smartphone. Text becomes illegibly small, requiring users to zoom in just to make it readable. Once zoomed to a viewable size, the user now has to scroll up, down, left and right in order to read the page or navigate the site. It's a nightmare that generally leads to a bad user experience. Often, the user will abandon trying to navigate that site, go back to the search results and choose another link in hopes that the next site will be easier to use. By not having a mobile-friendly website, that company just lost business.

Your mobile website is the first interaction a mobile customer will have with your business. Control that experience. Recognize that the needs of a mobile customer are different than those of a customer accessing the Web from a desktop or laptop. Design with that in mind. Use larger buttons. Keep the navigation simple. You have to learn to think "mobile" first. Ask yourself these three questions:

1. Why are they looking for my product or service?

The Spice Girls sang, "Tell me what you want, what you really, really want!" Your mobile website must immediately give your customers what they "really, really want." People don't buy products or services, they buy solutions to problems. No one wants a drill, they want a hole. The drill just makes that happen.

Think about what drives people to look for your business. What problem do they have? What solution do you provide? Answer those questions, then give the answers prominence on your mobile website.

2. What information would a mobile customer expect to find, once they reach my site?

There are some obvious elements that a customer expects to find on a mobile website. Since they are mobile, they are going to want your business hours, address, and phone number. You need to make this information available right up front and make it easily accessible from anywhere else on the site. Most mobile web browsers enable "click-to-call" and GPS directions by default, making it easy for mobile customers who want to reach you to do so.

Your business solution needs to be central to the site, after all, that's why they visited in the first place. If you're a restaurant, customers want to see a menu, complete with images, descriptions and prices. They want to see your specials, make reservations, and have the option of placing an order.

For retailers, customers expect to see products again with images, descriptions, prices and online ordering capabilities. They also want to be able to browse by category and to search for specific items.

Mobile users searching for consultants, professionals or other service providers expect to learn about your qualifications and the services you provide. They want to see testimonials, references and, if appropriate, videos of you in action.

3. What might a mobile customer be doing when they decide to look for my company, product or service?

What could they be thinking about that triggered the search? Maybe they saw your ad or read an article that made them want to find more information. Perhaps something came up in conversation or maybe they were already surfing the Web on their phone. You may be able to capitalize on the trigger with a related, immediate offer.

Next, where are they? …in the car? …walking? …or on public transportation? Mobile situations are generally not as "calm" as desktop or laptop Internet sessions. They are full of distractions and interruptions resulting in search sessions of much shorter duration.

Consider all of this when laying out your website. Your mobile experience has to accommodate these constraints. The content must be easily accessible. Keep the information that a customer wants only one or two clicks away. Don't make them dig for it. They just don't have the time to hunt around. The mobile website must also be engineered to accommodate the slower data speeds often encountered with mobile connections. Always be mindful when inserting images, video and other elements that might slow the customer experience. Nothing will make a potential customer abandon you faster than a slow site.

A well-executed, mobile web experience brings more customers and additional revenue to your business. Mobile searches are more valuable and have increased conversion rates because mobile customers are generally farther along in their buying process. Even if they are not ready to purchase, do it right and they'll bookmark your mobile site. A bookmark eliminates your competition. That customer no longer has to search when they are looking for the solution you provide. They just pull out their phone, open the browser and go straight to you! Congratulations, you just got in the pocket.

STAYING IN THE POCKET: YOUR MOBILE APP

Now that you're in there, you have to stay there. This is where having an app for your business becomes an essential part of your mobile strategy. What's the difference? A mobile website is Internet-based content which can be accessed using the web browser on any device. A mobile app is a software application, designed and coded for a specific mobile platform. It must be downloaded and installed onto the device.

An iPhone app will not run on an Android device and vice versa. When you see a popular mobile app like the game Angry Birds being played on an iPhone, an Android device, a BlackBerry or a Windows phone, know that individual versions of the Angry Birds app were written for each of those platforms. Although creating individual "native" apps makes things a little more complicated, this specificity gives mobile apps some distinct advantages over mobile websites.

When a customer downloads and installs your mobile app, it's validation that they are more than just "interested" in your business. You have become a trusted partner and resource. So much so, that they are willing to give you prime, pocket real estate on the home screen of their smartphone. This means that your customer is always just one click away from your business. By comparison, a bookmarked, mobile website holds a position three clicks from the home screen. The user has to open the browser, open their bookmarks, and choose your link; three clicks. This positioning difference alone increases customer engagement.

The development strategy for your mobile app will follow the same path as your mobile website, but an app can provide a more captivating customer experience. Graphic elements are downloaded and stored directly into the phone when the app is installed. This means that components like visual effects and animations can be made more elaborate and engaging.

Native apps also have access to hardware components within the phone. The camera, accelerometer, microphone, GPS and more become available for use by the app. A GPS, check-in, loyalty program (think of it as your company's private Yelp!) is something you just can't do with a mobile website. But, the biggest advantage mobile apps have over mobile websites is something called *push notifications.*

Push notifications allow businesses to use the app to send messages directly to their customers. Unlike email messages, push notifications have an extremely high "open" rate. People actually read them! This one tool allows businesses to share all kinds of information with their customers; blog updates, RSS feeds, coupons, discounts and specials. But the real power lies in the ability to use them to ask a question and get instant customer feedback. Think about it. If you were deciding what new product or service to offer your customers, wouldn't it be great if you could just ask them what they want? Your mobile app lets you have that conversation.

That's very powerful, but abuse the power of push notifications and customers will quickly delete your app. It's a delicate balance. Give them useful, timely, and relevant information and your app will deliver you customers for life. Apps deepen your relationship with your customers in a way mobile websites can't. It lets you stay in the pocket.

GETTING STARTED

Now that you know what you have to do, where do you begin? Like any other essential business project, your mobile website and mobile app strategy requires solid planning to execute and sustain it successfully. **POCKET** is a simple, six-step framework to guide the process and keep your efforts focused.

P - Prepare - Assemble your team. Most likely, this will be a combination of in-house and partner contributors. Get clear on how this project will complement your existing marketing. Establish your goals, designate a project manager and define the scope. Right here, at the very beginning, it is crucial that you set clear expectations and objectives for the customer experience. Get customer input, it's invaluable.

O - Organize - Identify and collect your assets. Gather any existing materials that you can leverage, determine where you have gaps, then fill them. Establish your timelines, key performance indicators (KPIs) and success metrics. Create your content calendar and establish an update schedule. It is essential that you keep your mobile app and website fresh. Give your customers a reason to keep using them.

C - Create - Design your mobile website and app. Test every single element and link. You want to find the errors here, before you introduce it to the world. This is also the time to create your app's promotional strategy along with any associated marketing materials. Take the time to identify any new processes, procedures and training your staff might need. They must be able to assist customers with features in the app or on the site. Be sure to thoroughly document everything.

K - Kickoff - Launch the app and mobile website, implement your promotional and content strategies. Measure everything you can at this stage. Later, you can decide what data is important and what can be tossed. Gather as much customer feedback as possible. Pay close attention to their likes and dislikes. This is critical information.

E - Evaluate - Review the data. Evaluate the analytics; number of visitors, number of downloads, click-through rates, etc. How are you tracking against your KPIs. Are you on target? Most importantly, track your ROI. After all, that's where the proof lies.

T - Tweak – Make adjustments based on your results. Keep what works and re-work what doesn't. You probably won't hit the mark with your first attempt. Keep adjusting. Continue the cycle of evaluation and tweaking. Failure is not an option. Commit to it until you get it right. You'll get there.

THE BOTTOM LINE

No matter what your business, a mobile strategy is not an option; it's a requirement. If you haven't already started building one, you need to re-think that. I guarantee, you have competitors who are already there. Start with a mobile website to reach more new customers. Then deepen the relationship with a mobile app. Remember, your customers are mobile. How mobile is your business? Take action today and start Getting in the Pocket.

About Damon

Damon Cockrel is a mobile strategist, entrepreneur, speaker and the author of the forthcoming book, *Getting in the Pocket: Mobile Strategies for Business Success.* He has counseled individuals, professionals, businesses, schools and government agencies on mobile strategies for over twenty years.

Strategies for small businesses and educational institutions are the core focus of Damon's mobility practice.

> *"I'm an entrepreneur. Through the course of my career, I've made a lot of money and I've been flat broke. Owning a business is hard. It took many small businesses way too long to take advantage of the Internet revolution. Now, we're in a Mobile revolution and I'm here to make sure that business owners stay ahead of the game this time.*
>
> *But it doesn't stop there. Today's students are tomorrow's entrepreneurs. We have a responsibility to give them the tools, training and strategy to be competitive in a global economy. Mobile technology is critical to raising student engagement and achievement."*
>
> – Damon Cockrel

An exciting and dynamic speaker, Damon has a unique ability to convey complex ideas in ways that educate, entertain and engage. As a teen, he was a local television reporter and a scholarship-winning actor. After college, he toured as a bass guitarist and lead vocalist. It should come as no surprise that Damon knows how to charm an audience. Technical and creative, he often refers to himself as "a geek with a personality."

Damon and his wife Christina live in Central Ohio. He is an alumnus of The Ohio State University and a member of the TBDBITL Alumni Club. A former competitive baton twirler, he enjoys donating his teaching skills to the OSU Marching Band Drum Major Training Program.

www.DamonCockrel.com

CHAPTER 8

YOU ARE ALL YOU NEED: The Power Of Authenticity

BY JASPER ARMSTRONG

As a teacher and a coach, I have worked with tens of thousands of people. Many of them have been children and the amazing thing about children is that they can spot a phony faster than anyone. As a result, in order to effect the most change in this arena, one must have the ability to know who you are and effectively communicate that to all you come in contact with. When your students find you out to be a fake, they lose all respect for you and your message. So it is in life, we get caught up playing the game so much that we forget what our true Self is bringing to the table. Living an authentic life entails knowing your worth, believing in your God-given power and living a lifestyle that is consistent with your purpose on earth.

You are fearfully and wonderfully made. All that is exists to see you reach your fullest potential. The difference between those that do and those who do not comes down to the choice you make to be your most authentic self. Being true to yourself when the chips are down is a major deciding factor between those who win and those that do not in the game of life. Every life has a specific purpose. What is yours? Why are you here now at this time, and what are you doing with the time that you have? If you have found your purpose, are you living it to the max? If not, why not? What is stopping you? Who gave you permission to mull around in the doldrums of life?

This is indeed the greatest time in history to be alive yet many of us are merely existing and not thriving in life. Fear (False Expectations Appearing Real) is what is holding most of us back. The fear that somehow if I am who I be, then the world will shun me or laugh at me or that I won't be sufficient. This is the greatest trick that is played on the mind of the winner and nothing could be further from the truth. You are exactly what the world needs right now. Being afraid to risk, reach out, fail or succeed is no longer the order of the day. The world needs you. Not the you that you have created from snippets of your three favorite TV shows, but the you that exists in the still of the night and the you that wakes up with you first thing in the morning before you put on the airs and masks of the day. What if you are the one that the world needs to create that tipping point in the battle of good versus evil? What if you are the last piece of the dam that is holding back the rivers of cleansing change? Nas, the great rapper and poet, poses a question in one of his rhymes that states, "Whose world is this?" …and the response is, "The World is yours!" However, this only becomes true when you step into what is already yours. It's a lot like the feeling you get on Christmas morning. Your gift lies dormant under the tree waiting for you to possess the gift with your name on it. However, until you grab hold of it and own it, it's just a box under the tree. So it is with the gifts life has for you, until you attack your life with the fervor of Christmas morning, you merely exist.

In our quest to dominate our lives, it becomes increasingly important to realize that we have all that we need to succeed. This is not to say that we don't need to develop what we have or should ever cease to learn and grow. However, we are equipped to not only survive but also thrive in this life. This is about using what we have and fulfilling our greatest potential. I believe we have a God essence inside of us that is just waiting to explode on the earth and make all of our dreams come true. This essence is of the original matter of creation, and therefore was produced under extreme heat and pressure. Much the same way the heat and pressure of our lives serves as the catalyst to reveal our true selves to our self. It comes down to us having the courage to succeed rather than the fear of failure. It further comes down to us having the ability to stand in the face of life's challenges and grow in the direction of our greatest dreams.

It was once said that winners have the same fears as the rest of us yet they are not paralyzed by that fear. To dominate life requires action that is born of a fierce will to win in life and an iron drive that states, "I will not lose." The challenge then becomes how to unify the dream in your mind, the will in your heart and your day-to-day activities to produce maximum results. The actions we take or fail to take are in direct correlation to our self-worth and self-concept. If we believe we are supposed to win and are capable of winning, then we act in a manner and according to our dominant thought. Conversely, if we feel inadequate to the challenge, then our actions will reveal that as well. As a coach, I have seen this scenario play out many times on the field. If a player feels adequately prepared and expects to play well, he does. This said player will continue to play well until a game situation or another player puts doubt or fear in that player's psyche. In contrast, a dominant player will always seek to find his advantage and use it to find success. He will draw upon his superior size, strength, athleticism or mental toughness to overcome every challenge. It is through the lens of the dominant player that we must attack the game of life. The thing we see with our players and our teams is that the only way to keep doubt and fear at bay is through superior preparation for the competition of life. The same principal applies to our daily lives. We have to continue to strive for superior preparation in regards to filling our cup with positive mental pictures and a positive sound track (self-talk) to prepare us for all that life will bring our way.

You are more magnificent then you know. When you were created the mold was broken. There never has been and never will be another you. You are a star. You have been created to manifest the glory of a perfect creation. You are sufficient; you have enough brain, enough beauty, enough strength, and enough stamina to get started. The question is: Do you believe in your star power? Do you know that your star is worthy of shinning? Are you willing to do what it takes to knock off the crust that prevents the world from viewing your light? Nelson Mandela states, "It is our light, not our darkness, that most frightens us." Primarily, it is our doubt, disbelief, anger, frustration and shame from our past that dims the light of our star. Your star is your gift; however, your star power must be developed. It is developed by meeting every challenge of your life as a victor instead of a victim. This is done when you view your life as a part of a greater whole and see your actions from the perspective that what you do now will affect the next four generations of your family tree.

Being in touch with your star power allows you to step into the future of your bloodline today and make decisions intentionally that will reach seven generations after you. When we look at our decision-making process through that lens, it becomes clear to see that the development of our perfect star power is not only a good idea, but also it is imperative for the future success of our families. Are you leaving a legacy of star power or stardust for your lineage to follow? Much of this is determined by how we speak to ourselves and the actions we take in the present. Star power is in complete alignment with the higher self; it knows what the self wants and needs. Star power is clear, intentional, and focused, and best of all it is purely original and can only come from you. When you develop your star power as only you can, it is at that point that you are experiencing the power of authenticity.

In our quest to live a life of authenticity and dominate our daily lives there are a few principles that we must adhere to in order to possess all that life has to offer us:

> Be a man/woman of your word. The Bible teaches us that "In the beginning was the word and the word was God and the word was with God;" it goes on to say "and the word became flesh and dwelt amongst us." This gives us some insight into the power that our words contain. Because of this, it is wise to choose our words carefully taking into consideration the effect they will not only have on our life, but the whole world. Our words unleash currents and laydown patterns for our lives. When we do what we say we will do, we feel better about ourselves – causing us to know there is nothing we cannot do, have or become. Conversely, when we fail to do that which we say, it sends us into an eroding spiral of anger depression and fear.

Because earth is a sphere and it encapsulates both physical and spiritual energy everything happens in cycles. Hence the saying what goes around comes around. The frequencies of sound govern all things, that's why everything was spoken into being in the creation (Let there be, and it was). This laid down a pattern for divine speech that we should adhere to. The rule is what comes out of your mouth will come to fruition. You are such a powerful and magnetic being that the things of which you speak will manifest themselves. Often times, we back ourselves into patterns of behavior based on the words we speak. For example, I met a woman who swore that if a man ever hit her she would shoot him. Many years later, being married with three children, her husband hit her and you bet she shot him. By making such a statement and striving to be a woman of her word, she was forced into a certain behavior by what she said would happen if this situation arose. And when it did, as it often times does, you are obligated to fulfill your word. This can be a source of great difficulty in one's life, especially if you are not in the habit of speaking that which will cause you to behave in an excellent manner. The things that come out of our mouths are a direct reflection of what is on our mind and in our heart. It then becomes imperative to check ourselves daily to ensure we are aligned with our Higher Self and that we are thinking properly. Further, our mental diet and exercise are paramount to our success. What are you putting into your spirit? And is that consistent with what you say you want to have, do or become?

When you find yourself in a proper relationship with your Self, you find that you have the ability to participate in the game of life in a way that makes magic happen. Where does your magic come from? It comes from the alignment or perfect peace you find when you are operating at your fullest potential and most authentic Self. You will know when this change has occurred in your life when your loved ones begin to compliment you.

When getting in touch with your desire to live an authentic life, it is your primary duty to come from a place of personal conviction. What is your stance? Where do you stand in difficult times? What do you believe in? To find answers to these questions is never easy and is often forged through a lifetime of turmoil and strain. Yet, your spirit, your true Self has always sent you whispers of this truth if you would only take the time to listen and heed its call you would find the answers have been with you all along. When you take a stance in life, you activate the cosmic forces of good that will come and assist you on your path of growth and development. Taking a stance in life requires a great deal of maturity and courage because whenever you take a stance, it will inevitably put you in direct conflict with some other way of thinking, acting, or being. And since we are social beings and have the innate need to be accepted by others, we strive to fit in. The problem arises when we suppress the truth that is exploding inside of us. Or seek to hide the beam of light that emanates from the deepest part of our soul for acceptance. This is the greatest obstacle to the human spirit that exists. It is important to know that this war is intrapersonal.

It is a battle fought between you and yourself and we all find out that you are indeed a worthy opponent.

In all, living a life of authenticity is about 'letting your little light shine.' It is about realizing that you are sufficient and up to the task of being all that you can be, and you don't have to try to be someone else to be it. Authenticity is about finding that respect for your own uniqueness and embracing that. For when you are comfortable in your own skin the world will treat you accordingly. It's about becoming your best Self through personal growth and development and striving to live at the height of what you know is right. Authenticity is about getting in touch with your higher Self and letting it guide you on your way. Authentic living is about living in the authority that God has granted to men, knowing the dominion you were created to express in the earth and being a good steward of your power. Authenticity is having the courage to let your 'ayes' be 'ayes' and your 'nays' be 'nays' and finding the peace that comes from having taken a stance, while having the wisdom to see when you have been wrong and change immediately. Most of all it is knowing that you are the complete package, ready to assemble and dominate life to the fullest. You have everything you need in order to be successful.

READY, SET, DOMINATE!

About Jasper

Jasper B. Armstrong III is a native of Aurora, CO. He currently serves as a licensed special education teacher at Overland High School in the Cherry Creek School District where he has developed an intervention program for African-American males focusing on self-advocacy, study skills, problem solving and empowerment. Armstrong's five years of instilling hope, self-confidence and determination with his students, their parents, and other colleagues has earned him a position of great respect with the school community. Mr. Armstrong has also served as a board member for several organizations and has sponsored and operated many student organizations, including the African-American Male Leadership, Black Student Alliance, and Black Men of Today.

Community engagement and teaching are important principals to Mr. Armstrong. In addition to his dedication to African-American males' empowerment and achievement in school settings, Mr. Armstrong has also had an extensive ten-year coaching career including positions held at UNC Greeley, Langston University, and Grandview High School. During his tenure in these positions, he has served in roles including educational coordinator where one of his main responsibilities was to mentor and coach the struggling athletes. Mr. Armstrong has dedicated his professional and personal career to uplifting and empowering his students and has served as an important role model for these young people.

CHAPTER 9

11 THINGS YOU SHOULD THINK ABOUT BEFORE SELLING A HOUSE IN TODAY'S MARKET

BY JEAN-PHILIPPE LOISELLE

The story begins with a youth. He had the "competition" inside him and always wanted to do more. One thing that was important for him was to set a higher and higher standard for himself. If you were supposed to do one mile to accomplish a goal, he would do two miles. In fact, he had a paper on his bedroom ceiling on which was written: Pain is in your head, and by beating pain, you can achieve your biggest dream.

I started to read like never before about motivation, business success, negotiation and how people think. What interested me the most was the reason why some people had different result than others, and I got many answers over the years. I was also interested in the psychology behind the negotiation. I then studied business, but it was not enough for me to work for someone else. My father, a notary *(the notary in Canada performs legal work for his clients)*, asked me why I wouldn't try real estate sales. I looked at the kind of work it was, and immediately fell in love with it. It is about giving one's best everyday and making things happen with good strategy.

The field of real estate is in the middle of many professions like notary, land surveyor, appraiser, inspector, mortgage specialist and much more.

Being close to people, and in love with psychology, he gives to others the use of his superb negotiation skills. Actually, the real estate job has a huge ripple effect on many lives at the same time. It was an amazing opportunity to learn so many different things. After two years, he was in the top 10% of all RE/MAX agents in the province of Quebec. He is now known as one of the top-growing stars in the industry. He has boundless energy and an innate business sense. His vast knowledge of the market and his negotiation skills allow his client to maximize their profit. His passion to help other people achieve their dreams is within his soul. I am telling you this: ''His service for his clients is anything but ordinary.''

A couple of years ago, a client wanted to sell his property for over eight months without any success. I decided to call her right after the contract ended. The conversation was clear and simple with her; she wanted to keep the same agent and she was going to lower the asking price. It was really interesting why she wanted to keep the same agent. I told her, I am sure he did everything in his power to sell your home, however, this time you need a different approach to make sure it will be sold, so that you can achieve your project. She finally decided to see me in order to give her some advice regarding a couple of changes to maximize the value and the time delay. She finally decided to go with me for the right reason, I was able to help her in her situation. We kept the price the same, changed the arrangement of the furniture, and adapted a specific strategy. The property was sold in the first eight days. Actually, I am like a doctor who has to give advice to a patient. For me, I say the right thing on the first appointment, and there will not be any surprises.

Many sellers have the goal to sell quickly at the best price with the best terms and conditions. However, many of them are disappointed because they make several mistakes that could have been avoided at the outset. The result of my study over several years show me that these errors often are very expensive.

ERROR #1 - ESTABLISHING A SALE PRICE WITHOUT HAVING DONE A COMPLETE ANALYSIS

Firstly, I do believe your home is one or your biggest assets. This part could be done by your real estate agent. You must insist on a professional analysis with comparables sold and for sale. He will be able to make an analysis with comparable house sales normally from the last 6 to 12 months. He is a specialist with the price of things in your house. However, you must insist having an aggressive strategy to sell your home, because it is the key to your success.

ERROR #2 - OVER IMPROVING YOUR HOME COMPARED TO THE SECTOR

When you are renovating your home, consider the fact that what you renovate is for you, and not for the new buyer. Furthermore, be careful not to improve your property too much compared to the sector, because the money you invest stays and it won't be possible to get this money back when you sell. Not because it is beautiful for you is it for somebody else. Make sure your property price is based on what you offer compared to the competition, and that you do not over-price because of what you add to the property. Normally, a property that is way over the normal price bracket of the sector will usually stay longer on the market and eventually be harder to get a better price than the competition that offers less to the buyer.

ERROR #3 - OMIT TO ENSURE THAT THE PROPERTY IS WELL-POSITIONED

Positioning the price of the property is one of the most important points. It is the same thing as looking at a race horse. In reality, the position of the house will determine the number of visits and how quickly you sell. One of the important points to maximize your profit is based on being well positioned at all times in the process compared to your competitor. Setting too high a price can be as dangerous as setting too low a price. The average buyer looks at between 15 and 20 properties at the same time he sees yours. If your home or condo does not correspond to the price range of homes or other comparable condos, you will not be taken seriously by buyers and agents. Your property is likely to remain very long on the market without moving and buyers end up thinking that your property has flaws. Asking the right price from the beginning gives you the chance to get the most visibility in the market. The visibility generate visits, and then hopefully mutiple offers simultaneously.

ERROR #4 - CHOOSING A REAL ESTATE AGENT FOR THE WRONG REASON

Do not choose a particular real estate agent based on the price that he evaluates your property. Choosing a great real estate agent is essential for selling your property for its maximum value. The real estate agent must be able to give a professional analysis of the property based on comparables sold in the sector. He has to be well-organised with a shielded structure. It is essential to have confidence in the real estate broker who represents you, to believe in his competence and experience. You want a broker who can easily explain the whole process of marketing, who knows the market very well, which holds a database of potential buyers and can give you valuable tips to increase your chances of selling. In fact, the professional you choose must show you a crystal clear strategic plan for the successful sale of your property.

ERROR #5 - TRUSTING MARKETING TOOLS FROM THE 90'S

The majority of tools formely used by brokers to sell a home are actually not very effective. People tend to have less and less time to look for homes. They will not take the time to drive to see the sign, they will go on the Internet after work or will call their real estate agent. Make sure your property is visible where it really counts. Over 75% of buyers have seen pictures of the property on the web before they come to see your home. The pictures have to be the best possible because great pictures are worth more than a thousand words in the marketing of your property. Make sure your description on the web is easy to understand and complete for the buyer of 2013. You must make sure they get the feeling when they read the description. If they receive the feeling by reading your description, you get a call and/or a visit.

ERROR #6 - NEGLECT SMALL DETAILS THAT MAY ENHANCE YOUR HOME

Also, no houses are perfect. Because of this fact, you have to take the time to look at your property and see what might be your obstacles. When you find those, you have to plan at which part of the process you will inform the buyer. Be prepared to face those obstacles and you can calculate the value for them to see if it is worth the reparation. Take the time to see if the problem can be fixed and at what price. It might be a good idea to fix it and increase the price in consideration, or even more.

Make sure you are ready to encounter the obstacles.

ERROR #7 - FAILURE TO TAKE THE TIME TO PLAN EVERY STEP IN ADVANCE

Selling a property in 2013 is not an easy game. In a market that only 60% of properties are sold, you must make a strategic plan and know each and every step in advance to be able to control the process. The process is not just an add-on on the computer, it is about being a master of each step of the process. You must be ready for any buyer to come and ask you questions on the property. If you are not ready to answer those questions, you might lose buyers. Make sure you know all the expenses of selling your property. You might need to buy a new certificate of localisation, pay a quittance for the mortgage, real estate fees, servitudes or insurance on your building. Make sure to check that your building conforms according to the certificate of localisation.

ERROR #8 - NOT TAKING THE TIME TO KNOW YOUR BUYER

In order to control the negotiation, you must know your buyer. You have to ask questions that will determine the motivation of the buyer. Does the buyer need to move quickly? Does the buyer have the money to buy your property? By knowing the motivation of the buyer, you will be able to control the transaction and the amount of money you get in your pocket. In fact each thousand dollars does not represent a lot for a buyer in terms of monthly payment on a mortgage. By knowing your buyer, you will be able to motivate him to reach your number.

ERROR #9 - GIVING THE BUYER YOUR REASONS FOR SELLING

Never tell any buyer your reason and motivation to sell because they might want to use it at the negotiating table. If someone asks you, just answer your housing requirements have changed.

ERROR #10 - NEGLECTING TO PROPERLY COMPLETE THE CONTRACT

When coming to complete the contract to sell or with a buyer, there are lots of emotions. Be sure to disclose all information about your property. If the buyer is aware of problems, a court action may result later.

Make sure not to look only at the price. Take the time to confirm all terms, conditions, costs and responsibilities are clearly mentioned in the offer to purchase. Resist the temptation to diverge from the contract. For example, if the buyer asks you to move before the closing date, say no. Make sure you stick to the contract. This is not the time to take chances and risk aborting the transaction. Make sure to follow up with the notary in between the completion of the offer to purchase and the time you go to the notary. Also, with the economy of today, it would be wise to have a short delay in between to make sure the situation of the buyer does not change.

ERROR #11 - MOVING BEFORE SELLING

My study shows that it is more difficult to sell a property that is vacant. The first reason is because by moving, you indicate to buyers that you have a new home and you're probably in a hurry and therefore highly motivated to sell quickly. This will give them an advantage in negotiations. It almost gives the same impression to a buyer as if the property is on the maket for a long time. They feel they have the control of the transaction and can negotiate more. The second reason is that the house being empty makes it not appealing. They also have a hard time to vizualise the property and their furniture. They have a hard time seeing if the size is too small or too big because they normally compare the furniture in the property to their furniture. Even more, it could cost you thousands of dollars.

The success of selling your home is not a question of improvisation. In reality, selling your home needs much more than just a sign or Internet advertisement. You must have a pro-active plan that is efficient for your type of property. It is about having a crystal-clear plan to use for a specific type of home. With these tools, you can maximize your profit, maintain control of the transaction and reduce stress surrounding the sale of your property. Good luck in your transaction!

About Jean-Philippe

Jean-Philippe Loiselle, also known as "The Hungry Machine," is a best-selling author and a dominant real estate broker, who is regularly sought out for his opinion on techniques that really work. Jean-Philippe is known for asking the question, "Do you want to sell your property or do you want to get the maximum value with wiser strategy?" Jean-Philippe is at the top of his business for many years. He tracks the market everyday and does minor adjustments every week to achieve his clients' goals. Jean-Philippe states that in every type of market, a strategy well adapted to today's market always allows him to get more for his clients. He identifies weaknesses with strategies and brings to his clients the newest and best evolutionary strategy. To learn more about Jean-Philippe Loiselle, "The Hungry Machine," visit: www.venduparloiselle.com.

Jean-Philippe Loiselle
Courtier Immobilier RE/MAX
514-766-1000

CHAPTER 10

YOUR SUCCESS STORY

BY DR. JEFF REBARCAK

We all want to succeed. There's not a person alive today who would willfully choose failure if it was properly packaged and labeled as such. Don't you wish it was? But life isn't that easy and choices don't always seem that clear. We are distracted, disheveled, and disappointed on a regular basis, and for some of us, a moment of clarity would feel like a cool glass of water in the middle of a long drought.

God has that glass of water for you, and the details of your success story are definitely on His agenda.

For I know the plans I have for you, says the Lord. Plans to prosper you and not to harm you. Plans to give you hope and a future.

~ Jeremiah 29:11

Sounds good, doesn't it? Who wouldn't want to be guaranteed a blessed and successful future? This verse is a promise to each of us from our Creator. There is one small spoiler alert though. The details of our success generally don't unfold in a way that makes sense to us while they're occurring. Looking back at situations, crises and obstacles, there are always a thousand lessons to be learned. Clarity is easy when we're connecting the dots backward and recognizing what we did right, what we did wrong, and how it all related. It's trusting the steps ahead when we can't see the way that frightens and threatens to overwhelm us. As for clarity, it rarely arrives with the degree of regularity we would like. Instead, it comes in small glimpses and ultimately, we have to learn to trust the Hand that's guiding us more than we trust what's currently happening in our lives.

Which brings us to the word trust. Let's talk about that for a minute. Trust has to do with vulnerability. Vulnerability has to do with honesty. Not the kind of honesty where you tell the cashier that she just gave you an extra ten dollars too much in change and she thanks you and tells you you're an honest guy and you feel good about yourself. The honesty I'm talking about is the kind that strips away everything you thought you could rely on, questions everything you thought was true, and leaves you standing bare, open, and exposed before God. It's a helpless feeling. It's supposed to be.

If you haven't reached your most honest moment yet, you will. We all do.

MY MOST HONEST MOMENT

My moment started out with the thought that I was a pretty good guy. I mean, that's not too unusual or crazy, right? Most of us have learned to capitalize on our strengths, practice positive affirmations and look optimistically at the road ahead. I had no problem with any of that. Optimism was my middle name. Always very goal oriented, encouraging to others, passionate, diligent, and kind of a serial-entrepreneur, it didn't take long before one of my ventures began to gain some real traction. It was a diagnostic testing business my wife, Coni and I had founded together. We put our all into it, hiring the top neurologists in the area and working very closely with the business to ensure its success. They say hard work pays off, and it quickly grew from one office into a nationwide, multi-million dollar neuro-diagnostic testing company.

Everything was perfect.

My family was healthy and happy, business was booming, and by most standards life couldn't be better. I had worked hard for this. I had been faithful. It was my time.

When an offer came in to purchase the company for 10 million dollars it seemed like icing on the cake of my life. Jeremiah 29:11 was really true, I thought to myself. It's God's plan to prosper me. I was a blessed man, indeed.

And then it happened.

The cool glass of clarity didn't come in the form of a certified check for 10 million. In fact, I couldn't have imagined in my wildest dreams the downward spiral of events that was about to take place.

As it turned out, the final team of neurologists we staffed had false credentials. Yes, false credentials. They were a part of an underground operation that I, still to this day, do not fully understand the scope of. Sounds like a B-rated movie plot, right? I wish it were. The moment we found out, we called each insurance company to report our findings and we immediately stopped billing our clients. Bringing in a new medical team to review all test results originally assessed during the "false credential period," we found ourselves in full-blown damage control mode. At that point things were happening too quickly for me to try to make sense of. The only clarity I had was the fact that the rug had just ripped out from under my life and my foundation was being rocked to its very core.

The day I found out the FBI was interviewing my colleagues and gathering information about us was almost surreal. We had done everything right. We had worked hard. We walked in integrity. We were supposed to be blessed. So, why was this happening?

For once in my life, I related to the disciples who were on the boat with Jesus when the great storm was filling it up with water. Beaten by the wind and waves, tired, alone and afraid, I had reached the same breaking point as the disciples who questioned the One who had looked at each one of them individually, and invited them to follow Him. "Come walk with me," he said to each one. So personal, so assuring, and now they were afraid for their very lives, pleading with Jesus and saying, "Don't you care that we perish?"

Don't you care? Don't you remember your promise?

How could everything that seemed so perfect just a few weeks ago, suddenly spin so completely out of control? An offer for 10 million dollars and an opportunity to move into another chapter of our lives now had us on the brink of bankruptcy, paying hundreds of thousands of dollars in attorney fees.

I wasn't sleeping. I was eating garbage. I was taking anxiety meds to get me through the day and sleeping pills to get me through the night. I felt like some sort of war ravaged, walking zombie. I looked at my wife and I felt utterly, completely helpless. I was supposed to be the provider. I was supposed to give her and our children the security and stability they deserved. It couldn't get any worse.

THE STRIPPING AWAY

"Jeff, I don't know how to tell you this," my attorney had known us for years and this conversation wasn't an easy one. "You're facing jail time. Maybe up to 20 years."

I felt like someone slugged me in the gut.

"I am completely innocent. You know that." I was so emotionally drained that I felt disconnected from the words that were coming out of my mouth.

"Innocent people go to jail all the time, Jeff. They're turning the whole story around now, and laying it all at your doorstep as if you organized and knowingly hired this team of imposters posing as neurologists. It doesn't look good."

CLARITY

Like a cool drink of water, it came to me. Right there, in the middle of the storm I had total clarity. I felt like the apostle Paul when the scales fell away from his eyes and he could finally see.

A million thoughts raced through my spirit, and all at once I knew where I was. I wasn't the good, deserving guy I imagined I was. I was sick. Spiritually sick, emotionally sick, and physically sick. In fact, I had been more than sick, I had been dead, and if I was to truly live, it was only because of Jesus.

Right in the middle of my storm, He walked in. Just like He did with the disciples in the boat, and for the first time ever, I stood there at my most vulnerable moment, completely stripped of anything I thought was true, and I had peace.

I looked at Coni and instead of saying, "Where are you God?" like I had a hundred times before, I said, "Let's do this."

THE REBUILDING PROCESS

I decided if I was going to jail, so be it. I'd tell people about Jesus every day. I'd help and encourage them. I got serious. I even got angry. I'd come too far with God to back down now. I was His, without question. He had looked at me just as He looked at the disciples and invited me to come follow Him. That day, I pushed all my chips to the center of the table, and I have to say, when you've got absolutely nothing to offer but the tears in your eyes and you choose Jesus regardless of the consequences, things get crazy. I didn't know where to turn, but God told me to get healthy.

"Get your mind healthy, your spirit healthy and your body healthy."

Everything else about my future was out of my control, but I could do this. I could get healthy. I started to walk every morning and listen to powerful teachings while I exercised. I was absolutely flooding my mind with God's Word 24/7. It felt like boot camp. The more of the Word I got in my spirit, the more I began to see things from God's perspective.

Naturally, putting the Word in my mind led to speaking it out of my mouth. This changed things for me, radically. The Bible tells us to speak to our mountains and they will be removed, so I did. Regardless of what things looked like, I spoke only words of life. I looked at myself in the mirror every day and told myself that God has a plan and purpose for me. I told myself that I'm more than a conqueror, that I'm filled with wisdom, that goodness and mercy follow me, and I'm surrounded with favor as with a shield. Not because my life looked like that, but because the Word says those things are mine.

The exercise and health part literally fell into place effortlessly. Once I got on the right path mentally and started to speak positive words that gave life to my situation, I exercised and ate the right foods without struggle.

That's how it works when you walk with God and put Him first. The Word tells us in: 3 John 1:2, *"I wish above all things that you prosper and be in good health, even as your soul prospers."*

FREEDOM

Right in the middle of our storm, we had a meeting with a Federal Agent. For over four hours Coni and I sat with her and laid out every detail of our story. We left nothing out. We gave her all the details and when we were finished, we just looked at her. For once I felt the assurance that my life and future were not in anyone's hands but God's.

"I came here with every intent to take you into custody today, Dr. Rebarcak. But for some reason, I believe your story." The cold drink of clarity was now met with the refreshing showers of God's unfailing love. They even used our testimony in court to convict the imposters; we were set free from all this mess. But the freedom didn't stop there. We were now free to be exactly who God created us to be, without fear of man, of circumstances, problems, obstacles, or anything that might come our way. We had found peace in the midst of our storm.

It was there that God built the foundation I stand on today, and this is why I'm completely passionate when I teach and mentor others on the steps to success. They worked for me during the biggest crisis of my life. They worked in my most honest moment, and they will work in yours.

BUILDING YOUR SUCCESS STORY

After experiencing your most honest moment, you'll see exactly what you have left. Anything that doesn't completely rely on Him and on His Word will be stripped away. For me, I had practically nothing left. I was starting at square one. I didn't even have the faith I thought I did. My relationship with God had a place when I had time. All that needed to change.

I felt overwhelmed and I found myself just looking for a place to start. I needed something simple. God gave me three: He told me to…

Engage My Brain - It all starts with developing a vision and deciding what you believe. Your belief system must be completely independent from what's happening in your life. What you put in is what you'll get out. That's why when I mentor people who want to change their lives and become healthy, we always start here. If your mindset isn't right, if you're not meditating on God's Word and allowing your mind to be renewed, all the exercise and eating right in the world isn't going to change your situation.

Engage My Tongue - Faith comes by hearing, and guess what? We can only hear what we speak. The second step to success is having your words line up with God's Word. When your words and His words agree, there is power there. Your words are constantly bringing life or death to every situation in your life. They are either building up or tearing down. Again, that's why meditating on and speaking the Word come before diet and exercise. You have to get your attitude right first.

Engage My Body - Food is fuel. We learn that in all of my workshops. Little by little we build the foundation for a healthy lifestyle, which includes plenty of physical activity and clean eating. This is not only great for weight loss, but it will jump start your immune system, fight and even reverse diseases, and provide you with the energy you need to do God's will for your life. If Noah were sitting on the couch all day eating potato chips, he wouldn't have been ready to fulfill his purpose.

When I was physically and mentally unable to think because of the place I was in, God gave me simple. Simple works without thinking, and these three steps lay a foundation that can be worked from regardless of what you're going through.

YOUR MOST HONEST MOMENT

Is that all it is? Three steps and I've got my foundation for success? Now you should know better than that. God is pursuing you, right now. Our stories are different, my story is personal. It is "my" story, but if you read between the lines, you'll recognize something very special. Although the characters, the obstacles, and the settings may change from person to person, the beginning and the ending are the same for us all.

God created you with a purpose and a destiny. You belong to Him and He wants to reveal Himself in the story of your life.

Here's hoping my story brought a cool glass of clarity to you today.

About Dr. Jeff

"Your health is your first wealth!"

Dr. Jeff Rebarcak's life mission has been to help others out of seemingly impossible situations by pinpointing and eliminating weaknesses and mental strongholds, while purposefully building upon strengths, especially where their health is concerned.

Never afraid to go against the grain, Dr. Rebarcak has made tremendous gains in the health and wellness community by getting back to the simple truths. Dr. Jeff takes a fun, three-step, holistic approach to total health, starting with your mind and attitude, and continuing through to your words and actions. "Most people do the process backwards, starting with exercise and food choices, which is generally a recipe for failure. Nothing works until your mindset is right. Once you get your mind and your words to line up with God's plan for you, the rest is easy!" His workshops and motivational seminars have been held across the nation.

Continuously on the road of self-improvement, Dr. Jeff Rebarcak has spearheaded numerous businesses while taking his education from the world-renowned Palmer College of Chiropractic to post graduate work where he obtained certification in MedX Spinal Rehabilitation from the University of Florida, a Certified Chiropractic Sports Physician Certificate and Master Certification in Neuro-Linguistic Programming. His education has served as constant fuel, purposefully adding to Jeff's passion to equip individuals to reach their full potential.

"Without your health, nothing else really matters. It's my mission to help individuals reclaim their health and experience their best life now!"

CHAPTER 11

THE 3 1/2 STEPS TO LIVING LIFE THE WAY YOU REALLY WANT TO LIVE

BY JOHN DICKS, ESQ.

What's most important to you?

What makes you really smile...and makes you laugh so hard that you feel like a kid again?

What do you really look forward to? What lets you drift off to sleep with the contentment of knowing that you can't wait to wake up in the morning and get going.

Well then, as we say in the South, "Why ain't you doing it?"!!

I mean, really...why aren't you?

Granted, we've heard for years the often used lines of ...

- *"you've only got one life to live"*
- *"life is short, make the most of it"*
- *"follow your dreams, not those of someone else"*

There's also the advertisers, like Nike, who use catchy lines made to inspire (or motivate spending) by imploring us to "just do it."

And then, of course, there's the music marathon and parade of hits urging us like Tim McGraw when he croons to *"live like you are dyin',"* or my personal favorite, George Strait's reminder that *"I ain't here for long time...I'm here for a good time."*

It's likely that I will get no real argument from anyone on this aspiration for "living life to its fullest." Most people generally acknowledge that God has blessed us with the potential for doing so. The true question, however, is how do we make it all possible?

Surprisingly, the secret to this success is not all that difficult. It takes determination; and certainly commitment. A bit of sacrifice is required, but the sacrifice makes the success all that much more sweeter.

Here then are the 3 1/2 steps to *Living Life the way you really want to Live.*

STEP #1 – DETERMINE WHO YOU REALLY ARE AND WHAT DELIGHTS AND EXCITES YOU.

Take a good long look in a full length mirror. Really ... do this. Take your time, don't make it a quick glance.

Mirrors reflect and that's what you really want to do. Reflect on your life thus far. Is that person staring at you in the mirror the one you really want to be...or is it the reflection of someone who you thought you should be?

Are you proud of that person? Is it the reflection of someone that you enjoy spending time with...someone who makes you smile and laugh and truly happy?

People spend much of their life seeking their soulmate (and I'm a firm believer in finding one), yet we forget that it is not the responsibility nor even within the ability of our soulmate to fulfill our life nor make us happy. Instead that responsibility frankly falls squarely upon the one who is staring at you within the mirror. This is the only one who can make it happen.

Success will never come our way when we shift the blame for our failures to other people. Do not, however, confuse "Blame" with "Shame." They are not synonymous. To blame is to assign responsibility. Shame, however, suggests dishonor, caused by doing something wrong or foolish.

We all have experienced failure; and frankly, will continue to do so throughout life. That's what the "learning" in life helps us through. The key to survive failure and learn from the experience, making it lead to success, is to accept blame, and hence responsibility, but to recognize that shame does not necessarily need to accompany it.

Thus it is fine to see blame (responsibility). It is shame that you must avoid. That does not mean to merely refuse to acknowledge it. Instead, recognize that shame is brought upon by doing something wrong when we know it is wrong to do so. Shame is a behavior to avoid if we want to accept and be happy with the one we see in the mirror.

While you are pondering that mirrored reflection and whether it's someone others would enjoy being with, consider, too, the physical condition it is in.

If you plan to start *Living Life the way you really want to Live*, you've got to be in shape to enjoy it.

I read somewhere not long ago the suggestion that nature makes us prone to be fat and lazy so that we will avoid things that can hurt us, keeping us safe to reproduce and replicate our species. What a bunch of bunk that is!

God made us with two legs in order to move ... to walk and run and swim and dance. And God gave us two arms with hands and opposable thumbs to waive and write and catch and throw. We're supposed to move, stay strong, and use our body in living life.

Granted there are people born without such physical abilities and ones who unfortunately suffer through accidents. My hope is that God will grant them other gifts, allowing them to excel in ways that we otherwise are incapable of. The renown physicist Stephen Hawking comes to mind; a man who's body is ravaged by ALS disease, yet his brilliant mind works wonders and through his special devices for communication is helping us unlock the secrets of the universe.

Still others are designed by God with unique and amazing physical abilities. We all are amazed by Olympic athletes whose fast twitch muscle fibers propel them effortlessly to speeds and heights which most of us can only dream of.

But these, of course, are the exceptions. What we must concern ourselves with is the reality of who we face when we stare at our reflection in the mirror. That is, in the context of what we each uniquely have; the body containing our being, the vessel in which we're sailing through space. Are we really using it to its fullest as we were so divinely designed? Or rather, are we sadly simply abusing our bodies and wasting away the only one we'll ever have?

Are we making the most of the situation? Or are we filling it with poisons and fats and sugars and just plain stuff that we know is not healthy.

For perspective, consider my longtime friend who raises race horses. He feeds them the best oats and hay he can afford. He told me recently that to celebrate the Birthday of one of his horses he fed her some shelled edamame. Never would he dream of rounding up table scraps to toss her way. She's a racehorse, after all. He's got to take care of her!

Which begs the question, of course, of how well are we taking care of that someone reflecting back to us in the mirror? My friend's race horse was quite expensive to buy and even more to raise, train and maintain. I dare say, though, that you are much more valuable. Are you taking as good care of the person staring at you in the mirror as he is of his racehorse?

Living Life the way you really want to Live requires that you take care of yourself. With any luck, you'll only need some fine tuning.

Fortunately, with the gee-whiz technological gadgets and gizmos that we have today, there's really no excuse for us not to take care of ourselves. A common complaint from those embarking on an exercise program used to be boredom, but that's hard to fathom today when you can listen to thousands of songs carried in your pocket or catch up on the news through free podcasts or get lost in an exciting audio book.

My own exercise routine includes that of swimming. Staring at the black line of a pool over and over can get boring; and of course it's impossible to carry on conversations with swimming partners. But consider my mornings with a waterproof iPod. Yep, they work quite well and I enjoy the time in the water listening to podcasts on business, finance and travel.

Frankly staying in shape is easier today than ever before since there are so many fine, and free, diet and exercise programs detailed all over the

Internet. Fortunately, they can all be summed up in just four words...eat less, exercise more!

It's good for you and saves you money, which will help with the Step #2.

STEP #2 – MONETIZE A PLAN FOR *LIVING LIFE THE WAY YOU REALLY WANT TO LIVE*.

How do you get your money? Do you earn it? Does it come to you through investments? Or is the amount and source of your income the problem to begin with?

We've all heard the old saw about how "money doesn't buy happiness." It's true, we must admit. But the simple fact is that it's much easier with money than without to enjoy *Living Life the way you really want to Live*.

Here then is the single best bit of financial advice that I have ever received:

Develop multiple sources of income!
It simply means to never rely on just one thing.

As the saying goes, "Stuff happens!" And when (and not if) it does and one source of income falters, you'll have others left to rely upon.

It's much like the advice you hear from financial advisors when they emphasize diversification. It's the old "don't put all of your eggs in one basket" approach.

I've been around long enough to see plenty of economic cycles. I've had friends who lost fortunes in real estate and others who have had it vaporize in the stock market. Some, too, have suffered while their business drained them dry.

In developing these multiple sources of income, I've worn many hats in my lifetime. Some I still do. In no particular order, I've been a lawyer (still am), farmer (still am), real estate broker (still am), stock trader/investor (still am), real estate investor (still am), financial advisor (not now), rancher (not now), teacher (not now), author/writer (still am) professional speaker (still am) and politician (not now ... but then politicians never say never).

Looking at that list, some might suggest (particularly my political opponents) that I couldn't hold a job! But the reality is that I always had an abundance of curiosity and early on chose to follow that advice about developing multiple sources of income.

The key to success in this endeavor is to choose to develop the sources of income which are closely attuned to enabling your *Living Life the way you really want to Live*.

For example, very important to me is traveling. I've been fortunate to have worked (through public speaking) in all 50 states of America. I've been paid too, to speak overseas, even in far away places such as South Africa, Dubai, Abu Dhabi and Saudi Arabia.

Wherever I've been, I've taken extra time to visit with the locals and take in the sights and sounds and smells of the area. It's always made me a better speaker for the occasion and location while at the same time allowed me to pursue my passion for travel.

My wanderlust or pursuit of travel led also to writing, which became and still is another of those sources of income. Early on, while we would travel, I would write articles and submit them to magazines, being paid for publication. It led to writing books and manuals which I still greatly enjoy doing today.

The point here is to recognize that generating income versus work are two distinctly different things. What you do in life is only work when you don't love what you do. Find the things that you love the most; the things that energize and inspire you. Develop ways to generate sources of income in those areas...even if it requires reinventing yourself. That is, become the person reflected in the mirror rather than the one living dreams that were created for you by someone else.

STEP #3.5 – LIVING IT!

Granted. It's a bit silly to name this final step 3.5. But the point is that for many people this last step is the most difficult of all.

It's the one that requires you to get up and start living it!

That can be hard to do. After all, for better or worse, we all develop habits. Some are good ones, like brushing our teeth before bedtime, while others are not, like smoking. Silly, but you get the point.

Bad habits, and even the not-so-good ones, are the toughest to break. We get comfortable doing things over and over. They become part of our routine. Breaking them requires doing something new. That creates anxiety. It makes us nervous. Our nature is to avoid change.

Why is it that so many people remain miserable in unhappy marriages, or toil onward in jobs that they hate, or continue to work for people they despise? It's simple, really ... people generally prefer the comfort of familiarity and routine versus the unease of uncertainty.

Taking that first step is difficult when you are afraid that it might lead to an abyss.

It is in such times that I am reminded of the important lesson I learned, strangely enough, from my dog, Dicksee.

Dicksee is, as of this writing, a 14 year old Jack Russell Terrier. That means she is a determined breed. But then, she is also blind.

However, when Dicksee is determined to do something, she moves forward, relying upon her senses of hearing and most particularly that of smell, which seemingly has become heightened by the loss of her vision (much as we each have our own superior abilities while also possessing inferior ones as compared to others so otherwise blessed).

Dicksee will bound ahead, sniffing, smelling, listening. And oftentimes she will bump into things right on her snout. But she continues to move forward, weaving and turning, never stopping to whine or cry out. She's my inspiration!

Like Dicksee, we are not perfect. We will surely falter. But focus will set our course and determination will dictate our destiny.

Living Life the way you really want to Live is not something that just happens. It is a lifetime journey that we commit to embark upon. It is what makes living life an adventure!

PS...as in a PostScript.

In case, dear Reader, that you have made it thus far, I thank you for hanging in there with me and reading these reflections on *Living Life the way you really want to Live*. I suspect that other than my editor, I can count on at least two to actually have savored these words. Okay, make it three, with thanks to my dear wife, for many things, including and especially for producing our two sons, for whom this tome is really written.

Thanks, sons, for making your Dad so proud. You both are already well on your way to making your life an adventure and I am loving watching you *Living Life the way you really want to Live.* Now get busy and pass it on to the next generation. For as the Good Book (The Bible) says in Genesis 1:28, "*Be fruitful and multiply...*"!

About John

Mayor John Dicks has traveled the World in his pursuit of *"Living Life The Way They Really Want To Live."* Early on he developed a plan to monetize his passions for travel and teaching others the secrets for a prosperous, happy and healthy life that can accompany financial independence.

Having lectured before audiences both large and small, John has shared financial and investment strategies with well over 1,000,000 people throughout all 50 states in America and several countries abroad, including Dubai, Saudi Arabia and South Africa. His expertise has led to appearances on ABC, CBS, NBC & FOX affiliate TV and Radio stations and he has shared the stage with such luminaries as Zig Ziglar and Brian Tracy.

John is an Attorney, having graduated from Florida State University College of Law after receiving his undergraduate degree in Public Relations from the University of Florida. He also studied at Oxford University in Oxford, England. John is a Real Estate Broker and was a Senior National Instructor for the National Association of Realtors. While a Registered Investment Advisor, John was also a Senior National Instructor for the Real Estate Securities and Syndication Institute.

John is the author of several books and texts, including *The Bookshelf Lawyer, Business Power Strategies* and *The Personal Financial Planner.* He is an entrepreneur, having founded Synergy Communications, a marketing and communications consulting firm.

With a firm faith in his family and commitment to his community and Church, John focuses his energies on public service and helping others achieve their dreams. He served his home town as Mayor for three terms and works on a variety of Boards and Foundations.

Along with Sharon, his wife of 35 years (so far), John is most proud of and enjoys spending time with their two sons. One is a successful attorney with an MBA while the other is an F/A 18 Jet Fighter Pilot in the Marine Corps and John is quick to note that they both are well on their way to *"Living Life the way you really want to Live."*

CHAPTER 12

HARD WORK AND PERSISTENCE ARE CHANGE AGENTS THAT DRIVE SUCCESS

BY JOSE LARA

"The heart of your idea of success should always be one without limitations." ~ Joey Lara

Through the course of my life's journey, I acquired my own definition of success as being a never-ending staircase. I began measuring my own personal degree of success by my ongoing capacity to always keep climbing upward no matter what type of adversity I should encounter along the way. I endured quite a few setbacks in my life, yet I appreciate how every bit of hardship helped me develop a strong foundation and a deeper understanding that if you follow your own destiny, you will become no more or less yourself, just exactly what you were meant to be, a success.

My first steps began in a small South Texas town of Victoria, TX with a population of about 48,000 at the time. I grew up in a humble, yet very happy home and was the second youngest of six children. Fortunately, I had loving and encouraging parents who always did everything they could to guide us towards the right paths. My childhood memoriès of my father are filled with his continuous reminders to always be anticipating the future and how he instilled the importance of doing something meaningful in our lives. My most favorite memory of my father was one that had the greatest impact on my career life and completely changed it for the better. It was a typical Saturday afternoon and I was visiting my parents at their house while I was on Spring Break from college. My Dad was reading the local hometown newspaper like he did on a regular daily basis and came across an article about becoming an insurance agent. I still remember to this day how he clipped the article out of the newspaper and handed it to me with great confidence in his eyes saying, "You should look into this."

Needless to say, I am very happy that I took his advice. I held on to that article, carrying it with me everywhere I went and I still have it as a reminder of where my career journey began with a touch of my father's blessing. The childhood memories of my mother are full of her absolute great faith and her constant willingness to give. My most favorite memories of my mother were the Sunday morning services at church. All five of my siblings and I would sit next to each other in a row and take up half the whole pew at church. When the time came to tithe, I remember my mother reaching into her purse and grabbing a handful of pennies. She would give a few pennies to the child sitting next to her and we would pass them along down the line until we each had a few to place in the tithe basket. We may have not had much to give, but the lesson learned was one that would continue to speak volumes in our adult lives and our future generations.

All through grade school and high school I was a straight A student and known in all my classes as the smart kid. Making good grades was never an issue for me because I was constantly reminded by parents growing up about the importance of education. After graduating Cum Laude from high school, I attended the local junior college with the plan of acquiring an Engineering degree to place a successful job after graduation and make a lot of money. Much to my surprise, I made my first grade of a C ever in my life as I struggled with these Engineering classes. I quickly learned that when your main focus is making money and you disregard your true interest you will struggle. I became discouraged seeing some of my high school friends enjoying and excelling in their Engineering studies.

From that point on, I switched my major many times in the hopes that I would soon find what I was destined to do with my life. I moved on to the University of North Texas where I started in Health Promotion studies, then changed to Nutrition, then Microbology, then Information Systems. Then, circumstances would have it that I moved again to attend the University of Houston and I started in the Computer Programming field, then changed to Medical Technology, and then to Finance. I believe I would have stayed with Finance, however, by this time I had exhausted all my college funds. I took out a short-term semester loan which needed to be paid back at the end of the semester, yet when I was unable to pay it back I was not able to attend any longer. My last semester of college ended with over 140 credit hours, a 3.5 GPA, and no degree. Knowing now what I did not know then, the whole time I was attending college I was not doing what I really felt I wanted to be doing in my life, so college was the worst place I could have been.

At this point in my life, I felt stuck and would wake up in the morning in my one bedroom apartment alone on my bed staring blankly at the four walls surrounding me watching the sun peek through the blinds. I remember thinking to myself, "Is this all there is for me?"; "Am I ever going to get out of here?"; "Will I ever get married?"; "Will I ever have children?"; "Will I ever find a rewarding career?" Being one of six children, I watched as all of my siblings found their career paths in life, get married, and all have children before me. My feeling at the time was that I had to put my whole life on hold until I had a career. I was just waiting for my moment.

I cannot tell you that the moment I decided to become an insurance agent that I ever dreamed of being a successful business owner. As a matter fact, I can honestly say that as a child growing up in a small town that I was never even exposed to the thought of owning my own business one day. Nevertheless, not knowing entirely what to expect, this was the moment that I took my father's advice and pursued my career as an insurance agent, and with this decision came many feats of struggle and ultimate sacrifices. Much to my surprise, becoming an insurance agent required that I have minimum debt and a bit of capital, which was definitely something I did not have at the time due to all my previous college semester expenses. I soon realized that the only way for me to pay down some of my debt and to establish some capital was to get rid of my biggest expense, my rent.

I can tell you personally that once you ever make a drastic decision to give up the roof over your head and a place you can call home, that a sense of fear and disappointment seem to haunt you as you constantly worry and wonder if you will ever bounce back. I could have easily moved back with my parents, but my stubborn pride and the will to make a drastic change in my life outweighed any logical reasoning. So coincidentally, my falling apart 2001 Ford Escort with 90,000 miles and wrecked driver's side door became my new home while I packed all my basic necessities in my trunk. I soon discovered a handful of empty parking lots where I could park nightly and get a restless night sleep. Consequently, I almost forgot what a good night's sleep was like while I began to work 16 hours a day as a full-time pharmacy technician, a part-time early morning stocker, and a hopeful insurance agent. It may have been sad and a bit depressing to think, but even though I was working countless hours to meet this required financial criteria, I appreciated the times that I was actually at work because I at least had a roof over my head.

My most challenging times of my life were ahead of me, yet I took comfort in knowing that I was never a stranger to hard work and struggle. It so happened that my full time and part time jobs were one hour driving distance from the insurance agent training center I was attending. Often times I would find myself falling asleep at the wheel while I was driving between jobs with all the many hours I was working. In particular, I take into account one time when I had fallen asleep while driving on the freeway at 70mph and my car was drifting sideways into a concrete barrier. Fortunately, I woke up in a life-saving second as my car hit the barrier and I was able to regain control of my car. I hate to think what would have happened if there had been any other vehicles around me at the time. That day I arrived at the training center with a smile on my face so thankful I was alive and remember my peers in the class saying hello to me and asking how me I was doing in normal casual conversation. I just smiled back and acknowledged that I was fine, yet thinking to myself, "If you only knew." Being practically homeless at the time and going through all the sacrifices and struggles that came with it, you would first think that I was at a big disadvantage. *Yet, it was exactly these hardships that equipped me with a never-give-up attitude as I continuously excelled above all my peers in class week after week.*

In the midst of my struggles came events and meetings that would one day complete the very most important part of my life. As part of becoming a new insurance agent, I began attending business-networking events in the hopes of developing business relationships with people in related industries. In particular, I had just arrived at this one networking event one evening and had introduced myself to a young professional woman just to see where this encounter would take me. As it turns out, this woman was at the event with a friend who came over and introduced herself to me, her name was Angie. Angie and her friend were actually on their way out the door but I made certain to ask for and hold onto her business card. As a matter of fact, I found myself childishly and periodically checking my pocket throughout the night after they had left making sure I still had her business card and had not accidentally misplaced it. *As fate would have it, my mother reminded me on our wedding day years later that when I was a young man still living at home that I told her one day somewhere out there I was going to find an angel and I was going to marry and spend the rest of my life with her. Well, that day had arrived on this night and I had met my angel and her name was Angie.*

In getting to know Angie, I quickly discovered that not only was she the perfect match for me, but she was definitely an angel because she was my answered prayer. In just a few weeks of getting to know each other, she offered to assist me in my business venture. She was a full-time accountant and would leave her eight hour workday at 5pm and join me at the insurance training center and would work side by side next to me into the late hours of the night. Just having someone there with me sharing my struggles made all the difference in the world because I was not alone anymore. Needless to say, with each passing day and Angie right by my side, my struggles slowly became less and less enduring. I knew right away that fate had finally intervened while everything in my life began making perfect sense with my new-found relationship and new career. I was finally certain that this was exactly who I was supposed to be with and exactly what I was supposed to be doing in my life. As a matter of fact, when I provided my very first client with an insurance policy, the sheer gratefulness I received from her helped me develop an instantaneous passion for being an insurance agent and building a successful insurance agency. I believe this passion stemmed from my father's childhood reminders to do something meaningful with my life, and my mother's lessons to be a thoughtful giving person.

In essence, I was finally doing something that I loved and was making a difference in the world. As my passion for being an insurance agent grew, I suddenly realized the possibility of creating the business of my dreams and it was this realization that took me to the next level. I centered my results on value and purpose that had an actual true impact on people's lives. I would now wake up in the morning everyday looking for a way of how I could give back. In realizing my purpose, I pursued it with all my heart and got rid of things that were holding me back. I went into business knowing that if I just followed my purpose that everything else would come together. I discovered that everything is a system and once you understand the system, and begin to see where your business is and where it can go by understanding the correct principles in the things that you do, the sky is the limit.

I took into account that in every type of business in every single industry in the world there will always exist some type of struggle and competition. Many times in your own business you must know that your biggest competition might be change itself. You must be willing to change and always stay in front of the change. Always adapt and have your mind open to new ideas and techniques. Accept struggle and challenge, yet never defeat. Know and believe in your heart that where you stand today will not be the same place you will be standing tomorrow.

Most importantly, become a Change Agent. Take a step back and look at your life and look at your business. Ask yourself if you are where you want to be and if you are happy where you are. If the answer is No, then now is the time to act, now is the time to change. Only you have the power to mentally make this decision and physically take action. Start by changing your negative thoughts to positive ones and change the way you look at yourself and your business. Change your attitude, change your routine, change your disbeliefs, change your words, change your actions, and change your goals and your purpose. Your staircase awaits you, take one step forward, take one step forward....

About Joey

Jose (Joey) Lara, also known as "The Quoting Genius," is an insurance expert and the CEO of Lara Agency which is a thriving insurance agency comprised of a highly trained team of insurance professionals located in Houston, TX. The Lara Agency has proudly helped thousands of families all over Texas in providing comprehensive insurance packages that are specifically designed for each client's unique insurance need and financial situation. Among these essential insurance coverages are: Auto insurance, Home and Renter's insurance, Health insurance, Business insurance, Umbrella coverage and Life insurance. During Joey's first year as an insurance agent, his agency was awarded the title of a Championship agency, which is the top 1% of Farmers Insurance agencies in the country.

The Lara Agency's track for success is clearly displayed in constantly being recognized as the #1 Auto insurance agency in the District and the #1 insurance quoting agency in the South Texas division for Farmers Insurance agents, averaging 800 to 1000 quotes per month. In addition to these outstanding achievements, the Lara Agency team has been recognized in Farmers Insurance's most recent Year End numbers as being among the Top 15 for Auto insurance production, the Top 20 for Home insurance production, and the Top 30 for Life insurance policies issued throughout the South Texas division.

Joey attributes the Lara Agency's success to its persistent focus on providing world-class service and always striving to make an immeasurable difference in the community. Joey is always known for saying, "Insurance is not our commodity. Insurance is our business and service is our commodity." In addition to providing excellent service to its clients, the Lara Agency is also a big believer in giving back to the community. Joey regularly visits low-income middle schools and high schools to speak to students about their powerful inner potential to become business owners. Mr. Lara is committed to his goal that every student should at least be exposed to the fact that the opportunity for them to be business owners is definitely an attainable dream for each and every one of them, if that is the path they should choose. As an advocate for student entrepreneurial leadership, Joey takes pride in the positive difference and incredible impact he is able to make in young people's lives at a critical point in time when they start to think about and plan their futures.

Joey Lara resides in Houston, TX with his beautiful wife, Angie, adorable son, Antonio, and precious daughter, Toryana. He is a loving father who is passionate about being fully engaged in his young children's lives and ultimately cherishes every moment with them.

CHAPTER 13

DRIVE IT HOME: Digital Marketing Designed To Deliver Your Business To Your Customer

BY BRETT SUTHERLIN

I grew up in the auto industry. My father owned over 30 new car dealerships, across multiple states. He was an automotive mogul and he strongly encouraged me to attend the highest reputable college with an intense focus on the automotive industry. So I attended Northwood University in Midland, MI, which specializes in automotive-related degrees. In fact, the National Automobile Dealers Association (N.A.D.A.) selected Northwood University as the college to develop the only collegiate degree program in Automotive Marketing & Management. In May 1995, I earned my Bachelor of Business Administration with a degree in Automotive Marketing.

To follow in my father's footsteps was an honor. He is a well-known, highly respected, powerful businessman in the automotive industry. He is admired, influential, honest, extremely hard working and philanthropic. My father is a family man and a man of good character. My love and admiration for my father continues to be the driving force behind my success. From washing cars as a young teen at my father's dealerships, I listened in wonder as my father taught me the car business. I worked in every department of the dealerships, learning every facet of the automotive industry.

My father always had impeccable timing for just about every business decision he made. Over the years, he acquired an empire of dealerships and brilliantly sold them with flawless timing. In 1997, he sold the vast majority of his dealership empire to AutoNation, Inc., the largest publicly owned automotive dealer group in the country. After fulfilling a non-compete, he successfully re-entered the automotive industry.

After years of immersing myself in the retail automotive industry and growing up with an entrepreneurial spirit, I knew I had to create my own success. This internal passion propelled me to seek a new adventure. My experience and education naturally led me to find a new avenue of prosperity within the fold of the auto industry. I have since successfully built my business in digital marketing to automobile dealerships.

Ten years ago, an auto dealership might have employed 25 commissioned salespeople. Today that dealership has primarily "Product Specialists" to answer questions for consumers who have already visited a dealer website. Instead of a burgeoning sales force, many business's—not just auto dealers—largest focal point area is the business development center. The BDC's primary role is to enhance the efforts of the digital marketing program.

A favorite quote of mine from J. Paul Getty, "Formula for success: rise early, work hard, strike oil" might seem a bit tongue in cheek, however, its message is true. "Striking oil" becomes easier when you know where to drill, and for any business today, but especially for the automobile industry, the place to drill is online. In the auto industry, 88% of buyers begin their process online. Any dealership not drilling in that area will miss striking oil—miss their sale. Knowing where to drill and knowing how to drill are two very different things. In the past eighteen years, I have perfected a digital marketing approach that enables companies to tap into their market in the shortest amount of time and with the greatest results.

For most industries, but certainly for the automobile industry, engaging customers through digital marketing campaigns is paramount. No intelligent business would ignore the well from which 88% of their business springs forth. There are still businesses following antiquated ideas such as closing on Sunday and ignoring the digital age. Those businesses are not realizing their full potential. The businesses that wish to thrive and strike oil are obligated to rise early, work hard and most essentially, maximize their presence in our ever-so-present evolving digital world. One can think of digital marketing as the base model of a vehicle. The add-ons that cause people to take notice amplify your digital impact, just like the fins on a 1959 Cadillac, bigger can be better. Before adding features, however, the base model—a successful business website-- has to hit the road.

WEBSITE BASICS

Make sure you show up for the party. A website, in and of itself, is only useful if your potential customers can find it. The goal is a fully optimized website that performs well for search engines. SEO - Search Engine Optimization - is what brings your webpage to a top ranking within search engines such as Google. Have you ever driven past a business that you did not realize was even there until they put out a large "Going out of Business" sign in the front? The same is true of a website. If the webpage is not visible to the search engines, your customers will never see it. For auto showrooms and any other sales-driven business, number one is the only place you really want to rank with the search engines. Start by hiring a company that knows SEO. Anyone can have a great looking website; very few can have a great ranking website. Once the customer finds the website, having a good experience and having a site that converts well, meaning it will attract and engage the customer and produce leads, determines the success of earning that customer's business.

ONLINE RELATIONSHIPS – CONVERTING CLICKS TO CUSTOMERS

From the moment a customer clicks his/her way to a business's webpage, the goal is to convert them to a qualified lead before they leave the page. In the case of an automobile dealership, the customer wants to know the price of the vehicle, the trade- in value of their vehicle, and their financing options. If a customer leaves a website after only 30 seconds, he/she is going to a competitor. The website that can acquire that customer's contact information, email address, etc., will be ahead of the game and likely will earn their business. A business needs to establish an online relationship with their customers in a very short time.

Retail websites need to have multiple facets of engagement. This will increase the overall conversion rates to your website and produce many more leads and sales for your business.

Common website engagement tools that can increase conversion:

- Credit applications or "Click here to Apply for Financing"
- Conversion tools for price, e.g., "Click here to get your Best Price"
- Subscribe to our Monthly Savings or Monthly Newsletter
- Schedule an Appointment Now

LIVE CHAT

One of the busiest times on the Internet is between 8 p.m. and midnight when families have put their kids to bed, and adults can settle down and concentrate. Of course, most businesses do not have a storefront open at these times for questions. Therefore, it is imperative that the website have a Live Chat feature to engage customers and meet them in their homes, at the time when the customer is available.

Our business employs a 24 hours a day, 7 days a week call center of fifty Live Chat agents to answer automobile customers' questions for the dealerships whose websites we service. Live Chat keeps customers engaged on the website for a longer period; length of the customer stay also aids in boosting a website's ranking. An IP address tracking system determines which customers show the most interest. For example, when an automobile shopper visits a webpage looking at mid-sized sedans, the system tracks that IP address and will acknowledge a return visit by the same customer looking at similar cars again. At this point, a Live Chat window would pop up and an agent might ask the client "I see you looked at these vehicles here yesterday, would you like me to send you an online brochure?" thus engaging the customer.

Coupling Live Chat with the Google Re-targeting Network generates the most bang for the buck. Google Re-targeting is essentially a cookies-based system that tracks where an IP address has been. It then prompts advertising based on the data collected. When your potential customer shops "down the road" at your competitor or even at another unrelated vendor, the system collects this information and offers the customer a pop-up ad for your business, effectively re-routing your competitor's potential sale back to your domain. Re-targeting generates about 150,000 impressions per month. These tools are wonderful, but not every customer originates his search at Google.

YOUTUBE

YouTube is now the second largest search engine in the world next to Google (Google owns YouTube) and more and more customers are beginning their search for just about anything on YouTube. Once reserved only for music and political speeches, now a YouTube video presence is a must-have for businesses seeking to increase their target audience exposure. Using the automobile analogy again, ten years ago air bags were not standard on vehicles; now a car will not sell without them.

One of the first things we do before we launch our website solutions to a new digital marketing client, is schedule our video production crew to shoot video at the dealership location. Our crew creates video of the dealership and takes testimonials, which give the customers a general idea of what it is like to do business at our client's dealership... In the same way as SEO, video gives the customer reasons why they would like to do business with "Dealership A."

Often times, YouTube advertising will generate a 30-35% increase in traffic to the dealerships website. My business often considers this a secret weapon, as many retail establishments don't realize the power of video search engines.

SOCIAL MEDIA

Facebook, Google+ and Twitter offer great soft-sell approaches. Our Social Media team will actually write the Facebook posts for clients, tweet about new products, build the Facebook site for an auto dealer and even embed inventory into the Facebook page so that customers can search for new cars, used cars and even schedule service appointments. These tools cross over effectively to many businesses. If you, for example, post seven days a week, then maybe one day a week you would post a "special" about a vehicle of the week. Do not be surprised if your business's social media presence generates your next big sale, but be ready to meet the customer's online needs.

ONLINE FINANCING

Online credit applications with automated approval for financing are imperative now since, in some dealerships, nearly 65% of auto sales are completed entirely online. The customer orders the car with the exact features desired, establishes financing online and waits for the dealer to deliver the vehicle to his/her home. Professionals with experience safeguarding customer identity should design website elements such as credit applications protecting sensitive customer information.

INVENTORY MANAGEMENT SYSTEM

Searchable online inventory motivates online sales. We offer our clients an inventory management system for their pre-owned vehicles that makes adding and removing vehicles and their data more manageable for a dealership. Most dealers take their own photos of pre-owned vehicles, and our system allows them to upload easily 25-30 images per car. Online shoppers can quickly browse the available cars and find one they would like to see in person. If the customer wants a new car, chances are he or she has a specific vehicle with specific features they want. We designed our virtual inventory—that is exclusive to us—to bring our clients 3-4 times more leads than their competitors.

VIRTUAL INVENTORY

Customers love choices. NADA reports that the average consumer visits at least four dealership websites in order to find the exact car that they desire. We created our Virtual Inventory program to allow customers to specify every feature they would like on every different vehicle made by that automaker. Therefore, if a customer wants a red Dodge pickup truck and we show him/her every possible configuration of that vehicle on our dealer's website, it keeps the customer on our client's webpage and he/she will assume that this dealership has the exact car for which she has been searching. The customer then at that point has no problem with filling out a lead.

Furthermore, when a client is still shopping and comparing various vehicles' makes and models, we offer them a comparison shopping application on the dealer website to help strengthen the dealership's position.

COMPARISON SHOPPING

One of the chief benefits of shopping on the web is the ability for customers to view many items in a short time, to comparison shop. To that end, we have created a user-friendly interactive Comparison-Shopping tool on our dealers' websites that customers can use to compare cars from various manufacturers. This program shows the vehicles of a particular automaker to the best advantage for that dealership by highlighting the best features to the customer

Lastly, the creation of even a stellar website is not enough to improve Google ranking or drive the business home. My company consults with car dealers to bring fresh ideas to the table and uses the latest advances in web technology. We maximize Internet presence by reaching the largest consumer audience to facilitate the greatest sales volume and increased bottom line. If you are not in the auto industry, your company can still use many of these tactics such as Social Media or Online Financing to increase your traffic and revenue. Find qualified professionals with the expertise and experience that your business requires.

About Brett

Brett Sutherlin, CEO and Chairman fusionZONE automotive, Inc.

If you smell that "new car smell" wafting through the Internet and into your living room while shopping for your next new vehicle, Brett Sutherlin is likely the man responsible. Sutherlin shattered the antiquated idea of driving dealership to dealership in search of the perfect vehicle by creating **fusionZONE automotive's** robust digital marketing system. Now, automobile shoppers can locate the perfect vehicle from the comfort of their own home!

Sutherlin spent the majority of his formative years working in his family's automotive dealership empire. Prior to this, he earned his Bachelor of Business Administration from the coveted Northwood University in Midland, MI where he studied all facets of Automotive Business and Marketing. His foray into the family business was cut short when an unprecedented opportunity came knocking and his family sold most of their dealership empire to AutoNation, Inc. Sutherlin knew at this time he must follow his entrepreneurial spirit. His mind never far from the auto industry, he recognized the increasing need for Internet marketing customized exclusively for automotive dealers. He leveraged his heritage, education and experience and launched **fusionZONE automotive**–a company that drives the good-ole-boy automotive industry into the digital marketing age.

fusionZONE automotive's advanced products have revolutionized a stagnant industry by merging cutting-edge digital technology with the heart of the automobile shopper. Sutherlin's digital marketing techniques are unparalleled in the industry, and net significant results in increased lead generation and sales completion for his dealership clients.

Sutherlin has grown **fusionZONE automotive** to be one of the largest automotive digital marketing providers in the nation. In less than 10 years, Sutherlin has grown **fusionZONE automotive** to over 700 dealer clients nationwide.

FusionZONE automotive is based in Los Angeles, CA where Sutherlin resides. He is married and has two sons. Brett Sutherlin appeared recently on television in "Americas Premier Experts" which aired on NBC, CBS and Fox.

www.fzautomotive.com

CHAPTER 14

WORK-LIFE BALANCE IS HAZARDOUS TO YOUR HEALTH

BY DR. SERENA REEP

As I sit down to write this chapter, I already envision a lot of resistance from you, the reader, to the idea that the pursuit of work-life balance as a goal is hazardous. After all, you have spent a lot of time and energy invested in the idea that it is a good thing; and you have been told that the more balance you have, the better off you are. Then, here I come to tell you that everything you were told, and everything you believed in up to now, is bad for you.

I understand. But, the greatest wisdom any of us has ever received came as a surprise. They were words that shocked us into a new reality. The conversation I hope to have with you here provides a fresh perspective on how to process the realities of your everyday life a little differently. After all, you are not an observer to the happenings in your life's journey. You are the captain. You guide the ship. My goal is to provide you the courage to embrace the things you know are right for your life, discard erroneous concepts, and reshape that invaluable piece of art called YOU!

My goal here is to show that you need a paradigm shift from the status quo (i.e. work-life balance is good) so that you can truly lead a more productive and rewarding life.

NEED FOR A PARADIGM SHIFT

Let us first look at what is meant by the concept Work-Life Balance in common every day parlance, before we look at what is wrong with it and why you need a paradigm shift. Believe me, adjusting to new realities takes hard work, but pays high wages.

Work-Life balance is generally defined as balancing work priorities and home priorities by adjusting the time spent on each, so neither becomes all-engulfing and crowds out the other areas of life.

Here are some common threads in most of the definitions of Work and Life:

- WORK is what we do from 9 to 5, and what we do after 5 is LIFE.
- What we do for a paycheck is WORK, and what we do for fun is LIFE.
- What someone else tells us to do, and judges us by how well we do it, is WORK; what we choose to do and how we judge ourselves by the outcome is LIFE.

Clearly, the assumptions behind these ideas are that:

- Work is not life, and, life is not work
- When you are doing one, you are not doing the other
- They are on two ends of the spectrum, and need to be in balance in order for you to live a satisfying and rewarding life.

When you dichotomize work and life and see them as two ends of the spectrum, it brings about what psychologists call "cognitive dissonance." You feel cognitive dissonance when you believe in one thing, but end up doing the opposite. For example, your value system says your family is the most important thing in your life, but you end up spending most of your wakeful hours at work. So, when you devote too much time to work, you feel guilty about neglecting the home and personal life; when you are at home, or on vacation, you feel guilty about the unfinished work.

But the greatest conflict is found in the work-a-holics on the one end, and the house wives and house husbands (and those forced out of gainful employment) on the other; they feel the most cognitive dissonance about the "lack-of-balance."

Most of the writers in the area of work-life balance contribute to, and even exacerbate, the problem. Why do I say that, you ask? The most common "prescription" coming out of work-life balance writers and bloggers is essentially the same: "Prioritize the different aspects of your life and schedule an appropriate amount of time for each."

Here is an example of such a recommendation from Laura Berman Fortgang, the author of "Now What? 90 Days to a New Life Direction." She suggests these five steps:

1. Figure out what really matters to you in life
2. Drop unnecessary activities
3. Protect your private time
4. Accept help to balance your life
5. Plan fun and relaxation

That sounds like reasonable advice, right? But, what happens if you cannot segregate your life into neat little chunks of time capsules or fit into a rigid schedule on your appointment book? Are the calendar and the appointment book really the appropriate tools for solving the work-life balance problem?

Problems arise when you don't see life as an "integrated whole" but as a "combination of pieces." The consequences are guilt, overwhelm, inner conflict, disappointment at not being the superwoman or superman and magically accomplishing everything on your plate.

One of the immediate consequences that I see in my interviews with people is the "blame game" –

1. You blame yourself for not having the "discipline" to balance the various activities in your life, and for becoming overwhelmed and frustrated;
2. You blame your work or your employer for de-humanizing you by blackmailing you with a paycheck and making you a slave to the desk, or the computer screen, or the clock.

Obviously, neither of these are productive responses to the resolution of cognitive dissonance. So where do we go from here? Is Work-life balance an exercise in futility? Why do efforts to sequester personal life from professional life only lead to greater frustration and less satisfaction while they are lauded by the experts as the panacea for a better quality of life?

It is because when you try to "protect" personal life from work, you are subscribing to an untenable dichotomy. When you place your time in porous mental compartments, you will invariably be frustrated when one bleeds over into the other. The overarching theme of such a dichotomy is the idea that happiness at home and at work can be achieved by giving equal weight to each side and keeping them in balance on the scale of life.

Does anyone really believe that life and work are of equal weights?

Let me start by saying that work-life balance is a myth. It is like a goal post with wings. As soon as you get a little closer to it, it moves a few inches away. Pursuing that myth and trying to balance work and life, as if it were the 11th commandment of life, has serious negative consequences; overwhelm, guilt and confusion over what one's priorities are in life. By getting busy balancing the things you do, you escape the need to question what you do, and its relevance to who you are. To solve the problem, you buy books and go to seminars seeking the holy grail of work-life balance.

The work-life balance concept has many accomplices such as time management and stress management. This has become an industry all unto itself. Motivational speakers and books claiming to reveal the secret of success give us temporary highs that are rarely sustained.

While good time management and stress management are valid concepts, they do not fully reflect the issues of balancing work life with personal life. For quite some time now, the work-life balance frustrations have been addressed by looking at how to be more productive. As a society, we have become committed to the concept of greater productivity. But here is the critical point you miss. Being committed means nothing if you are committed to the wrong path. The balance should really be between what you do and who you are, what your purpose and passion is in life. It's not between you and your job or your appointment book.

It is accomplished by balancing your daily activities with your true self. It is the alignment with your core identity that makes you feel alive and even *thrive*.

According to the Bureau of Labor Statistics, 67% of American workers are unhappy in their present work situation. Imagine the mental health consequences of spending most of your wakeful hours in an unhappy environment. If the best you can muster at work is the feeling of "I just work here… it is not my life," it contributes to the malaise. It disconnects you from being your best and doing your best. It is certainly not conducive to tapping the best in yourself. And, when you are weighed down by unhappiness, conflict, frustration and stress, the physical and mental health consequences for the overall quality of life you lead, are gigantic. Considering that you spend a large amount of your wakeful hours at work, your unhappiness at work undoubtedly spills over into unhappiness at home. That is a double whammy for your physical and emotional health!

WHAT IF

- What if you could obliterate this dichotomy of work and life by infusing both together into one?
- What if you could make life into work and work into life and make them both fun?
- What if you could create a scenario where work and fun are not opposites but complimentary?
- What if you could see them as two sides of the same coin?
- Will this change the happiness quotient? Would this improve your quality of life?

Working for a "job" vs. working for an identity that is rewarding and life sustaining—that makes all the difference in the world. Time and energy spent on your life and giving it more meaning and joy will help put other aspects of your life in proper context. And even though you must return to the doldrums of corporate work, having the subtext of knowing why you are there will change how you view what you do on a daily basis. The same duties, the same phone calls, the same things that once got under your skin will start to lose their fever.

Look at it this way. How long could you dig a hole if you know $10 million in gold nuggets waited for you a hundred feet deep? The answer is you could dig as long as it took to get to it. When you find your heart, your true identity, you'll be able to dig without frustration because you know what you're digging for. Your identity represents those pieces of gold.

The most balanced people I know have sharp distinctions between making money and making meaning. They use money to fuel meaning, not use money to create the meaning for their lives.

Here is a woman named Cheryl who had some insightful comments to make in one of the Internet forums about how she arrived at her personal sense of work-life balance. "I would say finding flexibility and/or control over my work schedule is my number one work/life balance issue. Although I am an empty-nester with the ability to work 100 hours a week if I wanted to, I don't want to! I am a dependable, dedicated, passionate worker with varied skills but I want some flexibility in my work schedule. I do not want to sit in an office M-F from 9-5.... I have aging parents, new grandchildren, many friends and a retired husband. We like to travel or have lunch together during the week."

Anne-Marie Slaughter, the first woman director of policy planning at the State Department recently left her "foreign-policy dream job" as she described it, to care for her family and fulfill her parental responsibilities. She felt the stress of her work identity playing a greater role in her life than she felt was desirable. This was in spite of the fact that she had a very supportive husband who picked up a lot of the slack when she left for Washington.

On the opposite end of the spectrum of choices, the Daily Mail in UK recently published an article by Isabella Dutton who says having children was the biggest regret of her life, which raised a considerable storm of controversy. Here too, we find that "balance" according to other peoples' definition does not bring you happiness or personal satisfaction.

Sheryl Sandberg's new book, "Lean-In" talks about the internal as well as institutional roadblocks to achieving work-life balance in women and how they can climb those walls. Interestingly enough, her book has also received considerable support as well as criticism for not adequately addressing the issues of balance for working mothers. One critique leveled against her is that most working mothers operate under extreme social and economic impediments leading to guilt and conflict between work life and family life, rather than because of a lack of lean-in self-confidence.

These feelings of guilt and conflict over life choices point to the mixed messages from society to the professional women as to what is the right balance between the priorities of work and life. The conflict of balance also afflicts men but to a much less extent, since it is a more inner need than societal dictates on how they "should" balance their lives.

These conflicts and cognitive dissonance are not limited to the high profile cases such as the ones I described above. After playing the game of climbing the corporate ladder for twenty or thirty years, many of us look down this ladder only to find our healthiest, most vibrant days gone. And sadly, we spent these days working on the dreams of others. This is what men and women of all walks of life have been struggling with for decades. The general sense of running without getting anywhere is not because people are inadequate, but because our value system is. We have to stop simply talking about the paradox of work-life balance and the guilt of choosing between the professional life and the personal life. It's time to fix it.

How do we fix it? Start redefining your life around your purpose and passion in life. Everything you do in your life needs to revolve around that sense of identity and self-definition. Ask yourself the question: "Who am I? Where am I going? What do I want out of my life? What would make me feel at the end of my life that I have lived a purposeful, meaningful and satisfying life?"

In this context, let me bring what I call the "Principle of 3Ms" and what we can learn from it. The 3Ms I refer to are Mother Teresa, Mahatma Gandhi and Martin Luther King, Jr. By most people's definition, their life was one-dimensional and very unbalanced – they had one purpose, one goal and everything else was secondary to that purpose. My contention is that indeed they were the most balanced; not the people who tout balance as a jigsaw puzzle where you try and fit many disparate pieces together. They had clarity, instead of confusion, about who they were and what their life was about.

You don't need to be a carbon copy of Mahatma Gandhi or Mother Teresa, to learn from them and benefit from their life's lessons. They can be valuable guideposts in redefining your own life that rejects the old, outmoded concepts like work-life balance and replaces them with more meaningful concepts that celebrate your own unique purpose in life.

About Dr. Sereena

Dr. Serena Reep is the President of Transformational Communications. She is an ex-College Professor, communication and relationship management coach, corporate project management trainer, author and motivational speaker. She considers herself a social-entrepreneur and likes to promote social causes in all her ventures.

Serena Reep received her Ph.D. in Social Psychology. Her specialization is Social Structure and Personality. She also holds an active PMP (Project Management Professional) certification. She frequently speaks on best practices in communication for successful project management as well as successful interpersonal relationship management. She spent eight years as a Professor at Rutgers University, and has been a consultant in the corporate world for almost two decades. She has worked as a contractor/consultant for clients ranging from private corporations such as CA, NCS and IBM to government agencies such as the DOE, CMS and FDIC.

Dr. Serena is the recipient of the National Association of Bestselling Authors award in 2012 for her work in the book *Success Secrets* with Jack Canfield. She has been seen on NBC, CBS, ABC and Fox affiliates. She has been interviewed by Arielle Ford on the "Meet the Experts" program. She is an Expert Blogger for the Fast Company and the Huffington Post. Her book *Work-Life Balance is DEAD!* is a very thought provoking and paradigm-shifting manifesto on living an authentic life, unfettered by the weight of outmoded constructs about balancing work and life. She also sounds a wake-up call to the corporations on the effectiveness of the work-life balance perks they provide and offers a fresh perspective on increasing their ROI.

To learn more about her work or to contact Dr. Serena Reep for your speaking or training needs, please visit: http://serenasez.com.

CHAPTER 15

MAGIC FUTURE: Becoming Your Own Change Agent

BY STEFAN WISSENBACH

Be the change that you wish to see in the world.
~ Mahatma Gandhi

Do you see your future as misery – or as magic?

Do you see the years ahead as a never-ending struggle that leaves you exhausted and drained – or as a series of new and exciting opportunities that will lead you to higher levels of achievement and satisfaction?

How you view what's to come affects your "here and now" - in a profound way. I personally believe in a future that's filled with magic. But here's the real trick – that so-called "magic" is really what we ourselves create through our own thoughts and actions!

Think of the many devices we all use on a day-to-day basis – and take for granted. Your smartphone, your iPod, your iPad...all of those, in the not-too-distant past, would have appeared to be "magic" to residents of that time – when, in reality, they are merely gadgets rooted in a technology that was painstakingly built step-by-step, piece-by-piece, until they became modern-day "miracles."

You can make yourself into a similar miracle – through the culmination of a building process that results in what appears to be a magical transformation to those around you. That's how you become the ultimate "Change Agent" of your own life.

Since I was very young, I've always been about creating a more powerful, positive future. It started with my own, and then it was my clients with whom I concerned myself.

Now I'd like to help you with yours.

MY "MAGIC" TUTORIAL

Money was a scarce commodity when I was being raised by a single mom in the U.K. Perhaps that's why I became obsessed with magicians and wizards as a boy – they took me away to magical lands that were far more fun than my everyday existence.

As I grew older and came to the realization that wizards weren't going to be showing up anytime soon at my doorstep to grant me any special enchanted powers, I looked elsewhere for evidence of some kind of magic existing in everyday life. And I saw it in the lives of the rich and famous, who seemed to enjoy plentiful helpings of abundance and excitement on a regular basis.

That kind of life journey truly did seem magical to me - the people in my neighborhood certainly didn't get to have that level of life experience. Why not? Why were some blessed with miraculous success – while others seemed resigned to trudge through their days, just scraping by?

I came to find out that those who, like me, came from humble beginnings created those magical lives out of relentless self-improvement, with a heavy emphasis on setting goals and achieving them; in other words, that step-by-step process I mentioned earlier. As I studied their secrets of success, I at last devised a powerful Magic Formula of my own - based on what I saw were the five essential elements that went into their accomplishments.

Let me spell out that Magic Formula for you:

- **M**otivation – We all must be motivated to achieve goals of a higher order.
- **A**pplication – Successful people get things done. If we don't apply ourselves to needed action, we don't achieve.

- **G**rowth – We must be open to doing what it takes to grow our intellect, our physical health and our spirit, so we are able to achieve more.
- **I**ndependence – Both personal and financial freedom enable us to live the kinds of lives we want to live, unfettered by arbitrary restrictions.
- **C**ommunity – Networking with other successful people helps you create a strong and supportive community that enables you to do more than you could achieve on your own.

Yes, if you put them all together, you end up with **MAGIC**.

This Magic, however, is not based on mystery, but on *mastery* – mastery of building a life that leads to an exceptional outcome. Fortunately, my mother instilled in me a belief that anything was possible if I put my mind to it. So...I did.

More importantly, this kind of "magic mindset" became an integral part of my professional career. I founded The Wissenbach Group in 1994, through which I have advised wealthy private investors on how to achieve their personal and financial goals. After two decades of success, I'm fortunate enough to enjoy a very different lifestyle than the one I experienced as a child. I have a large country property—with staff—and travel all over the world with my fabulous wife and three delightful children. I've enjoyed staying in many fine hotels, experienced different cultures, learned to snowboard, fly helicopters, and I'm able to drive any car I want.

Again, these are very different circumstances than my childhood. And I wouldn't be enjoying them now if I didn't believe I could attain it all back then.

I had to believe in my own Magic Future. And, more importantly, make it happen.

BRINGING YOUR MAGIC FUTURE TO LIFE

The question is, do you believe in your own Magic Future?

Do you have a plan to get what you want? Do you want to get to a point in your life where work is optional? Where you actually become one of the people I admired as a child, because you chose success over an ordinary existence?

If so...what are you doing about it?

Perhaps you've placed all your chips on one element of your life. Many of us do. We think, "What if I could just change this certain relationship? Get this particular job? Move to this particular place? Have this cosmetic surgery done?" And we believe these superficial things will make our problems disappear.

That is the kind of magic I *don't* believe in.

The only thing we can really control is ourselves, our attitudes and our actions. I always find it interesting that people will take the time to make a detailed will - so that they have a written plan of what is to happen after they're dead. And yet, they have no real plan for their actual life!

Then there are those who would love to make a life plan – but have no idea how to go about it. In the past, we may have felt we could rely on direction from the governments or the financial institutions that formerly gave us a sense of stability. Trust in those traditional bodies has been severely eroded, however, thanks to the 2008 economic crisis and our political leaders' uncertain responses to it. Many people have been left paralyzed into inaction and don't really know where to turn.

But that financial crisis is absolutely nothing, in my opinion, compared to the crisis that is currently building in the background – which is people who are not looking after themselves and not taking care of their financial futures.

Because we cannot rely on these institutions any longer, it's really up to all of us to take responsibility and take control of our individual fates. We all deserve a future that's better than our past.

I want to help everyone get that future. That's why I created Magic Future®.

I've invested over three million dollars in this initiative, which you can explore at MagicFuture.com, to help those who are in need of direction and assistance in reaching their goals. Human beings, despite their faults, are still wonderful things. When we move forward with passion, when we are engaged and we connect ourselves to a bigger and brighter future, we begin to close the gap between where we are and where we wish to be.

Those who have used the tools on our website have seen the magic work for themselves. Because of how they have connected themselves to their goals, they make different decisions – which they ordinarily wouldn't have in their day-to-day lives – because they are directed towards what they want to achieve.

In other words, they are beginning with the end in mind.

OUR MAGIC TOOLKIT

I believe it's worth reviewing the "Magic Toolkit" we feature on the site – because these individual facilitators are vital to creating real change in anyone's life. Even if you don't become a user of our site, it's important that you understand the powerful concepts that inform these tools – and shape our futures:

MagicGoals

Many people set goals, but never reach them. We've researched years of human behavioral research to discover how to improve the chances of goals being realized.

Here are a few empowering facts:

- ***Writing your goals down increases the likelihood of accomplishing them by 42%***
- ***Sharing goals with peers increases the likelihood of accomplishing them by 50%***
- ***Having a friend receive weekly progress reports increases the likelihood of accomplishing them by 77%***

A common thread to all of these statistics is this: Goals need to be removed from our imaginations and brought out into the real world. When we write them down or we share them with those around them, the more "real" they become – and the more committed we become to making them happen.

With that in mind, our MagicGoals tool simply asks you to write down your goals, construct a few simple short-term steps that are easily completed to help you attain those goals, and share those steps and objectives with your friends.

Yes, it sounds simple, but how many of us actually go through this kind of process? How many of our goals, instead, end up left by the wayside, simply because we didn't take the few moments to facilitate their completion with these easy steps?

MagicHabits

Negative patterns that we've developed can often prevent us from getting what we want; we actually end up obstructing our own progress. That's why creating new and powerful *habits* may be necessary in order to develop our own personal success stories.

For example, maybe you want to get in better physical shape. You can create new habits to make that happen. Perhaps you commit to taking the stairs at your workplace instead of the elevator – and you end up becoming so accustomed to this new pattern that it feels strange to do otherwise.

You should create new positive habits that correspond to your achieving your MagicGoals, as we encourage on the Magic Future® website (and, by the way, we recommend repeating a habit 21 days in a row - that will usually cause it to become part of your normal behavior).

MagicVision

Seeing is believing – we've all heard that pearl of wisdom. That's why putting a "MagicVision" to work can be incredibly empowering when trying to reach an intangible goal. Our MagicVision website tools allows for the creation of customized "Vision Boards," where users can gather together images that represent their life dreams – and give those dreams a physical manifestation.

If you know where you want to go, why not give yourself a sneak peek before you get there? Pretend it's the trailer to the movie of your life – and picture it as having the happiest possible ending imaginable.

MagicNumber®

This last tool is, to me, the most important one in many ways. It was the first "magic" tool I ever developed and I used it extensively to help my private clients formulate a real plan to attain the complete life freedom they were after.

What is the **MagicNumber**®? Quite simply, it's the amount of money (or assets) you need to have in order to make work optional at an age of your choosing. Our website allows you to determine that number in less than ten minutes – and also permits you to see how much wealth you need to accumulate, per day, month and year, to reach that number.

If that sounds complicated, it isn't, thanks to our academically-verified algorithm that simplifies what would seem to be a complex task and helps you make smart choices to achieve what is most likely your ultimate life goal.

MY MAGIC MOMENT

Recently, I used my own Magic Toolkit to achieve a goal – and I ended up experiencing a magic moment that might seem very trivial to you – as it merely involved my tying a shoelace.

I know I've achieved my success because of my dedication to personal development. But success can have its consequences as well – and, to tell the truth, I neglected my health along the way. I didn't exercise enough, and I enjoyed the good life a little too much in many a restaurant. Result? In my early forties, I found myself beset upon by the kind of culprits one encounters when in my shoes – early onset diabetes and high blood pressure.

This was a big wake-up call. After all, without good health, everything else is rather pointless!

Well, there it was in front of me one morning, my Magic Future website staring in my face. So I thought – why not use it to set a goal to eliminate the diabetes and lower my blood pressure – and, in the process, get fit and healthy?

So I used my Magic Toolkit to construct the goal, change bad habits and be an agent of my own change in my waistline! As I believe strongly in working with the right people, I took on a leading person in health and nutrition – someone who advised the Olympic rugby squad – and shared my goal with him. Every Monday morning, he received a progress report from me through the Magic Future site.

Well, as of this writing, I've lost over 30 pounds in weight and feel better than I have in a long time. My blood pressure is down to safe levels and just last week, my doctor confirmed I was no longer diabetic. Magic or mastery? Now you know the answer...

One morning, as I was going through this process, I came downstairs and, without thinking much of it, put my foot up on a kitchen barstool and tied my shoelace. Yes, this was the magic moment I spoke of earlier. What made it so magical?

My wife spotted me and said, "You wouldn't have been able to do that four months ago!"

And it was true – I wouldn't have, and suddenly, in that moment, I was incredibly happy, because I had seen, in that very small moment, the achievement of a very real benchmark in my pursuit of a much larger goal.

So it is with any objective you set your mind on. You experience long periods of effort, punctuated by sudden bursts of ecstasy as you reach a very real milestone. Of course, with every silver lining comes a dark cloud – and, in this case, my new health regimen has left me with an entire expensive wardrobe that no longer fits me!

AND YOU?

So, then, what about you? Do you believe you can achieve the Magic Future that will fulfill you? Are you willing to tackle yourself at a micro level to achieve on a macro level?

You too can be a huge Change Agent of your own life. You too can make small but powerful changes on an ongoing basis that will transform your life beyond recognition.

Believe in magic. Believe in yourself. Believe you can do what's necessary to create the life you really want. And believe me – you will!

About Stefan

Stefan Wissenbach is an entrepreneur, author and speaker. From a humble but happy childhood, he has built and sold several successful businesses and is an advisor to a number of leading business figures.

In 1994, he founded The Wissenbach Group, providing strategic advice to wealthy private individuals, helping them manage their affairs in harmony with their personal goals. Whilst developing his unique process, he created the concept of MagicNumber® – the amount of money or accumulated wealth needed to live your desired lifestyle where work is optional.

Having spent many years helping wealthy people, Stefan's mission is to now also help a wider audience. He is passionate about providing education and inspiration to enable others to fulfill their potential and bridge the gap between aspiration and achievement. His unique approach is to simplify the complex and provide a framework for people to take action, distilling a lifetime of learning into simple success strategies that anyone can master.

In 2010, he formed and launched magicfuture.com to achieve this mission. His revolutionary Magic Future corporate benefit programs have created thousands of successful, engaged and happy employees delivering greater value in the workplace.

Stefan has a lifelong commitment to personal development and travels to Chicago four times a year to meet with Dan Sullivan – one of the world's leading entrepreneurial coaches. Magicfuture.com takes the best practices from his lifetime of learning and applies his proven strategies in an easy-to-use, fun, inspirational online platform available to anyone with access to the web. Stefan's personal success is behind every feature of the tools.

His book, *Slaying Dragons & Moving Mountains, A beginners guide to a happy fulfilled life* and his audio program, *Your Magic Future™: A Proven Magic Formula for Making Work Optional* both teach practical and timeless skills, techniques and knowledge that enable anyone to create greater levels of happiness and success. Stefan is happily married with three children. He enjoys living life to the full, flying helicopters and travelling to new places. He is also the Founder of The Magic Future Foundation.

To learn more about Stefan Wissenbach visit: stefanwissenbach.com.

CHAPTER 16

BECOME A CHANGE AGENT WITH STORYSELLING: How The Right Narrative Can Transform Your Brand Into A Marvel

BY NICK NANTON & JW DICKS

Stanley Lieber, at the age of 17, had no idea what to do with his life. Fortunately, however, he could at least earn a paycheck, thanks to the time-honored practice of nepotism. His uncle owned a comic book company and installed the young man in the offices as an assistant in 1939. Stanley saw it as just a temporary situation; he knew that one day he would write the Great American Novel.

A couple of decades later, he was running the place – only there wasn't much left to run. A crackdown on bloody horror comics in the 1950's had caused many organizations and parents to ban them altogether – and the ones that had survived were so heavily censored that they didn't generate many sales on their own. Stanley had supervised over twenty people; now there were only three left, creating silly monster stories for boys and harmless teen romances for girls.

But DC Comics, the perennial industry leader, had just had some success with a new superhero group, The Justice League of America, which brought together Batman, Superman and a bunch of other costumed crusaders – so Stanley's uncle suggested that he create one as well. Stanley wasn't happy with the whole idea. He didn't want to write another copycat comic: he was convinced he needed a career change if he was ever really going to make his creative mark.

So he went home and talked through his frustrations with his wife. She was frustrated with those frustrations and finally told him, "Look, don't just quit. You've been going through the motions for years, doing what everybody else was telling you to do. Do this one the way you want to do it, put everything into this new comic and see what happens. You can always quit later."

Stanley thought about it and finally decided, why not? He didn't have anything to lose – he might as well go for it. So, using his pen name of Stan Lee, he created *The Fantastic Four* with artist Jack Kirby - and was as shocked as anybody when huge sales figures came in a few months later. His uncle quickly ordered him to make more superhero comics, so Stan did. In short order came an incredible creative burst that produced *Spider-Man, The Incredible Hulk, The X-Men, Iron Man, The Mighty Thor* and *The Avengers* – it was like something inside Stanley had been finally unleashed.

And that something began to find its way into every part of the business. Stan rebranded the whole line, calling it "Marvel Comics," and gave every cover the same distinctive design. He pushed the boundaries of traditional comics in every way; in-jokes abounded, and adventures were continued from issue to issue for the first time, just like soap operas. Stories were also more adult; they were an entirely new combination of the boy-girl dramas Stan had concocted for his romance comics and traditional superhero sagas. Also, for the first time, an irreverent humor that permeated almost every page.

The world at large took notice of the big Marvel movement. Soon respectable magazines like *Esquire* and *Rolling Stone* were publishing serious profiles of Stan and Marvel. Their readership now didn't stop when kids turned twelve; college kids were reading his stuff and loving it.

Stan "the Man" Lee suddenly found that he had become a comics legend by creating an entirely new narrative for the industry. By the mid-70's, he had made his mark and, finally, was ready to move on.

And he did – to Hollywood.

It took Stan Lee another couple of decades to find big success in superhero movies, but *The Avengers* was crowned the box office champion of 2012 – as the popularity of all the Marvel characters Stan Lee created fifty years ago hit its all-time high, mostly because many of the storytelling techniques Lee used in the comics were finally applied to the film adaptations.

Stan Lee created a narrative for himself and Marvel that produced a hip, fun and smart image that was personality-driven and fit perfectly with the growing youth movement of the 60's. More importantly, he applied it to every aspect *of the Marvel business* – creating a money-making mythology that culminated recently with the Disney Corporation purchasing the company for *four billion dollars.*

THE SUPER POWER OF STORYSELLING

StorySelling is all about using a personal or professional narrative to make your brand more high-profile and more profitable – and what Stan Lee did is one of the ultimate examples of how StorySelling can spark an incredible level of ongoing success.

In this chapter, an excerpt from our book, *StorySelling: Hollywood Secrets Revealed*, we're going to analyze the "Marvelous Steps" that Stan Lee took to implement StorySelling concepts – and show you how those concepts can be applied in a *practical* way in a business, as well as your Celebrity Brand.

Before we get into those Marvelous Steps, however, we want to point out something: What's *really* interesting about Stan's story is that the idea to create a new superhero comic wasn't his, it was his boss's. And the idea to create a new *kind* of superhero comic wasn't his, it was his wife's.

What was his idea? *The StorySelling.*

If we were to actually put down on paper the overall brand narrative he had in his head, it would be this: "An upstart with no money and few resources challenges the world's biggest comic company on their own turf. Through humor, intelligence and innovation, that upstart creates an entirely *new* approach to comics that brings in a whole new audience."

The four most effective StorySelling plots are these:

1. **"Overcoming the Monster":** defeating an overwhelming adversary
2. **"Rags to Riches":** achieving massive success from humble beginnings
3. **"The Quest":** Searching for a new solution to an old problem
4. **"Rebirth":** Like the fabled phoenix, rising from the ashes to live again

All FOUR are contained in Stan's narrative. DC Comics (home of Superman and Batman), was the "Monster" that had to be overcome, Marvel quickly went from "Rags to Riches," "The Quest" was Stan Lee's journey to find a new way of doing comic books that would give him some career satisfaction, and "Rebirth"...well, Stan Lee and Marvel both experienced that after both almost went out of business.

So, practically speaking, you can see how those four plotlines are directly responsible for a great deal of Marvel's successful StorySelling. Now, we're certainly not saying Stan ever consciously articulated any of this – for him, it was a simple matter of doing things the way *he* wanted to do things. But, being a natural-born storyteller *and* promoter (the combination is crucial), he instinctively understood how to put these principles into action, so he could stop blindly *reacting* to the competition and create his own narrative – which is precisely what StorySelling is all about.

And comic book readers dug that story; he and Marvel became *authentic* in a way he had never been before and suddenly, next to Spider-Man and Iron Man, Superman and Batman looked like the squarest dudes in town.

And is that any different than what Apple did to Microsoft? Nope.

With that in mind, let's examine a few steps Stan took to make his StorySelling a vital part of the Marvel mythos from top to bottom - and how you should think about doing the same for yourself.

MARVELOUS STEP #1: START SUBTLE

Stan Lee never came out and said he was going to change the face of comic books. Instead, he let the work itself do the talking and attract the attention.

When you begin your StorySelling efforts, do the same. Concentrate on bringing your narrative to life in your actual Celebrity Brand – or your product or service - before you make claims you might not deliver on. When you see something is starting to work, you can then exploit that successful narrative. The Hall of Failures is littered with overhyped products that fell with a thud heard around the world when they didn't live up to the expectations created by their parent company (The infamous Ford Edsel, "New Coke," Microsoft's Zune line of media players, etc.) – so don't hype unless you're sure you've got the back-up to prove it.

Implement this Step by Asking Yourself: *What "proof" can I generate of my own expertise or product/service superiority? Will it take the form of outstanding performance, believable testimonials, branded books or videos, or simply product popularity?*

MARVELOUS STEP #2: BE BOLD WHEN IT'S TIME

Stan didn't know he had a hit on his hands until he was ready to go to press with the third issue of *The Fantastic Four*. At that point, he decided it was time to go full throttle – and he boldly put across the top of the comic cover, "The World's Greatest Comic Magazine," a claim that continued to stay put for decades. Similarly, Steve Jobs, *after* Apple had attracted a devoted group of customers, spent a record-breaking amount of money on a commercial entitled *1984* that ran only one time during the Super Bowl of that same year to make his own monster StorySelling statement.

When you've got proof of your greatness, go with it. Until then, wait it out until your StorySelling is recognized in one way or another.

Implement this Step by Asking Yourself: *How can I best exploit my proof? What's the most memorable way to promote this fact that's consistent with my StorySelling narrative – and appropriate to my audience?*

MARVELOUS STEP #3: STORYSELL EVERYWHERE

Just like a great cook can make dishes from virtually every part of an animal, Stan Lee decided to look for StorySelling possibilities in every inch of his comic books – even the features into which publishers rarely put any thought or energy. Stan gave the letters pages hilarious names (Iron Man's was *Sock It to Shellhead*), he filled a page in each comic with what he called *Bullpen Bulletins*, spotlighting and cross-promoting other Marvel comics, and he started a wacky fan club, The Merry Marvel Marching Society (or MMMS, for short), that was a huge success. He took what other comic books saw as obligations and approached them as *opportunities* – and stood out from the other publishers by creating an awesome bond with its readers.

Implement this Step by Asking Yourself: *What overlooked opportunities are there in my industry that I can use for StorySelling purposes? How can I insert my narrative into those areas in a creative and impactful way?*

MARVELOUS STEP #4: DON'T FORGET THE FACES

There was something else Stan Lee did that was unprecedented in his industry – he began to give the artists and other writers (and even the guys who lettered the word balloons!) funny nicknames in the story credits – in a business where nobody had even put credits on stories before. Not only that, but he frequently talked about them in the Marvel *Bullpen Bulletins*.

Result? The men and women *behind* Marvel Comics became almost as important as the superheroes were to the readership, creating an even stronger bond. Stan, of course, put himself the furthest out front, with his own regular column in the B*ullpen Bulletins* and regularly commenting on his own stories with goofy footnotes.

The lesson? Always make sure to have some kind of strong personality involved with your StorySelling efforts, whether it's you, someone who works for you or even a hired spokesperson; people identify, of course, with people and create the emotional involvement you want to create with your narrative.

Implement this Step by Asking Yourself: *Who will be the face (or faces)* *of my StorySelling? How does the chosen personality (or personalities) fit into my narrative?*

MARVELOUS STEP #5: ALWAYS ENGAGE

There's one specific strong element to everything Stan Lee did – he engaged comic book readers on a level than had never happened before. Through his letters pages, Bullpen Bulletins, credits, story footnotes and fan club, *he was constantly talking directly to his readers in an entertaining way*. And he found unique ways to turn even negatives into positives with this attitude. For instance, the Marvel Universe grew so complicated that readers began writing in to complain when a story got something wrong or contradicted an earlier story. This was a growing problem – so Stan decided that every reader who correctly identified a mistake would win a "No-Prize." What was a No-Prize? Well, the winner would receive an envelope in the mail with a big announcement printed on it that their No-Prize was inside.

What was in the envelope? Nothing.

Implement this Step by Asking Yourself: *What opportunities do I have to engage in a new and unique way with my customers? How can I make that engagement as memorable as possible?*

MARVELOUS STEP #6: CONTINUE TO EVOLVE

Stan Lee's StorySelling evolved in a very organic way over time; he kept spotting new things to do with the comic book format as his StorySelling efforts continued to gain traction. He also deepened the Marvel narrative as it progressed. As more and more readers regarded Marvel as the cool "alternative" to DC, Stan made more and more fun of DC in his editorial content to reinforce that positioning and to reflect Marvel's growing success.

That growth occurred in the actual comics' content as well. In the late '60's, Marvel became the first major comic book company to break the Comics Code Authority's long list of rules. The Code had it that you couldn't portray drug use in any comic story – but, as addiction was becoming a serious problem with teens in the late 60's, the only way Stan Lee could take on the problem in *Spider-Man* was disregarding the Code – so he did, and created a very memorable, talked-about series of issues.

Implement this Step by Asking Yourself: *Is my StorySelling keeping pace with what's happening with my business? Am I reflecting the present – or only the past?*

Stan Lee's big mistake during his first twenty years in the comic book business was seeing it as a job and not an opportunity. Most of you have probably made that same mistake at one time or another – it's the difference between an employee and an entrepreneur. When he finally saw that he had the power to make something completely new happen with his comics, he used that power – and found out that it packed a lot more punch than any that The Hulk ever threw.

When you develop a strong StorySelling narrative and implement it correctly, as Stan did, it feeds on itself, it grows stronger and stronger, and it opens up more and more layers of opportunity as you move forward with it. There were very few businesses in 1961 sillier, more inconsequential and perceived to have less of a future than comic books – and yet Stanley Lieber took that business and transformed it in such a dynamic way through StorySelling that, a half-century later, it's paying its biggest dividends ever – both for himself and the company.

And for that, we salute Stan with the one word he uses as a sign-off in whatever he writes: "Excelsior!"

About Nick

An Emmy-Award-Winning Director and Producer, Nick Nanton, Esq. is known as the Top Agent to Celebrity Experts around the world for his role in developing and marketing business and professional experts through personal branding, media, marketing and PR. Nick is recognized as the nation's leading expert on personal branding as Fast Company Magazine's Expert Blogger on the subject and lectures regularly on the topic at major universities around the world. His book *Celebrity Branding You®*, while an easy and informative read, has also been used as a text book at the University level.

The CEO and Chief StoryTeller at The Dicks + Nanton Celebrity Branding Agency, an international agency with more than 1800 clients in 33 countries, Nick is an award-winning director, producer and songwriter who has worked on everything from large scale events to television shows – with the likes of Steve Forbes, Brian Tracy, Jack Canfield (*The Secret,* Creator of the *Chicken Soup for the Soul* Series), Michael E. Gerber, Tom Hopkins, Dan Kennedy and many more.

Nick is recognized as one of the top thought-leaders in the business world and has co-authored 26 best-selling books alongside Brian Tracy, Jack Canfield, Dan Kennedy, Dr. Ivan Misner (Founder of BNI), Jay Conrad Levinson (Author of the Guerilla Marketing Series), Super Agent Leigh Steinberg and many others, including the breakthrough hit Celebrity Branding You!®.

Nick has led the marketing and PR campaigns that have driven more than 1000 authors to Best-Seller status. Nick has been seen in *USA Today, The Wall St. Journal, Newsweek, BusinessWeek, Inc. Magazine, The New York Times, Entrepreneur® Magazine, Forbes,* FastCompany.com. and has appeared on ABC, NBC, CBS, and FOX television affiliates around the country, as well as CNN, FOX News, CNBC, and MSNBC from coast to coast.

Nick is a member of the Florida Bar, holds a JD from the University Of Florida Levin College Of Law, as well as a BSBA in Finance from the University of Florida's Warrington College of Business. Nick is a voting member of The National Academy of Recording Arts & Sciences (NARAS, Home to The GRAMMYs), a member of The National Academy of Television Arts & Sciences (Home to the Emmy Awards), co-founder of the National Academy of Best-Selling Authors, a 16-time Telly Award winner, and spends his spare time working with Young Life, Downtown Credo Orlando, Entrepreneurs International and rooting for the Florida Gators with his wife Kristina, and their three children, Brock, Bowen and Addison.

About JW

JW Dicks, Esq. is America's foremost authority on using personal branding for business development. He has created some of the most successful brand and marketing campaigns for business and professional clients to make them the credible celebrity experts in their field and build multi-million dollar businesses using their recognized status.

JW Dicks has started, bought, built, and sold a large number of businesses over his 39-year career and developed a loyal international following as a business attorney, author, speaker, consultant, and business experts' coach. He not only practices what he preaches by using his strategies to build his own businesses, he also applies those same concepts to help clients grow their business or professional practice the ways he does.

JW has been extensively quoted in such national media as *USA Today, The Wall Street Journal, Newsweek, Inc.*, Forbes.com, CNBC.com, and *Fortune Small Business*. His television appearances include ABC, NBC, CBS and FOX affiliate stations around the country. He is the resident branding expert for *Fast Company*'s internationally syndicated blog and is the publisher of *Celebrity Expert Insider*, a monthly newsletter targeting business and brand building strategies.

JW has written over 22 books, including numerous best-sellers, and has been inducted into the National Academy of Best-Selling Authors®. JW is married to Linda, his wife of 39 years, and they have two daughters, two granddaughters and two Yorkies. JW is a 6th generation Floridian and splits his time between his home in Orlando and beach house on the Florida west coast.

CHAPTER 17

GOING TRA*DIGITAL*

BY ANGELA JOHNSON & NADEEM DAMANI

Do you recognize this?

You've acquired a list of prospects. You do what sales people have done since the advent of the telephone:

"Hello, Mrs. Smith. I'm Angela Johnson with Farmers Insurance—" and before you can say anything else, you hear that horrible, heart-sinking click. Not to mention the restrictions of the Do Not Call list!

How many of you drive through a neighborhood and secretly wish that you could just knock on all those doors and introduce yourself? Door-to-door sales were tough, but what a great way to meet and get to know new prospects—for that magical price all salesmen like, free. Unfortunately, there aren't many people home during the day anymore and restrictive city ordinances have virtually ended this form of marketing.

Fortunately for us, there is an inherent lie in the idea that technology is killing the traditional. Consumers still need to be able to communicate with *someone* to find the best product for them.

It's just that the way that's done in the twenty-first century isn't over the phone or on someone's front porch anymore. The end result is still the same—connecting to potential and actual customers, but the way it's done is changing. Now, it can be done on-line via social media.

To give you an example of what we're talking about in terms of using social media for prospecting, let's look at a very successful traditional prospecting technique and how you could easily take it online: the direct mail campaign. Angela was able to grow her business fast and steady through direct mail marketing. However, she also realized that direct mail can get very expensive very fast.

Sometimes it can be shocking to stop and calculate the acquisition cost of a new client, Angela knew how much she spent per month on all of the costs associated with the mailings. But as the years went on and she had gathered all of the low hanging fruit, a wise friend suggested she calculate the current cost of acquiring a new client. Can you believe it was $167?

Now, Angela still does direct mailing because mailing directly to her community does generate leads. However, she's also taken the idea behind her direct mailer and has posted the same information online. When she posts the information from the mailer online it gets results. When she sends out the mailer it still gets results. The latter costs money, the former costs time—but that's what we have to spend to ensure our businesses have a constantly filled prospect pipeline. And that's what makes Angela a successful tra*digital* business owner!

Likewise, Nadeem has successfully used social media to generate sales as well as develop his personal brand. Through consistent social media usage, Nadeem has branded himself as a life insurance expert.

In one Facebook post, Nadeem posted a YouTube video about life insurance. A Facebook fan that saw the post contacted Nadeem, and made an appointment for the very next morning. In salesease, that is now a "hot prospect" And hot it was. That appointment resulted in seven permanent life insurance policies, generating over $10K in commission! This doesn't happen every day, but it does happen. When a prospect is ready to purchase but is unsure who to call, a status update from you can spur them to action and land them squarely in your lap.

Our goal is to help your business Go Tra*digital* as easily as possible. We're the first to admit it. Figuring out how to harness the incredible power social media offers isn't always easy. We have made our share of mistakes. We have accidentally found social media strategies that work. We have done our due diligence and have slogged through the research. Through it all, we have honed our social media skills.

At one point, many years ago, many thought that social media would never supplant traditional forms of marketing. They were wrong. Social media allows us to do everything the traditional forms of marketing once did—letting people know who we are, finding new prospects, but because it personalizes the whole transaction on line, it gives us something the traditional never could: more access and wider spheres of influence.

Please allow us to show you what we have learned so you don't have to make the same mistakes we did. For our goal is to have you enjoying the fruits of social media far quicker than we did. Here are six tips to get you on your way!

1. BLEND TRADITIONAL AND DIGITAL

More and more businesses are using social media to attract new clients, to keep existing clients and build relationships with clients at a deeper level. But many have shied away from using social media because they're scared of it or they don't understand it, or they've used it and it "didn't work."

We coined the word tra*digital* because we believe successful business owners use both the traditional and the digital to be successful. Have you ever heard the expression, "don't throw the baby out with the bathwater"? That's exactly our motto with Going Tra*digital*. You don't have to stop using traditional marketing and servicing methods. You can still do business in ways that you're comfortable and that many of your clients prefer too, which is face-to-face in the office or over the kitchen table.

But you can also integrate all the Internet has to offer, both in your marketing and in your daily interactions with your current clients and prospects because there is now a large portion of consumers (and growing daily) who are more comfortable connecting online.

2. COMPLETE ALL PROFILES

No matter which social media platform you use, thoroughly completing your personal or business profile information is critical. A completed profile will help others find you. We can't stress enough how important it is that you don't leave your profiles unfinished. That would be the equivalent of mailing out an incomplete resume or telling potential customers about only part of your expertise.

Furthermore, a partially completed profile could send the message that you aren't thorough or don't follow through on tasks.

Having access to only partial information that was frequently outdated was the demise of the phone book. Consumers today expect more. When a person who prefers to conduct research online can't find you, or finds incorrect or incomplete information, they won't take the time to search for your phone number and call for more information. They will move on to the next business that does have their information online.

Nadeem is a perfect example of this type of client. There is a bikram yoga studio in his area that he has gone to several times, but always on the weekend. One weekday recently he had time to take a class and went to their Facebook page to find out the weekday schedule. However, they didn't have a Facebook page. Strike one. So he did a Google search for the business and went to their web site, but it was no longer active. Strike two.

We're all accustomed to hearing "Three strikes, you're out" but in this case, Nadeem only allowed this business two strikes. He was (and remains) unwilling to look up their phone number, call, leave a voicemail and wait for a return call to find out their class schedule. Instead he is now attending yoga at a studio with an online presence that even has an iPhone app showing their daily class schedule.

This example isn't the exception. It's the rule with those who prefer to do research online. Be sure those folks can find and interact with your business online!

3. GROW YOUR ONLINE NETWORK

Once you have created your profile(s), connecting with people is the next step. Your social media success depends on developing an engaged audience for your posts and getting people interested in you as you become genuinely interested in them. That's when the good connections (the ones that can lead to new business) start to happen.

Just like building any network, online or off, you connect first with people you know, and all the platforms have made it very easy to do just that.

Your existing contacts are like a gold mine. These are your key contacts, friends, clients, family members and current and former co-workers. They know you well and will not hesitate to add you and may even feel complimented that you invited them to join your networks.

This can be done quickly and easily. Simply download a list of contacts into a workable Excel spreadsheet and then upload the contacts to the respective platform.

We have found that once you're connected to friends and clients on social media, they will start introducing you to old friends and contacts that you may have lost touch with. You will come across old college buddies, high school friends or co-workers from previous jobs and have the opportunity to connect with them.

If you are working in an office with staff, have your staff repeat this exact same process. This is tapping into the networks of your immediate network. This can generate great activity on an ongoing basis as staff and close contacts start advocating your business and start getting involved on your business page.

However you do it, by connecting with people you already know, you are building your prospecting and referral database for the future.

4. FIND YOUR ONLINE BRAND AND VOICE

Consumers are using social media to personally connect with friends and family, so know that when consumers connect with your agency as a small business, they expect a personal touch from you as well. For best results, the business owner should take responsibility for developing the digital brand and voice, then train and monitor the staff or social media management company on proper usage of that voice and brand.

We see a lot of businesses pass on the responsibility of social media management to low- level staff members. This is not a good idea, and the results show it. The posts are usually unemotional, unengaging, and inconsistent. If you must assign some social media responsibility to a staff member, make it the marketing manager who already understands the company brand you want to project.

If you decide to hire a company to manage your digital brand, be sure that you purchase the largest package of options they have available.

They will need to do more than just post content daily; they'll have to create and manage your business brand and voice, engage with fans, keep all profiles current and updated, connect with referral sources and lots more. It's probably cost-prohibitive for most businesses to hire a company that will create a truly personal touch, and in the end it's not something we recommend. Social media is about connecting personally, but if you hire a company to do it, they're not always going to have the passion or the purpose that you do, and it will be evident to your fans.

5. USE SOCIAL MEDIA TO INCREASE CUSTOMER SERVICE

Using social media marketing for business consists of creating new business or servicing and retaining existing business. Moreover, take out the "social media" part and that's exactly what business owners have been doing since marketing was invented.

We've talked about creating new business prospects through social media. Now how do we use social media to service and retain existing business?

As service levels in other industries rise as a result of social media, we need to look into ways of increasing our service levels. There are a ton of ways customer service can be handled thru traditional methods. More and more companies are using social media to identify customer service issues and resolving them on social media platforms. Connecting with clients through social media puts your business in a position to just do that.

For instance, one of Nadeem's auto insurance clients was in Germany and was in process of renting a vehicle. He had a quick question about whether he should purchase the insurance coverage being offered by the rental car company. Knowing how active Nadeem is on Facebook and not having a way to easily call from Germany to Houston, the client sent a Facebook message to Nadeem. He received it instantly in Houston at 10:30PM. Nadeem was able to answer the question without hesitation and the client got an instant reply while at the rental car counter. This was such a delightful experience for client that when he returned to Houston he sent a thank you email praising the quick service he received.

Many customer service questions, no matter how small, are time sensitive to clients. They expect an answer or response in minutes or hours, not days. We can also hear what some of you are saying. "I can't be constantly connected to my PC or smartphone. I can't be constantly checking all of my social media networks for questions." The good news is this is not necessary. Rest assured you can remain connected and still have a life!

Most social media platforms have the options to set alerts and notifications. To be sure questions are answered in a timely manner, just simply make sure those alerts are set up to let you know when someone has sent you a message or mentioned your name in a comment. By doing this, you can make sure you don't miss an interaction with a client or prospect who is reaching out to you without having to constantly monitor your networks.

6. "BEGIN WITH THE END IN MIND"

Stephen Covey's famous quote is a good one to consider when starting to develop (or retool) a social media presence. Whatever your business social media goals, "the end" should always include a vision of connecting with others in a sincere way. Whether you are currently utilizing zero, two, or ten types of social media, it is really important to bring a human connection to posts, tweets, and messages.

It is a common misconception that online friends are not real relationships. It is very easy to quickly identify those who feel this way. When viewing their Facebook page, it is a long series of posts broadcasting about what they sell, with no user engagement. None of their fans or friends "share" their status updates. No one comments on the posts. In short, no one cares what they say because the business hasn't done anything to show that they recognize their fans as real human beings on the other side of the screen.

Keeping this in mind, your primary goal for everything you do using social media should be to build a genuine friendship with our connections. It is only when this occurs that the true value of social media will begin to show itself. If you've been unsure of what to post or have been posting content that isn't getting the results you desire, don't worry. It's never too late to change! Changing this one little thing will dramatically ramp up the amount of interest your pages receive, and that's the secret to successfully using social media.

About Angela

Angela Johnson obtained a BA in Literature in 1996 and after working in mid-level management with a major phone company, started her career as a Farmers Insurance Agent. Angela started a scratch agency in 2005 and currently has 3800 PIF. She has achieved Topper Club and Championship multiple times and is a member of President's Council. Angela has been honored to address her fellow Agents at many events including Town Hall, Topper Club, State Conferences and many social media seminars around the country. Although she began using Social Media solely to keep tabs on her daughter, she quickly embraced it as a way to build relationships with long lost friends and then as a way to make new ones.

Angela and Nadeem are co-authors of *Going Tradigital: Social Media Made Easy for Insurance Agents* and are in the process of expanding the book into a series for a variety of industries. By focusing on five key areas, they teach business owners how to use social media to Increase Prospecting and Sales, Increase Customer Service, Improve Retention and Cross-Sales, Gain Referrals and Humanize Your Brand.

To learn more about Angela Johnson, Nadeem Damani or how you can Go Tra*digital*, visit: www.goingtradigital.com or www.facebook.com/GoingTradigital.
www.GoingTradigital.com

About Nadeem

Nadeem Damani graduated from UT in 1993 with a BBA in Marketing. He has been an Insurance Agent with Farmers Insurance since 2002. His agency is located in Stafford, Texas. His accomplishments and awards include seven-time Championship designation, eleven-time Topper Club attendee and one time Million Dollar Round Table qualification. In 2005, Nadeem Damani was number one in the company out of 16,000 Agents in writing term life policies. Damani has been actively using Social Media for the last four years to build his insurance business. He speaks at various company events regarding his Social Media strategy. He has over 40,000 connections in various Social Media networks including Twitter, Facebook and G+.

Angela and Nadeem are co-authors of *Going Tradigital: Social Media Made Easy for Insurance Agents* and are in the process of expanding the book into a series for a variety of industries. By focusing on five key areas, they teach business owners how to use social media to Increase Prospecting and Sales, Increase Customer Service, Improve Retention and Cross-Sales, Gain Referrals and Humanize Your Brand.

To learn more about Angela Johnson, Nadeem Damani or how you can Go Tra*digital*, visit: www.goingtradigital.com or www.facebook.com/GoingTradigital.

CHAPTER 18

FOR QUALITY OF LIFE

BY BRYAN KISER

In 1991, when I was graduating High School, I signed my classmates yearbooks as such: "In life find that perfect wave and surf the f*-- out of it, living everyday like it's your last, and loving every minute like it's your first." As you might have guessed, I grew up in a coastal town and I enjoyed the beach, the water, and of course, good surfing waves.

I am long out of High School now and look back on those days fondly. I am now a Professional Gymnastics Coach, Personal Trainer, and Business Developer having my own Gymnastics facility in Sugar Land, TX, USA. Health and fitness has been and is a major part of my life because of that I am often asked the question from friends, family, students, and clients: "In such a busy world, with the economy so shifty, how do I balance MY life so that I can find, and more importantly STICK TO, a fitness plan without disrupting my career and family life?" The answer I give is the same, but has different limits and parameters for everyone, let me explain.

In finding a balance to life, and for our topic, one's personal health, fitness, and general well being "is all in the approach!" You must first ask yourself a series of questions and may even have you concurring with family and friends to derive your answers. These are the same questions that you would ask if you were starting a new project at work, a new business, or even a new relationship. First, decide where it is you are going or would like to go, "What is the end result that I desire?" The next questions relate closely to one another but the answers won't be correct if you haven't "laid in stone" the answer to the first. What is the amount of time and money I am willing to spend? How does this new goal affect MY life, MY family life, and MY professional career? What parameters or limits should I set from the start so that I don't go overboard or let vanity run amuck? Is this something I could or am willing to share with my friends and/or family or this time I need to have to myself? Like I said, the answers are the same for everyone, but maybe with different limits or parameters. The questions are the same as you would ask in business or relationships however, the one MAJOR thing that most of the time gets missed, skipped, and/or omitted in the answer to ALL of these questions is the "ME" part.

"What is the end result that I desire?" In business, it maybe to make a certain amount of profit or move up the ladder to a specific level of recognition or position. In family life, it maybe to take the family on a special vacation, move to a bigger better home, or save a specified amount of money to retire at a desire age, but when looking at health and fitness, YOU have to decide what YOU want YOUR end result to be... the "REAL" answer is going to surprise you. Is the desired end result to look like Mr. Olympia? To be capable of lifting a specific amount of weight by a specified time? To run a mile? A marathon? A triathlon? or maybe to just make it thru the CrossFit class down at the local CrossFit studio. What is your vision for YOU? This is where that "all about ME" part I spoke of earlier comes into play and when answering this question you must be VERY selfish, this is YOUR health you are planning out! Another thing that has to be part of this answer and part of the "ME" within it, is that this plan actually should have NO END RESULT. What? Why would I say that? The question was, what end result was desired and now I am very clearly stating you shouldn't have an end result? Hmmmm.

As in life, business, and relationships, this starter question will be used at the end and the beginning of each and every "perfect wave" you surf, meaning that each "goal" you accomplish you will reflect on, take from, adding the experiences and lessons learned, and then start over asking the same question as YOU move to the next "wave" or chapter in YOUR life... The "end result" being accomplished or pronounced is an "EPIC FAIL" only when you die.

The next four questions that I outlined all relate to the answer of the first and CANNOT be answered until the first question is successfully defined. To get whatever the desired result may be out of the first question, you will have to spend a specified amount of money, which in turn will affect your budget, which will alter your life, the life of your family, and even your professional career. Setting the parameters and limits on the desired result will also dictate who you are willing to share this with or if this is needed time spent doing your own thing. WOW! Bryan, you have just taken such a simple thing, "starting an exercise program" and made it so complex and complicated, does it really needed to be so?

The simple answer is YES! Why do you think so many people each and every year set as a "New Years Resolution" to join a gym or get in shape, and by mid-February have already QUIT? This is a LIFE decision, not really a WORKOUT decision. Here in the next few paragraphs the reasons for having "Integrity to Yourself" is probably the most important set of words for you to use. Set for YOURSELF those limits and parameters that will allow you to accomplish the TRUE desired results. It will BALANCE your life and give you peace knowing that YOU have set YOURSELF in a position to accomplish your health and fitness goals in sync with your family, friends, and career. The peace comes from knowing that YOU accomplished a rewarding balance in your life that most people long for, but only a few will take the time to do the due diligence to produce that balanced outcome.

Most people think "Integrity" (the adherence to moral and ethical principles; soundness of moral character, HONESTY – as defined by Dictionary.com) applies only toward beings outside YOU. So in essence, you are honorable and honest to the outside WORLD all the while lying and cheating YOURSELF. It is actually how most of us were raised, to self-sacrifice, take the hard road, and help your fellow man...don't get me wrong, these are ALL good principles and ALL should apply in one's life, HOWEVER, YOU must also apply "Integrity to YOURSELF" in YOUR life. YOU must learn to make decisions that are HONEST and that do not cheat YOU; treating your health and fitness goals as you would every other important part of your life is not only essential – IT IS IMPERATIVE! Keep this quote in mind, "The best investment you will ever make is the investment in YOU!" Without your health and well-being you really have nothing...

Balance, try Googling that word, oh the definitions you can find...no wonder it is so hard to achieve! Dictionary.com has it is as: "a state of equilibrium or equipoise; equal distribution of weight or amount." The answer to the desired end result of your health and fitness program is not actually bringing it to a conclusion, but finding BALANCE! As I discussed earlier, YOU are not looking for an "end result" that is final and you are done, YOU and many like YOU are looking to find a program or regimen that YOU can enjoy and STICK TO that does not overtake YOUR life but rather can be done long term in BALANCE and HARMONY with YOUR life. Without approaching it like you would any other part of your life, in a planned out, systematic, realistic manner; this cannot be done! It is easy to rob Peter to pay Paul, but in the end one of them winds up taking a hit... Just like it is easy to focus on just ONE AREA of YOUR life, but in the end the other aspects, ALL OF THEM, TAKE THE HIT. I would have to call that, "EPIC FAILURE!" Why? ...you may ask, simple, because what you desired to achieve YOU allowed to ROB from other areas of YOUR life bringing about shortfalls, pitfalls, and lack of effort all because YOU did not take the time to be HONEST and TRUE to YOURSELF and that lack of "Integrity to YOURSELF" breeds a lack of Integrity to the whole.

Don't get me wrong, the path you may have chosen without taking the time to answer the above questions may have made you the fittest or richest person on the planet, but you neglected and/or lost your family, you gave up your friends, you blew your career and NOW your level of "Integrity" is not only questioned by all of those you let down, but even by your inner self that by not taking the time for due diligence on a plan, has brought you to ruin. This can happen in ANY and EVERY area of your life! YOU may set parameters for success in business that breed the same lack of "Integrity to YOURSELF" producing a YOU that is overweight, on 20 or more toxic prescription medications, giving you NO REAL quality of life and thought to the world around you. YOU display the utmost "Integrity" however, because you have lacked showing the same to YOURSELF and you get the same end result, EPIC FAIL!

Who knew that the words I wrote in my classmates High School yearbooks would be emblazoned in my mind all these years, and if you ask people that know me well, I live each and every word of that to the FULLEST! I have however, translated my "philosophical lines" and use them daily as a guide to stay within the parameters of balance that gives ME "Integrity to MYSELF" and allows ME to show and bring "Integrity" to my ENTIRE life. What the 18-year-old kid missed in writing those lines is that in YOUR life, YOU are not riding "one single wave," but you are riding several waves SIMULTANEOUSLY, it is each of our jobs to keep them in HARMONY and BALANCE so that we TRULY can "live everyday as if it were our last and love every minute like it was our first"; to me personally, the "surfing the f*-- out of it" will ALWAYS apply, I just believe a person should always do each and everything to it's fullest and enjoy it!

As the Country and Western Superstar George Strait sings in his award-winning song, *Here for a Good Time*, "When I'm gone put it in stone I LEFT NOTHING BEHIND, I'm not here for a long time; I'm here for a good time!" So to live up to "GO BIG OR GO HOME," the focus can NEVER be on "one wave" or "one area of life," it MUST be on the whole knowing that for each one of the "waves" or "areas of life" being ridden, they all connect as a part of us to create what we all call LIFE and now knowing, and understanding, even better that if YOU allow one to falter, YOU lose that "Perfect" wave, that BALANCE OF INTEGRITY TO LIFE AND SELF.

Oh I almost forgot, the workout programs!!! Ha-ha! I think you have figured it out by now, the "program" or "activity" you choose to participate in doesn't really matter. There are hundreds if not thousands of programs, regimens, routines, etc. The "program" or "activity" really is not a problem or an issue. I will preface the previous statement that due diligence must be done here as well, but that is mostly to find and figure out what you like and dislike. In finding what you like, is it a "lifetime activity or program"... this is important and this will have to be reviewed as you age to determine factors of benefit. However, do what you can as long as you can, do what you love as long as you love it! Like I just suggested, be sure to find ones that you like and enjoy doing. I suggest picking more than one and changing the activity, program, routine, or regimen every 3 to 6 months.

Now, in taking a better look at this, you can clearly see it is not an exercise activity that matters, and it is my desire that you take from this chapter the knowledge of how to integrate a workout program, stay fit and healthy, and give yourself TRUE QUALITY OF LIFE AS LONG

AS YOU LIVE. The key to that process is NOT THE ACTIVITY, the key is BALANCE and "Integrity to Yourself" don't rob Peter to pay Paul! Do yourself the honor of taking the time to do the due diligence of your LIFE and put in place the proper parameters and limits that fit YOU. After that is done, sky's the limit! Not just in achieving your fitness and health goals, but in achieving your life goals. The peace of mind and quality of life that you create will be noted and envied by those around you...tell them to read my chapter in this book I can help them achieve it too!

About Bryan

Bryan K. Kiser, BS, CSCS, CPT is a Professional Gymnastics Coach, Personal Trainer, and Business Developer.

Bryan has been a Professional Men's Gymnastics Coach since age 15, where he started out as an Assistant to the Head Coach at the Corpus Christi Athletic Club. At age 18, he moved to Stafford, Texas where he graduated High School and coached for Bill Austin's Gymnastics. After some successes at Bill Austin's, Bryan moved to Houston Gymnastics Club at the JCC of Houston, where he worked under now long time friend and mentor, Tim Erwin. With the guidance and influence of Tim, Bryan achieved many of his goals and assisted Tim in growing the Houston National Invitational, which is now one of the largest Men's, Women's, and Tumbling/Trampoline Competitions in the country. To date, Bryan still teams up with Tim to assist in the fundraising, equipment layout/setup, and actual running to this prestigious event.

Bryan just finished a "business turnaround" for Sugar Land Gymnastics, where he took a run-down gymnastics facility with 120 total students and made it the "Premier" Gymnastics Training Facility in the area boasting just shy of 1500 students! In between all of this, Bryan has trained and worked with, since he is also a personal trainer, competitive bodybuilder, and strength and conditioning specialist, some of the top athletes in various sports. People of note would be: Light Weight World Champ Juan "Baby Bull" Diaz, who Bryan worked with during his Golden Gloves career, and Jennifer Becerra, IFBB Ms Fitness Pro.

Bryan has had numerous State, Regional, and National Champions now on the Men's and Women's side of Gymnastics. Bryan and his partners, now known as "TEAM OLYMPUS," are currently in the final part of the process to open up OLYMPUS ELITE GYMNASTICS in Sugar Land, Texas.

CHAPTER 19

THE 12 PRINCIPLES OF HIGHLY SUCCESSFUL REAL ESTATE AGENTS

BY CARIN NGUYEN

"People Don't Care How Much You Know Until They Know How Much You Care." ~ John Maxwell

When I got my real estate license a decade ago, I expected to get some direction on how to be a successful real estate agent. It took me a few months to realize that was not going to happen, so I hired a coach. It was the most strategic decision I made. It provided me with structure and gave me a preview of success before the market tanked in 2006. The switched flipped and I found myself surrounded by underwater homeowners and what seemed like an overnight change in my business. I quickly learned about BPOs (Broker Price Opinions) and REO/ foreclosure sales. I combined that knowledge and the skills learned from coaching and built an REO empire. I started with only a part-time assistant and rapidly grew to a team of 18 selling 896 homes in my best year. Along the way, a culmination of events happened that would lead me to open my own real estate brokerage. As the market worsened, more and more agents fled from the business. I was perplexed by the reduction of services provided to agents from both existing and start up brokerages, so I decided to go the opposite direction and do all I could to offer as much I could to the agents. The most valuable tool would be coaching and we would not be a "virtual" office. I wanted to bring accountability into our industry and specifically into our brokerage. Accountability became the cornerstone of our business model. I thrive with change, and believe me, I know I am in the minority. Versatility is a <u>must</u> as the market is constantly in a state of change. I expect that my business will grow with every shift. Each time we have experienced a severe swing or shift in the market, I have been forced to react and think outside the box. The more I embrace the changes, the faster I grow and the more successful I become. I am on a mission to teach others to embrace change along with the other Principles of Success listed below. Let's dive in so you can experience success too!

PRINCIPLE 1: THE LEARNING PROCESS IS NEVER ENDING

The more you know, the more you can control. If you have the desire to succeed at a very high level, you must be consumed by learning and mastering your craft. You too must remain relevant. You must keep up. The real estate industry is ever changing. No one will ever know all there is to know because it changes fast. You have to learn to move with it! For me, this is one of the most appealing aspects of the business.

While most of the obvious sources provide traditional industry information and education, they generally lack creativity and relevance. I've found the most valuable are real estate agents who are already succeeding at a high level (within as well as outside your market), and seminars outside of the real estate industry. Many of the most effective ideas I have ever implemented in my business are a direct result of masterminding with other top agents. Sadly, I did not discover that goldmine earlier in my career. Looking back, I was probably too proud and too intimidated to pick up the phone and ask a competitor. Now, I get calls from agents across the country as well as in my market asking me for help. Top producing agents are usually pretty giving of their knowledge, so if you have not already, swallow your pride and ask for help from someone that is doing more business than you.

The second goldmine is engaging outside the industry. If you have been to even a handful of real estate seminars or workshops, you know that most are repetitive. Other industries face similar challenges when it comes to marketing, leadership or general business operations. It is exciting to venture onto their turf to hear and learn about how other industries are addressing some of our same issues I encounter. Do whatever it takes to gain as much knowledge as you can as fast as you can, and never stop the thirst for knowledge.

PRINCIPLE 2: GAIN EXPERIENCE

Many "How to Find the Best Agent" articles mention the importance of experience. I agree that experience is by far the #1 trait to look for, but be careful not to confuse experience with tenure. The value of an agent comes from how many transactions they have completed and how well they know the market, contract, addendums and overall process. As with any trade or skill, you begin to master it after thousands of hours of practice. You need repetition, not just time.

The dilemma is how to gain the experience if you have not closed a large volume of business yet. It's a 'Catch 22.' You need the experience to gain the business and you need business to gain experience. The way to gain experience quickly is to shadow a top-producing agent or join an established real estate team. By shadowing an agent or joining a team, you will be exposed to the entire process many times over. They will already have a steady stream of business that you can begin working with immediately. With this immediate volume of business, you will gain experience at an exponentially faster rate than the average agent. Eventually, you will reach a point that you can break away from shadowing or working on the team and establish your own self-sustaining business.

PRINCIPLE 3: BE A PROFESSIONAL AND ALWAYS KEEP YOUR COOL

This may sound like an obvious one, but I can tell you from experience that emotions run high more often than not. Nothing good ever comes from drama or high emotions and this behavior is not limited to one particular group. It will come from your clients, lenders, escrow officers, attorneys, cross sale agents and inspectors. If you are not an even-tempered person by nature, you must quickly learn the skills of how to keep your cool and remain professional. Your response will dictate the outcome. Your calm and professional approach will be the Super Glue that keeps the deal together. Everyone within the transaction has the same end goal...to close the deal. Many times, we are viewed more as "opposing teams" since we may each represent a different side, but we need to remember "the win" is the same for both sides. Keep your cool while you keep your focus.

Here are some deal-saving tips to try when a problem or challenge arises:

a) Do not call your client and tell them about the problem. Now, I am not saying to withhold important information from them. What I am saying is that you want to problem solve on your own first so that you can come to them with a solution. Avoid the emotional roller coaster. They are already stressed enough as it is. I have lost several deals because I was too quick to involve my client. I inevitably found a solution on these deals, but because they were mad or frustrated with one of the other parties, they cancelled.

b) Exhaust all of the options. Brainstorm for a resolution and if you are unable to come up with one, ask your broker and peers for suggestions. Sometimes an unrelated party provides immediate clarity.

c) If it is a lending challenge, call other lenders to see what options might be possible.

Most objections and issues that occur can be resolved, but we throw in the towel too soon or we create more drama. I am often told by my clients that my job looks easy. This used to upset me, because I know the job is far from easy. I took on the drama they never saw, so everything appeared smooth and easy to them. I then realized they were paying me a huge compliment. I made it look easy and that wasn't a bad thing.

That was my job! Now I strive to hear them say I make this look easy! It means that I have done my job well.

PRINCIPLE 4: UNDERSTAND AND KNOW THE NUMBERS INTIMATELY

All top producers look at the statistical data of their local market daily and keep abreast of stats in their state and the country. Why is it so important to know market stats? Besides the obvious reason to monitor supply in order to gauge demand, you are looking for trends that will affect your clients as well as your business. You must also know the numbers within your own business. You need to track what works and what does not. Constantly look for changes in the trends so you can immediately implement changes in your business. Being proactive versus reactive will have an immediate, positive impact on your success.

PRINCIPLE 5: LISTEN MORE THAN YOU SPEAK

Listen intently with the intention to understand, not respond, debate or defend. It is imperative to fully understand the end goal of the homebuyer or seller. If we are not intentional in listening, we will miss their true wants and needs. By nature, when we listen to someone speak, we tend to only hear select words because we are busy formulating our response. As a result we miss the entire message of what was said. This "selective listening" can cause us to make false assumptions. Get out of assumption and into understanding! Always ask questions. This is the ultimate sign you care and are focused on the end result for your client. There is no such thing as asking too many questions. Once the deal is over, the questions should not stop. Don't forget to ask for feedback. One of the most powerful feedback questions is, "On a scale of 1-10, please rate ... (the quality of service, etc.)." On anything less than a 10, ask what it would take to make it a 10.

PRINCIPLE 6: FANATICAL FOLLOW-UP AND OUTSTANDING CUSTOMER SERVICE

By far, the #1 complaint about Real Estate Agents is lack of communication and follow up on their part. The process of buying or selling a home is usually not a familiar one for the buyer or seller, and because of the amount of money at stake, they want and deserve constant contact and information. Invest in a powerful CRM (Customer Relationship Management) system to keep organized. For consistency, automate any parts of the process that you can. But also be sure to pick up the phone frequently. Do not assume the clients know you are "working." Communicate the activities you are doing on their behalf and once they are under contract, increase your contact with frequent updates. You can never update them too often. Even when there is nothing to report, report that. By having a process and system in place to constantly communicate with the client, you give them incredible peace of mind. In exchange for the peace of mind you give, you have now earned the trust and confidence of your client.

PRINCIPLE 7: VERSATILITY

My mantra since I started in real estate has been, "get comfortable with being uncomfortable". We are faced with changes in the market, the economy, our brokerages, with technology, our clients, contract terms, etc. Change is inevitable and you decide how you will respond to it. The harsh reality is the more you resist change, the faster you will fail. That's right, fail! I wonder where the agents that refused to use the Internet are now. They are out of business since all listings are posted to the MLS online. What about the agents who buried their heads in the sand when the market shifted in '06? Do you think they survived the last seven years? Probably not. Are you noticing a pattern? If you can embrace change and become very versatile, you will be far more likely to succeed. Technology is the area that seems to change most often. Just as you learn one new system, the next best thing comes along. Consumers have spoken and they want tech-savvy agents. Not to mention, using technology makes your job easier. You should be able to obtain electronic signatures, scan, resize and email documents. You also need to have a smart phone and know how to send and receive email and text messages on it.

PRINCIPLE 8: HAVE A BUSINESS PLAN AND SET GOALS

Who opens a business without a business plan and goals? Real estate agents, that's who! When you obtain a real estate license and "open" for business, no one asks you for your business plan. The "goal" is usually to pay this month's bills. The Successful Real Estate Agent, however operates like a business owner with a written plan and written goals and they refer to them often. Your business plan should include the specific tasks you need to accomplish to hit your goals. Your goals should be written, very clear and specific, and broken into long-term and short-term goals. Determine the annual goal and then work backwards. If you want $X in profit, how many transactions will you need to close this year, each quarter, each month? How many contracts will you have to write, appointments will you need to go on, and how many calls will you have to make, etc.?

Something very powerful happens when you write down your goals. A study of Harvard graduates found that after two years, the 3% who had written goals achieved more financially than the other 97% combined.

Visuals also assist us in reaching our goals. They keep us excited and motivated. Print out a photo of the new car you want, or the vacation spot you want to visit once you hit your goal. Make several copies and plaster them on your computer, refrigerator, bathroom mirror, television, etc. You want the constant reminders so you can stay motivated. It will inspire you to do what you do not like to do especially on the days you do not want to do it!

PRINCIPLE 9: NEGOTIATION SKILLS

An agent who is highly skilled in negotiation can 'net' their clients thousands more than the average agent. Conversely, it can cost them thousands if the agent is not experienced. A good negotiator is always poised and confident and has the ability to read people. In negotiation, you can push too hard and lose the deal altogether. If you can accurately assess your counterpart, you can come out ahead. The agent that yields the most money for their client will always be better at asking questions. You would be surprised what agents will say. Sometimes they answer without any hesitation. Others will present more of a challenge, and you will need to re-formulate the same questions in several different ways before you can get the answers you are seeking. The bottom line is that you never want to be the one to leave any money on the table. Also, remember that you negotiate for other items and terms that are important such as closing date, possession date, contingencies and earnest money.

PRINCIPLE 10: POWERFUL MARKETING STRATEGY

According to NARs 2012 Member Profile, more than half of real estate agents gross less than $35,000/yr. Why is this an important statistic? Marketing is expensive so if an agent is not closing a high volume of business, they simply cannot afford to market their listings. Do not fall into this category. Put aside 10% from every closing and apply it to your marketing strategy. As you close more deals, you will have more marketing dollars to invest in your growing business.

PRINCIPLE 11: HIGH ETHICAL STANDARDS

You should always adhere to high ethical standards and morals. I could write an entire book on the subject, but if you follow three simple commandments, you will always maintain high ethical standards:

1. You must always put your client's needs over your own.
2. You shouldn't do business with those that do not have equally high ethical standards.
3. Make the commitment to always be honest, no matter what. Sometimes this will be difficult because you do not want the client to be upset with you, and you will have to tell them things they do not want to hear, but they will respect you for being honest.

PRINCIPLE 12: POWER IN NUMBERS

Running a highly successful business is almost never a one-person operation. We all start out that way, but as we apply the previous principles listed, the success and growth will occur. As it does, take note of your weaknesses and hire to compensate for those first. There are other people that can perform those tasks better than you. Once you can fill in your weak spots with competent people, you will find that you will have more time to grow your business and a growing need to hire more people.

About Carin

Carin Nguyen takes the business of real estate very seriously and she has the track record to prove it. She has been ranked the #1 REALTOR® in AZ multiple times and The Carin Nguyen team has been ranked as high as #2 in the US, and featured in *The Wall Street Journal*.

Carin has been in the real estate industry for over 10 years full time, having honed her expertise during years in the finance and mortgage industries. She has sold over $200 million in real estate and completed over 2200 transactions. She has owned a real estate brokerage, coached and mentored top-producing agents and knows what it takes to succeed in the real estate business. A rich resume built with a tireless commitment to her clients and agents, undeniable proven past success and an uncompromised vision for the future, create the recipe for continued success.

If you are interested in learning more about hiring Carin and her team to handle your next real estate sale, please visit: www.SoldByCarin.com or: www.LuxSold.com

For coaching or public speaking information on Carin, please visit:
www.FireItUpNow.com

CHAPTER 20

CHARACTERISTICS OF HIGHLY SUCCESSFUL PEOPLE

BY DENNIS MCGOUGH

How is it that some people rise to high levels of success while others do not? The reality is there are many characteristics that successful people tend to have in common. In this chapter we will touch on three of them: a desire for financial security, self-awareness and a desire to be coached.

A DESIRE TO BECOME FINANCIALLY SECURE

One of the biggest questions that I get asked when discussing the topic of success is, "How is it that some individuals are more successful than others?" In my early twenties I asked myself the same thing. See, I didn't come from financial security, nor did I believe I would ever have it. I thought that if I just worked hard I could make enough money to get by. Where I came from, success was solely defined by your ability to put God, family and others first with no regard given to creating financial security. To this day, I still believe financial security alone will never make you happy. Lucky for me, I was blessed to have a few great mentors and coaches in my life who taught me that if you follow your passions, happiness as well as financial security will follow. The key to success is to discover your passions and follow them wherever they may take you, without losing focus on a work-life balance that fits you and your family.

Let's not confuse financial security with being rich. The concept of being rich is a subjective concept in itself. What one person deems rich or wealthy, others may not. We might define "how rich" someone is by the cars they drive, the house they live in, the vacations they take, or how big their toys are. On the other hand, we might define how "financially secure" someone is by their ability to not worry about current income to maintain their lifestyle for many years to come. Let's say you live in a moderate home, drive used cars, take one vacation a year, and have enough money in the bank to maintain this lifestyle for the next twenty years. You may not be considered rich, yet you are financially secure. On the other hand you may have a $10 million home, drive luxury cars and travel the world, but without the money to maintain this lifestyle for the next twenty years I would hesitate to call you financially secure.

Highly successful people have a strong desire to be financially secure. They aspire to have enough money in the bank or in financial investments to maintain their lifestyle for the next twenty years. This is very difficult to do when working at a job. It is not impossible, but most people are not willing to or do not have the ability to put away 20 – 30% of their income each month. Maybe it's because people will live at or above their financial means. Studies have shown that in today's economy, most people actually live at about 110% of their financial means. This practice in itself locks people into their current jobs and positions, which they may not be passionate about.

A very successful business coach once told me the word "JOB" was an acronym that meant, "just over broke." Somehow this always seems to hold true. This is why you'll find highly successful people looking for opportunities outside of the employment arena to help create financial security for their future.

There are a lot of myths out there about how to create wealth or how to become financially secure. In fact, the widest spread myths in today's economy would have you believe that most wealthy people inherited their wealth or that they made millions in the stock market. This could not be further from the truth. The reality is that the majority of wealth in todays economy is first generation wealth and it was not generated in the stock market. In fact, statistics show that 80% of the "financial market experts" lose their own money in the markets, so if the "experts" in the financial markets cannot make money in the long run, the chance of you or me doing it is very slim, and not a chance I want to take.

Here are a few facts to consider. We live in the wealthiest country on earth with 50% of our wealth being created in the last 25 years. There were 5,000 millionaires in the early 1900's and there are now over 9.8 million millionaires in America (most of them were self-made millionaires). 80% of the millionaires in today's economy made their wealth by starting a business. This makes sense when you consider the average income in the United States is $42,000 a year. While it is possible to put away 20 – 30% of your income each month and become financially secure in the long run, the fastest way to financial security is not in the stock markets. Highly successful people have found a way to create value or add value by starting their own business.

There are over 35 million businesses in the United States, which means 1 out of every 9 people in the United States own a business. Starting a business in the US is easier than in any other place in the world. More people will become financially secure in the next few years than ever before. My belief is that you should become one of them. This is a choice that I made many years ago for myself.

I came from a very humble background. Money for college was just not available. I knew early on that if I wanted to go to college, I would need to get a good job. My parents worked very hard to provide for three boys, but at the end of the day there just wasn't much left over. I took a job at a local department store when I was 16. This was a locally-owned department store where I soon realized I would have no advancement opportunities. At 17, I had the opportunity to go to work for Sam's Club, which I knew was run by the Wal-Mart Corporation. This was a concept store and the first of its kind. It could fail, but if there were a chance it would be as successful as Wal-Mart I just knew I had to give it a shot. I had to start out pushing carts in 104 degree heat to get on board, but shortly after I turned 18 I was able to move inside and start working my way up. I did what I needed to do; I worked hard during the day, went to school in the evenings and worked every weekend. I aggressively attached myself to mentors that could coach me to the next level. By age 23 I found myself in management and by age 26 was running a Sam's Club location. We were growing rapidly and learning a lot. Mentoring and training in a very fast paced environment was just a part of the job. After a few years of setting up and opening new locations, working long hours, every weekend and every holiday, moving and relocating, I had just had enough.

For the next three years I worked diligently to finish college. I worked a full schedule in my management position and full-time hours in college. I can't say that I ever really had a plan, I just knew there had to be a better way. Money was tight. Trying to pay for college and living expenses was overwhelming. My wife was working two jobs and trying to take care of everything at home. Between work, school and the commute I was gone 100 hours a week. Somehow we did it. I graduated with an honors degree in finance, insurance, real estate, law and accounting. But with no plan, I stayed in my current job for several more years.

My wife and I had to make some hard decisions. Our quality of life was terrible and we knew we needed to make a change. The only way we were going to find the financial security we were looking for was to start a business. So after 17 years in a "job," I made the leap of faith and decided to become self-employed in the insurance industry. It was risky and scary, but I knew that if I worked hard and had good mentors, I could find success. I had to give it a shot.

In the past 12 years of being self-employed I have started several businesses. I have had some great success and am well on my way to the financial security that I set out to find. That's not to say that there weren't struggles along the way.

A POSITIVE ATTITUDE AND SELF-AWARENESS

It was never easy. It has always been hard work. It has always been challenging. Through those challenges, the security of my family as well as the pride of ownership has made it all worth it. You must maintain a positive attitude at all times, through the good times and through the tough times.

So how do successful people maintain such a positive attitude? How do they stay in a constant state of self-awareness and learning? Why does it seem so easy for them to start businesses? What do self-made millionaires think about?

The biggest breakthrough for me was the concept of self-awareness and attitude. I learned that the way you see yourself on the inside will dictate how you act on the outside. You become what you think about most of the time.

Successful people think about results and not excuses. They understand you can have results or you can have excuses, but you can't have both.

They accept that there is a chance of failure or rejection. They internalize the fact that it is this fear of failure and rejection that prevents people from starting their own business and finding financial security for them and their family.

They practice frugality during their early earning years so they can enjoy long-term rewards.

They possess a "long-term way of thinking," meaning that they are willing to make short-term sacrifices for long-term gains. They do so by getting out of debt, and attempting to no longer be dependent on their current income.

Ultimately, they believe in themselves and surround themselves with like-minded people that can mentor and support them. They purposely disconnect themselves from people with a sense of entitlement and negative attitudes. They accept where they are today as a starting point. They accept their past as the past, understanding that their past shortcomings or failures will not dictate their future successes or failures. In fact, they embrace what they learned from their past and use it to help others succeed. I've never met a successful person that was not willing to share their past failures and what they learned from those failures in order to help others succeed.

A DESIRE TO BE COACHED

Highly successful people become experts at sharing their vision, inspiring others to act and take incremental steps towards their goals. I have also discovered that successful people have mentors and coaches that help them learn to do this. I define this characteristic as "being coachable." By that, I mean, highly successful people are in a constant state of learning. They do not rely solely on their own abilities or knowledge. In fact, I discovered in my early twenties that behind every successful businessman, athlete or thought leader you will find a mentor or coach that helped them develop a written vision, clearly defined goals, and the incremental steps they would need to take to achieve these goals. Successful people realize that relying on themselves is a limiting behavior in itself. They allow someone to hold them accountable to their own vision of success and goals.

The underlying, learnable characteristic behind "being coachable" is simply to keep your mind in a constant state of learning. There are many ways of doing this. You might decide to get a personal coach or professional mentor or even become a member of a mastermind group. However you choose to "be coachable" and "held accountable" is up to you. I personally choose to do all of the above.

In addition to attaining personal and business coaches I joined a group of Agency/Business Owners to create a mastermind group called Ambassadors for Change. This is a group that is committed to helping each other "embrace change" and build our businesses together. Not only do we assist each other, but we are committed to mentoring and coaching others with this "vision of change." Below you will find our written, signed and published commitment to each other. While this commitment may not apply directly to your business, it may serve as a template that you can use to create your own mastermind group. The concept of mastermind groups comes from Napoleon Hill, one of the great writers on success, and is one of the most powerful mentoring and learning tools you can apply to any goal you would like to achieve. The concept is simple; find a group of individuals that share a common goal and commit to holding each other accountable and to meet regularly to share ideas, successes and struggles.

As one of a select group of Ambassadors for Change, I am committed to:

Sharing the Vision of "Unthinkable, Unimaginable, Unreasonable Heights through Change"

Sharing the Vision of "No Agency Left Behind", "Team Excellence"

Desiring to see 90% of District 30 Agents make Achievement Clubs

Desiring to see the District and their Agents achieve President's Council

Carrying the torch and sharing this Vision of Change

Adopting at least one agency to inspire, motivate and share this Vision for Change

Publicly sharing this Vision for Change in District/Division/State Meetings

Meeting monthly with the Ambassadors for Change Group

Monthly coaching sessions at the District office

Monthly CSR coaching and the CSR Training Program at the District office

Building larger Agencies defined by number of licensed Sales Agents and CSRs

Balanced Agencies defined by balanced production across product lines

Successful Agencies defined by progress toward my written vision

A Business Owner, not Sales Agent mindset

A Happy and Balanced Lifestyle defined by quality family, health, business, community, personal time

Picking up any agent that stumbles in any of the previously mentioned commitments

One of my mentors told me many years ago, "A person that desires to do more and know more will find success." Having realized that it was the things that *they do* and the things that *they know* that made the difference, I have spent my working career doing just that; trying to *do* more and to *know* more everyday. For me, working with personal and professional coaches as well as masterminding with like-minded individuals has played a huge role in my personal and professional success.

So, decide today to do what successful people do. Take control of what *you do* with your time. Make a decision to get out of debt and stop living beyond your means. Work towards becoming financially secure by starting a business, even if it is a part-time business on the side. Accept where you are today with a positive attitude and set some goals for where you are going to be by a specific time in the future. Create a plan and write it down. Take action every day toward that plan. Get a mentor or coach or join a mastermind group that can help you stay on course with those goals and plans. If you adopt these characteristics of successful people you'll be well on your way.

About Dennis

Houston, TX–February, 2013 – Dennis McGough, business coach and mentor, was recently seen in Forbes with other leading professionals as part of a feature called "America's PremierExperts® Presents: Forecasts & Strategies For the New Year & Beyond." In the Forbes feature, Dennis McGough and other leading experts from various industries were asked for their "top tips on health, wealth and success to help you thrive in the New Year and beyond." Mr. McGough remarked, "Be coachable. Success comes from accountability through coaching. Coaches empower you to develop and define a personal and professional vision of success, usually greater than that which you are capable of developing yourself. However, you cannot personally be accountable to your own vision. If you want to succeed quickly, allow a coach to hold you accountable to your defined vision."

Dennis McGough was also recently seen on ABC, NBC, FOX and CBS affiliates across the country as an expert guest on The Brian Tracy Show.

Before joining Farmers Insurance, Dennis was a Competitive Market Business Development Manager for Sam's Club, where he recruited, managed, trained and developed thousands of employees and managers. Being mentored by Sam Walton and his team for 17 years has given Dennis a strong sense of vision, passion and purpose.

In addition, Dennis worked on a variety of projects including agency training and recruiting. Dennis brings a track record of success to his district operations and looks forward to helping current and future agents reach their highest potential. In 2010, 2011 and 2012 Dennis was honored at both Championship and Toppers Achievement Clubs and is currently ranked in the Top 1% of District Managers/Business Coaches in the Nation. He is looking forward to the growth of an even greater award winning team in the Houston market.

Learn more about Dennis McGough at http://www.farmersdistrict30.com/
or contact him at 281-408-2500

CHAPTER 21

PICTURE THIS!

BY DAVID LORMS

Growing up in a small town had some advantages. I grew up in Lake Jackson, TX with a population of about 10,000 where everyone knew everyone. Well, for me it was true since my Dad taught High School, owned a Roofing Company on the side, and he and I share the same name. So, someone in the town always knew a David Lorms, if not both of us.

When I was young and wanted a new bike, I got into sales. My parents always encouraged me to earn my own money. For example, when I was 7, I sold flower and garden seeds door to door making pretty good money. I would also go door to door using my Dad's business cards asking folks if they wanted a free quote to replace their roof upon which my Dad would give me $100 for every roofing job I referred to him. Later in High School, I sold Cameras at J C Penny and was the "go to" person in the mall if someone wanted to know how to use their camera. So, I guess sales and promoting me as my brand has always been in my blood.

In college, I majored in Marketing and took two aptitude tests, which both said I should be in Insurance Sales. No wonder I am in Insurance Sales today and I love what I am doing now as a Farmers Agent. And, from my sales experience over the years and being an Insurance Agent, I have learned a few tricks to Market my brand, ME!

Everyone knows Farmers Insurance, so I don't need to advertise them. However, I do need to promote myself. How do I do that? Well, the first thing I do is put my picture on everything. From my website, my email, my business cards, mail outs, note pads, fax cover sheet and advertisements. Anything I can put my picture on get's one. Not that I think I am that good looking, but my face is my brand so I splatter it everywhere.

One thing I do is always carry my business cards with me everywhere I go. You never know when you will meet a prospect. And, when I do, I not only give only give them my card, but write their contact information on another card so I can follow up with them. I also place my card on public post boards that I may see in places like restaurants or where businesses allow you to place your card. I have several businesses where I am a client and who allow me to place my card/brochure in a stand at their place of business. I use about three dry cleaners and each one allows me to put out my cards, even my Dentist has my cards out in his waiting room. As it turns out, my Dentist and one of the Dry Cleaners are now customers.

Another thing I do is to wear Agency/Company branded shirts. I don't even need to talk to people about insurance because they will always ask about what I do for Farmers. When I tell them I am an agent, many people inquire about something I can help (sell) them with. Either at the grocery store, the gas station or a party, insurance is always brought up by someone else because of my shirts. I also wear Agency/Company made T-Shirts for when I work out at the gym, advertising my business. I met a prospect through jogging at the local jogging trail from my T-Shirt.

For every quote my office makes and every sale, we write a handwritten thank you note. If a quote is not taken, I send a thank you note with a packet of "Forget-Me-Not" seeds and my business card. A gimmick I learned from my days of selling seeds as a kid and people to this day will say to me "Hey, you used to sell us seeds." I also send handwritten notes to friends or customers if we hear of, or see on Facebook, about an event in someone's life such as a birth, wedding, illness or death. I have a staff member who also sends out written Birthday cards to clients. I sometimes get calls from the customer saying it was the only card they got that year.

Once I make a sale, I send postcards to their neighbors, with my picture, with the address of the new client, stating what kind of insurance they bought, and asking them to contact me if they see an emergency at my new insured's address. I don't put the name of the client to maintain some type of privacy for them.

Another thing I do is to keep a "Real Estate" and "Attorney" email address list that I collect from local publications, where I may email information about homeowner's policies, flood insurance changes, or so that we can get their client an SR22 on the same day requested. Many Real Estate Agents appreciate this information to share with their clients. In fact, I visit many Real Estate Offices to get to know the Real Estate Agents so they will hopefully refer business to me. I usually take a bag of candy, and stop at each desk with my card, my agency branded pen and some candy, making small talk. I don't take donuts or cookies to offices because it doesn't give me a reason to visit each person individually. However, with a bag of candy I have a reason to drop a handful at each desk. I also offer to run flood zone reports for free, on addresses where they may want to know if they are located in a flood zone. This really helps me get to know the Agents on a personal basis, and build my reputation and brand. I also leave my cards scattered all over the office too.

Getting involved in the community is very important to my success as well. I partner with several elementary schools in providing them money, usually $500, to sponsor a "Perfect Attendance Award" program for students. This is well received as the schools don't have money in their budget to fund such a program and are paid by the state based upon attendance. The more students they have in school per day, the more money the school gets from the state. Plus, it encourages the student to have perfect attendance so they can win prizes at the end of the semester. In exchange, I get my name on the School Marquee thanking me; I am linked to the school website as a partner, and I am included in the school flyer that goes out to the families, along with my picture. In addition, I get to take a photo with the Principal when the check is given to the school, and photos with the award winners. These photos go on Facebook, my website, and other social media. I also write a small article along with the photos and submit it all to the local newspaper.

Sponsoring the Elementary Schools also gets my foot in the door for Parents Night, Festivals and Fairs, where I set up a booth and hand out safety information kits to parents. These safety information kits are provided by Farmers for free, and I usually include some type of agency branded trinket and have candy on the table to attract the kids (and also the parents) to my booth. Thus, more opportunity to post photos on Facebook, my website and other social media. I also hang a banner above my booth with my picture on it.

For the same reason, I sponsor the local Intermediate and High School. For the Intermediate School, I donate to various school programs and participate in the "Real Men Read" program, reading once a month to students. And for the High School, I donate to "Project Graduation," which funds an alcohol-free party for the seniors. The High School also invites me to visit their senior classes to speak about how "real world business" operates outside of school. And, all of these events are documented by photos and placed in social media and the local paper, if possible. In addition, all schools have invited me to participate on their "Parent's Board" as well. Sponsoring schools has given me access to the teachers as well as the parents at each school, building my brand, resulting in more clients. Some of the teachers have even become clients.

Getting involved in your neighborhood association is another way to get to know my neighbors, as well as to let them know I am a local Insurance Agent. Many times, people want to use a local agent even though they may never visit my office. I also advertise in their newsletter.

Becoming a member of a Church also helps. I volunteer as an Usher, so I am seen by the whole congregation on Sundays, and I also advertise in the bulletin. Many times I see people looking at the bulletin, and then my picture in the bulletin advertisement, which makes me smile. Some people like doing business with other Church members. One of the Pastors has ended up referring prospects to me.

Advertising should be done as well. I advertise in the local newspaper (helping me get articles submitted into the paper), the local news magazine and by billboard at the local kids baseball league. Folks see that I am supporting the league by seeing my billboard (with my picture) at their field. Subsequently, I insure the league as well and the news magazine sales person. My picture is in each advertisement.

Participating in March for Babies, the AIDS Walk and the Avon Walk for Breast Cancer with my Agency/Company T-shirt also helps advertise, and lets people know that my Agency gives back to the community. Of course, photos are taken and posted on Social Media and my website.

I also send a "Reasons to hire David Lorms" flyer with every quote. This flyer lists 10 reasons why the customer should select me as their agent or my agency over any competitor. Some people won't usually know about the great things I do in the community so letting them know up front can make them feel better about buying from me.

Creating a blog may help drive traffic to my website. I will post articles and pictures that show I am staying current with insurance, knowledgeable about the products, and offering advice for free. I have had clients tell me that after reading my website and blog, they feel more comfortable using me as their agent.

I mentioned Social Media earlier, which is a free way to promote your business and keep my name out in front of my friends, family and customers. Facebook, Twitter, Pinterest and Google are just a few that come to mind. I post photos of events, vacations, events, awards, accomplishments, donations, community involvement, safety tips and humorous items (non offensive). I stay away from political or religious postings or responses that might offend anyone, as hard as it might be to refrain.

I also use phone apps, such as Foursquare, that people use to "check in" wherever they are located. Each time I "check in" my name pops up where I am located. I also "check in" on Facebook, and submit photos of what I am are doing, keeping my name out there.

Another Social Media that I use is Linked In. I have a detailed profile, with my picture, and allow anyone to view my profile. I have solicited customers for recommendations which I have copied to my website and blog. Prospects appreciate reading recommendations and while they may not buy from me, they may refer someone else to me.

As funny as it may seem, I also use car magnets, advertising my agency, with my picture. Sure, I may get teased about them now and then, but people remember me for that reason. I have had people waive at me, write down my number from the magnet at a red light, and then call me later. Of course, you better drive safely and not cut anyone off, as they could get your phone number and call you up!

Regarding email, I have my picture in the email, as well as a tag line, that includes several "local office" numbers for other cities in Texas. I use "Vonage" that allows me to set up "local" phone numbers in any zip code, which then roll to my office number. So, when I buy leads in other cities, the customer will think I am local due to my phone number and may be more likely to do business with me. These office numbers in my email tag line also give the impression that my organization may be bigger than it is and people like to do business with businesses that are successful.

Naming my Agency was another creative way to get noticed. I call my Agency "Farmers Insurance by David Lorms" – so that when I am listed in the phone book, there will be a name associated with the Agency vs. simply "Farmers." I continued using this name when creating free profiles on search engines on the Internet. It also helps to sign up with "Yelp," a free website for user reviews and recommendations on shopping and dining.

I also have a personal laptop computer that I use, and on the lid, I have a laminated advertisement, with my picture, advertising my agency. So, when I visit places such as Starbucks and work on my computer, people see that I am an Agent and will come over to me to ask about insurance.

Belonging to business organizations or networking groups is another way to promote your brand. I belonged to a Business Network International (BNI) group for over 5 years and almost every member is a client, as well as the clients that were referred to me by the members. You may also consider Chambers of Commerce, the Rotary, and other business organizations for referrals.

My office is located at the entrance of our building, with windows for walls. Although we are not allowed to put signage on the windows or outside, I park my car out front with the magnets on the side, and hang a huge banner, with my picture, in my office which can be seen through the windows. Often, we will celebrate a holiday, like Veterans Day, and hand out flags, with my card on them, and donuts to building employees and visitors. This helps remind building tenants that we are here and are friendly. We also keep our door open so that people can walk by and feel more comfortable to pop in with a question, to say "hi", or get a glass of the Ozarka water we have in the office. We now have many building tenants that are customers now.

So, if you haven't realized by now, my brand is ME! I even answer my phone "Farmers Insurance by David Lorms" to reinforce the brand. I am always looking for new ways to promote my brand and image and the ideas are limitless. Creativity is the key.

About David

David Lorms is a Top Farmer's Insurance Agent, a Best-Selling Author, and a Blue Vase and Toppers Club Award recipient for his achievements in the Insurance Industry.

David spent several years in the business handling insurance claims, which gives him a unique background as an Insurance Agent. He sees the process of getting insured from all sides, but most importantly, from the human side. He prides himself on providing the right product for the right person – which is why he is so highly regarded in his community of Houston, TX.

In addition to his business, David is heavily involved in his community as a member of his Home Owners Association, an Usher at his Church, and donating time and money to several local Elementary, Middle and High Schools. Seeing the importance of school attendance, David founded a perfect attendance program which awards high achievers with bikes, medals or other items deemed appropriate by the schools. David is also involved in the March of Dimes, AIDS Walk, and Cell Phones for Soldiers, a program that collects old cell phones to exchange for minutes for soldiers to use to call their families.

In his off time, David enjoys traveling, photography, and tennis. He also enjoys spending time with his God Kids, Niece and Nephew.

CHAPTER 22

AMY'S CLEARINGHOUSE: Never Underestimate The Power Of Clarity

BY AMY SCOTT GRANT, MBA

When I was a kid, I knew things, but I couldn't explain how or why I knew them. I don't mean I was a smart-ass (although I kind of was. Still am, actually.) I often knew unusual or important or secret things, which surprised the adults in my life. I remember going to my first Chinese restaurant at the age of five or six. My family was floored to watch me use chopsticks with ease, and when my mother asked me, "Where did you learn how to use chopsticks?" I casually replied, "I don't know, I just picked it up somewhere." The whole table burst out laughing, but I had no idea why.

Eventually, I noticed the adults' sideways glances and nervous laughter every time I joined "grown-up" conversations, and I could see I was different. I soon realized that other people were not as comfortable with my insights as I was, so I tried to blame it on my imaginary friend, Chookel. (My brothers teased me incessantly about the name, pronounced "chew-kull," but what could I do? Sure, I would have liked "Jennifer" just fine, but when she first showed up, she said "Hi, I'm Chookel" and that was that.) But news of an imaginary friend who told secrets and taught me interesting things wasn't well-received. Then, one day, after receiving particularly disturbing feedback on one of my "knowings," I shut down my intuition completely.

A funny thing happens when we deny our true nature. We suddenly feel lost, confused, and uncertain. By age 13, I had made multiple suicide attempts, convinced that I did not belong in this world. The idea of living life without being truly known or understood by another human being felt like too much for me to bear. I needed answers, and desperately fast.

Have you ever heard someone say, "And then I had a moment of clarity," after which everything shifted?

My moment happened when a book fell into my life. I won't mention its name here, because some people absolutely love it and others positively hate it, and I'm not in the mood to spark a rousing controversy right now. (Maybe later, though. Check back with me on that.) Let's just say it was a 1950s book about an age-old concept: changing your thoughts in order to change your life. That book was exactly what I needed at that moment in my life. In fact, you could say it saved my life.

Changing my thoughts got me over the hump, but positive thinking couldn't sustain me for long. I quickly saw (in another moment of clarity) that it takes a tremendous amount of vigilance and willpower to police those pesky negative thoughts – especially when times are toughest.

It was hard, because I don't have a lot of willpower. (See? You and I have a lot in common.) Which is why – in another moment of clarity – I realized it makes more sense to shift our *beliefs*. After all, isn't it fair to say our most repetitive thoughts stem from our deep-seated beliefs?

Unfortunately, most "new thought" teachers will try to convince you that the way to change your beliefs is with affirmations, which requires writing out a new thought statement, and repeating it *ad nauseam*. Yawn. While this method does work – eventually – it is both redundant and exhausting. In search of a better way, I returned to my natural intuition and my own process of "knowing." It was through this process that I learned to swiftly and permanently shift beliefs, and sure enough, the corresponding thoughts followed naturally.

Hot damn! Clearing your limiting beliefs is highly satisfying, bordering on addictive. The resulting clarity brings a sense of freedom that cannot be compared to anything else. I immediately fell in love with the process, and the results. Imagine your biggest stumbling block – the one that keeps you up at night, consumes your waking thoughts, and prevents you from achieving what you desire. Now, imagine this block was gone *forever.* How would that feel? What could you do if you no longer had that block? What would now be possible for you?

That's right – *anything* would be possible. Doors that were once closed would bust wide open, and opportunities would abound.

I was so exhilarated by my own results, it felt like a natural transition to help other people do the same. I quickly realized I had a knack for this, and I turned clearing into my profession. Over the years, I have cleared millions of limiting beliefs for thousands of individuals, subsequently allowing them to become far more successful in life, in love, and in business.

I use my true nature – my intuition – to go to the root and figure out why you created the beliefs in the first place, and what we need to do to shift it. This shift, or complete release of the old belief, is what I call "clearing," because we clear the underlying cause of your stagnation/self-sabotage/lack of results. In a clearing, we get rid of the beliefs that don't serve you, and sometimes we replace them with new beliefs, designed to support achievement of your goals. This is when you feel "clear," and anything is possible.

Releasing limiting beliefs is a fast and powerful process, because as soon as the limiting beliefs are gone, your thoughts will naturally change. And when your thoughts change, your results change. And when your results change, this is when you can see the transformation – this is success! The process all begins with clarity. You'll be happy to know that you don't have to wait for a moment of clarity to randomly strike like lightning. You can *invoke* clarity. The clearing process acts like a lightning rod, drawing clarity to you and helping you to create that oh-so-yummy pivotal shift.

The first thing I do when I'm working with someone is teach a scientific technique (like muscle testing or dowsing) so the person can check for truth and accuracy. By the way, if you think dowsing is just for the new-age "crunchy" circuit, you might be surprised to learn that water utility companies *still* use dowsing rods to find water when maps and technology fail.

I teach the technique for a couple of reasons. First, it's a handy tool because it helps you make sound decisions and choices, and figure out whether someone is telling you the truth. The other reason is because you shouldn't have to take my word for anything. I'm a huge advocate for independent thinking, and if you have a reliable truth testing method, then you can check objectively any time your B.S.-meter suddenly goes haywire.

For example, let's say you and I are working together, and I tell you that your fear of exposure is keeping you from achieving the level of success that you desire. If you think, "What? That makes no sense," you could use your preferred truth testing method to ask, "Is what Amy said true and accurate?" Then you'll know for sure, instead of just believing me because you've paid me quite a lot of money to tell you such things.

Additionally, you can use these "truth testing" methods to figure out what needs to be cleared, how best to clear it, and whether or not the clearing worked. I offer a Truth Testing e-course at: InfoyesNo.com. But before you go on a wild clearing spree, there are a few caveats.

1. YOU ARE AN ONION. BUT NOT SO SMELLY.

First, consider that you are a complex individual, and any long-standing challenges you've had are multi-layered and multi-faceted. In other words, don't expect to do one or two clearings and suddenly find yourself holding the winning Powerball ticket. While it's true that clearings occur swiftly and dynamically, and rapid results occur more often than not, it's also true that the deeper the issue, the more clearing that's required to produce a dramatic result. Think of your internal belief network as an onion, comprised of layers upon layers upon layers. If you've got a longstanding issue with confidence, we may first need to clear your body issues or your financial issues or your childhood issues before we can get to that *bam-pow!* instant confidence you seek.

After all, you didn't become fearful or wimpy or broke overnight – your current condition is the cumulative result of countless choices and decisions and beliefs, accumulated over time. We clear in layers, and you can't get to the inner depths (your deepest issues) until you've removed some of the outer layers. The good news is that you feel better, stronger and more powerful with every layer that's cleared, and most people begin to see results immediately.

2. PRACTICE MAKES BETTER. (FORGET PERFECT!)

I believe anyone with desire and a willing spirit can do what I do, but it takes practice to get good and fast at clearing. When I first started, clearings took me hours and sometimes days to complete, but now it takes mere minutes and in some cases, it's instantaneous. Like any other skill, practice brings proficiency, speed and accuracy. Luckily, we're all far from perfect, so there's no shortage of practice opportunities. The upshot is that every clearing brings you greater peace, joy, freedom, and potential for success. I recommend that you celebrate every win, because life's too short to stress about how much you haven't done. If you can look back on the past few months and think, "man, I used to be a real tool," then celebrate that win! It means you've shifted and now you're that much closer to being the person you want to be.

3. RESIST MUCH?

As you embark on clearing work, you'll want to watch out for a little mental gremlin known as "resistance." The simple definition of resistance is a refusal to accept something, and the sticky wicket to watch out for is how well it can be camouflaged.

For example, I've been on the phone with clients and just as we strike gold, their phone dies, their doorbell rings, their baby wakes up, their dog starts barking wildly, their pipes burst, or their kids suddenly need immediate attention. I just smile, because I know it's that sneaky little resistance trying to interfere with our clearing.

No one is immune to resistance. When I'm resistant, I get angry or irritable, and my husband will tell you – I'm no picnic when this happens! It's simply a sign that there's something for us to see, which we don't want to see right now. But, like ripping off a bandage, it's best to just "nut up" and muscle through it. On the other side of it, you'll find freedom, joy and peace, plus a huge sense of relief, which will have you asking, "Why was I being such a baby about that in the first place?"

Resistance can rear its ugly head in many forms. It can stymie your progress and make you want to give up, even on the verge of your biggest breakthrough. Knowing how to deal with resistance is elemental in managing effective clearings for yourself and others.

4. THAT GUY/GIRL NEEDS FIXING.

It's easy to fall into the trap of wanting to "fix" people in our lives. The trouble is twofold – one, they're not *really* broken, and two, people don't often appreciate unsolicited advice. I have mentored many individuals who wanted to "fix" their spouse or business partner and I'm not talking about the kind of "fixing" a veterinarian does (though some clients have that issue, too).

It's no secret that the people in your life often mirror yourself back to you, including your underlying fears, doubts, blocks and limiting beliefs. But perhaps the most fascinating phenomenon is the way we can change something in ourselves, and suddenly, other people begin to act differently.

I once helped a hairdresser change her perspective on her mother-in-law, who was overly opinionated about how she was raising her young daughter. The hairdresser was very resistant to my recommendation at first, but was open enough to try something new, and during a conversation with me, she changed just a single perspective. She called me the very next day, demanding to know what I had done to her mother-in-law. She could hardly believe that her own clarity could have such a massive impact on her interactions with another person. She was convinced that I had "done something" to her mother-in-law, because she had never before seen the woman act so kindly, so graciously, so un-meddlesome-ly. (Yes, I do make up words from time to time. If the precise word for what I mean doesn't exist, I invent it. Chookel says you should humor me.)

The hairdresser finally accepted the fact that changing her own belief was enough to immediately improve such a volatile situation. I spoke with her recently, and their family dynamic is better than ever, all because she shifted one simple belief. When you change yourself, your whole world — including the people in it will shift, too.

When you begin to understand that we have chosen all of our beliefs because each one serves us in some way, then you may see why some people choose to hang onto their hang-ups, when in fact, they could easily release them. You cannot clear anything that a person is unwilling to clear. Your best bet is to focus on getting yourself clear, and let the rest take care of itself.

5. WE'RE ALL MAD HERE.

While your best results will come from your own clarity, be mindful not to get lost down the rabbit hole. Considering how many experiences you've had, how many beliefs you've accumulated, and how much clearing work could potentially be done, you might be tempted to fall into a bit of navel-gazing. I, myself, have gone through periods of intense self-improvement, where an obsessive need to transform my life drove me to fill my days and nights with endless clearing work. I can tell you from experience, it pays to work with someone who can keep you on track and ensure that you're exercising balance in your clearing work.

A skilled mentor such as myself can provide you with an objective perspective, and the clarity necessary to help you break through to the next level of success. My goal for every client is to place them in a position of self-sufficiency by the end of our time together, so that they are free and clear from their greatest obstacles and self-sabotage, and can also be empowered to tackle their own clearings as future issues arise. It might not be my smartest sales strategy, but it's the best win-win scenario I know.

You have greatness inside of you. But when the waters are muddy, it's difficult to see the true you under all those smelly layers. Clarity is what helps you see your true potential. When you get clear, you get results. And isn't it your quest for results that led you to read this in the first place?

About Amy

Without apology, Amy Scott Grant, MBA will call you on your stuff. Known as the Spiritual Ass Kicker, Amy's dedication to her own joyous freedom from self-imposed limits carries her commitment to helping anyone else who wants the same. Her raw boldness, unbridled enthusiasm, wicked sense of humor, kick-ass style and huge heart make her an amazingly effective catalyst for change.

Since the tender age of thirteen, Amy has captivated audiences of all ages and demographics with her razor-sharp wit, contagious enthusiasm and bold authenticity. Blessed with a gift for reaching people at their core, Amy has grown and cultivated this talent to pursue what she is most passionate about: assisting people in transforming their lives from "ordinary" to extraordinary.

Always passionate, occasionally brash, but never mainstream, Amy calls it like she sees it in every situation. She has coached and mentored thousands of individuals to create rapid breakthrough results by permanently clearing millions of blocks, doubts, fears and limiting beliefs, at the deepest core level.

Amy has also created a number of successful courses and digital products, including HIY (Heal It Yourself): Higher Power Tools and MindTime™ meditations for kids at KidCentered.com.

You can find Amy's writing all over the Internet, as well as in the Best-Selling book *Inspired Marketing* by Dr. Joe Vitale and Craig Perrine; *Chicken Soup for the Soul: Life Lessons for Mastering the Law of Attraction*; and the young adult novels known as the Annabel Series. Amy's blog is a massive resource of original articles, resources and unique perspectives: http://AmyScottGrant.com

You can get more information at: http://AskAmyAnything.com

CHAPTER 23

A NEW AND MORE PROFITABLE MARKETING SYSTEM

BY BENSON AGBORTOGO

The huge problem we have in the market place today is the avalanche of advertisements forced down our throats from TV, radio, newspapers and the Internet. Every week I receive hundreds of marketing emails in my inbox from people and companies trying desperately to me sell their products and services. Most of those emails end up in my trash folder. I skip ads when watching my recorded TV programs, and the snail mail I receive from companies that I do not recognize also end up in the trash. Maybe you do the same. Why am I, and perhaps you and many others ignoring these well-intended messages? For me, I ignore them because I do not have a relationship with these marketers. I see them as “takers.”

Some of these marketers are driven by **greed** and they are partly responsible for the economic crisis we are experiencing today. They are still marketing using the old approach of sell, sell, and sell without delivering enough value in return.

The good news is that the economy is changing. A new breed of marketers is rising and using a new marketing system where they give first and are focused on adding value to their clients. This new breed of marketers are *Change Agents*. They love their clients and they are “givers.” The ancient and proven writings tell us: “it is better to give than to receive.”

I used to hate marketing and sales, because I was of the opinion that selling was nothing more than manipulating people to buy stuff. I had been conditioned to think that way due to my experience with marketers who were driven by greed, so that their primary focus was to "take" from their clients. When I started my coaching and management consulting business, it was a challenge for me to sell my services because I did not want to be a "taker." I did not want to be pushy or manipulative.

However, when I discovered the new system I will be sharing with you in this book, my perspective about marketing and sales changed and my annual revenue increased by 31%. With this change in perspective, I began to see marketing and sales in a new light. I began to understand that marketing and sales are simply a process of finding people who have a problem, need or want and persuading them with love to buy solutions that solve their problems or meet their needs.

I had to go through the painful process of undoing that old mindset of "taking" and develop a new mindset of "giving." I had to learn how to focus on my client's problems and be determined to find solutions for them. If you have an excellent product or service, and you are not persuading people to purchase from you, it is like having the cure for cancer and hiding the cure from people who are suffering from cancer. If you have the cure for cancer, and you know that people are dying from cancer and you love them, wouldn't you persuade them to use your product or service to receive healing?

Now when you begin to see marketing and sales as offering quality solutions to people who have problems, needs and wants, it takes away the feeling of manipulation. In fact, it makes it a moral obligation for you to get the word out about your product or service. If you have a solution for an existing problem, and you don't present it to the people who have the problem, you are being selfish. Selfishness is the old system of marketing. *Change Agents* are selfless. They are givers. They are problem solvers.

If I could change my perspective about marketing and sales and increase my revenue by 31%, you too can do it and I will show you how.

There was a time in my business, especially in my first and second year, that I operated as a "taker." At that time, I went to meetings thinking, "What can I take or get from the meeting?" instead of, "What value can

I give when I attend that meeting?" I was doing things backwards, and because of that, my business continued to struggle until I discovered this new marketing system.

When you change your approach about marketing and sales from "taking" to "giving," you will:

- Increase your revenue.
- Reduce your expenses.
- Increase your profits.

This new approach is going to multiply your business because giving is multiplication, not subtraction as some people think. When a farmer plants (gives) seed, the law of sowing and reaping kicks in and the seed is multiplied.

- In this chapter, you are going to learn about this new marketing system. You will learn how to:
- Discover what your clients want.
- Offer your clients what they want without manipulating or pushing them to buy.
- Help your clients get better results.
- Identify what is working and what is not working in your business.

THE CURRENT STATE

According to the Small Business Administration (SBA), more than 66% of businesses fail within the first 10 years. Why are so many businesses struggling and failing with all the advancement in technology? This failure rate can be attributed to the fact that most of these struggling businesses are still using the old "taker" marketing system. The rate of failure clearly shows that the "taker" system is not working. We need a new system to enable us to market and sell our products and services effectively. The people who are going to win using this new system are businesses that are going to be "givers." They are businesses that are going to care for their clients consistently. The businesses that are going to lose are those that will only try to sell, sell and sell without adding adequate value. Businesses that are not willing to build relationships will fail.

HOW I OVERCAME MARKETING AND SALES PREJUDICE

After struggling with the "taker" approach for several years, I knew there was a better way to market and sell products and services, so I began to dig. I read every bestselling book I could find. Two of the many books I read were very impactful.

- *The Greatest Salesman in the World* by Og Mandino
- *Think and Grow Rich* by Napoleon Hill

The common thread in both books is love. People who love are "givers."

In this book, Mandino mentions love as the greatest secret of success in all ventures.[1] Hill also points out that love is the most powerful emotion.[2] Armed with this understanding, I decided to make love my greatest weapon as Mandino recommends.[3] I also discovered that asking people questions shows that you care and it is easy to make recommendations thereafter. From these discoveries, I developed and began to use a new marketing and sales system called, **A.R.I.S.E.** This system has transformed my business and it is simple and easy to implement.

THE A.R.I.S.E SYSTEM

Let's look at the system that will enable you rise to the occasion and sell your products and services effectively. When the opportunity to sell arises, **A.R.I.S.E**

Each letter in the acronym stands for a word that will enable you to help your prospects and clients get results.

A. *Ask* wise questions.

R. *Relate* and make *recommendations.*

I. *Implement* the recommendations.

S. *Sing* their praises.

E. *Evaluate* the results.

---

1 Mandino, Og (2011-01-05). *The Greatest Salesman in the World* (p. 59). Bantam. Kindle Edition.

2 Hill, Napoleon. "Faith." *Think and Grow Rich.* Electronic Facsimile Edition ed. Meriden: Ralston Society, 2000. 52. Print.

3 Ibid

I. ASK

Always *ask* wise questions and listen. What are wise questions? These are questions that will enable you to gather enough information about your prospects or clients to help them achieve their goals. Here are four typical questions I ask prospects or clients in regards to profits:

1. What is your current annual profit?
2. Where do you want your profit to be in the next 12 months?
3. How will you achieve your goal?
4. What obstacles are you currently facing or anticipate encountering?

Those questions help me to understand where my clients are now (departure), where they are going (destination), the strategies they plan to use to move from departure to destination and the obstacles (road blocks) they need to overcome.

What questions do you typically ask your prospects or clients? Why do you ask such questions? If you do not yet have typical questions, this is a good time to pause and ask yourself, "What do I need to know about my prospects or clients to help them accomplish their goals?" The answer(s) to that question will help you formulate some typical questions for your prospects and clients.

Based on the answers you receive from your prospects or clients, you can relate with them and make some recommendations.

II. RELATE AND RECOMMEND

Questions are powerful. They are conversation starters. They give you an ability to start or foster a relationship. Remember that as a *Change Agent*, your focus is to build great relationships. How do you use the information you receive from your prospects or clients to *relate* with them?

Ask more questions such as: What have you done to tackle your obstacles? What was your experience? The answer to these questions will enable you determine the kind of product or service to *recommend.*

Most of the prospects I meet know where they are now and where they want to be, but do not usually have a clear strategy to move from departure to destination.

For example, recently I started talking to one of my clients about his goals. After asking him some questions, I could relate to his goals and the obstacles he was encountering. I could easily relate with him because when I started my business, I knew where I was and what I wanted to accomplish, but I did not have a systematic approach at that time to move me from departure to destination until I discovered the simple system that changed my business. Relating with my client made it easy for me to recommend the table I have been using as a guide to reach my revenue and profit goals. This table covers five major factors that impact your revenue and profit.

Let us assume a starting point as shown in the table below. 20% increases in the five key factors (shaded) in this example will more than double your profit.

Starting point – Departure		**Destination Goals (20% Increase)**	
Leads	1,667	Leads	2,000
Conversion Rate	10%	Conversion Rate	12%
Clients	167	Clients	240
Transactions	1.3	Transactions	1.5
Average Price	$1,000	Average Price	$1,200
Revenue	$216,710	Revenue	$419,412
Profit Margin	20%	Profit Margin	24%
Profit	$43,342	Profit	$100,659

III. IMPLEMENT

Implementation is the key to getting results. When you make products or services recommendations to your clients, help them to implement the changes so they can get results. Here are some ways you can help them *implement:*

Provide clear instructions for them to follow.

Follow-up with emails, follow-up with direct mail, follow-up with phone calls and follow-up with face-to-face meetings if possible. I know it sounds like a lot of work. Remember you are building long-term relationships with your clients who will buy from you year-after-year or multiple times during the year. The investment of time is worth it. This single action will set you apart from your competitors.

Provide tools, templates, and checklists to make it easy for your clients to implement the recommended solution(s).

When I recommend the table above to my clients, I encourage them to print it and place it somewhere they can see regularly. The table is a guide showing them at a quick glance the numbers they need to pay attention to – in order to accomplish their goals.

I give them strategies to use to get more leads, increase their conversion rates, increase the number of transactions per client and increase their profit margins. I also provide them with tools and templates to *implement* the strategies.

IV. SING THEIR PRAISES

When you ask clients wise questions, relate with them, make recommendations and provide encouragement, tools, templates and checklists to enable them implement the recommended product or service, …they will get results. They will succeed. The results they get will change their lives and businesses. You see how you can become a *Change Agent* simply by following the **A.R.I.S.E** system? Immediately your clients get results, join them to *sing their praises*. Celebrate with them. Congratulate them and make them feel special for getting results. This will encourage them to implement more and get more results, and the cycle continues on and on. You see the picture? Cool! I know you are smart. When my clients get results, I get on the phone and tell them I am proud of them and then I share their praise with others to make them feel special because my clients are truly special business owners.

V. EVALUATE THE RESULTS

Finally, help your clients *evaluate* their results. Success is progressive. After singing their praise, help them improve their results. There is always room for improvement. Select key performance indicators (KPI) beforehand to evaluate the results. The best way to evaluate is to ask questions then relate, and then make recommendations and help them implement the changes, then the cycle repeats.

Evaluation enables you to determine strategies you need to abandon and strategies you need to improve in order to get better results. My favourite performance indicators in evaluation are conversion rates and profit margins.

CONCLUSION

You now know how to use the new marketing system to make more profit for your business. The old "taker" system does not work anymore. You are a "giver." You are a *Change Agent.* Continue to use the **A.R.I.S.E** system. Ask questions, relate and recommend, help them implement, sing their praise and evaluate their results. The **A.R.I.S.E** system enables you to show your clients that you care. It is easier and better to make recommendations than to just "sell."

WHAT SHOULD YOU DO IMMEDIATELY?

Develop or refine the typical questions you ask prospects or clients. These questions should enable you get the information you need to help them achieve their goals.

1. Ask those questions consistently.
2. Make recommendations consistently and watch your revenue and profit soar like an Eagle.

MY CLIENT'S STORY

When I met one of my clients several years ago, she was contemplating selling her business. She was tired and stressed with the daily rigors of running her business for more than 20 years. I simply asked her some questions and made some recommendations. I helped her implement the recommended solutions and in less than 24 months she doubled her revenue and became a millionaire.

NOW IS YOUR TIME!

Now is your time to arise and shine. **ARISE** and join the growing army of ***Change Agents***. Let us change lives, let us change businesses, let us change communities, let us change the economy and make the world a better place. You can make a difference because you are different.

About Benson

Benson Agbortogo, MBA is a marketing systems expert and the author of the book, *The Business System That Never Fails*. He is also an International speaker who has gone to three continents and spoken more than 1000 times to live audiences, online and on radio and television.

He founded the A.R.I.S.E Marketing System, a company that provides clients with a new, simple and easy way to implement a system to market their products and services. The A.R.I.S.E Marketing System focuses on five key factors that impact your bottom line: leads, conversion rates, number of transactions, prices and profit margins.

Benson specializes in moving small to midsize business owners from where they are now (departure), to where they want to be (destination). He does this strategically and systematically, making it simple to overcome obstacles (road blocks) along the journey.

Benson holds a B.S. in Business Management from The King's College, New York and an MBA from Keller Graduate School of Management, DeVry University, Milwaukee. He and his wife Zilpha have two children, and they currently live in Fort Worth, Texas, USA.

To learn more about Benson Agbortogo, visit: www.arisemarketingsystem.com

CHAPTER 24

THE WINDOW INTO YOUR FUTURE — An Unfair Advantage

BY CON ANTONIO

I cannot say whether things will get better if we change; what I can say is they must change if they are to get better.

~ Georg C. Lichtenberg

The world is in a constant state of change and the only constant is change itself.

Look around you, change is everywhere, humans grow old, trees grow tall, buildings deteriorate over a period of time and technology is forever improving.

At first, this may seem alarming: however, there is a certain calmness in this reality as we begin to understand what is actually happening and accept that this cycle is a universal law, and we no longer become eerie when change occurs.

Learning to accept that in a natural cycle everything has a beginning and everything has an end will bring you much greater peace and acceptance. The journey could be far smoother when a change agent paves the way for change.

Change is life in motion; when it stops we fade away.
~ Con Antonio

WHAT'S A CHANGE AGENT?

A change agent could be a natural event, institution, technological or medical advancement, or a person that initiates change. In this chapter we will discuss mostly the person who acts as a promoter of change.

Hi! My name is Con Antonio, and I will share with you my first encounter with a change agent. As I wasn't excelling at school, most of my teachers believed that I should leave and get a job. I also believed this to be the case until an incident occurred that changed my path forever. It was one day on a morning break at high school that a senior teacher approached me, and during our conversation showed me "through a window into my future," what could be possible for me to achieve if I was prepared to change. He explained that in order to change, one must first understand himself, he continued on to say that the answer to most of our prayers is in our mind, the most powerful instrument. Once we learn how to use our minds we can exert control over ourselves and our environment. I took on the challenge and never looked back. Today I own and manage a successful multi-disciplinary accounting firm and devote most of my time to assist my family, team and clients in achieving their personal and business goals. This is a pursuit that makes my professional and personal life a meaningful venture.

Life for most people is static, the vast majority of people perform a useful service to their communities and organizations, but they cannot make themselves go, and have to be pushed or pulled by someone else. Only a few people have the discipline and drive to not only move themselves, but also countless others; without them we would have no progress and no inspiration. My high school teacher was my change agent.

I believe each human being has the potential to change, to transform one's own attitude, no matter how difficult the situation. We just need to develop the courage to take the first step towards change.

LEVELS OF CHANGE

Processes of change have become major milestones in many organizations' life cycle. As organizations face relentless changes in their environment, the need for individuals who are capable of turning strategy into reality has created a new legitimacy for the change agent role.

In order to deal effectively with change, we will need to examine the three fundamental levels of change, namely:

- The motive of change
- The process of change
- The role of the change agent

In this chapter we will discuss briefly the first two levels and expand on the role of the change agent.

I. THE MOTIVE OF CHANGE

This refers to the **why** in regards to the subject of change. Understanding the motive for change is one step towards intentional accomplishment. Assisting individuals to develop a common motive for change will ensure greater acceptance of the vision. The subject of change is indicated in the proposal (e.g., through a logical framework), resulting from a thorough analysis of the organization and its context. During the planning process, the motive of the change is indicated as well as the overall objective of the change, together with the results that need to be achieved and the activities that will be undertaken.

II. THE PROCESS OF CHANGE

This refers to the **how**. Clear understanding of the process of change helps to address major issues and minimise resistance. When we implement change, we need to consider how we are going to carry out the activities indicated in the logical framework – resulting in the motive of the change. We have to consider the consequences of these activities, the effect on the people involved, the hindrances we might encounter along the way, the people who will carry out these activities, the order and time schedule of these activities and so on. We have to organise the process of the change so we can develop a strategy towards the implementation of change.

III. THE ROLE OF THE CHANGE AGENT

"We cannot change our past, but our actions can shape our future - we must change in order to survive."
~ Con Antonio

A change agent is a person who indirectly or directly causes change.

A change agent lives in the future, not the present. Regardless of what is going on today, a change agent has a vision of what could or should be and uses that as the governing sense of action. For example, a change agent may work within an organization to lead or cause the change that affects how the business is conducted. They may be assigned the role or may assume the role naturally.

To a certain extent, a change agent is dissatisfied with what they see around them, in favour of a much better vision of the future. Without this future drive, the change agent can lose their way.

A change agent possesses a strong ability to self-motivate and is fuelled by passion. They also have a strong understanding of people, and in doing so inspire passion in others. In some cases this may be misunderstood and underappreciated as the realisation of the vision may be too far in the future to be conceptualised.

As a result there is no 'ideal' change agent. It is about the motive and process as perceived by the person that will define the definition.

Seven Characteristics of an Effective Change Agent

Below are the seven most significant characteristics a change agent can possess to successfully implement organizational change:

- A person with a clear vision
- A person who is an effective coach
- A person who is an excellent architect
- A person that is tolerant yet persistent
- A person that asks tough questions
- A person who leads by example
- A person who builds lasting relationships

1. Clear Vision

Vision plays an important part for all individuals in leadership roles. In organizations where people have a clear vision of where they are going, they understand that this vision is vital to their success. A vision is necessary to bind the organization and give people direction. People tend to feel frustrated if they sense that the direction of this vision is blurred. Without clear vision, a business is like a ship without a rudder and is in danger of drifting aimlessly. As a change agent, your vision should be concise and give purpose to the organization, you are capable of motivating yourself and others by helping to link action to the business strategic goals from a clear understanding of the values they will create. If a vision is not clearly communicated it will not be remembered, it will not be transparent and therefore will be open to misinterpretation and create hidden agendas that will dilute the benefits of change.

With a clearly communicated vision, an organization will facilitate buy-in from its team and create a sense of shared vision that will enable the organization to realize the benefits associated with a strong sense of vision.

2. Effective Coach

It is essential for a change agent to create a mutual trust among all interested parties by supporting, guiding and teaching others the process of change. Only then can individuals be honest enough to bring their fears and concerns to the surface quickly so they can be resolved. By facilitating the exploration of needs, motivations, desires, skills and thought processes, this will assist individuals in an organization in making real, lasting change.

A change agent understands the process of convincing others about the necessity of change and the applicability of the vision to this change. One of the first elements in a change process is to create a basic awareness of the key factors in the organization that need to be improved. A change agent will establish a sense of urgency to take action and at the same time also create a belief that it is possible to reach the state of change necessary. This in turn will encourage the organization to develop the skills and abilities needed, enhance commitment, as well as instil a willingness to take risks towards achieving a common vision.

A change agent must also have sufficient personal skills to influence the human behavioural side of change by encouraging participation, sharing information and seeking and rewarding early adopters who will serve as advocates of this change.

3. Excellent Architect

A change agent plays a key part in shaping and fostering continuous improvement and business transformation initiatives. As they live in the future, not the present, they are responsible for creating a design concept that meets today's evolving business world. This driving force is needed in order to create the ability to change quickly and to make this ability a core competency in the organization. Creating this ability to change quickly and effectively is critical. To survive, organizations must be flexible and be able to quickly implement strategy and improvement processes. I believe that any organization that does not create this "change-based" culture will not survive, no matter how big they are or how successful they have been in the past.

Change agents must not only see the big picture when looking across multiple process and improvement initiatives, they must also have business strategy knowledge, a wide range of process discipline skills and methodologies in technological expertise. It is this rare combination of business domain knowledge and a winning personality that helps with communication and business change management.

All change agents must embrace this visionary role, focusing on how the solution delivers real value to the users, and how the system's structure meets the needs of all interested parties.

4. Tolerant Yet Persistent

A tolerant behaviour is vital for a change agent, they must be able to show respect for the rights and opinions of others. Change does not happen overnight, it's moulded by people who don't give up and most people know that. To have sustainable change that is meaningful to people, it is something that they will have to embrace and see as an important factor. Most people need to experience something before they can really understand it and this is especially true in organizations. With that being said, many can get frustrated that change does not happen fast enough and they tend to push people further away from the vision instead of getting closer. Persistence becomes present when you take on opportunities to help people who are ready to embrace change and get a step closer to this goal without giving up if they fail the first time. Organizations have to move people towards their vision with the understanding that individuals do not respond to change at the same rate. Every step forward is a step closer to the vision. People will also not change if they are given unrealistic goals; every time a person fails to change their behaviour, they become less capable of future change. Change agents just help to make sure that people are moving ahead with minimum stress.

5. Ask Tough Questions

Asking questions is a valuable tool for understanding the other person and determining his or her perspective. However, when you truly want to find out more about the other person's motivations and feelings, you have to ask tough questions that will help you formulate better advice and ideas about how you can help them to move closer to the process of change. When people feel an emotional connection to the proposed change, this is when they will truly progress towards the vision. When asking questions, it is focusing on what is best for all parties and helping people come to their own conclusions based on their experience, this is when you will see people displaying ownership in what they are doing. Keep asking questions to help people think, don't alleviate that by telling them what to do.

That doesn't mean that they aren't willing to have tough conversations. Trust is also built when you know someone who will deal with situations even if it is uncomfortable. Trust is also built when you choose to do what is right for your community or organization, as long as it is always done in a respectful way.

6. Leads By Example

As a change agent, you must lead by example. You have to not only be able to articulate the vision, you must also show them the way by doing it yourself. It will demonstrate your dedication to the organization and your team and help to develop inspiration and trust.

We at HID Group practice "what we preach," otherwise, how can our clients trust the process that we recommend for them to follow.

How can you really know how something works if you have never experienced it?

7. Building lasting relationships

For relationships to be lasting, you must create "goodwill" that you consider as an asset in your respective business. This goodwill is achieved mainly through business relationships and the reputation you carry as a business and as an individual too. There are many methods that can be used to build lasting relationships, however, all of the above means nothing if you do not have solid relationships with the people that you serve. People will not want to grow if they do not trust the person that is pushing the change. The change agents I have seen are extremely approachable and reliable, usually they will go out of their way to connect with you.

There are many methods that can be used to build lasting relationships, among them is networking, being accessible and visible, showing you care and solving problems immediately.

It is very crucial that as a change agent you preserve these relationships. Co-existing is the key to success and survival. Lasting relationships will assist in retaining good talent and this is one of the most important aspects of any business survival.

For change to be of any value, it must be shared by all relevant parties. It would be easy for someone to come in and tell you how things should be, but again that is someone else's solution. When that solution is someone else's, there is no accountability to see it through.

ABOUT CON

Con Antonio is the CEO of HID Group, a trusted business leader and coach.

HID Group is also dedicated to reviving the small and medium business community by providing business coaching to business owners. Con uses his 30 years of expertise in accounting and business knowledge to create efficient systems – which create profit, but he also works in-depth with the personal development of the business owners. Con realized years ago in working with various companies, from the medical industry to the car industry, that for a business to have lasting success – it is not simply about changing systems – it's about changing the mindset and habits of the business owners running the company.

He graduated from Victoria University with honours in Tax Law and Organizational Behaviour, and prior to completing his accounting degree, at the age of 19 he was granted a Tax Agent's licence and that provided him with the opportunity to prepare tax returns for individuals and small businesses - that was Con's first taste of business, and the self-satisfaction of helping individuals and businesses to manage their tax affairs.

After several years working for small companies, he joined AMCOR Pty. Ltd, one of the largest packaging companies in Australia and overseas. For the following 13 years, Con dedicated most of his waking hours to learning and developing his knowledge. He was promoted to different levels of management, working together with some of the most disciplined and toughest professionals of the group, who taught him all he knows today about business and the discipline and commitment that is required to become successful.

Although Con enjoyed achieving success in the accounting profession, he also knew that his passion was to inspire and empower people to achieve their personal and business dreams. So, at the height of his career, he decided to resign and went on to join the HID Group. For the past 13 years he has successfully coached a number of small and medium-sized businesses that, over a period of time, have more than tripled their bottom line.

To learn more about Con Antonio, please visit: www.hidgroup.com.au

CHAPTER 25

SURVIVING THE JOURNEY OF GRIEF

BY DAVID RISPOLI, M.DIV.

Ed and Shelly lived the storybook life. They met on a blind date in High School. Shorty after graduation, Ed enlisted into the United States Marine Corps and Shelly went to nursing school. Ed was a veteran of World War II. After the war the couple married. They were best friends and soul mates. They faced and overcame every struggle life offered and seemed to always come out on top, together. After the kids were raised, they sold the family home, retired from their jobs and intended to travel the world. Life had been grand. Their world came to a crashing halt when Ed suffered a massive heart attack. He fought hard, but eventually died. Shelly was devastated. Ed's death changed everything for Shelly. Other than the two years that Ed was overseas, this was the first time in fifty years that the two of them were not together. Now, six months later Shelly came into my office. She was feeling depressed, lonely and scared about her future. She started the conversation by saying these words, "David, I think I am going crazy!"

I have been hearing the same story from people coming into my office for the past twenty years. These are people of all different ages, from all different walks of life and from all over the world. While their journeys are all unique, they all have two things in common. First, every one of them has lost someone that they loved very deeply. Secondly, every one of them feels as if they are going crazy. These people come to my office for help. They have been told by others that they should be over it by now. They have been told that they should be feeling better. Sometimes they state how long it has been since the loved one has died and will say, "Well, it's been six months" or "It's been two years," as if the allotted time to grieve has clearly expired. The end result is that the people coming to see me frequently feel worse. They feel guilty, they are still in pain, and they feel like they are going crazy.

Usually, I am the first person to proclaim a message of hope. It is the same message that I shared with Shelly. The message is, "You are not crazy, you are grieving." As my grieving friends begin to share the story of their loss, they find that their grief journey is more similar to others than they had originally imagined. They also begin to realize that the feelings and thoughts they have been experiencing are not signs that they are weak or nuts, but signs that they loved deeply and now they hurt deeply. This realization is the beginning of a journey to hope and life again.

For the past twenty years, I have worked as a Hospice Chaplain and Bereavement Coordinator. I have also worked as a grief coach, a grief counselor for a local funeral home, and am the founder of Grief Journey Coaching. During this time I have had the opportunity to walk with thousands of families and individuals on their grief journey. The grief journey is the most painful journey this life offers. It is a journey that no one volunteers to take, but every one of us will eventually experience. Grief is not a medical condition that comes upon people who are sick; it is the human condition of losing someone that was loved. To this end, grief is not a condition that you get over; it is a journey that you go through. The only way to get to the other side of grief is to go through it.

My goal in working with people on their grief journey is to help them honor their loved ones, survive the journey and begin to live again. In my grief work, I have learned that people who successfully survive the journey of grief have left clues as to how to survive the journey. I call them the six keys to surviving the journey of grief. These six keys have helped hundreds of people honor their loved ones, survive the journey and begin to embrace life again. I know they can help you as well.

UNDERSTAND THE ENORMITY OF THE LOSS

Tom came into my office, thinking that he was going crazy. He said, "I don't know what is wrong with me. My Mom was old and I knew that she was going to die. But I just feel so sad all the time. It has been seven months and I really don't feel any better. Am I crazy?" I asked Tom to tell me about his Mom. He shared some wonderful stories about this woman who seemed to always be there for him. One particular story he shared was from his high school days when his Mom showed up at an event and screamed louder for Tom then any of the other parents. It seemed that his Mom had always been his biggest supporter.

I shared with Tom that he was not crazy, he was grieving. The reason Tom felt so bad, was that he loved his Mom so much. He had expected to be over it, as if he had lost a round of golf or a poker game. The truth is he lost his Mom and his biggest supporter in life. People who have survived the journey of grief come to the point in the journey where they understand the enormity of the loss.

Our challenge is that we live in a world that tends to deny and minimize death. This causes many people to react like the black knight in the movie *Monty Python and the Holy Grail.* There is a scene in the movie where King Arthur is trying to cross over a bridge that is being guarded by the black knight. After a short battle King Arthur slices off one of the arms of the black knight. There is the assumption that the battle is over but the black knight announces "tis but a scratch" and continues to fight. King Arthur then slices off the Black Knights other arm. The Black Knight then announces "Its just a flesh wound" and starts to kick at King Arthur. It is a ridiculous scene of a knight minimizing his pain and injuries. No one survives the journey of grief by minimizing the loss. The reason you hurt so much is that you have suffered an enormous loss.

EXPERIENCE AND EMBRACE THE EMOTIONS OF GRIEF

John and his son Bob attended one of my grief groups. They had lost a wife and mom to a long bout with cancer three months earlier. As we went around the group the first night and shared introductions, Bob shared that he was not grieving. He said that he was there to support his Dad, but that he was fine. He was a great young man who clearly loved his Mother and Father very much. In the weeks that followed, Bob began to open up to the group. He admitted that he was grieving and that he had felt like he needed to be strong for his Dad. He confessed that he often felt like crying but was embarrassed. Bob is surviving the journey of grief today, because he learned how to experience and embrace these emotions of grief.

The truth is grief is the inward response to a significant loss. It is like a capsule that opens up and spills on your insides. The loss triggers the cracking of the capsule and there is nothing that you can do to stop the grief liquid from leaking on your insides. This liquid produces certain feelings and emotions. One of the keys to surviving the journey and honoring your loved one is to embrace the feelings. Lean into them like you would lean into a wave at the ocean. Give yourself permission to experience all of the emotions.

Some of the common grief emotions include sadness, helplessness, worry, anxiety, fear, anger, guilt, emptiness, and loneliness. The natural thing might be to run from these feelings. Many people try to stuff these emotions and pretend that they don't exist. The problem with this is that the unexpressed emotions end up coming out in unhealthy ways. Frequently, grieving people will deal with their emotions by eating, drinking, shopping or other forms of self-medicating. The end result is that they get stuck in the journey. Lean into these feelings and give yourself permission to experience them. You feel this way, because you loved so deeply. The way to survive the journey is to give honor to all of these feelings and in time these feelings will change.

PRACTICE EXTREME SELF-CARE

A common phenomenon that we experience in hospice is when a husband or wife loses their spouse of many years, they end up landing in the hospital themselves shortly after their loss. One of the most common reasons for the hospitalization is dehydration. When you are grieving, it is sometime very difficult to focus on self-care. Many of my clients have expressed that they don't feel like eating or drinking and have a hard time getting motivated to do anything. Others have shared that they have made themselves so busy, so as not to have to deal with the grief, that they don't have time for self-care. People who successfully survive the journey practice extreme self-care. Give yourself permission to be selfish during this journey.

One of the things that you might consider doing on your grief journey is keeping a grief journal. In this journal you can write about feelings that you are experiencing and other issues related to your grief. You can write about memories or specific times that you felt your loved ones presence. Many people keep a journal in the form of a long letter to their loved one. In this grief journal include self-care items as they relate to diet, sleep and exercise. Be certain that you are taking care of yourself.

BE YOUR OWN GRIEF EXPERT

When you are grieving you will have friends, family and well-meaning individuals come up to you and say, "I know exactly what you need…" When you hear these words run. Give yourself permission to be your own grief expert. If you want to be alone, be alone. If you want to be around people, get around people. If you want to celebrate Christmas by putting up a Christmas tree, put the tree up, but if you don't feel like it that is OK as well. People who survive the journey of grief learn that they must be their own grief experts. No one knows exactly what you need but you. No one fully understands your grief, because everyone's grief journey is unique. People who survive the grief journey learn to listen to their heart.

BEGIN TO REORIENT YOUR LIFE TO THIS NEW REALITY AND GIVE YOURSELF PERMISSION TO SURVIVE THE JOURNEY

On December 28, 2007, David and Leslie woke up to a breaking story on the news. It was a story that would change their life forever. There had been an accident on Hwy 70 in St. Louis closing the highway to both east and westbound traffic. It was an accident with fatalities. Apparently a Walgreens truck had run into another smaller truck. There were prescription drugs all over the highway and the highway would remain closed for hours. All of St. Louis was in a traffic stand still. When David and Leslie looked at the TV, they were horrified by what they saw. From the Channel Five helicopter camera, they recognized their son's truck. They would later learn that there was only one fatality that day, their 27 year-old son.

That same day, I had been presiding at a funeral at Stygar Funeral Home and had just finished the service when David and Leslie came in. I had no idea who they were or what their story was, but I knew I had never seen so much pain on a couples face. They shared what had happened with me and we cried together. The next day they called and asked me if I would preside over Joshua's funeral. The funeral was on New Year's Eve. The song right before my message was Leonard Skynard's *Simple*

Man. It was one of the most difficult funerals that I had ever attended. In the mist of the tragedy, that New Year's Eve I proclaimed a message of hope with tears in my eyes.

One year later, David and Leslie began attending one of my grief groups. We became good friends and through the years we have done life together. I have been able to observe them on their grief journey and they have taught me much about loss, life, change and surviving the journey.

There were many days on their journey where they did not think they were going to make it. They would both share that there were many days where it would be easier for them to die. At some point they began to reorient their life to this new reality. It was not a new normal, for them nothing has been normal since December 28, 2007, but it was and is their reality.

Several weeks ago we celebrated their fiftieth birthday party. We gathered with all of their friends and family at a rented hall. Many of the people I had not seen since Josh's funeral five years earlier. David and Leslie have survived the journey. They still miss Josh and they still cry. We are always amazed how we will be out and hear the song "Simple Man." Now when we hear the song, we remember and honor Josh. They are good memories. They say the pain is still there, but they also experience a profound sense of Joy. Their friends, their faith, and having leaned into their grief gave them the ability to take each day as it came.

One day I asked David, "What do you think Josh would say to you today?" David replied by saying Josh would say "I am OK, be happy." The truth is, Josh is ok and David and Leslie have reached a point where they experience happiness. They have survived the journey of grief.

If you have lost a loved one, you know how maddening the journey of grief can be. I hope that the stories and suggestions in this chapter can help you continue to honor your loved one, survive the journey of grief, and begin to live again. I have a hunch, that if you were to ask your loved one who has passed away what they would say to you today, they would respond much the way Josh did to his parents, "I am ok, be happy."

About David

David Rispoli, M.Div., has been assisting people on their grief journey for the past twenty years. In the last two decades he has helped hundreds of individuals and families during the most difficult days of their life. He is the president and founder of Grief Journey Coaching. Grief Journey Coaching is an international coaching firm based out of St. Louis, Missouri. The mission of Grief Journey Coaching is to help people continue to honor their loved ones, survive the journey of grief and begin to experience life again. David has worked in the hospice industry as a Chaplain and Bereavement Coordinator for the past twenty years. He also serves as the Continued Care Coordinator for Stygar Funeral Home in the St. Louis area, and is the Senior Pastor at Joy Community Church.

David is the host of the monthly "Grief Call" a free teleconference where people who are experiencing the pain of losing a loved one learn the six keys to surviving the journey of grief. He is the host of a monthly radio talk show called "The Grief Show". He does public and corporate speaking, hosts grief groups, and does one-on-one grief coaching.

David has a Bachelor's Degree in Philosophy from Slippery Rock University and completed his graduate work earning a Master's of Divinity from Gettysburg. He is currently working towards his PhD. He is an excellent communicator whose passion is helping people survive the journey of grief.

To learn more about David Rispoli, visit: www.griefjourneycoaching.com
or call Toll Free: 1-800-877-3470.
www.griefjourneycoaching.com

CHAPTER 26

MOVING BEYOND CHANGE

BY DIANA TODD-BANKS

Change is not a mental battleground, but we're conditioned to believe it is.

I was.

The mere thought of the word change terrified me as it did and still does many people today, because it instantly appears to mean a time of major upheaval, even trauma.

Now having experienced change in many forms throughout my life, I know that moving beyond change can bring joy and a positive new beginning.

Having packed up possessions of others after 5 deaths, had 19 different occupations, with 8 different companies, in 3 different countries, 2 ½ husbands, and had a major health setback lasting 3 years represents a lot of changes. But those experiences created 50 physical moves packed into 48 years in business and more years of life. I do now know about change and moving beyond that *status quo*.

But when I first heard the phrase "for things to change, 'you' need to change" four decades ago, I found that hard to comprehend because there was always a clear reason why 'things' didn't work out. It never occurred to me, to look at me for the reason things didn't work out. I knew why; it was always the same one reason. I was scared, because I was just not good enough.

How that came to be is a very sad story. Some readers may have similar stories.

On the way home from kindergarten my mother said she had a big surprise for me laying on my bed. When we arrived home, of course I rushed into the bedroom and there on my bed lay two sets of clothes, two sets of boy's clothes. One was brown and white, the other navy blue and white, shorts and shirts with 'proper collars.'

My Mother proudly said to me, 'these are for you I thought you'd like them. We wanted a boy - you were supposed to be a boy. You can keep them!' Even as a tiny little child, I was crushed! I can still see my stomach crunching up into a tight knot. Right there I knew I was a failure, I knew I wasn't good enough. I wasn't that little boy they wanted.

That feeling of being a failure and not good enough stayed with me and anytime I tried something new and it didn't work, I knew why. Affecting me all through my school life, as soon as I could, I left, got a job at a newspaper and soon after was raped. Getting on with life, I later realised leaving home was the only positive solution and the best way to leave was to find a good kind man who would marry me. And I did.

Six months later, my conscience took hold. I sought help, but no one would help me. Where I found this wisdom I just don't know, but I knew I had to take responsibility for my actions and the outcomes. That decision taught me a major but painful life lesson.

Of the two solutions, desertion was the best option, so I left and disappeared overseas. It was a very traumatic time, yet ultimately, I came back to Australia, met a chap, married, then we moved to the US, sailing on a meat cargo ship which later got stuck in the ice in the Great Lakes. Fortunately, we had left the ship early to get to Chicago for the University year.

But, with our luggage stuck in the Great Lakes, we had no cooking equipment and no winter clothes. On top of that we only had one dollar a day to live on, 33 cents a meal, 15 cents for each of us, and neither of us was allowed to work. Add to that University housing was in a ghetto area.

It was an utterly terrifying, seemingly hopeless situation compounded by the cold winter with the wind chill 30 degrees below freezing. How could we possibly exist? I had to find a solution so we could eat well and survive the bitter winter.

In doing that, not only did I learn about nutrition from library books, but I also found a way to feed my mind, because that also needed to be richly nourished. I had to find a way to do that other than reading.

Where there's a will there's a way, and studying classical guitar filled me, and my mind with such joy, pleasure and peace that the harshness of our poor life wasn't foremost in my mind.

When my husband graduated we moved to southern Indiana, and before moving there, I started out doing what became a foray into my own first small business. Teaching classical guitar to young adults. But how can you get clients in a new area where you know nobody?

Using some bold creative thinking to find a way, two weeks later 40 private students were pounding the pavement to my door each week. But life stepped in again and unexpectedly another major change occurred. I found myself suddenly back in the windy city of Chicago. I moved back there alone, but with no income, no family, few friends and a ton of fears. My husband thought I was having an affair, how wrong he was. Well maybe I was with my classical guitar.

A Chicago University awarded me three scholarships, and I graduated a few years later with a Music degree majoring in Classical Guitar. All through those life change experiences, there were two underlying major issues I had to somehow overcome. It was that feeling of failure and not being good enough - both kept providing fuel for my fears and my constant negative internal chatter.

I knew without dealing with those issues, I could not successfully move forward in any new direction, a direction where I felt strong about my self where I could hold my head high.

That decision forty years ago was the start of my foray into the world of self-improvement and further development of myself, which continues to this day and that won't change. That decision and the ensuing knowledge I gained has enabled me to now help others through their periods of change and transition.

Later when I moved to California I did experience more changes, and also achieve some remarkable unexpected highs, from being Australia's first female wine importer in the US, to having a small US company listed on the New York Stock Exchange. But those and other stories are for another time.

Sure I took risks, sometimes I fell down badly and very low too, but I got up and moved forward, again. Friends have said, 'Di you've had some big knocks and many changes why aren't you jaundiced about life, how come you always pick yourself up, get going, move on and are still positive about life? What's your secret to all that?

My reply is quite simple:

"I won't let worries about my tomorrow destroy my today! We're all in this physical world once, and for me, I don't want to miss any new opportunity of an unlocked interesting door that comes into my life."

Learning how to move beyond those changes, beyond those seemingly hopeless situations to one of strength, is one of the most powerful lessons I have learned, and in doing so, my personal and professional life helping others has flourished. That makes me very happy and I know I've found my mission in life.

Reflecting on my life change experiences, the most powerful tools I learned are ones I used to deal with, and ultimately overcome, in these two significant areas: 'identifying what's holding me back' and 'internal negative chatter.'

While each of the tools did benefit me, ultimately they also had a positive impact on the success of my business. Had I not consciously dealt with those issues within me and taken 100% responsibility for me, I would not be where I am today.

Now, it's time to be brutally honest with *yourself*!

1. Just as I needed to do with all my life changes, take a cold, hard, honest look *inside you*, and ask, '*what is one issue that has continually and negatively interfered with my life?' Could it be, you are holding yourself back? If so, how?* If an answer does not emerge immediately, it will later.

   Generally two issues emerge, and each is within you, one being there's something holding the person back but they don't what that 'something' is (there are some simple ways to unearth the reason). The second area is your internal chatter, that inner critic and what it's saying.

2. If you find yourself facing a major change in your life, be it due to divorce, death of a loved one, job loss, financial loss, moving, business loss or your business is not going as you had planned, then there's a good chance the stress and anxiety of the situation can cause your internal inner critic to become profoundly more vocal and negative.

For most people that inner negative chatter becomes such a normal part of their daily life they are not even aware the negative conversation is happening and undermining them. It can severely affect one's ability to think clearly, function logically and in turn move forward with a good sense of direction, unless you learn how to manage, deal with, tame and turn around that negative inner voice.

While the left side of the brain does have a protective role, the negative chatter can quickly get out of control, and for most people that is what happens – affecting their entire personal and professional life.

Don't let that negative chatter run rampart like a spoilt, uncontrolled, adolescent teenager. Deal with it immediately. While the process is more involved than the steps listed here, these will be of significant help. So please keep an open mind.

- The first step to managing your change experience is accept, it need not be a mental battleground.
- Be aware negative internal chatter or the inner critic is just that … a critic!

We've all encountered the naysayers, negative people in life, but thankfully there are also the positive encouraging creative people. Now imagine two people are having a conversation: one represents your left brain, the other your right brain.

Each time you become aware the critical voice has emerged, right away adopt these six steps to address taming it:

Your ultimate goal is to turn your inner critic, that negative naysayer, into your inner cheerleader.

Step 1: Be aware - Notice it.

Step 2: Acknowledge It.

Step 3: Determine Its Purpose.

Step 4: The Power Of Choosing A New Thought.

Step 5: Detach From It.

Step 6: Slow Down, Breathe.

Step 1 - Learn to become aware when the Inner Critic pops into your mind. Don't try to push it out of your mind it won't permanently go away. Start to notice when it occurs: when you're tired, hungry, stressed, alone or lonely or facing a challenge.

Step 2 - Acknowledge It – Remember it's a critic, so thank it, for it's opinion.

Step 3 - Determine Its Purpose – Is it a protective voice coming from truth or caring, or is it critical and negative, coming from fear? Whatever it says does not mean that's the truth. Begin to look at the chatter from an objective viewpoint if it's a thought trying to stop you from doing something. Then challenge it.

Step 4 - The Power Of Choosing A New Thought – You have a choice of what you think. Consciously replace the critical voice with an empowering positive opposite voice. Say it confidently, aloud if possible if not then silently. Even if you don't believe it, say it aloud firmly. It will quieten the critical voice. This is extremely powerful.

Step 5 - Detach From It – Let go of the thoughts that are not supporting you.

This will begin to occur the more you immediately, positively respond.

Step 6 - Slow Down And Breathe – The best way to slow down the rate at which you think, is with meditation. Meditation creates distance between you and your thoughts. You are able to observe them like clouds drifting across the screen of your mind. Meditation can simply be sitting and focusing on your breathing, walking in nature, sitting on the beach at dawn or dusk alone, or listening to guided meditations or meditation music.

Stop thinking a negative thought, when you do that it will eventually disappear. Your thoughts only continue to replay in your mind because you support their existence by thinking them, just like letting that spoilt, uncontrolled, adolescent teenager run rampart when it wants to.

So, why not choose your thoughts deliberately?

Turning around your inner critic, so it works for you and becomes a positive voice, is a vital skill that can benefit you for any aspect of your life.

A FINAL FEW WORDS ABOUT MOVING BEYOND CHANGE

- To many people, *Change* means loss of some kind, rather than what will or is being gained by the Change.
- Even if a situation seems totally hopeless, there is always a solution, but 'beyond the box' thinking needs to be implemented.
- Any life Change, whether planned or unexpected, involves a range of different emotions, similar to those experienced with loss of a loved one, or loss of any kind – whether a pet, a job or a business. The common denominator with each experience is grief, which is a natural response to loss of any kind as are the related emotions.
- Any life Change is a very personal experience and cannot be hurried.
- If the Change experience is viewed as a loss, then address what is being lost, why it is perceived as a loss, and what 'new' things, or experiences will replace that loss with a view to looking positively to the future.
- **Change your view about Change** – Change is not frightening, nor a mental battleground, it represents an exciting new opportunity. Why?

The world is rapidly changing every few years. A new world presents new challenges ... and new opportunities for people of all ages.

It makes sense, if you don't want your life to be the same in 5 years time as it is now, it is necessary for you to adopt new strategies in your thinking, attitude and actions for your wealth, health, happiness and overall wellbeing, and doing so will involve a lot of change. Only you can do that by taking 100% responsibility for your actions and outcomes, and in doing so, your business will also benefit.

Don't let worries about your tomorrow destroy your today! Get used to Change, learn to love it, because Change will always happen. You can never tell what's around the corner.

Be bold, take a step into the unknown, it *can* change your life.

About Diana

DIANA TODD-BANKS is a Speaker, Coach and Award-winning Best-Selling Author. As a leading authority on Life Change, Diana Todd-Banks shares her considerable business and life experiences via seminars, speaking engagements, and private coaching.

A very down-to-earth woman, Diana Todd-Banks has received extensive print and electronic media coverage in the US appearing in most major dailies: *USA Today, Washington Post, New York Times, LA Times, Chicago Tribune, Orange County Register,* and many more including major Australian TV, radio and print media. For twenty years she lived, worked and owned businesses in the US.

Diana is a woman who has had an incredibly varied life, has conquered very high hurdles to make things happen, and overcome many deep lows. Picking herself up, dusting herself off from these lows, she has moved forward with a positive outlook on life which ultimately has opened up many new doors and opportunities.

Combining her vast wealth of experiences and insight with practical strategies, Diana works with clients to help them achieve a new beginning following the loss of a loved one, or a job, business or financial loss, divorce, retirement, health or relocation setback. As well, she works with clients who have other specific goals they want to achieve.

She was a US wine and food importer, and an international marketing consultant for Australian businesses seeking new niche opportunities in the US. Prior to that, she gained a degree in Classic Guitar in Chicago.

In 2012 Diana was a co-author alongside several top world inspirational speakers and best-selling authors. In *The Success Secret, The World's Leading Experts Reveal Their Secrets for Success and Life* Diana co-authored with best-selling author Jack Canfield, named by Time magazine as the "Publishing Phenomenon of the Decade."

In another book, entitled *Cracking The Success Code*, released in 2012, Di was a co-author with the legendary best-selling self-development author Brian Tracy. *In The Spirit of Success* is another book also released in early 2012, and Di wrote with Deepak Chopra, Dr. Wayne Dyer, Esther & Jerry Hicks, Mark Victor Hansen, Neale Donald Walsch & Sandy Forster.

In Australia, her groundbreaking book drew significant media attention, since it was a world first on the subject: *Wrapping It Up - Packing Up Possessions & Other End of Life Matters.* This was followed by *Estate Organizer – The Ultimate Guide to Recording Your Life Matters.*

To learn more about Diana, visit: http://dianatoddbanks.com/
Or email diana@dianatoddbanks.com
Also visit, www.wrappingitup.com.au to learn more about the book *'Nobody wants but everyone needs. Read it before you need it.'*

CHAPTER 27

JUST LIKE SPORTS, YOUR BUSINESS IS ALL ABOUT THE HALF-TIME ADJUSTMENTS

BY ED CANTU

Charles Darwin's Theory of Evolution applies to the survival of each species and it also applies to sports and your business. "It is not the strongest of the species that survives, nor the most intelligent that survives. It is the one that is the most adaptable to change." This chapter was written to help you adapt and even embrace change.

I am a 28-year-veteran in my industry and am considered by most of my colleagues to be an expert in my field. Since being an expert alone is not a guarantee for continued success, in this Chapter I will share my personal story with you so that you will learn from my mistakes. You will gain the knowledge necessary to avoid common pitfalls that can ruin your business.

You may be asking yourself, what business am I in and how can this Chapter help you? Well, like you, I am in the people business. I just happen to help clients build and protect their assets. And maybe like you, there were times as a business owner that I searched for help. I wondered if I was alone and was searching for ways to get my business back on track.

It was November of 2002 and after ten straight years of great success and massive growth, the political environment of my State was about to derail my business after seventeen years of hard work. It happened quickly and unexpectedly! Within three months, my annual revenue was slashed by 53 percent and my income decreased by $105,000. I didn't know what to do or where to turn, but I knew the way we ran our business would have to change.

By following processes and procedures that we developed, my office had been in the top five percent (out of fifteen hundred sales offices) in Texas for five years in a row. Now those processes were worthless. The way I saw it, we had three options: We could continue to do the same things and hope we would get better results, we could sell my business for pennies on the dollar amongst all the uncertainty or we could change and adapt to our new environment and develop new processes and procedures. So, like Darwin envisaged, I chose to adapt in order to survive and eventually thrive.

We tried our own changes at first and floundered like a fish out of water for a few months, until I came across a "business coach" who thought and operated outside of the box. It seemed too different at first, especially for a conservative person like me from a conservative Industry, but I was willing to try just about anything new since what we were doing was not working and we still hadn't figured things out on our own.

Up to that time, I operated as a technician within my office. I worked in my business and my new Coach showed me how to work on my business and how to delegate less important activities to my staff. He showed me how my business could Make More Money, Gain More Control and how I could Take More Time Off to spend with my family. After all, aren't those the main reasons we started our businesses?

I then took a deep breath and did some soul searching to discover my business' strengths and weaknesses. We needed to capitalize on our strengths and make changes to overcome our weaknesses. I learned to better understand my clients and how to discover the inner-conversation already going on in their mind, so that my staff and I can better meet and exceed their needs and expectations. I also learned how to discover my "inner gift," what I enjoy and do best, and the "inner gift" of my team, so that our efforts would deliver a Wow experience to our clients every day.

Here are the **Top Seven Changes** we made that saved my business and will improve and save yours. These are easy-to-copy ideas that will help you grow and make this year your Best Year Ever…

You must set goals and these goals must be S.M.A.R.T. (Specific, Measurable, Attainable, Realistic and Time-Bound). You must look at your goals every day. You must review your goals every quarter and adjust if needed. And of course, you and your gifted-team must believe you will achieve your goals.

1. **Challenge your Team and give incentives**. I challenged my team and developed a Team contest with a special bonus they could earn. We would share profits. Their share of the profits could easily add an additional 10 percent to their paycheck at the end of the year. That was their long-term incentive but I knew I needed to reward them throughout the contest period so that there was constant positive reinforcement for their accomplishments.

   They got cash for each activity they performed that I knew would eventually turn into opportunities for us. Getting them to change their habits became easier each week when they saw results and earned more frequent rewards.

   In addition to the individual goals and activities that were assigned, we made sure that there were team incentives too. All or none incentives so that each team member would benefit only when the entire team accomplished things. The goal was for each team member to encourage each other to do better and do the activities that would turn into opportunities. These rewards motivated team members to act as a team and to keep each member accountable to each other and the team.

   Results: My team talked to an extra 126 people about our services during a 73-day time period – an increase of 200% over the same time the prior year. This resulted in 31 new appointments that led to 27 new sales. We not only earned our bonus for that quarter, we continued to earn our bonus each of the following 3 quarters because they loved the rewards and because they proved to themselves that when they developed good habits, more opportunities would come. The opportunities they provided allowed for new sales that would protect our clients better.

   My Return on Investment (ROI) was 4.38 to 1… for every $1 we paid to a team member in incentives, our Business made $4.38.

Paid Staff: $9,552 for Incentive

Office earned: $41,849 Total Bonuses

2. **Added a Fun Referral Program**. Referrals are the lifeblood of your business. In fact, the only thing better than a referral from a satisfied customer is a new sale to a repeat customer. Why not give one reward and make two sales? How, you ask… It's easy; you reward your customer for telling their friends and family to do business with you. Send your customers a personal thank you note and small gift of appreciation when the person they referred contacts you.

   When you send a thank you note and gift for each referral they send you, the odds they will send more referrals will increase. The "Law of Reciprocity" assures they will continue to send you referrals when you meet your client's expectations. We established our referral program eleven years ago and the ROI is still 4 to 1. The positive reinforcement of each referral assures they continue to tell their friends and family to do business with you as long as you take care of them and the people they refer. *Check that gifts are legal in your State.*

3. **Re-contact your Customers.** We wrote 130 new items in a 90-day period by reminding our clients that they need protection. We compiled a list of clients that had gaps. We contacted them and then updated our list each week and followed up regularly. 130 items X $253 (average price) = $32,855 new sales.

4. **Improve your repeat sales and prevent buyer's remorse.** Sending a Welcome Kit to new customers to remind them why they chose to do business with you will reinforce that they made a wise choice to select you. They will buy again from you sooner and give you referrals and testimonials when you ask them shortly after their first purchase.

5. **Use Testimonials**. People are more likely to believe what someone else says about you than what you or your team says about you.

6. **Control Your Business with better processes.** You must automate your systems so that you work smarter and spend more time on your business rather than in your business. I completely rebuilt my team within the past twelve months and will continue to make improvements as time goes on because like it or not, things change. Only my

office manager has been with me throughout the rebuilding process. I added a part-time assistant recently who spends her time assisting my sales team with clerical duties, so that they can spend more time helping our new customers and visiting with our current clients to help them avoid dangerous protection gaps.

7. **Review your year-to-date results with your team each week.** We choose Tuesday morning to track our goals and to keep each of us accountable. "What gets measured gets done."

More helpful tools you should use to achieve your goals and to make sure you have your Best Year Ever:

Delegate more… when possible; give the things less likely to earn you money to the team member that costs you the least wage.

Chart Your Game Plan... Make yearly goals and then update them each quarter. Assign the required duties to each employee.

Chart a Team Game Plan... Make sure each team member knows the importance of their duties and how they help reach the team goals. Give them a copy of your plan.

Unleash Your Skill... Do the tasks that you enjoy and are good at so that you will enjoy your day and get important things done. If you are not good at a specific task, delegate it to someone else.

Unleash each Team Member's Skill... Determine what they are best at and assign tasks to them that will help you reach your goals. As the CEO, you are the Coach, it's up to you to maximize your team's strengths and minimize their weaknesses. After all, a good football coach wouldn't send their 300-pound lineman out for a deep pass, would they? Of course not, that is not his strength, so you would be setting him up for failure and it would prevent you from reaching your goal.

Nurture your customers… Stay in contact with them to make sure you are at the top of their mind the next time they buy your product or service. A monthly newsletter or mailing, regular mail or e-mail, is a good way to stay in contact. Let your clients get to know you and keep them informed on how things in your business affect their daily lives.

Join or create a Mastermind Group of other Business owners... There are things that only another business owner will understand and be able to help you improve. Ask them to keep you Accountable for your goals.

My business has seen a complete turn around since I first found help eleven years ago. The growth did not happen overnight, but the growth has been consistent and our revenues are back where they need to be. We accomplished all of this because my team and I adapted and embraced necessary changes. Not just once but several times by using the tools in this chapter. You see, we learned how to anticipate necessary changes, how to keep up with technology and how to better serve our clients. I've also learned the importance of having a coach or mentor and reading more business success books.

My first business coach and mentor was Michael Jans with a company called Quantum Club. He coaches Insurance Agents, but his teachings are universal. He taught me how to implement each of the tools I've described in this chapter, so I suggest that you find a mentor or coach to help you. If you can't afford a business coach right know, then continue to read success stories. Learn as much as you can from other successful businessmen and businesswomen by watching what they do and by reading what they write. They don't have to be in the same business that you are in. In fact, sometimes the biggest breakthroughs come from outside your industry because they are new and will set you apart from your competition.

Here are some of my favorite Coaches and books you should check out:

"The E-Myth" by Michael E. Gerber... This book is a must read for all Entrepreneurs and for everyone who wants become an Entrepreneur. Michael Gerber explains the difference between someone who is a good technician but has a failing business because he works **in** his business unlike the successful entrepreneur who works **on** his business.

"Influence: The Psychology of Persuasion" by Dr. Robert Cialdini… How to help people choose the best option so that it will mutually benefit them and you. According to Dr. Cialdini, influencing others isn't a trick or magic- it's science. His book uses proven principals of influence:

1. **Reciprocation**- You give, then I give.

2. **Social Proof**- Gather and use testimonials.

3. **Commitment and Consistency-** People like routines and hate change.

4. **Liking**- People do business with people they like and with people that like them.

5. **Authority**- People follow authority. Knowledge, Credentials.

6. **Scarcity**- Fundamentals of economics relate to supply and demand.

Dr. Cialdini's book is a classic you can find at bookstores and on the Internet.

"Eat That Frog" by Brian Tracy... 21 great ways to stop procrastinating and to get things done faster. It's a best seller that has sold over three million copies. "You cannot save time; you can only spend your time differently." I first meet Mr. Tracy in 2010 and I highly recommend you contact and follow him at: www.briantracy.com

Finally, **"Think and Grow Rich"** by Napoleon Hill... The hidden secret in "Think and Grow Rich" can help you tap into the Millionaire Mindset you need to gain financial freedom.

In summary, today is your half time and regardless of the score, the only thing you can count on in the second half is change. You must adjust if you want to win the game because your competitors are going to make adjustments, and from know on, change will happen faster. Be prepared to adapt to your customers as their habits change.

Follow and implement my tools for your success and remember this. More money, more control and more time is great but what good is it if you don't do good things with your time and money. I am grateful for what I have and I know that none of it would be possible without the love and support from my God, Family and Country. Owning a successful business isn't as satisfying if you don't help others become successful too. I enjoy helping others and that is why I decided to contribute to this book.

I hope you enjoyed reading this chapter and hope you put it to good use. For more information, contact me at: www.facebook.com/edcantuinsurance and watch for my new and upcoming website at www.edcantu.com.

One last thing... Don't try to do everything at once. Start by choosing just ***one*** *or* ***two*** of the tools. Choose the one that gives you the greatest ROI. Implement and gradually add more. Remember you sometimes have to go backward just a little in order to go forward a lot. After all, you can't jump very high without first crouching down and you can't throw a ball very far without rearing your arm back first.

About Ed

Ed Cantu is a top performing veteran agency owner of 28 years with numerous achievement awards who represents some of the largest insurance companies in North America. Ed's Agency is highly recommended by his clients and his peers because he and his staff members are knowledgeable agents with excellent customer service skills who know how to treat their customers' right.

He is one of the great insurance minds in the field and is constantly learning the newest information to pass along to his customers to help protect them better.

Ed received his BBA from Texas A&M University-Corpus Christi in 1981 and is a native Corpus Christian who understands the ever-changing Texas Insurance market.

He and He and Pam, his wife of 20 years, are active in their community with Church and organizations like March of Dimes and The Coastal Bend Emmaus Community. Ed is an Alumnus of Leadership Corpus Christi and serves on the boards of the Greater Corpus Christi Chamber of Commerce and the Texas A&M University-Corpus Christi Athletic Foundation. He is also an active member of the Corpus Christi Association of Realtors, Builders Association Corpus Christi Area, The Greater Corpus Christi Hospitality Association, and helps raise funds for March of Dimes through his Agency's referral program and MOD's annual golf tournament.

CHAPTER 28

BUILD YOUR PLATFORM: Launch Yourself With The Power Of Digital Publishing

BY FARHAN JAMAL

The magical world of publishing is now in the palm of your hand. Books with promise no longer hide out in sock drawers. Instead, you are likely to find them frolicking around within the e-reader on your nightstand.

The publishing industry is rapidly changing and where there is change, there is opportunity. Authors today have many options available to them. Aside from traditional routes, they now have eBooks, the clever platforms that go along with them and social media. Digital editions may not have the bulk and weight of their printed cousins but their lack of physical presence certainly hasn't stopped them from making a splash!

You may be looking to build a platform with a non-fiction book or perhaps you've always wanted to write fiction – whatever your situation may be, eBooks are a great way to get started. The complexities that once existed with traditional self-publishing are starting to disappear and authors who are succeeding in the digital world are getting picked up by agents and publishers more frequently these days. The opportunity to self-publish online is most certainly ripe and ready for the taking. However, the big question is where do you begin? After all, the Internet is vast and there are so many ways in which to approach this strategy. Indeed, digital publishing is much simpler than traditional self-publishing, but releasing a book online is the easy part. Making it a success is another story. Many authors are starting to realize that they must see themselves as online entrepreneurs in order to succeed. The good news is that the necessary skills can be acquired with a little determination.

Readers today are enjoying a massive selection of titles that are available to them on demand and their hunger for quality content seems to be increasing with each passing day. Even if you plan to publish traditionally, including a digital edition in your publishing strategy is a wise option.

IT'S A GREAT TIME TO BE A WRITER

A new chapter in publishing has begun and this is precisely why it is a great time to have an eBook out there. Once you've launched yourself online, publishers and agents may approach you, but most importantly – and this is the ultimate prize – you will start to attract readers, cultivate an audience and build your platform.

- Why not go digital while you break into traditional publishing?
- *Your contribution is valuable* and your message should be out there.

I was watching *Oprah's Life Class* the other day and Joel Osteen was on the show. At one point during his discussion he said, "*As long as you have breath somebody needs what you have.*" His words immediately resonated with me. Everybody has something unique to bring to the table. Think about your writing and what you want to say, whether it is through fiction or non-fiction, and realize that your unique perspective on life ought to be shared. You just have to find an audience that 'needs what you have.' The medium in which you share your message is not as important as getting your message out there. The audience you desire may very well be waiting for you, at this very moment, on millions of e-readers around the world.

TRADITIONAL PUBLISHING

Breaking into traditional publishing can be a challenge and it's a shame to see authors give up too soon. Once upon a time, I was one of those authors.

I discovered my joy for writing when I was sixteen and in high school. I caught the bug one day during English class. My imagination began to bloom in ways that I had not experienced before; writing was like meditation. By the time I graduated from high school, my first novel was complete. The plan was to continue onwards to university and get a bachelor's degree, but I was seduced with the idea of becoming a published author so I did both. I queried a handful of literary agents and it took about eight weeks to hear back from them. For the first few days after that eight-week period, I ventured down to the mailbox in earnest, fully expecting to find good news waiting for me. I was so excited that I even had several copies of my manuscript prepared and ready to go. Sadly, those first few letters all contained rejections – a simple form letter with a scribble at the bottom. I was crushed. The remaining letters were the same. All the advice that I'd received up to that point, from agents and authors alike, was to not give up and to keep writing, but I took a step back. I wanted to know where I had gone wrong so I spent some time learning more about the publishing industry.

The fact was that I hadn't really done anything wrong… It was just a tough business to crack into and I hadn't prepared myself for that reality. Publishers typically only looked at agented materials and agents were swamped with submissions and queries, making it a challenge for them to consume everything that came their way. My readers were out there, but the only way to reach them was if I had an agent. The name of the game was to get an agent and land a contract with a major publishing house.

Publishing is a subjective business and agents have their own personal tastes. It takes time to find the right person who believes in your work. Once you do find an agent, they have to get on with the business of selling your book. *If and when* it sells, you will then be waiting at least a year before your book is released. In consideration of today's publishing environment, you may not wish to invest this time, at least not at the early stages of your writing career.

DIGITAL PUBLISHING

Today, things are much different. Authors can follow an alternative path... While attempting to break in traditionally, authors can self-publish online with relative ease. Quite literally, they can start to build an audience of readers within days and if a book has promise, agents and publishers will eventually find them.

Everybody wins.

The simple truth is that agents and publishers want to find good books, but having to vet through the bulk of materials they receive is time consuming, which ultimately slows down the process. Digital publishing, on the other hand, allows authors to demonstrate the market viability of their book *in real-time* as soon as they're ready to publish. This is truly the beauty of digital publishing.

By releasing an eBook, authors can accomplish several objectives all at once. They can:

- build an audience
- generate royalties almost immediately
- possibly attract agents/publishers
- establish a platform

These days, most publishers look to their authors to get significantly involved in the marketing process anyway, particularly with online promotion. In light of this, why not flip the model around somewhat and start out with digital editions, especially since an eBook has the power to launch an author in today's environment?

Your work may turn out to be a goldmine, but the only way to find out is if you take a leap of faith and get it out there.

THE PATH TO SUCCESS

The path to success is not always clear.

Despite how attractive digital publishing looks, many authors are still confused about the direction they should take. My advice is to follow your intuition. The path to success might not always be straight forward, but intuitively, you will always know *what your next step is*. When something is meant to be, it will always fizzle up to the surface.

Take my story for instance. Even though my initial brush with rejection motivated me to stop writing, the need to write never evaded me. I just found a way to ignore it. My attempts to brush it off proved futile, because shortly after stopping I was writing again. Intuitively, I just couldn't give it up. Instead of starting a new project, I dug my manuscript out of the closet, took a serious look at it and changed a few things around. Once I was good and ready, I mustered up the courage to query a few more agents. I sent out the letters and endured, with great trepidation, the eight weeks that followed.

And then the unthinkable happened... I got an agent!

I was beyond ecstatic when I was offered a contract for representation. At last, I had broken into the inner circle and my dream was alive and well, once again. I immediately signed with the agent, but in retrospect, I should have hit the brakes. During our first (and only) month together, after two phone calls and a few brief emails, he concluded that I needed more attention than he was willing to give. Of course, that was completely ridiculous. I called and emailed him because I wanted to get to know him better, become familiar with his process, learn more about his plan to market my book, etc. After all, we had a long distance relationship and email/phone contact was the only way to get to know one another. While I was attempting to build a good working relationship, he thought I needed my hands held. His abrupt decision to move on was a slap in the face that I never saw coming, but I moved on pretty quickly. I had simply experienced a case of mixing with the wrong agent. I was still drawn to traditional publishing however arduous a path it was, but I was young and restless and there were plenty of other exciting opportunities on the horizon.

I decided to move on.

Fortunately, my intuition was as strong as ever and it guided me towards the next step. During my second hiatus from writing I forged a new path. My thirst for change led me to web development. The Internet was becoming commerce-friendly and tech startups and IPO's were the latest rage. I was drawn to this exciting new field so I started a web development company. It was a wise move: I learned a lot about Internet marketing, skills that serve me very well today. Once I got my bachelor's degree, the plan was to carry on to dental school, but my business was already doing very well. Intuitively, I felt compelled to carry on with web development so I gave up on dentistry and carried on with the business. As it grew, so did my experience. I didn't know it back then, but everything that I was learning was helping to prepare me for a future career in digital publishing.

My break from the traditional model of publishing ushered me into a whole new career, which I'm grateful for. Perhaps I should thank my former agent! In any case, I have come full circle, having found my way back into publishing, and the path that led me here was the right one. *There is a purpose for everything*. Had I not gone into web development and Internet marketing, I wouldn't have acquired all the skills and experience that has made for a seamless transition into digital publishing.

What path do you find yourself on?

The success you desire may not necessarily be showing up for you right now. That's okay. Let your intuition guide you – get to the *next step*. If you feel drawn to digital publishing, honor the urge and take the plunge. The rest will fall into place.

BE A REBEL AND TAKE THE PLUNGE

I don't think print books will ever go out of style. I for one love the feel of a real book, but eBooks are definitely *in style*! Not only are they convenient, they're a *game changer*. Looking back now, if this sort of publishing environment was available to me when I was getting started, I would have jumped on it.

Digital publishing has proven to be so lucrative that some authors are now *turning down* offers from publishers. *Writer's Digest* magazine recently featured an article on fiction author Hugh Howey. He is amongst a group of authors who have found great success with digital publishing. In the article, Howey talks about why he was willing to walk away from six and seven-figure offers from publishers. The publishers presenting offers wanted his digital rights, however if he sold them he would have been forced to put an end to his staggering monthly income. Howey was only interested in selling his print rights, but the publishers wanted it all, both digital and print. With the help of his agent (one of the many agents who had approached him *after his self-published books took off*) Howey finally got what he wanted: a lucrative print-only contract. The key to his success was that he didn't wait... ***he got started right away*** and then traditional publishing found him.

Once again, this is a scenario in which everybody wins.

Be a rebel. Get your book out there... Start building your own platform and dare to see what your writing can do!

THE BALL'S IN YOUR COURT

Your opportunity is here at last.

If you choose to publish digitally, success can be yours but know that this new mode of publishing, first and foremost, must be seen as a *business opportunity*. The complexities associated with self-publishing may have changed but the fundamentals still remain the same: you have to know how to create, market and distribute a good product.

Readers expect quality.

Traditional publishing has always been a provider of this. When readers visit the bookstore, they expect to find a professional product, complete with well-written and professionally edited text, a good cover design and interesting copy on the back cover.

Publishers are in the *business of selling books* and they can only profit if they produce quality products as well as the sort of titles that readers want. If you tailor your approach in the same way, everybody stands to gain. As long as the digital content being put out is of the highest quality, eBook platforms will continue to thrive for years to come.

To learn more about the author and launching your own eBook and turning it into a success, please visit: www.bookanchor.com/changeagents/

About Farhan

Farhan Jamal has a BSc. Degree in Kinesiology. He is a bestselling author, web developer and digital publishing expert. He has been involved with publishing and Internet marketing for over fifteen years and has helped many business owners develop a web presence. With his new venture, *Book Anchor,* Farhan is now helping authors launch their careers. To learn more about *Book Anchor* and the digital publishing programs available, visit: www.bookanchor.com.

Farhan is also the founder of *Upstart Success*, the popular personal success site and publishing company. For more information, visit: www.upstartsuccess.com.

www.BookAnchor.com

www.UpstartSuccess.com

CHAPTER 29

LIFE LESSON: Pick Two From Price, Quality And Service

BY FRED ECK, DDS

I was a junior in high school when I decided I wanted to become a dentist. I was absolutely certain that dentistry was the career for me. At that young age, as excited as I was to have chosen my path, I was unaware that I had my work cut out for me. For the next several years, I was told that I would need to have money in order to go to dental school. How discouraging and worrisome this was because I knew my family did not have any money. Hard work and borrowing money were the only way I was going to get through school. After I graduated from college, I learned that my mother was severely behind on bills because she had been giving me money every month for my rent. So, after ten years of school I was excited to be done and able to finally get above the mountain of school bills. I think I was as excited about being able to help my mom as I was about helping myself get ahead.

Following graduation from dental school, I was glad it was over, but still had a hunger to learn more. I wanted to learn as much as I could and knew that educating myself was going to play a large part in reaching my goals. So one day I was looking at a trade magazine and saw a continuing education course titled, "How to put your practice in the top 10%." I figured putting myself in the top 10% meant top 10% of income. Being fresh out of school, this was a very appealing idea, because I was constantly thinking and worrying about school loans, practice overhead and practice loans. Finding a way to position myself in the top 10% of dental offices would ensure that finances would not be a problem anymore.

On the first day of this course, it was proposed you could be in the top 10% of dental practices if you simply "did the right thing" for the patients. It was stated that if you did that little thing then the money would just come. This did not seem to be earth-shattering information. In fact, I was a little surprised that I paid money to learn what I thought was common sense. At the time I remember thinking, "who doesn't do the right thing for their patients?" I would not discover until several years later how important doing the right thing for the patient was. You see, during this course, we learned how to treat complete complex cases that many doctors were not learning to do. We were learning that doing the highest level of dentistry was beneficial to the patient and they would appreciate and pay for it. My next several years of education would be focused on learning everything I could about providing superior clinical results. The doctor I bought my first practice from would even routinely stop by just to see how different his old practice was becoming. He was fascinated with some of the dentistry we were providing.

In late 2007, the economy started to change and the real estate market bubble burst. Our patient's did not have the disposable income levels that they had enjoyed in the past. In Southwest Florida, where I practice, it was obvious that we had to change the way we were practicing dentistry. Our area was one of the hardest hit in the country and it was becoming increasingly worse as time passed. Our community is a retirement haven with a large portion of the residents whether full time or part time "Snowbirds" being originally from the Midwest. Many of these people had worked their whole lives in the manufacturing and automotive industry. They retired to Florida with great benefits, fantastic pensions and healthy stock portfolios. When the bottom dropped out the majority of our patients lost much of their insurance benefits, pensions, homes, investments and more. As it worsened, we realized that we were in a major national economic crisis. This of course was having an impact on our dental practice. More than 50% of the patients coming in for treatment were not able to afford that treatment. Not only were we slowing down, but also I was becoming very concerned about all the patients delaying treatment. I knew that money was the reason why these patients put off their treatment, but I also knew that it would lead to ever more costly treatment and make their financial concerns even worse.

Once I completed that first course following dental school, I changed dental laboratories and materials I used in order to provide the absolute best, most esthetic treatment available anywhere. We had to raise our fees to use these labs and materials, but it did not seem to matter. In fact, high-end dentistry became very popular and it seemed to be what people wanted. One day I had a patient come into the office who, like many other individuals, could not afford treatment. I really wanted her to get the treatment that she needed so I came up with an idea. I could use one of the old labs that I used before taking all this advanced training. Although I explained to her that there were a lot of advantages to the higher end work, in the end she was primarily concerned about the cost. After completing that case it hit me. I could create a menu or range of options so every patient could be treated. We could offer basic service, moderate service or high-end service depending on the patient's desires and budget. Often times now I will use automobile brands as examples. We offer the ability and choice to purchase a Hyundai, Honda, Lexus, Mercedes, etc. It's like we offer all these on one lot. Most patients, and I would argue most dentists, do not understand and are not aware of the cost differences available in dentistry. I myself had no idea until I took the course to learn high-end dentistry. We also learned that the high-end services we could now provide to our patients needed to be matched with a dental laboratory that possessed that same set of skills. In other words the average dental lab could not perform at that high level.

We have cultivated relationships with many different types of dental laboratories. We offer multiple options for almost every service in our practices. We are able to offer almost endless crown or cap options, several types of dentures, six dental implant options, etc. I would like to go into this aspect a little further and shatter some of the myths that exist with regard to dental treatment. I'm going to use a dental crown, or in layman's terms, a cap as my example, but the same rule applies to implants, bridges, dentures and partials and virtually every other aspect of dental treatment. Most people think that a crown is a crown is a crown. They are under the false impression that the quality is universally the same and the only difference is the price. They believe if they "price shop" for the best price they will be getting superior quality for a lower cost. This is most certainly NOT the case. In reality, it is quite the opposite. Let's say you want to go out for a nice steak but you don't want to pay a lot of money. They serve steak at Golden Corral so you could go there or you could go to Ruth's Chris. What you are not going to get is the Ruth's Chris steak at Golden Corral prices.

Patients were exceedingly happy with the availability of these new options. For those that have finances and budget as their primary decision-making factor, we could help them find an option that would work for them. We were now able to help almost any patient that came in to the practice. We began evaluating other areas in the practice that we could improve to make us a truly patient-centered practice. We want all of our decisions to be made based on what is best for the patient, more so than looking at what was best for the practice. All of the choices made for the benefit of the patient were to become so popular that we began to see rapid growth.

So it came full circle, do what's best for the patients considering the times and the business did thrive. Doing what was right for the patient now meant make something affordable. Giving up a little of the profits resulted in such volume, it was beneficial to us and especially to the patients.

I must say that there is one funny side effect of practicing this way. Offering anything from bare bones services to high-end services, some patients actually get offended once they learn there are multiple options available with multiple price points. The people that get upset are those that come in with only the cheapest thing in mind and are caught off guard or shocked that there are differences between one crown and another or one implant and another. Everyone knows and understands that there is a difference between a $50.00 DVD player and a $300.00 DVD player. Is a $700.00 55 inch flat screen TV the same as a $2,600.00 55 inch flat screen TV? Of course not, and that is not to say you need or want the $2,600.00 model. However, you have to acknowledge they are not the same thing. That same group of patients also doesn't want to take into account the fact that there is a vast difference in the training and clinical skill level amongst dentists. This group, for some reason, thinks the services and products we provide are all the same but that we all just have different prices. In fact, most dentists are taught to establish prices the same way. It's all based on industry norms, lab bills and material used. We used to hear a lot of our seasonal patients that live in Florida say, "I can get this done much cheaper up north." The reality is it doesn't matter what state you are in, there are dentists that do high-end work, dentists that do low end work and dentists that are somewhere in between. You the patient must decide what level of care you want because a $1,200 crown in Florida is a $1,200 crown in Ohio. The same can be said for a $700 crown.

Over the years there have been many articles written on the topic of price, quality and service. You can pick two out of the three. You can never have all three. I have illustrated this point with the following examples:

Quality and service: Companies like Mercedes Benz and Nordstrom base their business on quality and service. They are not trying to be low price leaders. It's not that their prices aren't fair, but what you are getting is not going to be cheap compared to other brands. A Rolex is a Rolex and a Timex is a Timex. You can get a fair price on your Rolex but you cannot buy a Rolex for the price of the Timex.

Price and quality: Costco and Home Depot come to mind when thinking of companies that base their business model after price and quality. Both offer quality name brand products for a lower cost. However, service is not a focus of their business. Costco does not hire or invest in a staff that can actually give you enough information to determine what flat screen TV best fits your needs. They will only read off the product card next to the price or read off the side of the box. Their product knowledge is typically no better than yours.

Price and service: as I mentioned earlier with the 55 inch flat screen TV example, just because the cost of something is low doesn't always mean that the quality is horrible. One must keep in mind however that there is a difference and you must accept and live with the difference before making a buying decision. The example that comes to mind when thinking of price and service as the leading factor in a business model is printing on hats instead of embroidering. We buy shirts and hats all the time with our logo on them. I really like the hats and shirts with our logo embroidered but if we are doing a big give away and trying to keep costs down we have the logo printed instead of embroidered. Obviously, embroidering is far superior in quality and longevity compared to printing so we are giving up the quality for price.

For those of you that have dental insurance, this is very important for you to understand. Insurance plans are sold under the premise you are getting huge discounts. After reading this, do you realize you're not getting a discount? You are simply getting what you pay for based on the fee structure of your plan.

We take great pride in being able and willing to provide our patients with enough information for them to make an informed decision about what type of dental treatment they want. By altering some of the ways we do business and by widening the product/service selections that are available, we have allowed many people who otherwise would not be able to afford their dental treatment to get what they need at a price that works with their financial capabilities. For the last few years, we have provided and will continue to provide free dental service for retired and active duty veterans as well as those with no means to pay for treatment at our Dentistry from the Heart and Salute to the Troops annual events. This is just one of the many ways in which we are able to give back to the community that has been so kind and supportive and allows us to keep our charity local.

We feel that we are unique in that most offices do not operate with the same business model that we have established. Other offices usually only have a single fee structure.

In the end the consumer has to pick between price, quality, and service. Most consumers know which one of the three that is most important to them. So when selecting a dentist, choose one with that most important attribute in mind. Then pick which of the other two is more important. In our office we have tried for several years to provide all three. I thought I would be the guy that cracked the code. I found that trying to provide the same quality at a reduced price to help those affected by the economy was resulting in not being able to provide the same service. I find things like adequate staffing, running on time (no waiting in the reception area), time to stop and have a conversation with a patient are critical for providing great service. We have actually separated our practice into two separate practices in order to treat everyone depending on which two are most important to them.

About Dr. Fred Eck

Dr. Fred Eck, DDS owns and manages some of the most premier dental and facial pain offices in the country. His philosophy is to employ and train doctors to be the most educated in the industry. Patients come to southwest Florida from all over the United States. In fact, many of their patients travel from other countries to be diagnosed and treated.

Dr. Eck is regularly involved in educating the public by contributing to newspaper columns, blogs, and patient education seminars. Dr. Eck's seminars were developed to educate the public so they can make an informed decision.

Dr. Eck devotes some of his time to educating and training dental professionals as well as other doctors offices, so this level of treatment and patient education can be more widespread in the dental industry.

To learn more about Dr. Fred, visit: drfredeck.com or call: 1-239-992-8555.

www.drfredeck.com

CHAPTER 30

EARLY LESSONS IN PERSISTENCE AND DETERMINATION

BY DR. JAMES MOSS

Looking back over the years, I can't help but think how my determination and persistence has kept me from quitting when faced with difficult life challenges. Just like many young boys, while growing up, I had aspirations of becoming an astronaut, a doctor or a policeman. I liked to watch Westerns and Saturday morning cartoons on television. I went to Sunday School every Sunday. I felt I was a regular kid. I was a Cub Scout and I did chores before my homework each day. I kept very busy. When I had time alone, I would dream of my future as a business man. I also dreamed of doing more important things, like finding new food sources under the depths of the ocean. Science Fiction stirred my attention. I enjoyed watching "Voyage to the Bottom of the Sea" and "Sea Hunt." I liked to watch animated cartoons such as "Danger Man", and TV shows such as "The Prisoner" and "Gun Smoke." Two of my favorite actors were Lee Marvin and James Arness.

I grew up with asthma and my mother sheltered me by not allowing me to play with other boys in the neighborhood. Sometimes I'd watch them play sports, like sandlot football or wrestling. A spectator was all I could be. Skateboarding was a popular activity in our neighborhood. We built our own skateboards using wood and an old pair of skates. My parents were poor and we had to move frequently because they could not afford the rent. I was often in a world of my own because my interests were very different from those of my brothers. I developed an interest in amateur radio, chess and science at a young age. As I became older I took an interest in Martial Arts. I felt this could strengthen my mind and body. I became less interested in the world and more interested in the things I liked to do. Soon, I overcame my physical shortcomings and learned many things which made me different from my brothers. I was always determined to be the best I could be at whatever I tried to do. I think that is why I liked gymnastics. My persistence grew as I did, and any Challenge I'd encounter I'd find a way to overcome.

My mother worked at restaurant jobs and helped me to get a job at a hotel where she had worked previously in the kitchen. I learned how to wash dishes and bus tables. It paid $1.25 an hour and I could eat free. So it was great for me. Since it was in the downtown area of Jacksonville, I had to catch the bus to get home. I continued to work it as I finished high school. I had to get up early to get to school because I walked about three miles daily to get there. I kept a wide-eyed enthusiasm about everything I was experiencing in my youth and tended to always look on the bright side of things most of the time.

I was raised by my grandmother and my godmother, who we called "Big Mama." They were very strict about disciplining me! I had a tight schedule, which taught me how to complete my daily tasks and plan for the following days, weeks and months. Big Mama worked as a maid for a private family and was a great role model for me while my mother worked. My three younger brothers always seemed distant, but we all loved each other as a family. I tried to be a good example as the oldest sibling and was the first to go to college and achieve my goals.

The discipline I received as a child played a big role in helping me to develop while growing up in the community. I was raised in a neighborhood where the parents cared and took the time to discipline their children by teaching them right from wrong and taught lessons in morality. I didn't know it at the time, but later I would come to value these times.

I focused much of my time on learning amateur radio because it allowed me to meet people and play chess. I spent lots of time listening to others speak about their communities and discovered we had many things in common. I was interested in Taekwondo and learned to focus my energy through meditation. Soon I was taking classes at a dojo in the downtown Jacksonville area. Later I formed a class of my own.

I seemed to learn best through repetition and was determined to understand things. Obstacles seemed to appear when I lost focus. This was an important part of my early learning years and I felt that I could accomplish anything I tried to learn.

Later, near high school graduation, I had a desire to help people and spoke with the Urban League who served our community. I had been a boy scout and was active in the church and the community. The Urban League was involved in a Law enforcement outreach and had a program called Jacksonville youth patrol sponsored by JSO. There I learned about the various areas of the Jacksonville Sheriff's Office and was exposed to several areas of the police department and the county jail. I later took the tests to apply for a job with the city and passed. Then I attended the police academy and was very excited that I would become a police officer and help protect and serve the community. Near my graduation, I was offered a chance to work in the Vice unit headed by Lt. Joe Kicklighter. I didn't wear a uniform but had a new opportunity to become a detective with the squad, so I worked hard and focused on being the best at whatever tasks I was assigned. I'd completed a number of cases and worked in an undercover capacity learning more about the interaction with State and even Federal agencies like FDLE and DEA. At one point I was working with Broward county Sheriff's office under the direction of Chief Nick Navarro, well known for drug intervention with Miami Vice. I gained experience on several large drug cases.

I married and had hoped to live a normal life but the relationship did not last and we were divorced. I ran into trouble at work too when my cover was blown, and I was nearly killed, so I made the decision to change careers. During a drug bust and raid, I was shot and later had to testify in the case. My life and my family had been threatened and I did not want to risk getting my family involved, so I resigned.

After leaving the sheriff's office, I sought to join the Air Force where I served in Okinawa, Japan and upon returning home to the US, I got married for the second time and we were happy for a while but the relationship ended. I went back to Florida where I wanted to complete my education and get into the medical field, so I worked toward completing school and also worked jobs to support my goals and myself. I studied at a few schools and worked in the medical field for a few years before deciding that I really wanted to learn to operate a business. So I started a part time vending machine company "Pablo Beach Vending," and started working in the fast food industry. I worked toward ownership of a franchise and learned a great deal about operating a restaurant and managing people. I enjoyed it so much that I took on large projects and multiple unit locations, eventually in a few southern states, which occupied most of my time.

I wanted to live in a major city and I had heard that the Olympic Games were coming to Atlanta, Ga. This was a perfect opportunity to start a new business venture and live in a progressive town. I'd heard many good things about Atlanta and the opportunities it could provide for a business, so I moved.

I drove to Atlanta and got lost. I took a a wrong turn and got on I-285, which circles the city, but I didn't know that at the time and after nearly two trips in a circle I got off to ask directions and get gas. I spoke with someone in Decatur who pointed me in the right direction finally and I arrived in downtown Atlanta (5 points area), parked, and went to the underground area to get directions to a local apartment complex in midtown. When I returned to the area where I parked my car I could not find it and moments later that sinking feeling of disbelief was creeping in. Someone stole my car. I had left money in it too, locked away in the glove box with my wallet. This was the start of my being homeless for about 13 months. A few years prior to the Olympics and in a city I didn't know, I felt overwhelmed but not defeated. I carried myself as I had always been taught with pride and dignity as I searched for help and resources.

I lived on the street for a few weeks before meeting someone who was sincere about helping me, Carl Booker. He could tell that I was in trouble too. I had not eaten for some time and grew dizzy when I stood for long periods. The first thing he told me about was the homeless shelter, which had free meals at noon daily. We stood in line and I was able to eat a few bites of a sandwich and some soup (it felt great to eat again). I met a few people who listened and helped me to get into a church outreach program "Cathedral of Faith" in South Atlanta where I lived, and got clothes and shelter for a few months while I wrote back to Florida to request a copy of my birth certificate to obtain an ID card again. I could not get work or temp labor without ID. Sister Jackson led the Outreach ministry and Dr. Jonathan Greer was pastor of the church.

A short while later I was working again and had started to regain my footing largely due to a few people who reached out to help me, and my new friend Carl and his family, who helped me to learn more about the city.

Being ambitious, I worked hard to leave the Church mission and get my own place to live. I worked odd jobs at Manpower (Temp labor) until I found work at Mayflower movers then I worked at WQXI, a local radio station selling advertising and doing some voiceover work. I had worked a part time job in radio previously and had some experience. Radio sales eventually allowed me to become an independent Marketing consultant and work on a contract basis with media advertising agencies, print and billboards.

It led to my growing my business to the point that I had to hire people to help me manage the company, and it seemed that my life was heading in a new direction. Within a few short years I'd gone from being homeless to running a multimillion dollar company again. I had struggled for some time to get things going, but now it seemed that good things were coming my way. I met a woman who seemed to like me and shortly afterward we got married but it ended only a few years later due to problems I could not help her to solve or overcome.

Even during the worst season of my life, when I was indicted by the Federal Government and accused of wrong-doing because I was doing marketing for a client that turned out to be a criminal, I wouldn't quit. That client and his associates were found guilty of criminal acts and fraud in real estate deals. Eventually, persistence and patience paid off and I was acquitted of all charges. After the stress of this four-year ordeal, I suffered a heart attack. I am alright now and much more health conscious. I am thankful for my mother and for Big Mama who raised me and for all of their prayers of support and protection. Most of all, I'm eternally grateful to close friends and loved ones who believed in me during these bleak situations.

I moved on to gain an even larger client base, and worked more than I'd ever been tasked to do before. I went back to school to learn and relearn, because technology was changing and many of the things I'd always hoped to do in marketing were now available for me to explore. I felt I had an advantage as a returning student, because I was mature in several ways and had learned to solve problems benefiting from the gifts they offered – often disguised as adversity.

In this chapter I'd like to provide a mental bridge to aid others who may encounter similar rough patches in life and let them know that anything is possible if you have faith and believe in yourself; you can overcome difficulties in time if you don't quit. I am involved in building an internship program to help Sales and Marketing career-oriented students and those who have good graphic arts skills online design mobile and digital ads for companies. As the concept gains popularity, I am developing a reality show format for students to compete for a space in the program on a national level. In addition, an accredited Business Marketing sciences program (Equivalent to an MBA) to provide basic understanding in Neuromarketing science and sales skills on an applied level with the students actually working with businesses and in the community. This will help small to medium sized businesses and help more entrepreneurs to get started now that the Internet can be used to level the playing field of business, and helps provide a digital platform for commerce.

About James

Dr. James Moss has been described as "a visionary thinker with a rare intellect." James coaches leaders of organizations on marketing strategies that result in more sales and higher profitability. His company uses applied Psychology and research (Neuromarketing) to New Media Marketing and Mobile Advertising solutions that produce sales through ads and promotions. Our digital/ mobile media and video content marketing solution uses a sophisticated yet simple strategy of Interrupt, Engage, Educate and Offer that has proven to be the most effective in converting suspects to prospects and winning sales.

James has been consulting with small to medium-sized businesses on marketing and business growth since 1988. James founded and developed a New Media digital Marketing/Mobile promotion system that is based on neuromarketing. James has built a vast network of marketing professionals and service providers throughout the United States, Canada, Mexico and parts of Europe and South America that he collaborates with in order to bring his clients best-of-breed solutions. AI SmartNet cloud solutions provide digital content and advertising to display devices (Billboards, placed based displays and mobile) over the Internet.

James is the Former Chairman of the US Global Marketing Alliance and he continues to speak and create outreach programs to help municipal business growth and youth development programs helping like-minded people to become successful in their own lives giving a hand-up instead of handouts.

James formerly worked for George S. May as a marketing consultant and business growth expert. His time with the May company gave him valuable insights into marketing and strategy that he still employs today.

James holds a Doctorate in Advanced Information Technology and Business Management from Robert Kennedy College. He is currently teaching marketing courses and providing career-oriented training for college and high school students.

James is an avid learner holding many degrees from various universities such as Harvard University, Massachusetts Institute of Technology (MIT), Mercer University, Florida State University, Baylor University, Florida College of Medicine, and the US Air Force. His vast education and expertise in the medical field allows James to understand how the mind works and how it will react to stimuli. His company then uses this information to produce the most effective marketing pieces possible.

One of the key things that separates James from other people in his field is that James has an extensive background in software application development. This allows James to blend his knowledge of how the brain works with marketing, strategy, and software in order to create the ultimate marketing solution for his clients. His clients rave about his customer service, follow though, and the value they receive from James.

CHAPTER 31

CREATING THE DREAM – From Cancer To Entrepreneur

BY ELIZABETH POTTER

Ever wonder ....what if? Ever had an event in your life that changed you forever? Good or bad, change is imminent. It seems the older we get, the harder it is to accept change. Sometimes if we do not embrace change it is forced upon us.

I was living my life raising my children like most do until one day I had one of the most heart wrenching experiences of my life ...change was forced upon me!

Everything changed in a blink of an eye it seemed. Your health is the most important thing cause if you don't have that, you cannot enjoy all that life has to offer to the fullest. After the fog lifted from my chemo brain I was in a place of now what? I can't go back, I can only go forward...but to where? Nothing was the same. Everything was different. I was different too. I was searching for some kind of familiarity. I blasted myself back to the past remembering when I was a child. Remembering when I would use the words "I Want". I remembered using them often. Did you? I also remembered the word "NO." "That was Then and this is Now!" I reminded myself. In my moment of perturbation I did after all promise the universe that I would do something really big and make a difference if I was allowed to live.

Due to my past experience my outlook on life had shifted dramatically. I dared to ask myself the question ...What if I became an Entrepreneur?

What would that look like? Who would I be? How could I make it happen?

The first and most difficult question I had to find the answer to was, "What do I really want?" Being a single mom, the only two things I knew for sure were...

(i). I wanted to be able to provide for my children

(ii). I wanted to be available for anything that they may need me for

I too was like a child …as I embarked on this new journey.

I began to do my research and read book after book. I purchased seminar after seminar. It almost became a rat race as the more I learned the more I needed to learn. People were calling me crazy and a seminar junkie. It did not bother me as I met many amazing people along the way that I had things in common with. Just like anything in life…. if you have no experience, you get to experience it all!

Being exposed to all the new ideas that I'd never heard before and listening to various speakers, influenced me to take action and spend on a continuous basis. Navigating the waters of the personal growth world can at times be very chaotic with information overload. The good news was that I gained clarity on what I didn't want. The biggest joke amongst my fellow seminar junkies was to create a seminar on how <u>not</u> to buy another one. But you don't know what you don't know and its all part of the learning experience. Everything is included!

According to statistics, the number one fear is public speaking. I am so thankful to all those who have the courage to talk on stage and share their knowledge. It's because of them I am where I am.

I had to keep reminding myself that just because something is for sale does not mean I have to buy it. There has to be a return on the investment.

As an Entrepreneur, learning how to manage your money can at times be very challenging. Never refuse a lender that wants to give you credit because when you need it most is when you can't get it. I remember when the bank wanted to give me a large Line of Credit. The amount scared me and I thought why on earth would I need that much? So I refused. Well little did I know that a year later I did indeed require that amount, but by then the lending boom had subsided and it was not available.

Ouch!!! When there is more month than money you have a problem! One of the biggest failures in business is underestimating the amount of capital required.

I remember worrying if I would have enough money to keep funding my education. There was still so much that I didn't understand or know. Amazing things can happen if you ask yourself the question "How can I?" I continued to keep growing myself and the result was my organizing business began to grow too. One of my mentors once told me, "If you want to earn more money, help more people!"

Sometimes it is not what you do but more in how you do it. I began to really listen to my client's concerns and I either provided the answers for them or found someone who could help them. By sharing ideas with my clients it became apparent that my investment was providing value not only to me, but also to them. Years later we are all still learning and growing together.

As time went on, something kept tugging at me. I realized that I was not fulfilling my earlier promise to the universe. I like my organizing business and working with business owners, but there was something missing – I just didn't know what.

Finally one day I found the answer. When I heard the concept it was one of those moments where a light bulb goes off. The ignition of an idea. The moment of inner knowing. The chance to be a part of something big in a community of like-minded individuals for the betterment of all. Martin Luther King's "I Have A Dream!" speech was ringing loud and clear in my heart and my mind.

With the economy heading into the downturn, I saw the opportunity to do something really big and make a difference. It was the opportunity to help many people thru' their adversities and come out the other side making it a win-win. It was the answer to my question of how can I make a big difference? Clarity and passion is the power to move you to action. Once you have a clear map of what you want, you become unstoppable regardless of the obstacles that arise along the way. As long as you never give up and keep on growing yourself to be bigger than the problem … anything is possible!

There are millions of people with credit issues and I understand how things can go sideways in a blink of an eye. When your world stops and everything keeps going on without you. When we are in the ditch, we know we are there and it doesn't help when people keep reminding us and demanding we get ourselves out without offering solutions.

I believe that most people are genuine and when things happen all they need is a helping hand just like when a child falls. We, as parents are there to pick them up, give them a hug and say its OK. They smile at us and continue on with renewed vigor.

One of my favorite quotes by Buckminister Fuller …
"You never change things by fighting the existing reality. To change something, build a new model that makes the existing model obsolete."

When I opened my credit buying company, it was not to be like the others, but to be different and be dedicated to treating people with dignity and respect.

As I started this new journey with excitement, I knew it would be a huge project and the main question I asked myself was, "Who do I have to become to make it all happen?" The answer was very daunting as I would have to become someone I was not at that moment. I would have to keep growing myself and really challenge myself to act in spite of fear. To live outside my comfort zone for a very long time. The road is scary when you travel alone. The first thing I thought of was to acquire a partner so I was not.

The word partner by definition *"the state or condition of being a* ***partner****; participation; association; joint interest."* To me, it meant that if we work together, it would make things a little easier and a little more enjoyable to have someone to share the experience with. Unfortunately a couple years in; that partnership was dissolved. The decision was extremely difficult to make for me. One more time pushing the boundaries of my comfort zone! It's that "Oh Crap!" moment that happens when doubt and fear tries to overtake your mind.

Once again I found myself in a place of now what? I was looking for people to tell me what to do. This was a bad habit to have as it caused me more grief than good most times. It took me several times to fall into this place of "now what" before I realized that was the wrong question to be asking. The right question is always "HOW CAN I?" Until I asked myself that question I was stuck in a ditch spinning my wheels going nowhere.

Because of my promise, the internal driver would never allow me to give up no matter how scary it is! The one thing I did know was that based on my past, I have the ability .... just like everyone else .... to always find or create a way.

The next thing I did was to seek out mentors specializing in whatever area I needed assistance in. One of my mentors once told me, "Don't do a word I say!" it took me several years to figure that one out.

The one thing I always remember is that I am thankful that I have choice. I can choose if I want to be a victim of my choices or be the hero of my choices. It has been my experience that if I learn to control myself it is more empowering. It's my mind and my life and how I choose to live it is up to me. The mind is very powerful and it will take you where you want to go as long as you know how to drive it!

Next I hired a business coach with an outside unbiased opinion that I could discuss ideas, doubts, and fears with. A coach can be a valuable asset as they are the best people to talk to because they are trained to hook your mind to find solutions. Just make sure you hire the right one for whatever obstacle you need assistance with. Most times I found that the answers lie within providing I have enough information to make a decision. Other times I ask for advice and consider the advice with relevant data.

The one thing I struggle with on occasion is to pay myself first in time and money. I always make sure everyone is taken care of first. I am not sure if it's how I am wired or if it's because I am a mom. Either way, it is a part of who I am and what I stand for, so I have learned to accept it and enjoy all that life has to offer. To me the greatest gifts are my children and one of the greatest inventions is the video game. It has taken many years of training to trust myself and at times when I am in the ditch, I just recall the Mario Cart game I play with my kids ...Whooo hooo! What a ride!

My commitment to continuously grow myself and to helping others along the way is a passion and purpose that makes life worth living. Things just keep getting better and better everyday!

In closing I'd like to share one more quote I read from Oprah Winfrey….

"I've come to believe that each of us has a personal calling that's as unique as a fingerprint--and that the best way to succeed is to discover what you love and then find a way to offer it to others in the form of service, working hard, and also allowing."

LIFE LESSONS LEARNED

- Everything is a choice. You can choose your life or let life happen to you.
- The best way out of your problem is asking yourself "HOW CAN I?"
- Change is imminent. Embrace it.
- Never underestimate the amount of capital required.
- Creating the right team is an essential to take you where you want to go.
- Find your passion and purpose and you become unstoppable.
- Trust yourself. Only you know what's right for you.

About Elizabeth

Elizabeth brings over 25 years of experience with logistics, production, customer service and financing. She opened her first business in 2006 offering book-keeping services. In 2008 she expanded as a Professional Organizer specializing in small business. Feedback from clients and realizing a niche for other services, Elizabeth formed a new company Systemized For Play Ltd in July 2010. (www.systemizedforplay.com)

She has a special talent that helps business owners work through their chaos and create simple systems unique to them. She has built a reputation as a reliable, effective, and proactive consultant. Elizabeth has worked with many small business owners by creating systems that help them understand and achieve greater efficiency, profitability and more free time.

Her largest project and passion was formed in 2009. **LP Credit Resolution, LLC a credit buying company that specializes in credit card accounts. The company is committed to helping at least 10,000 people re-build their lives by treating them with dignity and respect, utilizing the resources of CFS2 an outside the norm financial recovery agency who in 2013 won the "Friends of the Consumer Award." (www.lpcreditresolution.com and http://www.cfstwo.com/)**

In July of 2012, she co-authored *Cracking The Success Code* which made it to #2 Best Seller on Amazon. Elizabeth is a 2012 "Quilly Award" winner and was a guest on the Brian Tracy Show aired on ABC, NBC, CBS and Fox Affiliate stations. She was also in USA Today. In addition, she also appeared in the February 2013 issue of Forbes Magazine. Elizabeth Potter has also been a keynote speaker in New York with Steve Forbes.

Elizabeth has trained in the areas of computer science, economics, accounting software, business management, sales and marketing. She is a proud member of the Professional Organizers of Canada, CEO Space, as well as a member of the Progressive Group For Independent Business (PGIB).

CHAPTER 32

THE SATISFACTION OF SUCCESS BY GOING AGAINST THE GRAIN

BY JAY OLSON

When I grew up I always wanted to be an entrepreneur. In middle school and high school, I had a baseball card business where I worked with people all over the country buying and selling over 500,000 cards and just loved it.

For one, I like baseball, so that really helped. But the analysis of it, it was just a miniature stock market for me. It was the buy and sell; it was a thrill and I loved it.

At about the same time, I also had a lawn mowing business with another friend for a few years. We went door-to-door earning the business of 15 or so clients around various neighborhoods in Southwest Houston and maintained their yards until I had to leave for college.

Additionally, I was very good at math as an 18-year-old, and maybe just a slight bit arrogant about it. One of my teachers told me, "If you think you're so good at math, you should be an actuary. That's the best thing you can do with math." So, of course, despite not having any idea what that was, I took the challenge and replied, "Fine! I'm going to go and do that!"

When I got to the University of Texas, I sought out the Actuarial Program, figured out what it actually was and did really well with it. I was at the top of my class and had the typical 21-year-old aspirations. I was going to be a millionaire by age 30, retire when I got to 40; all your typical youthful blustery dreams: "Fast cars, big houses...."

Luckily though, because I took care of my studies during the school year, it afforded me the opportunity to travel during my summers in college. The first summer, a friend and I drove up to New York to be camp counselors in the Catskills.

The next year I ratcheted it up a bit and spent the summer in Europe working half the time and backpacking all over the continent for the other half. I was fortunate to have paid for the entire trip from the proceeds of selling the baseball card business when I got to college.

The Europe trip really gave me the travel bug, so as soon as I returned I started planning the next one. The following summer I bought a one-way ticket to Australia, having no idea when I was coming back or how. I would just figure it out as I went. Theoretically, I did study abroad there, but there was no actual studying going on (I only needed a couple of elective courses by this point). I made many friends and learned a lot about the culture and the people, but little of it was in the classroom.

After finishing study abroad, I traveled around Australia and New Zealand for a few months, then through Southeast Asia, the Himalayas, the Middle East and just kept going West until eventually I made it back home. And then it was time to start in the "real" world.

My travels changed who I was as a person and altered my priorities. I had seen the world and saw what my place was in it. I was more interested in really helping people, affecting change - the 'save the world' mentality. But it was time for a little bit of reality, so I went forward with the actuarial career as I had been trained to do. With my background, it was easy to find a job, so I was an actuary for an insurance company for a few years in Houston. As it turns out, being an actuary wasn't that interesting, at least not compared to what I had seen in my travels.

I was good at the job and it paid well. I moved up the ranks, but it just wasn't my passion. Whenever someone asked me, "What do you do?" I would quickly change the subject to travel, photography, sports - anything other than my job. In the end, it seemed that the main purpose of the job was earning a paycheck to afford to travel any chance I got, which was what I really wanted to do.

I looked into other careers, thinking maybe I should do something I'm more interested in. However, anytime I put my resume out there, several head hunters would call with offers of actuarial jobs all over the country. Eventually, I figured that I've always wanted to see what it was like to live somewhere else (which in a way is like traveling all the time), so I decided to try continuing as an actuary in a different part of the country.

I made a short list of cities I was interested in and told the headhunters, "If you can find me something in one of those cities I'll go." This resulted in a dozen or so interviews all over the country, which was fun and exciting, but also exhausting. As it turned out, a job in Boston worked out best, so I ended up in "The Hub." I lived up there for 11 years, met my wife Rebecca as well as many other friends, raised our son through age 3, and really enjoyed my time there. But still the same issue persisted with the actuarial career. It still was just a job. It was okay and it paid well, it just wasn't that interesting.

Finally in my last job as an actuary, I was able to position my role a little bit more to do the things I enjoyed doing. I found that, as opposed to staying in a cubicle and crunching numbers, that I really liked mentoring and training other employees, setting up the social events; all the things that were not your true actuarial duties. They were more pulling towards the other side of the personality spectrum of introverted analyst versus outgoing networking-type person.

Late in my actuarial career, my son Matthew was born and my parental instincts kicked in. Anyone who is a parent understands the feeling when you have a kid of taking stock of your life and thinking deeply about it. You wonder: is he going to be proud to say, "Yeah, my dad sits in a cube somewhere and pushes numbers from one side of the page to the other, and some millionaire makes a few more dollars based on what he did." Or do yearn to have him able to say "My dad really helps people and is a positive influence in their lives"?

So I said to myself, "That's enough. I've done this for 13 years; it's run its course. Now I'm going to go do what I want." I asked myself what was going to make me feel fulfilled and talked it through with my family and friends to get their thoughts. They all agreed that I needed to go after what I really felt was my calling – to help people and truly affect change. Soon after, I officially retired from the actuarial game, throwing a retirement party complete with champagne, friends, laughs and the whole production. The 21-year-old me was a little disappointed that I wasn't a millionaire at age 30 (although I didn't actually care at this point), but by age 38, I had retired. Hitting 50% on the lofty goals of a 21 year old isn't bad, right?

My father-in-law Harvey and his business partner David are financial planners, and I was always intrigued by what they did. The first thing I tried in the search for career fulfillment was working with them. I assisted in running their seminars and went along on their client visits, providing in-depth analysis to aid their discussions and found that I really enjoyed it. I loved working individually with people; teaching and showing them how they can help themselves and ways we could help and add value. The less enjoyable part for me was attracting the clients via seminars, as it seemed like too much of a sales role for me.

Nonetheless, I prepared to run my own seminars and was ready to do my first one when we decided to move back to Houston. The move meant starting from scratch no matter what I chose to do for work, so I had a decision to make:

- Should I set up my own financial planning business in Houston?
- Would I be best served going back into the corporate world?
- Do I start some other kind of business and do what I always wanted to do?

I decided to go for it and take that chance. I looked at several franchise opportunities and then it just kind of hit me – start an insurance agency.

I met my District Manager / Business Coach Dennis, who presented me the opportunity to run an insurance agency for Farmers Insurance under his coaching model. The standard insurance agent is a great salesperson first, and they may or may not know much about insurance. I had no interest in being a salesman, but knew that my in-depth knowledge of insurance and interest in teaching and truly helping people would make me a great fit. More than anything though, I wanted to run a business and with the coaching model Dennis was running, it was a perfect fit to my skills and interests and I could be very successful with it.

It is fortuitous that I met Dennis when I did. Frankly, had I met another District Manager who just said, "I'm going to teach you how to sell. You're going to be awesome." I would not have been interested and instead would have opted for something else. The key concept was to build a business and to build it big. So I didn't open an agency to be a salesperson; I got into this to be a business owner and to help people.

It's easy to wonder why I didn't think of running an insurance agency earlier. As an actuary, I had seen insurance agents before and thought that their roles looked much more interesting than what I was doing at the time. So, this was my opportunity to start a business in something I already knew very well.

My goal from the start was to truly help people. It was a huge advantage starting out that I could really sit down with clients and say, "This is the big picture. You're asking me about these little details over there. We'll talk about that, but THIS key piece is what you need to look at. THIS is the important thing." I was not just trying to sell them something; I really was trying to provide solutions. And, thus "The solutions guys" moniker was created.

The key premise in building the agency is treating everyone on the staff like an owner, and putting people in the right positions based on their personalities. If somebody is an analyst and they want to crunch numbers and work on processes, fine. There's that role in the agency. If somebody wants to do sales and they don't want to do paperwork, then we put them in that position. We also place a strong emphasis on balance in our lives, and I have had the fortune to spend great quality time with my family, including coaching Matthew's Little League team.

Coming from an analytical background, my personality type does not lead to the direct sales role. However, I love working with people, and have found I am really good at networking and branding the agency. In my mind, it is just being friendly. Additionally, I enjoy discussing with other business owners how we can help each other's businesses thrive and am pleased to be able to offer some excellent solutions that benefit us all.

Frankly, my product (insurance) is a commodity that can be purchased from over 1,000 agents in my city. It is our philosophy of collaboration with the client and providing them solutions that really adds value and differentiates us from other agencies down the road. I believe in this concept so much that our brand states – "We are the solutions guys."

This philosophy has worked well and the agency has grown at a fantastic pace. In our first six months, we earned the Toppers Club achievement, representing the top 10% of all of Famers Insurance agencies country-wide. Within the first year, we received the Championship designation, which is actually the top 1% of Farmers agencies. There are 14,000 Farmers agents in the U.S., and we are the top 1% of that. That is: the third largest insurance company and we are considered the top 1% - in the first year!

Perhaps the neatest though was that I won a production contest for the entire Houston area and as a reward got to throw out the opening pitch at a Houston Astros game. For this lifelong fan, it was a dream come true. And, despite being a little nervous and having my friends warn me not to bounce the pitch and end up on ESPN blooper reels, I threw a perfect strike!

Obviously, we are very proud of these achievements, but I know that we are just scratching the surface. Our agency is going to go way past that. We have so many cool things that we are in the process of setting up, and it will take the agency to much higher levels.

In addition to growing the agency and earning fantastic accolades, I take great pride in the fact that we are providing excellent solutions for both individuals and businesses and helping them prosper with our solutions. Also, we have found some great people for the agency; folks who, like me, were miscast in their previous roles but are thriving now that they have been put into places that fit their personality strengths.

The excitement of where we are going is evident. As an actuary, when someone asked me what I did for work I replied with "Well, um, ah… let's talk about something else," and quickly tried to change the subject. Now, I actually love to talk about what I do. I'm affecting change, not just for our clients, but also for the people within the agency. And I'm growing a successful business from scratch. It's a very exhilarating and fulfilling. I can't wait to see what we will do next.

About Jay

Jay Olson was born and raised in Houston, Texas and received his Bachelors degree in Finance with concentrations in Actuarial Studies, Risk Management, and Insurance from the University of Texas at Austin. He was at the top of his class, earning multiple scholarships, getting published in a national insurance publication, and twice being awarded the role of paid assistant to the head of the actuarial program.

He worked for 13 years as an actuary for companies in Houston and Boston, before returning home to be closer to family and start his own insurance agency with Farmers Insurance.

His hobbies include UT football, Astros baseball, skiing, fantasy baseball (his statistical background has helped him win several championships), biking and playing with his son, and coaching his son's T-ball team. An avid traveler, Jay has traveled to nearly 50 countries on six continents, including a year long "round the world" trip in college. Locally, he has visited 47 of the United States and is always planning the next trip in the back of his mind.

Since joining Farmers, Jay has achieved the prestigious Toppers Club and Championship distinction (representing the top 1% of all Farmers agents) in every year eligible and was the first agent ever in his district to achieve both in his first year in the business.

Perhaps his proudest moment was winning a city-wide Farmers production contest in the summer of 2012, where the prize was getting to throw out the opening pitch at a Houston Astros game. He is happy to say that despite being a little nervous and the taunting by friends to not bounce the pitch, he threw a perfect strike.

The Olson Insurance Group is located in West Houston and continues to grow at a rapid pace while remaining an excellent place for everyone to work.

Jay is very close with his family; his parents Art and Dixie, brother Kyle, as well as mother-in-law Andi, all live nearby and spend lots of fun time with Jay, his wife Rebecca, and their 5-year-old son Matthew.

CHAPTER 33

THE GIRL CAN TAKE A PUNCH

BY KARLA SILVER

It's August 2001. It's 3:00 a.m. I've woken up in the middle of the night. Again.

It feels like it's the millionth night in a row where I wake up in the middle of the night, totally burned out from my job, and I'm miserable. I hate it. The technology sector is almost in ruins and my life feels the same way.

The Internet/Technology sectors have been one of the best places in the world to work. I'd been part of the team in charge of creating the whole Internet business model at a company called Excite.com, and I'm enjoying the perks of stock options, stock splits, shareholder euphoria and a job that can't be beat with the pay to match.

And yet something doesn't feel right. Deep down something is bothering me but I just can't put my finger on it. I start to think about my life as a whole. Isn't this job and this career the dream career I always wanted? And suddenly it dawns on me. My life is so out of balance that I actually don't have a life at all. I am living and breathing my career. That's when everything began to change for me.

I jumped out of bed and started making a list of things that would make up my dream life. I had never thought of that before... *what I* really *wanted.* Not what was best for my next career step, the next big deal or promotion, etc., but what I really wanted my life to look like. *I began to define what I wanted.*

I'd have my own business, a beach body, speak French, live somewhere beautiful and travel the world. The list went on and on. You know… that list of things you've always wished for and wanted, even fantasized about? The list you have, but for some reason keeps getting pushed to the back of the to-do list over and over again. I was tired of that – I wanted to take action **now**. I wanted to live a life of my own design. I wanted everything on my list. I wanted my life back.

The next day I took a leave of absence. I was half relieved and half terrified. I was taking a huge leap of faith. I didn't have a plan, just a general notion and a feeling that a better life was possible. I didn't have the blueprint or the solution yet, but I was officially on the hunt to piece together how I was going to make this happen – in all areas of my life.

At that moment, I was so hopeful, so optimistic. But life has a funny way of giving you a reality check. It turns out optimism doesn't necessarily make anything easier.

Fast forward two months later, and I'm completely lost. I still have no direction. I'm listless and drifting. What should I do? Then my husband decided that he would leave me. See, he had felt so ignored in my pursuit of the next job/promotion/deal, etc., that he had had enough and wanted to find someone else that would actually BE in a real relationship with him.

That was the deepest pit of despair that I have ever been in. I crawled into bed for a month (or two or three) and just ignored the world. Those months were some of the loneliest months I have ever had. How could I have left my job at Excite only to end up questioning everything? More importantly, what the hell was I going to do now?

I couldn't help but wonder – had I made the right choices? Was I crazy for leaving Excite and thinking that I could ever build a business around the lifestyle I wanted to live? At the time, all I wanted to do was move forward… somehow. I had lost track of my quest to design my life, and just wanted to go a day or two without crying.

Finally I got out of bed. I travelled to visit a friend in Paris (about six times!), went to school in the UK at Oxford University, went on safaris in Kenya and Tanzania, travelled to Australia, and moved to San Francisco. It was fun, but it wasn't making a living or a life. I was really just avoiding life.

I looked at franchises, and considered buying an established business. I even thought at one point that I would open a spa, but all of those options felt like I was just buying myself a job. All of those options would put me right back where I was before, and look what that cost me.

I woke up every morning feeling emotionally drained. I can't remember another time in my life where I've ever felt so drained. So devoid of energy, I just felt lifeless... If you've ever been in this kind of circumstance, you know what I mean. It wasn't just the break up that had me down, it was finding myself embarking on yet another new path, more alone than ever and feeling very uncertain about my future. I was scared out of my mind.

Despite all the good things, and positive progress around me, I'm human and therefore susceptible to nature's "flight-or-fight" syndrome whenever I feel fear. And I do feel fear. I'm no different than you. We all do at some time.

You need to know you're <u>not</u> alone in feeling these feelings. I hear you - I've talked with literally thousands of you that experienced incredible lows...and I want to tell you, you're <u>not</u> alone. But it's these fears that may keep you stuck. And I was stuck.

But I could feel it - there was still something deep down inside me - gears churning, not as quickly as before, but enough so that I felt uncomfortable doing nothing. Slowly but surely I got up. If you want to succeed you need to override your natural desire to flee and stay and fight. Fight on for another day. Truly successful people make the choice to feel the fear and move forward anyway.

That day, despite my overwhelming desire to flee, I made the conscious decision to fight. As you can imagine - 99% of me didn't want to get up. Getting back into bed and sleeping for a year sounded much more appealing. But I got up... slowly and surely I forced myself to get up. And that was one of the best decisions I ever made.

Looking back at it now I've realized getting up is 90% of the battle. Life is going to knock you down and your ability to get back up is what makes all the difference in the world. And thank God I did get back up. Shortly after, I met the man of my dreams and began building a life with him. And just a few short months after that, I answered an ad online which led me to meet a group of crazy-fun and successful Internet marketers, some of whom have become my best friends.

I began to feel slightly more recharged. The fire inside me was glowing a little brighter and I felt that all may not be lost after all. The universe was giving me a sign. Over the course of the next few years, things started to slowly change for me. I'm not saying this was the only challenge I ran into...far from it. In fact I'd need a whole book to write down all the struggles I've overcome on my path to success. But I continued to persist, and this persistence has led me to one single realization that changed everything for me.

I'm going warn you - initially you may not think its revolutionary, and when you read it, you may think to yourself "That's it?" But those of you who "get it," you know that it's BIG.

It was the simple realization that if someone had accomplished it before I had, that not only was it possible for me too, but the rocky road ahead was now literally paved in gold.

Read it again.

There's something amazing about our ability to observe others - to ask questions - and to find the missing puzzle pieces in our own lives based on the experiences of others. Even though I was satisfied with how my business was going, I couldn't help but think about that list I had made years ago, just before I left Excite. Even though my business was going well, and my personal life was fantastic, if I had to grade my progress on all of my other goals it would be a streak of D's. Yikes.

It was honestly a little overwhelming thinking about all the things I hadn't gotten to do yet (sound familiar?) but were very much a part of my list - that list that I had made detailing that version of myself that exists in my wildest dreams. Even worse is that it wasn't until later that I had my second "a-ha" moment - when I finally asked myself:

Why don't I look to other people who have paved the way?

There are many people out there who have automated their businesses at the million (or billion) dollar level, more than I have, who live and work all over the world, who have learned to speak a second language, to dance, to surf, to rock a beach body, to play the guitar - you name it. That road has been paved hundreds and thousands of times for me, or anyone.

What's stopping me from applying the exact same process I used to build my business and apply it to grow my business bigger and better as well as in all the other areas of my life I want to improve? The answer is…nothing!

You're probably thinking ...how is this even possible? Listen, I'm not that out of my mind, I'm just dead set determined never to live a life of mediocrity in any area of my life. As far as I know, we have one life to live and it's ours to decide what to do with it. It's never too late to change the trajectory we're on.

It's not always going to be easy, but we don't need easy... we just need *possible. It was time to DESIGN MY LIFE.*

So… I went back to that list and added to it. I read a ton of books and blogs about other people who were living their best lives. I studied what other people had done. I consumed information like a beast.

I had met the man of my dreams. I was earning an income online without selling my soul to corporate America. Now it was time to step out on a limb and do what I had always wanted to do.

I wanted to live, love, work and travel all at once - to actually design my life!

So here is what I did:

1. I specifically defined what I wanted to do. I mean *everything.* What my perfect day looked like. What my perfect relationship felt like. What I felt and looked like. Everything. AND I wrote it all down – every last detail.
2. I found a business that didn't require me to **be** in any one place. That meant being able to work remotely, online from anywhere in the world. This way I could pay for my lifestyle as I lived my lifestyle.
3. I decided to take action. Making a move today is always better

than tomorrow, because as you and I know, tomorrow never actually comes.

On September 28, 2008, all of our stuff went into storage, and since then, my husband and I have lived all over the world.

We've walked the ancient streets of Rome, got married in Tuscany, learned wine-making secrets in Portugal, studied with personal development gurus in Hawaii, made tortillas in Mexico, lazed on the beach in Spain, and so much more. The memories and experiences and friends that we've created together beat anything I could have achieved while working a job, or simply accepting what came my way in the world.

Most importantly to us, we weren't travelling the world on a shoestring. No youth hostels, budget hotels, or rail passes. No third-rate villas, no teeny cars, mass transit or bad restaurants. That kind of travel is fine, but it isn't for us. We are "luxury vagabonds," not couchsurfers. If we were going to travel, we were going to travel in comfort, have someone else take care of our luggage, and go and do and see and eat what we wanted, when we wanted.

It hasn't all been easy. We've had enormous financial ups and downs, made incredibly bad decisions, and started in businesses that ultimately failed. But all these ups and downs have been on ***our*** terms, and each one has played an important part in our wonderful journey.

Part of me knows that I could be doing more. I'm still looking for new and better ways to automate my income, make more, save more and be more. There are areas of my life with room for improvement. I definitely don't have that beach body yet, I can't speak French or Spanish *yet*, there are many relationships in my life I could improve, I can't surf, dance, sing or play the guitar. But I'm excited to continue working on my to-do list and designing my future, even better than I ever imagined.

Are you ready to live a life of your own design? I've helped many people live the life of their dreams. When you are ready, I can help you. Just go to: www.KarlaSilver.com, or www.luxuryvagabonds.com.

I've designed my life. And you can too.

So, what are we waiting for? Let's go!

About Karla

Meet the "Luxury Vagabond" known as Karla Silver – an accomplished entrepreneur, best-selling author, and passionate advocate for Lifestyle Design.

Karla was born on the East Coast of the US, but calls the world her home. Living a non-traditional life, Karla and her husband elected to put all of their "stuff" in storage back in 2008 and have lived all over the globe since. As "luxury vagabonds," they have lived in California, Spain, Hawaii, Acapulco, Portugal, Italy, France, Bahamas, Mexico, and most recently Palm Springs, California.

Karla is a powerhouse entrepreneur, speaker and Internet marketer. Purely for fun, she dabbles in writing, art, cooking, and golf.

Karla Silver has a solid background in Business Development, Management and Internet marketing as well as Direct Sales. Karla's track record of success spans 30+ years, including working with various startups such as MTV: Music Television and Excite.com. She has built successful sales teams worldwide while creating innovative solutions for many of the top brands in the world.

In the last few years, Karla has:

- Launched a bestselling book
- Co-founded a company that provides online marketing solutions to local businesses in North America
- Helped thousands of entrepreneurs succeed online
- Co-created the Super Saturday Spirit Sale

Contact Information

Karla Silver
949 313 7968
karla@karlasilver.com

http://karlasilver.com/
www.luxuryvagabonds.com

www.linkedin.com/in/karlasilver/
http://www.facebook.com/karlakeysersilver

CHAPTER 34

THE 3 R'S: Referrals – Real Estate – Relationships

BY MARK RAFAIL

It was the 80's in Egypt and the persecution of Christians in the country was reaching a boiling point. This was no place to raise children, my parents thought. So Steven and Louris Rafail decided to migrate to a safe place to have a family. So my parents moved to Houston where my brother Ben, and I were both born. Funny how oblivious you can be as a child, but I can't even imagine what my parents must have gone through. Two immigrants who knew no special trades and having to learn English at the same time. Needless to say, my parents took work where they could get it, which means their opportunities were limited. My father worked in the fast food industry for 20 years and my mother worked in retail her whole life, just so my brother and I could have an opportunity to go to college and have a better life. Our family has always had a strong faith in Christ, and I thank Him everyday for my parents.

In 2001, I graduated High School and had no idea what I was going to do. Luckily one of my best friends suggested we apply to a Junior College, which was an educational path that led to Texas A&M University if you worked hard and got the grades. So I did what was necessary and I persisted. I ended up getting the grades I needed while working to support myself. It was at that time I would start to look around at all the students who didn't have to pay for things on their own and how they took it for granted. It made me think of my parents. That motivated me to work even harder and I graduated from Texas A&M University.

So now it was time to get a job, right? Little did I know that the economy was not that great and the only job a Bachelor of Arts in History could get was a sales job. So I took that job while living with my parents. I walked out every morning in a suit because I knew my parents were so proud I had graduated and gotten this great job. Little did they know I had to walk into 50 businesses a day DOOR-TO-DOOR and there was nothing great about it, at least that's what I thought. But as most struggles in life are...this job was a blessing in disguise. I ended up growing up as a person, and in business learning how to communicate with business owners and clients, and more importantly, I began to learn how to build solid relationships. I sold business telcom to businesses from 3-50 employees and began to understand the struggles and successes of small business owners. A year and half later, I began to receive top sales accolades and was offered a job in the insurance industry by my sales manager in telcom. His father owned an insurance agency and I was told if I can sell telcom I could sell anything! So I quit my job with my first mortgage and car note weighing on my back and thought, I can do this.

After several months, it turns out I was the worst insurance salesman ever! $600 paychecks and $20,000 in debt on credit cards as a 25 year old was a little much to grasp. So I started working multiple jobs just to get by. A good friend of mine from Junior High, Bryant Black, saw me struggling and was able to get me an interview with the oil and gas company he worked for. Thankfully I got the job! I was happy to have colleagues again, a name badge on my hip with normal hours and health insurance! I thought this was it, I will be a normal guy with a normal job.

A few months went by and America falls into a recession. A massive lay-off occurs, and I am the newest person there, so it was fair to say I was one of the first to get laid off. So here we go again was my thought, but that's when I met my lovely wife to be, when I was at my worst. She could never figure out what the heck I did. Was it insurance, answering phones at a flooring store, helping at a friend's restaurant? So she met me at the worst time and just happened to ask me if I needed part-time work doing health screenings for her company? I was so excited and played it cool as if I did not needed the money, but boy was she a blessing. I can truly say that meeting Sylvia, who is now my wife, was an amazing catalyst to the successes to come. Sylvia and I were acquaintances through our parents who were friends and had been going to the same church our whole life. We went to rival universities with her going to the University of Texas. It is sort of ironic that she became my boss then months later she would blindly be my business partner and a year later my fiancée. Unbelievable!

So even though I got some part time work with Sylvia, I still needed to do something, and for some crazy reason I felt I was getting pulled back to insurance. It killed me to fail at something so bad. I wanted to try it again. It had taken me down once, but I felt it was God's calling to try again. So in early 2008 I dove right back in to insurance and worked under a broker. The agent told me I would have to start completely over from scratch and the pay would be cut. I didn't care. With that said, their approach was dialing as many people as you can and "the sales will come," "it's a numbers game." Something about that didn't sit right with me. Well, I learned fast that I was not connecting with any of my potential clients at all because it was all over the phone from the Internet.

So I picked up the phone and called my Local Farmers Insurance contact Dennis McGough. Dennis would come to be my business coach, mentor and friend over the years. He listened to my struggles and said, "Why don't you start your own agency?" My ears perked up, me owning a business so young seemed far fetched. Dennis mentioned that I would be able to get a loan for the first two years. In mid-2009, with not many options, as the economy was at its weakest I decided I would open my own insurance Agency. I wanted to prove to myself and my family that I could be as successful as those business owners I was pitching telcom to. Although my family was pessimistic about the idea since I failed the first time; however, they realized I was going to do what I wanted. I then asked Sylvia and she asked what I would do differently than in the past? I answered that I would meet as many of my clients, realtors, apartment leasing agents and mortgage professionals as possible. I wanted to tailor my office to these centers of influence that always speak to clients needing insurance. So this is exactly what we did.

I handed Sylvia my cell phone to answer while I hit the streets like I was used to doing in the past with telcom. I was passionate about never providing bad insurance just to get the deal; instead I wanted to educate everyone on the importance of having the right coverage. I started by networking, going to apartment leasing offices, real-estate functions and getting involved in my community (when most people did not). People then saw my face over and over, so they gained TRUST in us.

That trust then turned in to REFERRALS, and boy was it much easier to discuss insurance with a client that called our agency. I knew in my first year that I had to be spending half my time out of the office to continue being the face of the business. Sylvia then took faith by answering my cell phone while I visited people. Then that turned into her getting licensed soon after, ditching the cell phone, and having eight phone lines three years later with a staff of seven. Sylvia has been the backbone of not only our business but to me as a person. Before we were even engaged, she knew I was struggling and lent me her savings to help start our agency. She knew nothing about insurance, but tried to help me succeed. She pushed me not to fail and I promised her one day things would get better and guess what…she believed in me. If it was not for Sylvia, I would not be in insurance today. So if you have a loved one that supports you in whatever you do, you are ahead of the game.

The next step was finding a "Gifted Team" as Coach Dennis would say. We all respect each other equally and truly see the big picture and where we are going. Nancy Flanary is the mother of the office and our Customer Service Manager. She has been such an asset to our operation and practices amazing customer service and knowledge of insurance day-in and day-out. Her hard work is out of passion to help others, and she can make someone that is crying from an accident laugh at the end, because she promises to hold our clients' hand. Matthew Wadyka was able to see our vision and left teaching to become an agent and now he runs our personal lines department. We were also able to recruit a telcom sales rep who learned the same values and determination that I learned to run our commercial department. George Abdelmessih already knew how to deal with business owners, which made it a perfect fit. Nancy and Matt actually car-pool in from the suburbs of Houston to our office close to downtown Houston. This has of course strengthened their relationship and helps pass the time in that awful traffic!

Finding a "Gifted Team" is a struggle so once you find the perfect fit, hire them and pay above the market to keep the staff! We have slowly added more staff to our operation and each member has specific duties based on their personalities. (People work better when they enjoy what they are doing!)

Having a gifted team has lead to a number of accolades from being in the top 1% of Farmers agencies, to being the only agency to have achieved top home/condo/renters production in our districts for 36 months straight!!! Apparently no agency has ever been even close to achieving this. This is based on our REAL ESTATE marketing, relationships we gained with people in the real estate industry, and the referrals that came from them.

We have been award the top-producing agency in our Houston district for the past two years and the largest agency in our district. Mind you - we are the youngest agency and have been in business the shortest time. The best part for me is I was able to change the way we market and build relationships with all our clients and find success in the industry I once failed in.

Those that saw us come up knew that we were something special, because we had a RELATIONSHIP with everyone - from our clients to all those in the real estate industry that continue to refer. Currently, we get 99% of business from referrals (with the occasional call-in from the web). Our relationships have built trust in those who know and do business with us. Price is not the first subject to discuss but the last. We really pride ourselves in providing a true insurance plan to protect our client's assets and families. Our passion can be seen even when we quote on someone's small 650 square foot apartment all the way up to multi-million dollar properties.

Competition – The word that scares us all. The truth is our agency believes in knowing our competition. In fact, we look at it more like an affiliate partner. We come across clients we may not be able to assist, therefore we would rather refer it to a friend in the industry than not be able to help the client. This goes both ways, if they cannot assist a client they will send them our way! It can be a beautiful relationship for many years and most people don't realize this.

We are on track to grow to 25 employees and give back more than we ever thought to our community, local charities and churches one day. It is four years later, we live across the street from our office and walk to work most days. I take my dog Chloe, which I have had since she was a pup and is basically our mascot. We look forward to being change agents and making this industry one that can be the center of their community with God's grace.

About Mark

Mark Rafail is a Best Selling Author, Top Producing Insurance Agent, and CEO of Rafail Insurance Group. His Agency is one of the top producing agencies in the Houston district and has been named "TOP 1% of Farmer's Agencies" in the country.

Mark is a specialist in the home, condo, life insurance and renters insurance niche and his agency has led production in this space every month for the last three years. Coming from humble beginnings, Mark's work ethic and persistence have allowed him to become one of the fastest rising entrepreneurs in the Insurance market. He attributes his success to a continual focus on the person, not the profits. Making sure his clients get the right policy is number one and building lasting relationships is the foundation of his business. Mark is involved with his Texas A&M Alumni Association and his church community.

Whether Mark is insuring a 650 square foot apartment or a multi-million dollar property, his passion for providing great service and a secure policy never wavers. He is proud to have his wife Sylvia as his business partner as well as having a staff he truly considers family.

For more information visit: www.RafailInsurance.com

CHAPTER 35

THE LAST REORGANIZATION – EVER!

BY MATTS REHNSTROM

I shut my eyes and breathe slowly, …deep and calm breaths. I can hear them around me. There are three, maybe four, of them. Their goals are to make me fall to the ground and to defeat me. It is a moment of concentration that seems like forever, as I know what will come. I hear a command and then all hell breaks loose. I move in the ways that I have been taught and I perform the techniques as well as I possibly can to defend myself. I have to change my balance, and my position, and as there are so many of them I also have to change the way that I usually respond to a situation like this. I need to stay calm and focused, otherwise I will lose concentration. My concentration is vital to handling the situation in the way that I have trained so hard for, and to make it possible to adapt to new attacks. All the years of training and experience pay off, as I am able to defend myself and control the opponents. After a couple of sweaty minutes, the command *jame*[1] reaches all of us.

As a practitioner of Ju-Jutsu for more than 30 years, I have studied the philosophies and techniques because they fascinate me. I have also studied other styles like Karate, Judo and Eskrima. When an opponent attacks you, the general technique is to use the opponent's force to your advantage. You also need to know the techniques very well. They need to be instinctive. You need to have good balance at the same time as you make your opponent lose his or her balance. You need to move around

1 Means "End" in Japanese

with full control of your body and mind, to be able to perform the techniques successfully. Your mind needs to be calm and focused on the challenge for you to be able to perform at your best.

The philosophy of Budo has also been a foundation for my work with enhancing organizations and making them more efficient. An organization must also be able to meet any challenges with full control and with well-known techniques. It needs to have balance to be able to be innovative and agile. As the organization is built on the people involved, they also need to have the calm mind, the focus, the balance, and the techniques to perform in the best way possible.

A CHALLENGING FAST-PACED WORLD

We live in a fast-paced world that changes rapidly. The speed of change is increasing every year. Our organizations stand before the customers increased demands for quality and speed of delivery. At the same time, demographics, globalization, and the fast-paced development of technology impacts our organizations' way of doing business. Also the number of organizations involved in delivering value to the customer increases as we move from a chain-of-delivery to a network-of-delivery.

You and your business have to be more skilled, focused and agile to not only survive in the future, but to thrive and to grow. If you are not improving, as the world around you is moving ahead, you will lose out to your competitors as they become better. If you do not want to go out of business you need to improve yourself and your business.

FROM CHANGE TO IMPROVEMENT

We talk about the need for change, but I believe that it is more important to talk about improvement. The world is changing and we need to improve ourselves to be able to cope with the changes. We cannot merely change. If I jump off a cliff, that would certainly be a change, but not necessarily an improvement. So you need to focus on improvement.

To improve is to do something in a better way than you did yesterday: to deliver better value to your customers than you did yesterday, to deliver higher quality than you did yesterday, and to have more fun and feel more satisfied with your accomplishments than you did yesterday.

To be able to improve, you need to know where you are and where you are heading, and you need to be able to measure your steps of improvement. If you do not know where you are, then you do not know what your surroundings look like or what your relationship is to them. If you do not know where you are heading, it does not matter where you are, as the Chinese proverb says.

Do not only change – improve!

NEED FOR ORGANIZATIONAL IMPROVEMENT

To be able to create the required improvement in your organization, you need to create an environment that supports agility. People need to focus on the right thing in their daily work, and they have got to take the time to think strategic thoughts and truly be a learning organization.

Agility

Agility in an organization is to be able to act in different ways based on the different demands of the customer. The agility is there to always act in the best interest of the customer; even if it is not according to the set plan. Agility is to adapt so that the customer finds the value you create outstanding. In that way they will be back for more service and they will point others in your direction.

Agility is also to be able to improve the work that you do as an organization. You need to adapt the processes according to the changes in the world around you.

Focus

To be able to deliver the outstanding value that both you and your customers want, you need to focus on those things that bring that value to the customer. If you do, then you can get rid of other things that do not create any value. There are three sorts of work: direct customer-value-creating work, indirect customer-value-creating work, and non customer-value-creating work. You need to get rid of the last one, as that is only waste. You need to be careful about the second one, as it must be as slim as possible. And you need to focus on the first one, as that is where the customer will experience your commitment to them.

Strategic thinking and learning organization

To be able to have an adaptable organization with focus, you need to have a structure that constantly allows for learning and for thinking the

"BIG" thoughts. These thoughts are the ones that will improve your business in the future. It is strategic and tactical thinking that puts the operational work in relation to the surroundings and where the organization is aiming to be in the future.

As a basis for those thoughts you need to have a culture and an environment where people may express themselves, and where their work is evaluated. That culture and environment does not blame people for doing something wrong, instead it raises issues and inspires the organization to learn from them.

A learning organization drives itself up the spiral of improvement, to constantly strive to be better tomorrow than today.

HOW TO THINK

How do you then create an organization that provides the aforementioned important components?

The 250-year-old remnant

The first step is to change, or improve, the way that you think about your current form of organization. You cannot be agile if you have an organization that is as stiff as a refrigerator. Most organizations out there are based on the more than 250-year-old linear organization. That form of organization is built on the basis of mass-producing goods that there is a high demand for, with employees that have a low, or non-existent, level of education, and that do not know how to read or write. There was also a way of thinking regarding the employees, that they were lazy and uninterested in doing a good job.

That is not the way the contemporary situation is. Today we have a very tough competitive situation where you have to earn the trust of the customer to sell your goods or services. The people that you have as employees are well educated, often with 12 to 16 years of education before they begin their career. They have all the information that they need by accessing the Internet, and they are more than skilled in finding it. Many of the employees also have the option of changing their place of work if they want to, so now they have something to compete for.

Trying to keep up

Organizations, both public and private, have reorganized themselves many times to cope with the changes. They do change but they do not improve much. The changes made are done in a way as if the linear organization, as a concept, is a constant that has to be there, and is only being altered in different ways on the same foundation.

To be able to meet the increasing demands in an even more challenging world you need to get rid of the linear organization. The linear organization is a stiff form that cannot be as agile as needed. You need to find another form of focusing on the creation of value for your customers and to make sure that your highly educated and committed personnel is giving their all for the customer and not wasting time on irrelevant work.

The new form of organization

You need to change the way that you think about the organization. You need to understand that there is a need to divide the organization into three structures. These three structures work tightly together with the focus of giving the customers an outstanding experience. Three structures that work together and that are agile enough to meet all the demands and changes that come in the future.

The three structures are:

1. The Process Structure
2. The Project Structure
3. The Competence Structure

To describe a layout of these structures in relation to each other, you could imagine them as two blocks: the left block and the right block. The left block contains the Process Structure and the Project Structure, while the right block contains the Competence Structure. The Process Structure and the Project Structure both deliver value to the customer, while the Competence Structure gives the processes and projects the right resources needed to perform well.

The Process Structure

A Process is series of repetitive activities that deliver value to the customers. A Process is not bound to one linear organization, but starts wherever the customer begins to have the need, and ends when that need is fulfilled. The Process Structure focuses on giving that value in a way that is cost-effective for the businesses involved.

As the process quite often is larger than just one organization, you have to see and understand the whole flow of the process. And your organization together with the others involved are partners in satisfying the customers' needs.

The Process Structure contains activities, and these activities require skills in order to be executed correctly. The activities are executed by roles, which have the required skills. Each role is then played by a person, who has the knowledge corresponding to the required skills.

Processes are constantly improved to be even better each time they are used – this is called *Kaizen* in Japanese.

The Project Structure

A Project is a group of people momentarily put together, to work together one time, to achieve a goal with a set and limited amount of resources. Projects are, today, a very common way of conducting work that is not suitable to be handled in the linear organization. Projects often consist of resources from several linear organizations, inside or outside the legal organization structure, e.g., a company or public authority.

To be managed in an effective way, a project must be guided by a project model. Unfortunately there are a lot of projects out there that do not have any model to support them, and if you look into the set-up of them, you will find that they are not actually projects at all.

Projects and processes work tightly together. A flow-through process that creates value to the customer can be seen as a project, sometimes large and sometimes small. A project on the other hand, that is run with the support of a project model, has processes within it, as the project model contains set activities in order to make the project efficient. These two structures never collide with each other, as they both work with the linear organization structure. They complement each other.

The Competence Structure

Competence is a resource to create and deliver value to your customers. Competence is the most important resource because it is packaged in us – humans. The human perspective, of course, differs from other resources like machines and computers. We, as humans, are more complex and autonomous than any machine today. That is why we need to take care of this resource in a special way. As mentioned, the people of today and tomorrow are quite different from people 200 years ago. We are not more intelligent, but we are more educated and know more, and we have a different conceptual view of the world.

The Competence Structure's only focus is to have knowledgeable people according to the competence strategy so that the Process Structure and Project Structures may conduct their business. The Competence Structure contains all personnel, and, together with these personnel, it is responsible for the development of knowledge. The personnel are divided into resource pools within the Competence Structure. These pools may be organized in different ways depending on where and how the business is run. The common method is to have different pools for different areas of knowledge, e.g. service, advance medical, IT, teachers and technicians. One pool can contain several sub-pools to refine the competence of the main pool. Pools may also float into each other, as there are multiple-knowledge crossovers that are important for some resources.

Within the Competence Structure there are resource managers that manage all resources regarding well-being, competence development and assignments in other structures.

Harmony and focus

The three structures work tightly together and each of them has an important role to play in the overall purpose of delivering value to the customers. As none of them interferes with each other, there is an even stronger force to create the desired value. All today's struggle between the linear organization on one hand and the projects and processes on the other is gone. And it is gone forever!

Forerunners

There are businesses out there that have already performed this transformation and some of them never had the old linear organization structure in the first place. Others are in the midst of their transformation.

Most of these businesses are doing very well. They have satisfied customers, proud employees and happy owners, since the financial results are excellent. Take the time to have a closer look at some of these examples: Google, W.L. Gore, Wholefoods Marketplace, IKEA, and Scania.

HOW TO ACT

What you need to do is to understand the above description of the new form of organization that must be formed. If you and your organization do not understand the foundation, it is very hard to make the necessary improvements. The first action is, therefore, to create an understanding within the management team of the organization that you want to improve. If the management team in today's linear organization does not support the improvements to be made, there is no way that you will ever succeed.

When the understanding and support is there, you have to start to model and design the business according to the above-mentioned structures. That work is described in detail in one of my other books. It is important to note that you need to have a project, supported by a project model, managed by a knowledgeable project manager, and with involvement from the employees, and, most importantly, the support and trust of the leadership of the organization.

This is the most important project you will ever have – you are creating a new bright future for you and your business!

Good Luck!

About Matts

Matts is appreciated for his skills and methods, with more than 20 years of experience of organizational development and leadership. He has held leading positions in several businesses and large projects. Matts has helped many organizations within manufacturing, service, and the public sector, to excel. Today Matts is working as an author, speaker, trainer and coach with assignments all over the world. He has helped his clients' businesses provide their customers with more value, while reducing costs and increasing revenues.

To read more about how Matts can help you achieve the same benefits, please visit: www.mattsrehnstrom.com.

References:

"Matts is a very competent and experienced operations developer. Based on his career and experiences, his leadership has influences from Sweden, the U.S. and Japan with Kaizen as the heart and soul. He is a structured person who supports and drives the customer forward, creates good results and is very appreciated by his co-workers."

- Patrik Samin, *Luleå University of Technology*

"Matts is genuinely dedicated to understanding how to make organizations more efficient. He unites his abilities and perspectives on both IT and operations in a unique way. This, combined with his strong social skills, enables him to handle the most difficult problems and to achieve ground-breaking results."

- Berne Landgren, *Gaia Leadership*

CHAPTER 36

THE ONE REASON WHY MOST PEOPLE FAIL TO REACH THEIR FULL PRODUCTIVITY POTENTIAL

BY MARLENE SCOTT

Often when I meet a new client, they will introduce themselves and tell me their job title: "I'm an entrepreneur and own a software company," or "I'm a manager at a University." In their mind, they have introduced themselves properly. To me, this is only the beginning. Why do I say this? Mainly because I work with clients to figure out how they can work more productively by understanding their personality. But, also, because most of them don't really know themselves.

And here is my confession—once upon a time, neither did I understand myself. When I was twenty-five years old, I thought I understood myself pretty well. After all, I had almost finished my studies that were encouraging me to reflect upon myself and my past. I had spent hours and hours talking and thinking about my upbringing, stories, and experiences. I thought I knew everything there was to know about myself.

Then I met a new friend. During one of our conversations, I explained to him that I am the type of person who really likes to know in advance what is going to happen each day. I have a longing for predictability, or so I told him. At first, he tried to be polite, but finally he couldn't help himself from laughing. I was shocked. Why did he not believe me?

When he later asked me to do a certain personality test and I saw the results of that test—confirmed by all kinds of experiences—I began to realize that I had made a big mistake. I had allowed expectations from people around me to take over my sense of who I was, and I had become "the girl who loved security." But, actually, I'm not that girl! When left to myself, I enjoy taking risks, traveling, and reading about all kind of new ideas. Also, I'm easily bored. It turned out I was a whole different person from what I thought I was. And I'm not the only one this has happened to. Now that I work with entrepreneurs and managers, I see the same problem happening over and over again to all kinds of people.

Do you really know who you are?

Let's be honest—it might sometimes be a painful process to get to the bottom of the truth about yourself. But in the end, it will bring you a lot of freedom and relief, even if you figure out that you are indeed the person that does crave security. Life becomes so much easier, as does working productively.

Together with that same friend and now business partner, TJ, I coach entrepreneurs and managers to become extremely productive. The first step in our program is always to get to know who you are—the real you. And I love encouraging people in that process.

Alex and Jeff are two business partners who were in our program.[1] They had worked together for over 10 years. We had been helping them find out where their respective strengths lied. Alex really liked having all the facts. He was sure to have all the information before he started a project, but could be slow in making decisions and spent way too much time doing the necessary research. Jeff, on the other hand, was like me, always wanting to take risks and wanting to get work started ASAP. He became bored if there were too many details in a presentation, and he ran the risk of starting new projects without a decent plan.

Can you imagine how you would work together with somebody who is your polar opposite? Consequently, it certainly did not look like they were too happy during our first meeting. But throughout the year, they started to discover their respective strengths and made some fundamental changes to their way of interacting. This allowed each of them to bring their best to the table, and, not only did this improve their working

1. I changed the names of our clients for their privacy's sake, but their experiences are real.

relationship, it also brought a new synergy to the business, which made them much more productive and able to provide more value to their customers.

HOW YOU NATURALLY TAKE ACTION, EVEN IF YOU DON'T REALIZE IT

Do you often drive home from work feeling tired and in a bad mood? Yet, you love being in business for yourself and would never want to go back to a regular job, but at the same time, there are many things that you don't actually enjoy.

You're not the only one. Many entrepreneurs love their work, but still feel drained at the end of each day. After a while, you even start thinking that this is how it is supposed to be. Many business owners end up stuck in their offices doing all kinds of admin, managing employees, writing up detailed proposals, and generally doing all kinds of things they never anticipated when they started their business.

Work becomes much more fun and satisfying when you can spend your time on projects that really fit your personality. Things nobody but you can do. What if someone else took care of all the administrative stuff? What would you do? What would your day look like? Could you use the time to think about the big picture, new products, and the future? How useful might that be?

So, exactly, how did you end up sitting there late at night collecting receipts for the bookkeeper?

One of the ways people work against themselves is by ignoring their conative profile. Conation means "natural tendency, impulse, or striving." It is the way you tend to do things, and some people call it "instinct." So your conative profile is the way you take action naturally.

You've probably never heard of your conative profile. Nobody ever learns this stuff in school. Everybody knows about IQ, most have heard about EQ, but somehow we have lost sight of "conation." The Greek philosophers talked about the three sides of the mind: intelligence, emotions, and conation. But, in the last couple of centuries, we have been so focused on the intellect that we have ignored instinct. Too bad, because "conation" is what it's all about when you want to get things done.

Fortunately, Kathy Kolbe has spent decades of her life researching conation and publishing her findings. She describes the four modes in which people prefer to take action:

- Fact Finder
- Follow Thru
- Quick Start
- Implementor

Kathy designed a test, called the Kolbe-A test, to measure which mode you naturally prefer. None of these modes is better or worse than the others—no one has a good or a bad conative profile. But if you score a high number on Fact Finder, like Alex, you'll probably have a whole different approach to life than when you score a high number on Quick Start, like Jeff.

Scoring high on Fact Finder means you need to have specific information and lots of detail to solve creative problems. And you run the risk of analysis paralysis.

Scoring high on Follow Thru, indicates you generally enjoy knowing what the rules are. Creating and following systems and procedures helps you do a good job. We actually do not encounter a lot of entrepreneurs among these people.

People who excel on Quick Start, like me, have a high-risk tolerance. We enjoy challenges, new adventures, and crave a certain amount of variety to spice up our lives. The stereotypical adventurous entrepreneur and "crazy maker," probably score high on Quick Start.

Scoring high on Implementor signifies that you enjoy working with tangible stuff—you like to work not just with your brains, but also get your hands involved.

One of the problems for Quick Start entrepreneurs is when they create something brand new, then they have to maintain it for a long period to see it succeed. Many of our clients are in that situation and we are glad that we can help them figure out better ways to work from their strengths.

WORKING WITH PEOPLE WHO ARE TOTALLY DIFFERENT THAN YOU

Are you frustrated working with your team? Your employees seem to drain more energy than they give back. They misunderstand you; you're often not satisfied with the quality of their work, and somehow they always find time to argue. You, frequently, fantasize about life without employees.

When you can rely on your team, work becomes much easier. What you want is for your employees to properly appreciate your role in the business. Your job is not just looking after them. They actually are a kind of supplier to your business—selling their time to you. So if your natural role is to be the visionary, you should be free to come up with new ideas. And your team should finish what you start.

A lot of entrepreneurs we meet have chosen a role in their company that didn't match their personality. For example, when you are an entrepreneur, it seems natural to be the leader. Your team members expect you to take that role. Society, in general, expects you to. But what if this role doesn't fit your personality? Do you like managing people? Or would you prefer research or developing ideas?

And maybe your own working experience has colored your expectations. We worked with a guy who learned to be a good leader from his uncles who ran the company before him. They taught him that a good leader is empathic to his employees. This style didn't fit his direct personality at all, so he has constantly struggled to adapt himself to their model. Imagine how much energy this has cost him!

The British professor, Meredith Belbin, did some interesting research on team roles, working with teams in management games. He identified nine roles that people fulfill while working on a team. Everybody prefers two or three of these roles.

Take, for instance, "The Generator." Generators are full of ideas, and they always come up with creative ways to solve problems.

"The Shaper" is another one of these roles. Shapers have strong wills, strong opinions, and take the lead in shaping the world around them. They are visionaries and will challenge others to break with the status quo.

Belbin discovered that teams that were the most balanced in the amount of roles got the best results. Generators, for instance, are extremely helpful to any team, but only if

there is one generator around. As soon as Generator Number Two shows up, problems are guaranteed to show up as well.

For extreme productivity, you have to make sure you know exactly which team role fits best with your personality. Are you a Shaper or a Chairman? Each will make for a whole different approach to leadership.

Once you know your role, make sure you surround yourself with people who are not like you. You want your employees to excel in other roles. If your secretary is as creative as you, you'll have a great time bouncing ideas off of each other, but in the end, not much work will get done.

HOW TO COMMUNICATE EFFECTIVELY FROM YOUR CORE

Do you feel an abnormal amount of internal resistance when having to call a potential customer? Does your stomach churn every time you have to pitch to investors? Do you keep postponing writing an article for the company's newsletter, because you don't know how to start? As you would expect, communicating has a strong link to personality.

When you start communicating in a way that follows your own preference and style, it suddenly becomes much more fun. If you listen to the "experts," you'll hear them say that there is one right way to communicate and convince people – though each expert teaches you a different way! A couple of years ago networking was the name of the game for filling up your prospect list; but if casual conversation is not natural for you, no amount of skill building will change that. Even if you become reasonably good at it, you have expended energy on something you'll never be really comfortable with, while ignoring other modes of communication that fit your profile much better! Not really productive, is it?

So we encourage our clients to do the free Marketing DNA test, which can be found at web address: http://www.marketingdnatest.com. This test measures how you naturally communicate and persuade. One of the things it will tell you is whether you prefer words or images. Chris, another one of our clients, found out that he had a strong preference for images. And this was a big eye-opener for him. It made him realize how resistant he was to words and gave him the freedom to let other people do all the writing, so he could focus on images himself.

WHAT TO DO NOW?

Knowledge by itself doesn't improve your productivity. You have to take action on what you learn about yourself and allow yourself to go with the flow of who you are.

Tests can help you discover more about your personality. But knowing yourself is only a starting point from where you can take giant strides forward. In another chapter in this book, TJ will tell you more about how to dramatically improve your productivity, based on your own personality.

For now, here are some things you can do:

- Write "*The Rules for Being Me.*" Create five rules for yourself in which you describe what things you should do, and what things you should avoid to be really productive. For example, "I like starting projects, but I don't like keeping them going. Therefore, I must get people to work with me right from the beginning, so they can continue what I start."
- Run through your calendar for the past three months and cross off everything you should not have been doing. Find ways to delegate those tasks to other people.
- Explain to your team what you have discovered about yourself, and how you want things to change. Ask them to take the tests, and discuss how you're going to help them become more productive, based on their personalities.

In the end, knowing who you really are and adapting your work so that you can use your strengths is much more effective than trying to force yourself into a box that you don't naturally fit into. If you can focus on doing those things you like to do the most, it will give you a much higher level of energy, supplied by a motivation from deep within yourself.

So figure out who you are, and how you can use that to create a business model in which you add the most value to your customers. And if that turns out to be a difficult process, give me a call—encouraging entrepreneurs like you is what I love to do.

About Marlene

Did you start your business years ago and now have moments where you wonder whether that was, in fact, a good idea? Maybe you are disappointed about the kind of work you have to do day-in-day-out. You are focusing on financial numbers, solving conflicts between your employees, making decisions about all kinds of minor things, and writing detailed proposals. This was not what you had in mind when you dreamt of being your own boss.

Marlene Scott loves to help entrepreneurs find joy in their entrepreneurship again. She helps them to transform their company into something that fits their personality instead of them being the slave of their business. Her clients feel relief because they don't have to push themselves forward anymore. Like one of her clients said, "It starts to become so much fun it scares me."

A lot of entrepreneurs forget to look at their own personality when they start a business. They have a passion for their product, but never thought about what kind of work they actually like or dislike. And when their business grows, a lot of things they do "just have to be done." But when your work is 80 percent "must do," it's no fun anymore—it drains you.

As a best-selling author and productivity expert, Marlene loves to help entrepreneurs find more time for the things they love to do. Together with her friend and colleague, TJ, she developed a proven system to help business owners get to know themselves and use that information to free up two hours every day for strategy, innovation, and growth.

As a productivity expert, she has inspired and trained professionals in businesses of all sizes, from small companies to multi-billion dollar enterprises like AkzoNobel, Vodafone, BDO, Boston Scientific, Damen Shipyards, Hennes & Mauritz, Heinz, ING Bank, KLM Air France, Toyota, Nestle, Pepsi Co, Philips, Reed Elsevier, Toshiba, and Unilever.

Marlene finds that she likes her work most when she can coach and train entrepreneurs who have the drive to change and the ability to take action. She loves to help and encourage them to create a business in which they can fully utilize their strengths.

If that's you, please surf to: www.FridaysOff.net

www.FridaysOff.net

CHAPTER 37

MAKING IT HAPPEN

BY RAUL VILLACIS

Change is inevitable, progress is optional.
~ Tony Robbins

If you are like me, you get excited with the new flavor-of-the-month strategy. You see someone on the Internet promoting a webinar about a product and you automatically want to do it. Next week you see someone else doing something different and you want to do that too, but you didn't finish implementing what you learned last week. I used to attend the latest seminar, download the newest program and found myself full of great ideas and intentions, but never following through and implementing what I just learned. I wonder why is it that I learned something that I'm excited about but I never follow through. One of the most important discoveries I have made in my life is the formula to implement immediate massive action. In this current economy, it is not enough to have the knowledge but you must implement immediately, because if you don't your competition will. That is why I love this quote "Change is inevitable, progress is optional." I want to share with you the five step formula that made my company not only survive but thrive in this new economy. **This is not brain surgery, this is a simple formula that if you apply even some of the steps you will create the drive that you need to implement massive action to follow through.**

I come from a Real Estate background, and as you can imagine, the recession hit my business pretty hard. I went from having millions in Real Estate assets to seeing my equity vanish daily as the property values dropped. I was just like everyone else waiting for things to get better, but as time went on, things got worse. I had sales people that worked for me that couldn't make any sales. I had investors and sellers that couldn't sell their properties. I was stuck with some properties myself because buyers couldn't get financing. It felt like I was in a scene from the twilight zone. Banks were going out of business, the stock market was crashing, people were not looking at Real Estate as a secure investment any more, foreclosures were at an all time high. It seemed that it was doomsday for anyone that was in the Real Estate business. My big competitors were going out of business, so I knew if I didn't change, that was going to be my future. I don't know if you call it luck but I call it grace, I got a call from a sales rep for a seminar called "Unleash the power within."

I don't know how she got my information since I never attended any self-development program before. At that time, I said I don't need a motivational seminar, I need banks that will lend money so my clients can move their properties. She said that the person that was presenting was not a motivational speaker but a strategist, and she believed that if I attended the seminar it would help me find the right strategy to get my business back on track. I asked who was presenting the seminar and she said, I'm sure you heard of Tony Robbins. To that I answered "Tony who?" I'm a business person I told her, I'm not involved in the self-development world. **My model of the world back then was if I wanted to achieve, I needed to focus on business strategies not in my personal belief system.** I wasn't depressed nor had issues with my family I said. I just want a good business strategy to get my business back on track. Well she finally convinced me to go, and to make a long story short, that weekend Tony had us walking on fire and the breakthroughs that came out of that seminar not only helped me survive the crisis, but I was able to positioning myself to build one of the top Real Estate sales organizations in the Nation according the *Wall Street Journal*.

I learned to condition my psychology to be able to see the opportunities available in any circumstance as opposed to sitting and complaining why things are not as good as the good old days. That is how I came to create this 5-step formula based on my needs to take massive action. Now that didn't happen overnight, that seminar was just the beginning of my journey in finding that the chokehold of any business is the psychology or the skill of the leader. I learned that business is 80% psychology and 20% skill. My skill took me as far as I could go until the economy meltdown happened, but I needed to have the right psychology in order to change my approach and see the opportunities that were in front of me. **The first thing I did was I made a conscious decision that I was not going to look at my situation worse than it was.**

So many of us do that when things go wrong. We automatically look at the situation as worse than it really is. In my industry, the problem was that we couldn't move any of our real estate inventory or take the equity out because the properties were losing value faster than banks could write a loan for the buyer. So I just accepted that fact, and moved on to the next step. **See where the opportunity in your current situation lies.** In my case, I saw the opportunity in working with financial institutions that got stuck with the bad assets from the mortgage crisis, and needed help in analyzing their portfolio and eventually needed someone to manage their properties and sell them. I became the 'go to' guy in my market for over 20 financial institutions including the US government. The only way I was able to do this is by taking massive action on what I just learned. I followed the 5 steps that I'm going to lay out for you. I have taught this to several CEO's in different industries, and they found that it gave them the clarity and leverage they needed to apply from what they learned. I call it the **Formula to take Massive Action**.

1- FIGURE OUT WHY IS THIS IMPORTANT TO YOU?

You need to decide first if what you want to implement is really important and relevant to your vision. I learned that if I wanted to succeed I had to say no to what was not relevant to my vision. What is the ultimate vision for yourself or for your company? Notice I said vision, not your goal. Goals are set to fulfill a vision. If you don't have a vision I suggest you start there before you decide to take on a new strategy or make a change in your company. I have an entire process just to create the "ultimate vision." That is not what his chapter is about, but if you want help on this just go to: *www.raulvillacis.com*. Every time I learn something that I want to implement in my life or my business, the first thing I ask is why is this important to me? And is this going to help me get closer to where I want to go? Once I have that answer I go to step two.

2- MAKE AN EMOTIONAL DECISION TO MAKE THIS HAPPEN.

I have learned that pleasure and pain are the two driving forces that makes a person take action on their decisions. That is why you need to make sure you have enough pleasure in what you want to accomplish and enough pain associated if you don't do it. To do this, simply write down what are the benefits in implementing the change in your life or taking massive action? What would you gain by doing this? Once you answer these two questions, answer what would you lose if you don't make the change or take massive action? What is the pain that you can associate with it if you don't take action? The key here is to decide and internalize your commitment by making an emotional decision.

Decision comes from the Latin word, *decisio,* which means – to cut off. Once you know the pleasure you will get by taking action on your decision and the pain it will bring if you don't, you will cut off all uncertainty that this will not happen. If you have enough leverage, this will become a must for you. The reason that so many people fail to take action is not because they don't want to take action, but it is because they haven't internalized it as yet. It's not enough to want to do it or to have a plan that you want to execute; you have to internalize it in your nervous system. A basketball player doesn't go to the NBA by just wanting to be a professional player or by knowing that all he has to do is shoot the ball through the hoop. He had to make an emotional decision that gave him the drive to take massive action and train daily to accomplish his vision.

One of the ways I internalize my decisions is that I magnify the emotion of pain and pleasure. When you answer the questions in step one, what emotions were you feeling when you were thinking about the reason this is important to you? What if you magnify the outcome and create an emotion that will trigger even more the need to take action. I do the same with the question of what would I lose if I don't take action. I amplify that emotion to exaggerate the pain it will bring if I don't follow through and take massive action. This is what I call the glue to taking action. If you are like me, you made a lot of decisions before in your life, but you never follow through. You have endless projects, ideas and aspirations but never had the time to complete them and you feel overwhelmed with knowledge, but never seem to organize yourself to take action in any of them. You may do them half way, then jump to the next new project thinking this time I'm really going to finish. Once I learned this technique of internalizing my decisions with pleasure and pain, I have been able to use it to accomplish more in one year than I did in the last five. The growth is exponential. I can't emphasize how important this process is, this is the glue that holds all the power in taking action on your decision.

3- TELL PEOPLE ABOUT YOUR DECISION AND ACTION PLAN.

Most people don't share their plans because they are afraid of what people may think if they don't accomplish it. Or perhaps we think that people may look at us differently because we are trying something new or want to change something about ourselves. We tend to look for validation from those around us and we play at the same level field as our peer group. We undervalue our success and exaggerate our failures just to fit in. But the truth is that by telling people what your action plan is, you are going to get two types of responses. One response is going to come from those that support you and believe in your decision, and this will help you feel more certain that you are in the right track. The second response is going to be from people that doubt you and think you don't have what it takes. Depending of your personality this may be the response you need. Some people hate to be told they can't do something and will do it just to prove that person wrong. I am living proof of that. **I built one of my businesses to be the number one sales organization in my market due to one of my competitors telling me that I could never accomplish it. She told me that I don't have what it takes and I will always be an outsider looking in. I used that as fuel to create a driving force to take massive action.**

There is something inside every one of us that knows that we are capable of so much more than what we think we are. I find that the more people I tell about my vision and what I want to accomplish, the more it's reinforced and conditioned in me. My brain goes, 'there is no way you are not going to make it happen after you told so many people about it.' You will build massive leverage by having people holding you accountable.

4- BELIEVE THAT YOU ARE GUIDED.

No matter what your religious background is, I think we can all agree that there is an external force in the universe that is bigger than us. So why do we rely only in our own ability to accomplish what we want in our lives. If I was to believe that everything I have accomplished in my life has been because of my own effort, I would be fooling myself. I truly believe that every human being has a purpose in this world, but it is up to us to find it or to expand on it. Every major event in my life, whether it was picking up a corporate client account, making the right connection or even the fact that you are reading this book right now, is for a reason. If you believe that there is a force bigger than you guiding you towards your vision, then the pressure of relying on your own ability is off. I know that in my life, once I got myself out of my own way and allowed God to guide me, everything came into place. Some people call it luck, I call it grace. I learned that life doesn't happen to you, it happens for you.

5- CREATE A DAILY SUCCESS RITUAL.

Remember what I said in step one. Figure out why your decision is important to your vision. Goals create the vision, but rituals make it real. Nothing happens overnight. But nothing creates faster growth than creating successful daily rituals. Ever heard the quote by Gandhi that says, "Habits create your destiny." I believe that habits are reinforced by daily rituals. When I discovered this, it was a game changer for me. If you follow the steps that I will give you to create a successful ritual, I guarantee you it will be like putting steroids in your drive to take massive action towards what you want to accomplish on a daily basis. I actually came UP with this formula out of desperation. A couple of years ago, while having one of the most successful years and growth in my company, I started to have sharp pains in my stomach. Every day that I would go to the office I felt great, our sales team was doing awesome, our clients where happy, but at night when I went to bed, I had a horrible pain that will be so intense that I would not be able to sleep. Every night it came in around midnight like clockwork. The doctors ran their tests but they couldn't find anything physically wrong with me. As I traveled to different seminars and learned how to re-condition myself I found that in certain environments and events I had no pain. The pain went away when I was doing fun or creative activities, and I found a direct correlation between my emotional state and physical pain. It wasn't that I was depressed or that I was overwhelmed with work, it was that my daily routine was causing stress in my health because I didn't have a beginning or an end to my day.

I was such an achiever that I was focused on my goals 24/7. I didn't have an ultimate vision at the time either; all I concentrated on was immediate results. I remember learning that if you want to take control of your emotions you have to change the state of mind you are in. So I started to apply the teachings of changing my state and I created a process that has evolved in what I call my daily success ritual. I have been constantly improving it through time, and I am happy to tell you that once I got it down to a science, my pain went away immediately, and I've had more energy and more clarity every day since I've been doing it. I will share this step by step process with you so you can create your own version of my morning ritual. If you need a visual you can watch my video in *www.raulvillacis.com*

MORNING RITUAL

I do this every morning as soon as I get our of bed and brush my teeth. I find that the benefit of doing this first thing in the morning enhances the conditioning process.

Here are the instructions: In order to change your state here are the 3 main factors that impact the way you feel.

1. Your physiology - which is the way you move you body, if you are depressed you tend to slouch your shoulders and put your head down. When you fell happy or strong, you tend to have your shoulder back and your head up high.

2. Your words - What you say to yourself is probably the most important thing you do. We tend not to pay attentions to the words we are using when we talk to ourselves. For example, when we say I'm always late for every meeting. Usually your brain says you are right and therefore you struggle to make the next meeting on time. Or you would say I can never save any money. Your brain says right, and you always spend all your money and you never save it. It becomes a self-fulfilling prophecy.

3. Your Focus - What you are constantly focusing your thinking on is what triggers how you feel. If you focus on why you are always spending money and how you can't save any money, that usually will trigger a bad emotion. Or if you focus on why you are always late, you create an emotion of stress and pressure. So whatever you focus on determines how you are feeling.

These three factors are what create our emotional estate. So knowing this, I created my morning ritual around these factors so I can change my emotional state and feel great at any moment just by triggering my physiology, words and focus. Here is what I do.

Step 1 – I spend about 5 to 10 minutes focusing on what is working on my life. I take a deep breath and stretch my body out and I focus on all the great things that are happening in my life. We usually don't make the time to really appreciate and look at all the things that we could be grateful for: family, business, and health. For this moment focus on everything that you are thankful for. I use music in the background so I can trigger the emotion even faster. I have the Gladiator Soundtrack playing in the back while I'm doing this.

Step 2 – I start with an affirmation that I have customize to my action plan. For example, I will say: "I am focused and determined. Everything I do brings me profits. I am blessed with abundance and I have all the time that I need. Every day I'm getting stronger and stronger, and my body knows exactly what to do to heal itself." I don't just say this, but I say it with emotion and intensity. I have about 20 different affirmations that are meaningful to me and apply to what I want to accomplish that particular day. I do this for about 7 to 10 minutes. I usually will play a song in the background so I do it for the duration of two songs. What I like to do is use the first song to get me in the state of "getting things done," like the song "I'm not afraid" by Eminem, and the last song will be an energetic song that will get in a "powerful state" like Teen Spirit by Nirvana. The key here is to use your body at the beat of the song to make power moves and use your tone of voice and words to anchor the conditioning of what you are saying. This is what is called incantation. I learned this from Tony Robbins and he says. "An incantation is an active belief structure. When you are saying it, you engage your entire nervous system with the full force of your focus."

a- the power of an incantation far surpasses any other belief you once had before.

b- empowering incantations have unmatched power to create the certainty and emotional intensity that you desire to create an extraordinary life.

c- by creating a new incantation, you guarantee that you have created a new cause-and-effect direction and destination for your life."

There Are 3 Types Of People:

- PEOPLE THAT MAKE IT HAPPEN
- PEOPLE THAT WATCH IT HAPPEN
- PEOPLE THAT SAY "WHAT HAPPENED?"

You choose who you want to be.

For information on this ritual, go to: www.raulvillacis.com

About Raul

Raul Villacis is one of the top Real Estate Sales Coaches in the country, as well as a Best Selling Author and CEO of Advantage Real Estate Group Advisors. Raul's work in re-strategizing the real estate portfolio of big financial institutions such top banks and also working with the US Government earned him the designation of "One of the Nation's Top Real Estate Firms" according to *The Wall Street Journal* and *Real Trends Inc.* With the creation of his "Next Level Real Estate" brand, Raul's focus is teaching innovative Real Estate strategies to top Real Estate professionals around the world, helping them get predictable results in all Real Estate environments.

There are three types of people....people that make it happen, people that watch it happen, and people that say "What Happened?" Although he didn't know it at the time, that is a mantra Raul has been living out since he was a young boy. His mother once had to tell him that she could not afford getting him a haircut every week even though little Raul insisted his hair had to be perfect at all times. After all, presentation is everything, right? Well that didn't stop Raul from achieving his goal. He simply went to his local barber and asked to be taught how to cut his own hair! Sure enough he learned, and hasn't had a hair out of place since. He MADE IT HAPPEN.

It is that same attitude he carries into his Real Estate Coaching; tenacity, repetition, and a hunger to learn. Raul is the creator of the "Successful Daily Ritual Formula" and the "Formula to take Massive Action" which have become a foundation for helping his coaching clients reach the next level in their Real Estate career. In addition to his coaching Raul has consistently bought and sold over $100 million a year in Investment Property. His knowledge of the industry from all angles, and his commitment to being mentally prepared for success, make him a unique asset to all Real Estate professionals.

CHAPTER 38

SHOW UP FOR THE SHOWDOWN

BY ROY VALE

Just remember: don't change you, just the TEA!

It all started the night my wife and I were getting ready to go out for her birthday! We were at a nice place, no kids around, (we have four), and the night was young. We are getting all decked out, excited and ready for the "show". And then, out of know where, the real *SHOW* is upon us. The bomb goes off! Figuratively! I will explain in more detail shortly. Because I wasn't ready to show up for the show down event in my life, I felt compelled to help others attempt to prepare for their own showdown. It will come, and in some cases, *the show* has already begun! You thought this message was about change? NO! Yes! Maybe! However, what if we don't change a thing about us, not our personalities, not our political philosophies, our religion, not even our hair, homes or career associates… yet, through some applied historical human science, we are now able to improve every outcome, remove one fear at a time, expand our careers as well as ignite our personal relationships! First, we must learn to examine the real "SHOW", because your *bomb* will go off! In the next 44 days, we will all start to get familiar with "Show up for the Showdown!"

When we hear the phrase "show up for the show down", we might presume it means things like, 'Show me your stuff', 'Put up or shut up', yada, yada! What exactly does that mean, "Show up for the Showdown?" Could it be who has more charisma, talents? It certainly doesn't mean 'act boldly' or 'no pain no gain' philosophy either. It does remind me of a comment I heard from a church lady on the radio simply talking about her teenage kids, and how they wanted a jeep with the biggest winch they could afford mounted on it. For some of us city folks, we do the same thing, don't we? We place big old brush guards on our trucks and jeeps and feel bravo! We really believe that we are going to *show up for the showdown*, right? What exactly does "show up for the show down" mean?

DON'T CHANGE YOU!

That's right! In many organizations, you might hear the slogan, "Did you drink the " Kool-aid " today?" In your new "show down" journey, you simply take in some new TEA! TEA ? Allow me to share with you what got me started on this TEA thought and my new 44-day journey. As you recall, on that night that I was to celebrate my wife's birthday, I lay on the floor crying and desperately seeking rescue. I had a horrible back pain, cramping of the muscles, the joints were not working, and the body was reacting in a way I still can't explain. And there I laid, on the floor, not able to move! I started wondering about the rest of the night, tomorrow and possibly my entire future. I started searching and seeking. Outside help, no – just inside my own heart and soul. Why me? When will this go away? Will it? What if my back gets worse?

Being human and scared, I opened my "old book" and asked for a special message from "above"…you know?, or maybe not, but sometimes we even play games with *HIM*. Remember, I am just like you, trying to improve and grow rich in all areas of my life as well. I am just as weak as you are too! So, I said, "Come on Lord, show me something right now to inspire me! Give me that one last shot of healing!" Uh, oh!! This next moment will never be forgotten, and this is why I am telling you about it right now! I closed my eyes, flipped the pages back and forth, then I said… "Now God, show me something now!" "I need your message. Guide me!" Wow ! As I open my eyes while still holding my finger on this one page, this particular verse is at the edge of my finger:

"Seek the Lord while you still can, call upon him while he is near." WOW - While I still can? What exactly did that mean? Call upon Him while He is near? Did *He* just touch my back with pain? Or did he warn me, with the "real show"? He '*showed up*' for the '*showdown*', and I wasn't ready!

About 2:30 a.m., (pain/*show* started at about 6:20 p.m.), I was lying on the floor crying and my wife asked, "Does your back hurt that much?" I was too proud and ashamed to admit the real reason I was crying, so I lied to my wife. My wife thought I was crying because of my back pain. I wasn't. Later, about 5:30 a.m. that morning, (still awake with pain and wonder) I had to share with her all my real pains. You see, I wasn't ready for showing up to the real showdown! The pain of the heart and soul had gotten larger than the pain of the back. This moment in my life prompted me to start the *new show* now! I too, am searching for a critical balance. I also know I had to make a specific time frame and I had to write things down. I believe that if you commit to the knowledge, coaching and insight you are reading today, and you make a commitment to act on it for 44 days, you truly *will show up for the showdown.* I needed some *new TEA* more than anybody else. A distinct target, environment and approach to the new me! I hope to someday not be an amateur on the journey of the real "show" as well as the much-needed TEA we all seek. If you simply take your new TEA, FOR THE NEXT 44 DAYS, you too, will start to *show up for the showdown*!

A friend of mine once told me, six hours before he died, "Roy, thank you for showing me a few paths to take, and a few TEA's to sip on, but I want you to know I met God and the Devil in a dream last night…and guess who scared me the most?…Now that, is powerful. He said, "You see Roy, the devil, the demons, the bad folks can only take your body, material things and such, but God wants your heart and soul, He wants all of you!

I could get tougher, but I just seem to be getting softer and more at peace with my new TEA. There are a lot of people that can confirm, that I am far from maturing for the *showdown* and the proper TEA! My wife Monica and maybe even some people reading this, could easily confirm that I have many chapters to go in my *show up* journey. However, even Jesus got hacked off and had to make some serious decisions and take aggressive actions to pursue *His own TEA and Show*.

> Mark 11: v.15 – *When they arrived back to Jerusalem he went to the Temple and began to drive out the merchants and their customers, and knocked over the tables of the moneychangers and the stalls of those selling doves and stopped everyone from bringing in loads of merchandise.*

Timid? I don't think so. Are you ready to drive out the demons and nay-sayers, knock over the hurdles in your way of your new *show*! For us, it just takes 44 days to start the journey.

Teddy Roosevelt was once quoted for saying something that ended like this:

… "If he fails, at least he fails while daring greatly, so that his place shall never be with those cold and timid souls who know neither victory nor defeat."

'I should have done this or that?' 'I should have not quit.' 'I should have given it my best.' 'If only I had done it this way!' ARE YOU WAITING FOR THE NEXT MEMO? Don't look back five years from now and say the same things. Whether you like Teddy or not, experience great failure while daring greatly! It's okay. Today, you have to find a way, *to show up for your showdown.* Don't CHANGE You, change the TEA!

Simply try this new TEA for 44 days now. Five in each area makes it 15 different TEA's.

Write down today's date here: ______________________________

Write down your new TEA:

1. Adjust **T**arget/s

2. Improve **E**nvironment/s

3. Create different **A**pproach/s

Please start today and please write them down!
Have at least 5 in each area !

____

____

____

____

____

____

A poem with the theme, Show up for the Showdown:

THE "SHOW"

Yes, yes; the best *show*
not stumble, nor grumble- the Time a fumble.
Where the wind not blow, best quickly… row
no heartfelt goal? none the show

The purpose of bold drives ye passion of gold,
Imagine the spirit, without the know
Release the soul, to start the show
The why be reached, w' love unleashed.

Yes, yes; the best show
Not fear, not cower- real purpose, power.
Boundless, soul to goal
O' purpose! the *show* a glow

With your new TEA, Discovering ye purpose, the *show* a glow !

My father was one of those guys who would never admit to pain, losing, giving up, disadvantages, none of those kind of things. I recall an incident which I will share with you with the hopes of adding value and support to my conviction of "*Show up for the Showdown*" mentality. As I recall, I came walking home from school crying because I had just had three school bullies beat on me. This was somewhat typical in the neighborhoods many of you grew up in as well, I'm sure. So, when I walked in the living room, my father heard me crying. This was the second bad thing to happen to me by now. Normally, my dad was out working, driving cabs. However, as things would happen, this time, he was home. I was scared to *SHOW* him my tears and weakness.

As you would guess, my father asked- "Why are you crying, son?" I thought for what seemed eternity and said….. "Dad, normally I never cry when I get into a fight but this time dad, there were three of them." I stopped and waited for his response. He quickly responded to me and said, "Do not lie son, I know for a fact that you are telling a lie". "Dad, I am not lying!" I replied. He says: "Son, You know why I know you are lying? Because of all the kids in school that I have seen, I cannot count in my hands any three kids, that if they all got together and tried to take you down on the playground, with the real you *showing up*, it simply wouldn't happen! They simply don't have the talent, speed, toughness and tenacity like you do. So, son, you say there was only three?" My dad always had this attitude that we cannot fail, we can win at anything and he did empower me and give me a sense of tremendous confidence to fight for the top, the best, the most.

So, my dad asked me to get in the car. We go and pick up the other three kids and head out to the playground for a second round. Needless to say, I was "driven" to victory. There was no way I would lose or be frightened in front of my dad. While this might not be the best way to teach a kid toughness and a no-quit attitude, it did teach me boldness and tenacity, and to not flirt with the other guys girlfriends. I had no choice, but to *show up for the showdown.*

My dad had a way of inspiring us that may not always work with others, but at the time, for me - it was the inner strength that I needed fed into my mind. The TEA I had to intake for Showing up for the showdown—my dad was part of the group that started that evolution. His constant philosophy was: *Never back down, never quit, you fake it till you make it!* In a twisted, weird sort of way, my dad did inspire me to bigger goals and visions. I still love him to this day for giving me such confidence.

A few years back, on a cool, beautiful Saturday afternoon, I sat there and watched four young boys, YOUNG MEN if you will, preparing for a track meet. They were part of a high school varsity track relay team, forming a circle. They start holding hands right before a huge crowd in the middle of the field. These four boys were getting ready to be in one of the biggest state track events of their high school life. They had been stretching for some time now. They had gone over the routine of hand-offs, steps, counts, etc. They were one of the fastest relay teams in their region. These four individuals also had four distinctly different faiths. I knew them well. Then all of a sudden, they bowed their heads and appeared to be praying. After about 30 seconds a coach from another school walks over to them and from what I could see , it appeared as if the coach was quite upset with them and reprimanding them. I wasn't sure, but I could see some frustration on the boys as well as the coach. After the race, I went down to talk to my son and congratulated them on their victory and the fastest time of the meet. Then I said, as best as I can recall, "Son, who was that coach that came over right before your race who appeared to be upset about your praying, or were you not praying?"

My son said, "Dad, yes, we were praying. We didn't ask for a victory, we *asked for no injuries* and a good day on the track!"

Then this coach that we don't even know said, "Boys, you didn't come out here to pray for yourselves, you came out here to run. Stop this nonsense and go show the fans that you can run, you can always do your thing later!"

My son, to the best of my recollection, said something like this. "Dad, just because he was a coach and I didn't want to disqualify my team, I didn't say anything, we just "showed" him everything. But one of these days, I know I will run into that man, and I will have my chance to *show* him his nonsense." I never asked my son what he meant by that, but I just hope he doesn't run into that coach. Sometimes, *showing up for the showdown*, is simply getting a *real* EKG of the heart. The next 44 days, start the new journey. Remember, don't change you – take in some new TEA: Target, Environment, Approach!

For ideas on your new TEA, email me at rlvale@yahoo.com.

About Roy

Roy Vale is a family man living in San Antonio, TX with his wife and inspiration, Monica. Roy also has four children and four grandchildren. He is a fan of sports, outdoor adventures and admits his fair talent of golf. Roy has also completed a few half marathons and marathons. In his younger years in athletics, Roy broke his neck playing football, as well as having four other major injuries. These injuries, and growing up in the government projects way down south near the border of Mexico as a child, were part of the mold that have created a person who simply won't let up when the wind won't blow! In the business world, Roy is also known as the Marketing Guru in some of his circles, as well as Big Dawg and the Godfather of Sales. The Godfather of Sales says, "Winning is not a slogan, it's a way of life!" This past year, he received the highest honor, Presidents Council Member, from his company, The Farmers Insurance Group of Companies. Roy has been in sales for 15 years, and business coaching and performance management for the last 16.

On a personal mission to help himself, his family and friends, Roy has also started a personal speaking seminar/tour of his own: Critical Balance. Roy tries to share inspirational, calculated and proven systems from the old book as well as guidance from popular people who have succeeded and failed, but learned well in their efforts to balance their lives in areas of relationships, money, health, careers and faith!

As a Sales Manager, he inspires, guides and coaches 40 agents and 80 reps. In 2012, Big Daddy completed an event called "Tough Mudder" in the Austin, TX area. His wife Monica and his son Ryan, as well as other friends and peers were there to witness the 3 hours and 31 minutes. Roy completed this grueling event (12 miles, 26 obstacles) while not being in the best of shape. When asked by his friends, "How in the world did you finish?" the Marketing Guru replied, "My son called me two days before the event and told me he remembered one of my favorite sayings." So I asked, "Which one is that?" He replied, "In life, when you can't reach your goals, you sometimes lack the tenacity or desire, so Dad, are you going to finish the Tough Mudder, or did you want to answer your own question?" Yes, Roy Vale is known for never giving up and finding ways to win! Roy Vale was also asked by a colleague as to why he had so many nicknames. He believes that as you journey through the days and years, we must change, adopt, create and react to different "curves" that come our way. He has been blessed to help others while maintaining some decent "nicknames" and yet, enjoy the benefits of the career he has and able to share his blessings with others!

To contact Roy or share your thoughts on this Show up for the Showdown chapter, visit: AgentCareers.com

Or: rlvale@yahoo.com

CHAPTER 39

FUNCTIONAL FITNESS AND FITNESS LONGEVITY™

BY SAM IANNETTA

My system and concepts have helped clients make great changes for the better. Regardless of how "fit" they were to begin with, be they sedentary to extreme athlete, infant to senior and every type in between, Fitness Longevity™ can help everyone. At Functional Fitness, we are experts in analysis and creating exercise programs for real life fitness. Fitness that changes the way your body adapts to the challenges of life, while paying attention to the positions and movements that can destroy your body long term.

In 1992, I started using the term Functional Fitness to describe my system of using analysis to decipher poor movement patterns that lead to pain, poor digestion, loss of energy, depression, and weight gain, not to mention excess physical wear and tear. In many cases, clients also saw significantly diminished symptoms of disease, illness and aging. After the initial analysis, we discuss and demonstrate the problems that we see and then create a corrective exercise and nutritional plan to change these poor patterns. Only after proving my techniques by solving complex mechanical and structural issues with hundreds of clients did I decide to open Sam Iannetta's Functional Fitness and Wellness Center in 2002. To date there is no other exercise facility using our analysis and techniques. Let me introduce you to the world of Fitness Longevity™.

SIX ELEMENTS OF FITNESS LONGEVITY™ PARADIGM

1. Alignment
2. NORMAL Joint Range of Motion
3. Gait
4. Functional Muscular Strength
5. Structural Stability
6. Eating and Food

Many of us go through life figuring that our body is what we were given at birth but this is not completely true. Each one of us is being built, rebuilt and repaired every second of every day of our lives. What I hear often is "this is just how I have always been." It is a common statement with my new clients and when I ask if they had tried to change it, in general they reply, "No, I didn't know I could." If we were to look at a professional bodybuilder, no one would say, "Well, that's how they were born." Everyone knows they work hard for the build they want to achieve. You have to work a bit harder to achieve quality changes in your body and work a lot smarter too. Learning about these six elements: your body's alignment, range of motion, strength, gait, stability and generally how/what to eat to make change is crucial to everyone who wants a body that lasts a lifetime. I am not saying that you need to become a professional, but you should know as much as possible about ***the body you were born to live in***©. Okay, so understand that each category below has hundreds if not thousands of books written about them so this is purely an outline of the most important features and how to attack them. The human body is much more complex than an automobile, but still, getting to know it starts with a single key – so allow me to throw you the keys to Fitness Longevity™ Paradigm.

Alignment systems in our body are always changing, but learning to change things for the better is critical for long lasting fitness. Start by taking a good look in the mirror beginning with foot alignment, knee alignment, hip and back alignment, upper back and shoulder alignment and lastly head alignment. You need to recognize where your discrepancies in alignment are and take action to remedy the situation. Odds are good that most pain-based issues in your own body are joint, alignment and posture related. Start by creating an awareness of how you are aligned and how you can move to correct it. See a professional if you cannot make a change on your own.

Joint Range of Motion is another factor in fitness longevity and I want to make something clear right off the bat. If you want your body to feel good and last a long time, you will be searching for **NORMAL** range of motion. Normal range of motion is not a set number of degrees but a range of degrees +/-. Unless you happen to be an engineer or an architect, you may not be familiar with this concept of "plus or minus." Simply put, if you are a few degrees off you can function normally whether it be relatively tight or loose. This said, if your joint is hyper mobile or immobile, it will not do what it is supposed to do and consequently, another joint up or down the chain will be affected negatively and become injured, painful, or have increased wear and tear.

Functional Muscular Strength sounds complex, but it really isn't as it relates to ninety percent of us. It is simply the strength that we need and will definitely use on a given day, week or month of our lives. Strong enough to lift a car is not really necessary as they make jacks for that. Strong enough to sit down and stand up effortlessly is pretty important yet most people plop into chairs as if the mechanics of their body are unimportant. The poor positioning of sitting and standing is as dangerous as a heavy squat! It might take a much longer time to see a resultant injury, but is no less disabling when that injury eventually occurs. Functional muscular strength incorporates strength, structural stability and movement technique. Only when these 3 areas are working properly can a person power through their myriad activities in any given day. As an example, consider simple tasks such as walking a flight of stairs which incorporates placing more than your body weight on one leg and performing a squat-like movement. Most people who have problems climbing a flight of stairs have a strength, stability, and power issue, and not a flexibility or balance issue.

Gait, or how you walk, is one of the most critical factors in being and staying in one piece for a lifetime. Not to mention crucial to maintaining the ability to stay independent and in your own home, for as you age, this can become the basis for whether or not you can get around independently. The problem with gait is that no one wants to think about it until it is a major problem. There are many opinions when it comes to how humans should walk but in all my research and teaching over the years I have found a simple formula. You heel strike, with toes up and slowly lower your foot to the ground as you roll from heel to big toe and gently push off the ball of your foot and big toe. Improved gait increases muscle recruitment all the way up to your hip. It stretches and strengthens calf and ankle, decreases risk of tripping, and helps to keep circulation in your feet. During a walking gait, our body functions like a pile of pendulums©. As such, your hips should rotate; shoulder blades should glide side to side, your arms should move forward and backwards, all in a clean and rhythmic pattern. This amazing gait is the reason humans can walk farther on two feet than any other animal on the planet.

Structural Stability is a bit of a strange concept but let me explain it simply. Structural stability is a way of looking at the body as a structure that is being pulled, pushed, twisted and rotated by movement every moment of every day. Even when sitting in your chair reading this book, gravity is pulling down on you not just as a whole but also as individual parts. It is trying to bring your head forward to the ground, it is trying to make you fall sideways and if you were to fall asleep right this second you would end up in a different shape as your body relaxed and sleep took you, changing your position.

Now let's look at other parts of your life. According to the laws of physics, when you pull on a door, car door or any type of door, it is pulling back on you with an equal amount of force. If you are structurally unstable, the car door will pull you off balance or pull you into a different position. This is especially noticeable in people who are slight of build. However, if the force is large or unexpected enough, your size and strength matter less. For example, even a really big guy walking down the street can be thrown off balance by a huge gust of wind. A 40 mph gust can pull that big strong guy off balance making him as unstable as a ninety-year-old nonna. Whether you are picking up a glass of water, a laundry basket or a feisty toddler, the passive applied forces may be small, a 10 ounce glass of water to a 10 pound stack of clothes in that basket or a 25 pound 2 year old, but the forces being created in your body can be extreme and if your structure is unstable, instantaneous injuries can occur.

A client came to me after suffering a bulged disc in her back. She assumed she had injured herself lifting something. I did a few minor tests which revealed her structural instability. She was amazed by just how unstable her body really was. The lifting incident that she felt caused the injury was really just the straw that broke this client's back. Many fitness professionals refer to this as core strength but I tend to believe that core begins at your feet and ends with your fingertips. In short, your entire body is your core and anything injured affects your movement patterns causing weakness and high injury risk. When all of the forces of your body can stabilize you properly, your core is stable and strong as well.

3 Q'S OF EATING AND FOOD

Eating and Food is not nearly as difficult as most so-called experts would have you believe. I have a few Q's for you that should fix it right up.

Quantity is generally the biggest problem (no pun intended) and is also the single thing concretely linked to longevity as there are several studies that show that reasonable restrictive intake of food increases life expectancy. That being said, going through life hungry will probably lead to poor relationships, anger management problems and increased conflict. In my experience, when we are hungry we are not very happy, yet when we are **over-full**, we are totally lethargic and relatively useless. Quantity is the easiest of the Q's to control, yet most people show no control when it comes to food. If you are heavier than you would like to be…eat less by leaving a portion of your plate clean or getting away from the table. Social gorging is just a mess, so come up with a better hobby and have some physical fun with your friends, family and coworkers. Distracted eating is the worst quantity control practice, and relates to the second and third Q as well.

Quality is the next factor to look at and is as simple as saying logically, "what is the quality of the food I am eating and could I do better right now?" If we are eating junk food, we are not only consuming useless, nutritionally void and potentially harmful junk (by the very name), but you are likely replacing an opportunity to consume something of quality for which your body may make great use. When I say "great use," remember the part above where I spoke of you being built and rebuilt and repaired every second of every day? Well, this is what quality food does best. Think about the amount of processing and coloring and chemical garbage that goes into what passes for food, something that has no nutritional value besides calories. Eat far less of that and more real healthy organic human food of the highest quality you can obtain.

I conducted an oral quiz with a large group of firefighters at a local Volunteer fire station and ***it was not amazing*** when everyone was able to tell me what foods are good for us. When asked the logical follow up question about how many of them actually actively sought to incorporate these better dietary choices into their meals, the majority admitted they did not. The same responses came from my daughter's third grade class a few years ago when I gave a talk on health and fitness. You know what foods are good for you so why are you making poor choices when your health depends on it. A quick reminder about our first Q however, quantity prevails, as too much of a good thing is still too much. Overindulgence in high quality food will affect us poorly.

The third and final **Q** of food is **Quiet**. Now I am not suggesting that we should create a sound proof room or join a monastery to have our meals, but rather that we should take the time to chew and eat our meals in a way that lets you relax, smile and enjoy our time nourishing our body. Remember it is the body we were born to live in©. For many of us, meals have become yet another burden to rush through, to multi-task or skip altogether. The peace and mindfulness one gains by employing this third Q each day reaps countless rewards in terms of stress reduction, far better benefit from our meals and overall inner calm. Most people spend their lives nowadays running from place to place "getting things done," but what they may not realize is that 15-30 minutes of this type of relaxation can reap huge rewards by giving us hours of refocused energy and quality thought, not to mention greatly improved digestion. Get out of our busy life and spend time focused on eating foods that help us heal from life's fast pace and thoughtless nature. When we do, we will surely feel the world open up with greatly increased energy and improved personal quality in our lives.

What can my company and I do to help you, your family or your company, school, school system or organization improve and enter the Fitness Longevity Paradigm? Seminars, workshops, and coaching for your company, one-on-one personal analysis and or coaching for individuals, in our location or yours, are all available. We offer fitness longevity professional training, certification and continuing education as well as goal oriented and injury prevention for individual athletes and sports team assessments and training programs. Analysis of your family, group or organization can be scheduled at our location or yours. Information is available upon request.

About Sam

Sam Iannetta grew up an exceptionally skinny yet perpetually hungry kid. Fortunately, having parents who emigrated from Italy meant there was never a lack of food in his house. At the age of 10, he got fascinated with weightlifting and exercise. He took little jobs for neighbors and a local store and purchased his first weights. A year later, a Police Athletic League opened three blocks from his home. He started working out with police officers twice to three times his size. There was a great passion in them because they needed that high level of fitness, their lives depended on it. Inspired by the people around him, he worked out hard and started gaining serious strength. Many officers had injuries, aches and pains. He had a deep desire to help them. He started researching rehabilitation, injury prevention, and biomechanics. He became the "go-to-kid" for problems with their bodies. He had no idea it would become his life's work. Currently with over 44,000 hours of one-on-one personal training and over 3,000 hours of group instruction of children to seniors, he is considered by some to be one of the most experienced personal trainers in the United States.

In 1992, Sam started creating a system of analysis of human movement that incorporated his years of knowledge and experience, but he added one more crucial element, **Common Sense**. He found out some time later it was not so common. In 2002, he opened a fitness center in Boulder, Colorado called Sam Iannetta's Functional Fitness and Wellness Center and trained others in his system. The trainers stated, "It was like having a new set of eyes." They could see problems in clients' movement long before an injury occurred. They train 700 to 1000+ sessions a month in a 2,800 square foot facility. Denver, Colorado is always among the top 10 fittest cities in the U.S. and Boulder makes Denver look lazy. In 2008, Sam Iannetta founded the concept of Fitness Longevity™ which is his system of fitness based not on how fit someone can be, but...**how long they want to stay fit**.

Here Sam was in what people called an incredibly fit city, yet clients came in with injuries, pain and premature wear and tear. In 1995, Sam created the concept of the S.P.O.R.T. Paradigm© standing for Specific Performance of Repetitive Trauma. This is the paradigm that he grew up in learning Sports Education in our Physical Education system. P.E. wasn't physical education; it was S.E. or sports education – teaching little or nothing about your physical body. His clients realized that in committing to playing any sport or sport-like activity, they were signing an unwritten contract, **"I am willing to sacrifice my body for my sport."** He coined the concept of the Fitness Longevity Paradigm© as a replacement for the current

SPORT Paradigm©. Let him help install the idea that maintaining fitness should be for life. This is **Fitness Longevity**™.

Find out more at: www.functionalfitnessusa.com, www.livingfunctional.com
or email: functionalfitnessusa@gmail.com

Or call: 303-440-1440.

CHAPTER 40

HOW TO START AND GROW A SUCCESSFUL DENTAL PRACTICE IN ANY ECONOMY

BY STEPHEN SEIDLER, DDS

Growing a dental practice or any successful business for that matter is no secret. If you decide to put in a lot of hard work, dedication and become committed to mastering your craft, anyone can grow the practice or business of their dreams. In my case, starting from scratch with no patients whatsoever, I grew a practice to the top 1% of all dental practices in the United States, sold it, then opened a new practice with no patients and did it all over again.

What makes me qualified to be viewed as a successful dentist? My name is Steve Seidler and I have spent over 32 years as a practicing dentist:

- Attending over 2000 hours in continuing dental education courses.
- Have performed all phases of dentistry on tens of thousands of satisfied patients. These procedures include cosmetics, veneers, whitening, root canals, crowns, bridges, surgery, implants, mini-implants, adult orthodontics, sleep apnea treatment and sedation (sleep dentistry).
- Have given numerous courses and taught my techniques to many other dentists.

- Top 10 provider of Mini Dental Implants in the eastern United States

- Have created a dental assistant school where I have helped hundreds of students with no previous dental experience how to become expanded duty dental assistants.

- Named to America's Best Dentists, Leading Physicians of the World and America's Premier Dentists as featured in USA Today.

- I am a Fellow of the Academy of General Dentistry, and a member of the American Dental Association, Florida Dental Association, Dental Society of Greater Orlando and the American Dental Society of Anesthesiologists.

My story begins after graduating from Georgetown Dental School in 1979. Having no experience and not much more self confidence, I decided to join the United States Navy. This would become the beginning of my never-ending quest to get as much continuing education in dentistry as I possibly could. In addition to gaining much needed experience by performing dentistry on naval personnel, I was able to learn from senior naval dentists who represented dental specialties from every field. During my time in the navy, I realized that dental school doesn't really teach you how to become a good dentist; it just gives you a license to begin the learning process.

After getting my dental 'sea legs' in the navy, I decided to open a brand new three chair dental practice in 1981 after serving my military commitment. I began with one employee, then quickly had the demand to hire a second and third, based primarily on a successful direct mail marketing campaign. Fast forward five years, the practice grew to eight chairs where I employed two dental hygienists, an associate dentist and five auxiliary personnel. During this growth process, I took as many continuing education courses as possible with an emphasis on sedation because I quickly realized two things about dental patients:

1. Rarely if ever does a patient want to be referred out for specialty services and

2. Most dental patients range from slightly apprehensive to absolutely petrified to undergo dental treatment.

During this five year period I successfully obtained my Fellowship in the Academy of General Dentistry, an honor only 2% of dentists nationwide achieve. It requires the passing of an examination and completion of over 1000 hours in continuing education. In addition, I completed a 100-hour internship at the University of Alabama in conscious sedation.

In 1998, I thought I might want to try something new, and a dental management company offered to buy my dental practice, do all of the administrative chores and allow me to just do dentistry. Sounded great, but I only agreed to sell because the company promised to allow me to operate the practice as I always had, with the same patient-comes-first systems. For the first 10 years or so, they kept their promise and pretty much kept a hands-off approach. The name on the door stayed the same and most patients were not aware of the change in ownership. When the economy was in the midst of its downturn in 2009, things began to change to where due to cost cutting measures, I was not able to deliver the type of patient care that I was accustomed to. As a result, in 2011 I finally resigned from the company and left the practice that I had started some 30 years before.

I felt too young to retire, so at age 58 I started the process all over again. Not many people are given the opportunity of a do over, but that's exactly what I got! I again started a new practice with no existing patients in an uncertain economy, with the belief that if I did it once, I could do it again. Utilizing the systems that I developed the first time around and by being totally committed to exemplary service to our patients, the practice has quickly grown to maximum capacity in less than one year.

So what's the secret of my success? The answer is simple; the very best customer service possible with a great staff and the development and the utilization of great systems. Four of the most important systems that will quickly grow a successful dental practice are:

- Having a clear ***Mission Statement*** with a ***Great Staff*** to support it
- The use of a ***Treatment Coordinator***
- Being able to do ***Conscious Sedation Dentistry*** and
- The ability to provide ***Full Service Dentistry***

MISSION STATEMENT SUPPORTED BY A GREAT STAFF

Creating a mission statement is a highly individualized process that not only encompasses the dentist's vision of what the ideal practice should be, but also must be fully supported by the staff. As an example, our mission statement is:

> *With advanced technology, state of the art equipment and extensive experience in a comfortable environment, we will always strive to provide the optimal level of affordable dental care and never compromise our treatment in any way.*
>
> *We will provide a compassionate, pampered, courteous and caring environment so that we can greatly exceed each of our patient's expectations.*
>
> *We will support, encourage, respect and inspire each other; we will have fun and communicate openly so that we can obtain all of our goals both personally and professionally.*

This mission statement is fully supported by our staff and in practice translates to exceptional customer service. Getting a great team in place takes time and patience. What I've learned is that most skills needed by a team in a dental practice can be trained except for the values and personality traits needed to achieve the customer service-based practice. As long as the doctor is clear that this is the type of practice desired, the task is simply finding like-minded individuals to fill out the staff.

USING A TREATMENT COORDINATOR

In today's competitive post-great recession environment, having great customer service is absolutely essential to having a successful practice. The key is treating people like you yourself would like to be treated and always trying to deliver more than you promise. The very best way to achieve this is by utilizing a treatment coordinator and providing what we call *"The New Patient Experience."*

The idea of having a treatment coordinator can be applied to any medical or dental practice. *"The New Patient Experience"* begins by having our treatment coordinator greet the patient and get to know the patient by asking a series of questions to find out specifically what the patient is seeking. She then takes all needed records including x-rays, digital photos and intra-oral photos. As she is taking the records the treatment coordinator points out dental problems and potential solutions to these problems to the patient. All of this is done before the doctor ever examines the patient. Following the doctors examination and treatment plan formulation, the treatment coordinator then goes over the treatment recommendations of the doctor and offers the patient affordable financial options in order to have the treatment accomplished.

By using a treatment coordinator for each new patient, it allows us to establish a relationship of trust and to give each patient an experience that's unlike any they have had in any other medical or dental office. We do this by making the patient feel special, listened to, and treated as a unique individual. Think about it ...don't you tend to feel better when you go to a place where you are recognized and fussed over?

Additionally, the treatment coordinator is able to form a bond with each patient. In order to do this, each new patient is scheduled for 2 hours although it may take less time than this. This gives the patient ample opportunity to ask questions and have all of their dental problems and potential solutions explained. Having a treatment coordinator and creating a "New Patient Experience" truly is a win-win situation. By having our patients truly understand their dental problems and having us know their concerns, it gives them the ability to accept any level of treatment they desire. It also creates the opportunity for the dentist to help many patients with their dental problems.

Once patients recognize the need to have dental treatment done, the fear of having the procedures done will often delay or even cause the patient to postpone treatment. That brings us to the next essential system for a great dental practice; Conscious Sedation Dentistry.

CONSCIOUS SEDATION DENTISTRY

There are many reasons to incorporate conscious sedation dentistry into a dental practice. Conscious sedation is very useful when patients have:

- High anxiety and fear of dental procedures
- A severe gag reflex
- A need or desire to have all of their dentistry done in one to two visits
- Chronic or acute jaw soreness when getting dentistry done

- Difficulty getting numb
- A desire to have dentistry done comfortably while fully relaxed

Conscious sedation consists of a combination of oral and/or IV medications. A single pill is given to the patient to take one hour prior to their dental appointment. This will produce a sense of calm and relaxation by the time the patient is ready for their dental appointment. For some patients, oral sedation is all that is needed. However for many patients that are more nervous or who have had a bad dental experience, an IV line is obtained and medication is given so that the patients is able to snooze through their appointment. It's important to note that this is not general anesthesia. The patient is always able to respond to the doctor when asked. Most patients though have very little if any recollection of the appointment so that a 3 hour appointment may feel like 15 minutes. In addition, due to the muscles relaxing from the sedation, there is no gag reflex and a greatly-reduced incidence of a sore jaw.

Patients will often ask if this procedure is safe.

- ➢ During sedation, we constantly monitor the patient's blood pressure, oxygen level, and heart rate.
- ➢ Since the patient is relaxed while sedated, there is much less chance of stress induced complications such as increased blood pressure, angina or hyperventilation.
- ➢ In 30 years of practice, I have never had a health complication as a result of sedation.

So, is it safe? In a word, yes!

Most dentists that advertise sedation are only able to deliver a single pill to provide the sedation. This has severe limitations for highly anxious patients. In order to provide true conscious sedation, I attended a 100 hour residency at the University of Alabama to have the necessary training to provide this valuable service. In addition, doing conscious sedation requires taking courses in advanced cardio-pulmonary life saving (ACLS).

This brings us to the third absolutely essential item in having a highly successful and rewarding dental practice; being able to provide full service dentistry.

FULL SERVICE DENTISTRY

What do I mean by full service dentistry? My definition of full service dentistry is "the ability to provide any and all dental services needed by each patient at least equal to the level of a dental specialist." Why is this necessary? Mainly, the reason is that most patients do not like to be referred out of your practice. They already know and trust you. By referring out a patient, you are asking them to go to a new doctor who they don't know and who probably will charge a significant fee just to examine the patient and make the same diagnosis you have already made.

Do I ever have the need to refer out a patient? Of course. The referral of a patient to a specialist is occasionally needed. There may be an unusual problem that requires another opinion. Or there may be a procedure such as impacted wisdom teeth removal where the patient would be better served by an oral surgeon because this is one procedure where due to the vast numbers of this procedure done by oral surgeons, this is something they can do quicker and thus more comfortably for the patient. The goal though is to be able to treat the vast majority of patients in your own office.

So how does a dentist become a full service dentist? There are no shortcuts. It takes considerable continuing education along with experience in doing the various procedures. I believe that when you become a dentist, you assume the responsibility to never stop learning. Your patients are owed nothing less.

Growing a highly successful practice obviously involves more than the factors mentioned above. Using these keys however is a great start to create the practice of your dreams during any economic conditions.

About Dr. Stephen

Dr. Seidler utilizes his extensive training and experience to treat even the most challenging dental situations. He has been delivering cosmetic, implant, and functional solutions to patients for over 32 years. His commitment to "doing it right" and ability to "handle just about anything" has won him the admiration of patients and other doctors. A big bonus is that Dr. Seidler uses his expertise to prevent big problems from ever happening.

Dr. Seidler graduated from The University of Florida with a Bachelor of Science degree in 1975 and graduated with special distinction from Georgetown University School of Dentistry in 1979. He then served in the United States Naval Dental Corps for 2 years. Since 1981, Dr. Seidler has been in private practice in Orange City, Florida for 30 years and the last 2 years in Sanford, Florida. Over those 32 years of practice, he has accumulated over 2000 hours in dental continuing education including a 100 hour course in advanced dental sedation techniques at the University of Alabama in Birmingham, Alabama.

Dr. Seidler has won numerous awards and received much recognition in his 32 years of dental practice. These are highlighted by being named to *Top Dentists in Florida* by the International Association of Dentists, America's Best Dentists by The National Consumer Advisory Board and *America's Premier Dentists* as featured in *USA Today*. He is a member of the American Dental Association, Florida Dental Association, Dental Society of Greater Orlando, Florida Dental Association of Anesthesiology and is a Fellow of the Academy of General Dentistry.

The fellowship in the Academy of General Dentistry recognizes the broad range of dentistry that Dr. Seidler's post-graduate education provides for patient benefit. He also operates a dental assistant school that teaches students the art and science of dental assisting and provides them with career opportunities to do his part in helping improve the job market. In addition, Dr. Seidler has provided lectures to other dentists on his practice techniques.

Dr. Seidler performs all phases of general dentistry with a special emphasis on implant and sedation dentistry. He is able to provide all dental services including oral surgery, implants, mini-implants, fixed and removable prosthodontics, cosmetics, conscious sedation, adult orthodontics, root canal therapy, operative dentistry and sleep apnea treatment. Dr. Seidler enjoys teaching what he has learned about dentistry to others. He also enjoys spending time with his 3 children aged 28, 26 and 16.

CHAPTER 41

HARNESSING THE POWER OF THE 100TH MONKEY

BY CHOY WONG AND YVONNE DAYAN

In the 1950's, as the legend goes (as per Lyall Watson's foreword to Lawrence's Blair's Rhythms of Vision, 1975), there were monkeys on the Japanese island of Koshima who loved sweet potatoes. However, they would not eat those fallen in the sand since they disliked the taste of dirt. One day, it occurred to a young adventurous monkey to wash the dirty potatoes in the river, which could now be enjoyed. All others followed suit. This started a different reality, a new future.

What's even stranger is that, at a certain moment in time, all monkeys on neighboring islands who had never been in contact with each other, simultaneously possessed the same knowledge and were doing the same thing, much like the instant assimilation and omniscience of the DNAs in our physical body.

This phenomena, known as The Hundredth Monkey effect, theorizes that there is an undetermined level of critical mass for every occurrence that, when reached, instantly transcends global consciousness and everyone's life instantly becomes endowed with the selfsame level of knowledge, emotion, ability and behavior.

In the same way, global change among humans starts with just one mind, one person, such as you or I. Change is the natural progression of life whether in nature, society or the world. There are many who resist change, but resisting change is futile since it is inevitable and will occur from moment to moment.

Sometimes, even when we know change is necessary, either personally or professionally, we still resist it, nevertheless.

We must distinguish between these two kinds of "change":

(1) change that occurs by force of nature and

(2) change that can be initiated by human will or desire. This is the kind of change that can eclipse the forces of nature, transcend human destiny and enrich human evolution.

The first monkey washed her potato, because of her own desire to satisfy her taste. By exercising her own will she transformed the group consciousness of all monkeys, thus empowering the free will of everyone to do the same.

Change brought about by exertion of human will can likewise advance the evolution of human consciousness through these seven meaningful steps: awareness, possibility, desire, evaluation, decision-making, activation/empowerment and commitment.

SEVEN STEPS TO BECOMING A POWERFUL CHANGE AGENT:

1. AWARENESS

Awareness is the agent that allows us to become conscious and discover the purpose of our lives. When people are not aware of who they are, and can't recognize their role in the world, they miss out on the power they wield to effect change.

Knowing that *You* are a change agent is the first step toward creating change. Recognizing that you're the one who can make the difference, and acknowledging that you hold the future of your life and of human destiny itself in your hands, makes it possible for you to remove any barriers and effect meaningful change.

You are the most important change-maker in your life and in the lives of those around you. To become an active participant in change, embrace the reality that **you** are the active part of that change. Too often, people wait for things around them to change because they're not aware that they can play a definitive part in determining the kind of change that occurs. You can definitely exert your power and influence over your own future. Thus, with awareness comes possibility.

2. POSSIBILITY

The world is filled with possibility and wonder. By becoming aware of your own power, possibility opens up. You can thereby activate the possibility within you to accomplish any significant change you desire. Remember that every possibility, every change on the planet started from just one, single change agent.

What changes are possible?

And which would contribute the most to your life?

The possibility of success?

The possibility of wealth?

The possibility of health?

The possibility of love?

The possibility of relationships?

The possibility of peace?

The possibility of happiness?

The possibility of contribution to humanity

The possibility of serving the world?

The possibility of higher consciousness?

Whichever possibilities align with your personal power will actually represent the changes you can manifest for yourself and for others. To do so, it is essential that you develop a strong will or desire to begin the conscious process of change.

3. DESIRE

As change agents, the strength and passion of your desire will make it possible for you to partner up with life and effect the changes as per your desired outcome. If your desire is not strong enough, then any change that happens will more likely be in accordance with the force of nature.

To create powerful, positive, change, make your desire stronger than your fear of failing.

Either you determine the circumstances of your life or others will. Thus, you are the conscious evaluator and primary influence in the evolution of your destiny.

4. EVALUATION

Before effecting any desired change, proactively evaluate your possibilities, as not all changes end up good or positive.

As you evaluate, avoid reacting impulsively. There's lots of spam around and it's never life's purpose for you to take on every random circumstance or occurrence that comes your way. Analyze all available options. Focus on achieving your purpose.

- Which are your best options for the positive changes you want to make in your life?
- What are the action steps you would need to make to achieve the destiny you desire?

Rather than having life's random events determine and shape your life, decide which to let pass and which happen to be opportunities that fit harmoniously into your own life's plans and goals, and thus, yours to engage.

Discerning which changes are the right ones for you is not always easy and may require much pondering and deep reflection, since the truth can only come from within yourself. When you connect to that place of trust within, and get to listen to your own inner wisdom, you will intuitively know what to do.

5. DECISION-MAKING

Every new decision you bring forth transforms your future and the lives of those around you. The future of the world converges at the juncture of every one of your decision-making processes.

As you make choices that honor who you are and also accept the right of others to make their own life's choices, whether you agree with them or not, you truly start growing, and becoming more expansive.

You start elevating your own energy, and vibrating at higher frequency, whereby your mere presence becomes a catalyst for change. Your whole energy field becomes a source for empowerment, creativity and leadership. You walk into a room, and suddenly you stand out like a brightly-lit chandelier. You have probably personally experienced at least one such magnetic personality who dynamically draws others to their light. At this level, you become this powerful pillar of attraction. This is the energy field that all true change agents generate around themselves.

At a quantum level, each change changes everything else on the planet. No one ever contemplated the fall of the Berlin wall as a possibility. However, as human will transformed global consciousness, there was no stopping the people from tearing down the Berlin wall. What had started decades ago in the mind of one thinker finally reached critical mass. A new directive became activated in global consciousness and people became part of that one global mindset and moved with one force to remove the wall, which was a metaphor for human imprisonment and limitation.

6. ACTIVATION/EMPOWERMENT

As the Chinese proverb says, a journey of a thousand miles starts with a single step. So it is with our lives; all journeys, even those of a thousand miles or more must necessarily start with empowering oneself to take the first step. Follow your sound, conscious choices that come from the highest place within you. Empower yourself to take the most effective action and commit yourself to its accomplishment and realization.

Business owners or managers who wish to effect change in their businesses, recognize the need for change and try to take the steps to change, but often, they do not realize that their staff is not yet onboard. Managers then, become frustrated and give up before the staff has had the opportunity to assimilate the proposed changes, thus resulting in failure. So, it becomes vital for any team leader to first achieve the effective enlistment and participation of their staff.

7. COMMITMENT

Be totally committed to any change you take on and sustain this commitment until your purpose has been achieved. Some changes happen quickly, but most of them take time to set in, some may even take years.

Change is not only a result that is achieved. Change is also a process that takes a certain amount of time and often, effort and sacrifice. Patience is a virtue.

Those who expect change to happen quickly are often disappointed and are missing part of the equation. In the business world, most new enterprises fail within the first two to three years. Frequently, this is due to the need for better planning and marketing or because people gave up too soon. Positive change requires lots of faith, strength and a sustained commitment until your goal is achieved. For change agents who wish to create an ideal world, the next step is to take on the following tasks and functions.

THE PROCESS FOR BETTERING YOUR WORLD:

a). ENROLLMENT

Destiny is the secret recruiter of all change agents on the planet. It enrolls us, often through adversity, failure and setbacks. Some of us necessarily go through crisis in life in order to grow and develop our strength and character for this purpose. Often we do not understand what is going on at the time, and cannot make any sense of it, but in hindsight we recognize these mishaps as the unique process destiny uses to mold us into the most formidable change agents.

Those who are aware of the flow of life become the most successful in creating change. They learn not to resist the changes that life throws at them, and instead partner up with and utilize change in new creative ways.

With some practice, you too, can learn to say: Yes! Always welcome change that comes your way, and trust that the changes happening in your life are for your greatest good. Instead of resisting, this new attitude towards life provides possibility for great opportunities for growth and contribution. Apply this old adage: "When life gives you lemons, make lemonade."

b). GROWTH

"Conformity is the jailer of freedom and the enemy of growth."
~ JF Kennedy

Personal growth is a necessary part of evolution, as it betters our personality and character. It calls for active leadership, continued learning, and taking action, while pursuing breakthroughs that push us to our max. These actions are the opposite of apathy, conformity and resistance. When we choose to resist, life will have us go through excruciating circumstances that help us understand we need to move on, until we catch on. As we let go, we grow and develop higher values.

c). DEVELOPMENT OF HIGHER VALUES

Development of our higher values such as compassion, understanding and acceptance for our fellow human beings impassions our quest to improve the world around us. As we enact these noble works of service, we ourselves become totally inundated by the overflow of the creative force that calls us forth to accomplish the mission we are finally privileged to own up to.

d). DESIRE TO IMPACT THE LIVES OF OTHERS

Developing higher values defines the quality and impact we can have in our business as well as our personal relationships. We have all been witness to the amazing power of the human spirit when another's life is impacted. It ignites our innate desire to contribute to others.

e). INTEGRITY

Integrity is the compass that determines that our impact on others will be one that fosters a constructive change that builds and unites. Integrity requires that you act from your authentic self. When aligned from your true self, you become the vessel and force for positive energy in the world, which can only manifest as success, prosperity, love, peace, happiness and higher consciousness. You start drawing to you the best opportunities and the most rewarding relationships. As we learn to live selflessly and give of ourselves, we can't help but become the 100th monkey for a whole new way of living on planet earth.

f). PASSIONATE INTENTION

Passionate intention is the mover and shaker of change. It requires the discipline to be constant and undistracted and to persevere and persist and not give up, even when things get difficult and seem impossible to achieve. And passionate intention keeps you committed to your mission.

G). MISSION

A mission's purpose is to concentrate your power. Therefore, allow your mission to keep you focused throughout your journey of exercising your "true" calling as a powerful and effective change agent.

Carrying out your mission channels your energy and power into the universe, contributing to a still young humanity in much need of leadership and guidance…

h). CREATING YOUR OWN TEAM

Reach out and create your own team of change agents. You can create change in your life by yourself, but to change the world requires that you form a dedicated team of change agents.

Recruiting your team and embarking on your mission as change agents must start out by first bettering our character, enabling our people skills, opening our hearts to unconditional loving and caring, committing to our values and principles without compromise, and dedicating ourselves to fulfilling our destiny through service and contribution.

As part of their mission, business owners and executives take on the world of commerce and industry by :

(1) Empowering management's and employees' character and professional capability (initiative, leadership, emotional intelligence, creativity, productivity, effectiveness).

(2) Improving management's and employees' lifestyle, prosperity and well-being.

(3) Creating better products and services that over-deliver true value since we are dedicated to truly serving our world.

WHAT ARE THE BENEFITS OF BECOMING A CHANGE AGENT

- o You get the opportunity to achieve self-realization, which means to know yourself – which is the greatest treasure in life.

- o You get to fulfill your destiny. Fulfillment is the only accomplishment that leads to true happiness. And when you're happy, you've become the 100th change agent for happiness on the planet.

- o You achieve the state of higher consciousness, which raises your vibrational frequency, endowing you with a cosmic force that allows you to become the master of your own destiny.
- o You start exerting instant influence over happenings around you. Ultimately, you become imbued with power that seems magical and your desires achieve instant 100th Monkey Effect.

For more information on the power of a change agent or details about embarking on your own experiential journey of self-discovery, self-mastery and self-enlightenment, visit: www.imastery.net

May the multitudes be touched by your example of giving and service, and use you as their role model to likewise become enrolled as conscious change agents as a force for good on the planet.

About Choy

CHOY WONG, entrepreneur, corporate trainer, life coach, and author, is regarded as a top specialist in leadership and business management, emotional intelligence, personal growth and self-mastery. Having achieved his own financial independence at the age of 26, he has helped hundreds of thousands internationally to achieve their life's dreams and goals by empowering his students with the same disciplines and systems he himself had to master.

Choy has devoted his life to teaching his unique technology on success, wealth and happiness. He possesses a unique insight into human nature and the mechanics of life. His programs have helped entrepreneurs, executives and professionals become more effective and accomplished, prosperous, loving and fulfilled, in both their professional and personal lives. He has taught his programs at several universities, lectured widely for the past 30 years, and appears regularly on radio and TV in the U.S. and abroad. He's just developed the latest cutting-edge technology on powerfully overcoming our modern challenges and succeeding in the *new economy*.

About Yvonne

YVONNE DAYAN – Entrepreneur, gifted author, and corporate trainer, is a pioneer in the field of human potential. Her expertise in life and success coaching has helped thousands achieve breakthroughs in their personal growth, emotional excellence, and wealth creation.

As an accomplished entrepreneur with various degrees in psychology and counseling, Yvonne is often sought by the media as an expert and spokesperson in the fields of success and social behavior. She has appeared internationally on numerous TV and radio programs, in magazines and newspapers and was featured in the documentary movie: *ANYTHING BUT ORDINARY: ORDINARY PEOPLE EXTRAORDINARY LIVES.*

In 2005, Yvonne produced the acclaimed DVD Series *"Creating Your Own Fountain of Youth," "Bringing Down the Light"* and *"Restoring Your Soul to Wholeness"* that created a paradigm shift in the way we can use our mind-body connection to impassion and heal our lives. She has also appeared with Harrison Ford and Kristin Scott Thomas in the movie *"Random Hearts."*

Driven by principle and passion Yvonne has dedicated her life to empowering others to reach their highest purpose. She specializes in coaching today's modern women in leading extraordinary lives.

Yvonne has been designing transformational programs for over 20 years, incorporating unique life-changing techniques she herself has mastered, and actively teaches her innovative seminars to both students and trainers in major cities throughout the U.S., Latin America, and Europe.

The Team

THE WONG-DAYAN TEAM brings together a rich and combined experience of more than 50 years in the fields of corporate and consciousness training, from which their students and members will benefit in any of their programs.

They are the best-selling authors of their "*24 hours to Master Your Life*" Book Series. The iMastery Group International, Imastery Seminars, Seminarios Imastery and Seminarios Caminos boast more than 350,000 graduates, and hold seminar events every week in more than 65 markets in the United States, South & Central America, the Caribbean and Europe. Their various teaching organizations, some established since 1980, hold over 1000 training seminars yearly, led by their team of 300 seminar trainers, and 1200 personal coaches, both in English and Spanish.

Contact information: www.IMASTERY.net and Tel. 1-800-756-1064

CHAPTER 42

NOT WITH THAT ATTITUDE

BY DR. THOMAS MATTERN

Did you know that your teeth continue to tell a story about you long after your death? The shape of teeth indicates ancestry, while the conditions of the teeth tell a story of their use. For example, we know that certain ancient tribes used rocks to grind their flour because when they consumed the rock-flour mix over a lifetime it completely wore down their molars. Similarly, day-to-day use of toothpicks will leave characteristic markings on teeth as well. Taking care of your teeth is not only good for your oral health and saves you money, but it will also leave a record for future generations of your oral health habits!

Fear is a major factor in people's avoidance of the dentist. Every year that a person avoids seeing the dentist adds about $1000 per year to their lifetime dental treatment costs. Therefore, if a person has not been to the dentist in 15-20 years, that person will likely need approximately $15,000-$20,000 of dental work to repair the damage caused by neglect. There are as many reasons why people neglect their dental health as there are people; however, the biggest barriers are often the easiest for a dental practice to address. Even celebrity chef Paula Deen commented, "I'm so glad I'm not a dentist. How many times does someone say, 'Oh, Doc, it felt so good when you were drilling my teeth'? Never. But when you give someone a wonderful cookie, you put a little of yourself in it, and you see someone's face light up – that's immediate approval." Many businesses face the same image issues that a dentist does. Rarely do people get excited about having to call a plumber, pay for routine maintenance on their cars or purchase life insurance. These businesses are perceived by the consumer as an inconvenience or a nuisance. Combatting the perception of one's business as a "nuisance" is a hefty order, but by focusing on the customer and minimizing their fears, with a fun and informative visit, a dentist can change not only the patient's perception, but their life. Changing the focus of the business even slightly can remove impediments that might otherwise keep customers, patients and clients from reaching a business.

The single biggest factor in developing my ability to focus my business was my decision to run my business in the same manner that I ran my life. My children can attest that whenever I hear someone utter the words, " I can't do that," my immediate response is, "Not with that attitude!" I knew that my staff and I had to approach a patient's fears with a completely positive and supportive attitude. We had to create an amazing experience for them so that their perception of a dental visit went from fear to comfort. Changing the way we think has encouraged us to focus on delivering more than is expected every day.

DELIVER MORE THAN IS EXPECTED

Our patients expect us to examine their teeth; they do not expect our concern for their overall health. While our patients might not brag about the great time they had getting a tooth drilled and filled, they will likely tell their friends about the service they received but did not expect. For example, we check every patient's vital signs (blood pressure, pulse) before we examine their teeth. Many patients do not understand the correlation between oral health and overall health. We once detected dangerously high blood pressure in a patient of 199/121. We immediately sent him off to the hospital for follow-up. He later called to thank us because he had none of the symptoms, like headaches, commonly associated with heart disease and could have died if the condition went unchecked. Whenever we notice something that might compromise a patient's overall health, we encourage them to follow up with their doctor. For example, a patient with greater than a 17 inch neck has a significantly higher probability of having sleep apnea. We offer dental appliances for mild to moderate sleep apnea, again, to improve a patient's overall health. We make patients aware, and we share our own experiences to improve their lives.

We know that dental emergencies such as a broken tooth do not always happen at convenient times or during normal business hours. Our emergency line is always available to our patients in need. Convenience for the patients, our customers, is a major part of a customer-driven business. Our multiple locations make us more accessible than our competition.

OFFER MULTIPLE LOCATIONS

Today's busy work schedules and family life can run a person ragged, and we do not want to add to the stress with a long commute to the dentist. In a large city like Phoenix, a single location means your business is only accessible to a small cross-section of the population. We choose to meet our patients where they are. By offering five offices, we provide our services near their work and their homes. We even opened an office in a town where a number of Phoenix residents spend their summers.

With multiple locations, we ensure a wonderful patient experience at each location by investing the time and energy into our staff. Repetition of our core office values at our morning huddle meetings keeps everyone focused in the same direction. Giving our staff the authority to fix patient issues while they are small is a key factor to our success.

CREATE A STRONG BUSINESS MODEL

I learned an important lesson when I was growing up and had my own lawn care service that later evolved into part of our business model. I mowed lawns all summer long, and generally took exemplary care of my customers. One year, however, I was more focused on getting back to school than taking care of my customers. I did not arrange for continued lawn care in my absence and unfortunately lost customers as a result. I learned that summer that it is far easier to meet a customer's needs than it is to find a new customer. We strive daily to meet every client's needs.

I carried that lesson into my dental business. We adopted the "Ritz Carlton" approach to customer service. We strive to deliver more than the patient expects and make the experience as smooth and as quick as possible. In these days when it is hard for people to get off work to come in, if we find something in an exam we try to do that work at the same time so the patient does not have to make an additional appointment. Providing same day treatment is a service that our patients truly appreciate. For those patients that need us immediately, we promise our customers that if they call before 10:00am for an appointment, we will get them on the schedule the same day. We are there for them.

As a dentist and business owner it is imperative to give your customers more than they expect. With that concept in mind I have spent a large part of my career attending high quality courses to add to and improve the services that I can offer to our patients. I travel between the offices to perform the more difficult oral surgeries, root canals or implants that patients require. This allows the patient the convenience of getting all their work done at one office. My focus on continuing education has been matched by my associates who also strive to add to their skill set. In addition, we have added specialists such as pediatric and periodontal dentists to our staff to add to the expertise that is available at one location.

Having all of this expertise available in one office requires good organization. The key to a smooth operation is our morning meetings. It provides the doctors with an opportunity to address the team, discuss any challenging procedures for the day, review patient medical requirements and identify openings in the schedule that can be used for same day treatment. Huddles are completed by reminding the team that our focus is always to make our patient's day. With the team all focused in the same direction, the work is more enjoyable. Being focused and aware of the schedule allows our assistants to know when they can offer same-day treatment and still maintain a smooth workflow. This provides an optimal experience for patients, doctors and staff. Getting started right allows us to work better. When we satisfy our patients, the practice thrives.

Our staffing method is another unique aspect of our business. We test and hire people not only for their technical skills, but their customer service skills as well. Staff must have the ability to perform their duties, educate the patients and reduce their anxiety. In order to create an amazing experience we understand we must have an amazing staff. We also empower our staff to fix, on the spot, any issues that arise with a patient. For example, if our staff is running late and an appointment gets pushed back when it is not our patient's fault, our staff will offer that patient a gift card to a store such as Starbucks or Target with a note thanking them for "being our patient and for being patient." Maintaining clients is not optional, it is imperative. Once we have created positive, memorable experiences for our patients, we ask them for referrals. The best new patients often come to us because another satisfied customer recommended our services. We want every relationship to be win-win; to that end, we also offer dental warranties on our work.

DENTAL WARRANTY

A warranty says, "I stand behind my work." We offer our patients up to a five-year warranty on our work as long as they practice the general maintenance necessary like cleanings and exams at least every six months. No questions and no exceptions, if they hold up their end we hold up ours. For an expensive dental procedure such as a crown, the likelihood of the porcelain crown chipping is about 1 in 100. The possibility of having to re-treat free of charge is a small expense for keeping the customer happy. The caveat that the patient must maintain their teeth, both at home and with regular office exams, encourages our patients to stay on track with their oral healthcare. Long term, these dental warranties save time, pain and money for both our office and the patient. A dental warranty is a moot point if the patient cannot afford dental care to begin with, so we offer a Dental Assistance Plan to our patients as well.

DENTAL ASSISTANCE SAVINGS PLAN

Our office has created a special dental savings plan just for our patients. Patients with insurance tend to keep up with regular cleanings every six months, however, when insurance is no longer available or is too expensive they forgo this general maintenance. Cleanings are to the mouth what regular oil changes are to an automobile. The lack of them can cause catastrophic damage down the road. We developed pre-pay plans for our patients that include exams, x-rays and two cleanings per year plus a 20% discount on our normal fees for treatments such as fillings. Additionally, we are currently establishing relationships with specialists to enhance the care and services we offer to our patients. While maintaining and building stronger relationships with our current clients, we of course want to reach new patients everyday, and we have found that online services bring us many types of new clients.

OFFER ONLINE SERVICES

Technology today requires that your business is available online. Utilizing your website and social media to offer online specials to make appointments, to review the dentist's credentials and to complete patient forms at home is not only a gamechanger, but a time saver. Online services allow our practice to offer specials that reach different types of patients and demographics. Our free exam and x-ray special or our free second opinion offer gets people in the door and begins the relationship-building process. After visiting our web page, the free visit allows the patient to decide if they like you and your practice. Discounted cleanings encourage current patients to come in more frequently for routine dental maintenance. Implant specials are a great tool to bring older or more mature patients into the office. Mouthguard specials remind the moms to bring in their young athletes. Specials on products such as Invisalign for straightening or teeth whitening treatments entices everyone. Being proactive with the search engines brings your company out on top with our technology savy customers. Our clients appreciate our online services, but they also appreciate our involvement in the community.

ACTIVE COMMUNITY INVOLVEMENT

Volunteering in the community gives the doctors and staff a higher purpose. I did not create Desert Dentistry to be just a job. My associates and staff are passionate about giving back to the community. Our office has always assisted with organizations like Give Kids a Smile that provides free dental treatment to children and Saint Vincent DePaul's dental clinic. We also volunteer with St. Vincent's program for battered women. When working with women that are trying to change their lives, we always get more out of it than we give. We encourage staff members to volunteer and support them in their charity of choice. From cancer walks, to dog shelters, Kiwanis Club to Feed My Starving Children, we have enjoyed watching our staff grow and get further involved. Last April, we even won an award for our volunteer work with Give Kids a Smile, but the award is secondary to the reward we receive by having done something needed.

We also collaborate with the organization Latin World Ministries (latinworldministries.com) to go several times annually to Atoyac, Mexico, a town about two hours north of Acapulco. Latin World

Ministries has created a full service medical, dental and optical clinic for the disadvantaged. The clinic has completely transformed lives with their cleft lip and palate surgeries as well as improved the medical, optical and dental health of the population. They have also drilled and continue to maintain over 200 water wells to provide clean, safe drinking water to the people. Donations are always appreciated. When in Mexico, we see about 100 patients a day for about 5 days. We generally take dental students with us on that trip so that the students also learn to give back. Although our mission trips in Mexico do not garner patients at our Phoenix offices—actually only one in many years—the change in perspective has altered the way in which we do business. Community involvement breathes new life into a business by creating a sense of purpose larger than bringing new clients or making more money does.

PASS IT ON

At the center of the practice, before all of the other elements fall into place, are our employees. The company is dedicated to improving the lives of my associates and staff.

Treating your staff like family goes a long way to keeping morale high in the office. If your employees are happy they will automatically pass on that happiness. Sometimes simple assistance to an employee, such as an interest free, short-term loan is enough to relieve stress in their lives and free them to focus on the patients. We take time to set personal goals with our employees and share them with the rest of the staff. This has caused staff members to shed pounds, go back to school, get degrees and achieve things they never thought possible with the support of their coworkers. Special opportunities that enrich an employee's life build a work family. During my annual missionary trips to Mexico, I offer employees the opportunity to go with me. A trip like that changes the employee's life and broadens their appreciation for the services we provide.

Don't think you can take a business that people frequently associate with pain and suffering or expense and inconvenience and change the way your customers perceive the experience? *Not with that attitude, you can't!* If you are willing to change the approach you use, to do things differently and focus your business on improving the ease with which your customers can do business with you, then you will succeed. Our patients might not ever brag to their friends about how great they felt when Dr. Mattern drilled their teeth, but they will likely tell their friends that they never had a dental experience as great as Desert Dentistry. I never tire of hearing patients say that our staff and doctors gave them the best dental visit they ever had. We want our patients to remember us for the excellent care they received and for future generations to be able to look at those teeth and see that our patients cared about their oral health.

About Dr. Thomas

Thomas M. Mattern, DDS graduated from Creighton University School of Dentistry in 1988 (the same day his daughter was born). He has been a member of the American Dental Association and The Academy of General Dentists for 25 years. Dr. Mattern is an alumnus of the Las Vegas Institute of Cosmetology program. He obtained his fellowship in the International Congress of Oral Implantologists in 2007.

Giving back to the community has always been a priority for Dr. Mattern. He has offered his office every year since 2003 to the ADA Give Kids a Smile program, providing care to hundreds of disadvantaged children. His monthly visits to Saint Vincent DePaul's dental clinic in downtown Phoenix and his on-going trips to the dental clinic in Atoyac, Mexico have been rewarding for both Dr. Mattern and the patients he serves.

Dr. Mattern enjoys all aspects of dentistry and due to his many hours of continuing education is able to provide all forms of treatment including implants, complete smile makeovers, root canals, dentures, orthodontics and all restorative work. Not only does Dr. Mattern treat patients but he also manages Desert Dentistry's five practices. His offices are recognized for the level of customer service they provide.

Outside of work, his passion is golf and spending time with his wife and four children.

CHAPTER 43

HOW SUCCESSFUL PEOPLE DO THINGS DIFFERENTLY

BY NJERU NTHIGAH

"When we are foolish, we want to conquer the world. When we are wise, we want to conquer ourselves!"
~ John C Maxwell.

What would your life look like if you were living to your fullest potential? That has always been a persistent question in my life! In the next few pages, I will be sharing with you a simple, practical and powerful four steps to creating your success blueprint so that you can live out your potential.

Let me start by telling you a little bit about myself. I was born in Kenya to a young single mother but I was brought up by my grandmother. She took me at the very tender age of three weeks and became my provider in every way. She was a simple, wonderful woman filled with love and great wisdom. I grew up in the city of Nairobi and as I jokingly say – we were upper poor! Truth is that there were poorer families and my grandmother who was a seamstress worked hard to provide me with the best that she could.

I had the good fortune to be influenced and nurtured by three very powerful women. My grandmother, my biological mother and my aunt. In spite of the financial challenges, I never lacked in love. They always reminded me that every situation was temporary and I had within me the ability to craft a future that was different from my environment. Unfortunately I lost my biological mother at the age of 18, my aunt at 19 and my grandmother at the 22. I lost everyone I loved and my life changed forever.

I became an entrepreneur out of the need to survive. I tried numerous businesses, growing through failure in most and eventually succeeding in one. I became a millionaire at age of 24 and I was living life on the fast lane. I had achieved "success" so I thought! I was travelling the world, belonged to the Golf and Country Club, dressed in expensive clothes and was busy partying my life away! I had the disease called SOS – Shiny Object Syndrome! I was driven by the acquisition of temporary material stuff. The more I got, the more I wanted and the less I experienced satisfaction. I was chasing all these things in the hope to validate myself, yet not realizing that I was engaged in self-sabotaging my potential.

At the age of 27 I got an amazing opportunity to represent Kenya's national airline in Southern Africa. It was a great experience. Even with the new-found success, I still struggled with the true purpose of my life. I had realized that the quest for material possessions was never going to offer true happiness. Two years into my assignment, I decide it was time for a major change in my life and I resigned. I wanted a fresh start and I was determined to find my true purpose and to grow myself. I also had a very compelling reason, as I was a father now. My daughter was four at the time and I knew that I had to get it together if I was going to be a great father to her.

I decided to come to America and even though I did not know a single person or where I was going, I was determined to make something out of my life at whatever cost. I was willing to pay the price. I walked into America with two suitcases, seven hundred dollars and a DREAM. The last ten years have been a journey of growth and I can say with confidence and clarity that I have found my passion and my purpose. Today the thing that gives me the greatest joy in my life is helping people discover their passions and realize their potential, so that they can live life fully and powerfully. I empower people to create a future filled with possibility for themselves and their loved ones, while having a positive impact in the world.

I like what Les Brown says: "Too many of us are not living our dreams because we are living our fears." Seize the opportunity to create a great life. This is your finest hour. My goal in sharing my journey was in no way to try and impress you, but to impress upon you the urgency and value of creating a success blueprint for your life.

"Success is nothing more than a few simple disciplines, practiced every day; while failure is simply a few errors in judgment, repeated every day. It is the accumulative weight of our disciplines and our judgments that leads us to either fortune or failure."
~ Jim Rohn

I am constantly studying successful people and have realized that they produce results by taking certain specific actions. If we become aware of what they do and mirror these specific actions, then we have the opportunity to produce equal or better results in our lives. In order to produce the kind of results and success we desire, here are my top three foundational pillars to build upon:

1. RESPONSIBILITY

When it comes to your life, your purpose, your dreams and your impact in this world – it boils down to simply a "You-and-You-only deal." This is about personal responsibility. Nothing will change in your life until you decide to change. You must first take responsibility for where you are now, and secondly, clearly define where you want to go. You start by determining who you want to be by raising your level of awareness of who you are. In that awareness, you develop the values that will guide you in what you need to do so that you can have impact and the lasting success you desire.

2. PERSONAL LEADERSHIP

In his book *As a Man Thinketh*, James Allen says: "Men are anxious to improve their circumstances, but are unwilling to improve themselves; they therefore remain bound." Personal leadership is simply the process by which you embrace, develop and engage in an intentional personal growth plan. Before we can lead others, we must learn how to lead ourselves first. In order to realize and maximize your potential, you must make your daily growth a priority.

3. GOOD THINKING

In his book *How Successful People Think*, my friend and mentor John C Maxwell teaches that good thinking creates the foundation for good results. He further says that:

- ➢ Unsuccessful people focus their thinking on survival.
- ➢ Average people focus their thinking on maintenance.
- ➢ Successful people focus their thinking on progress.

I like what Meng-Tzu says; "Those who labor with their minds govern others; those who labor with their strength are governed by others." Therefore in order to achieve our desired results, we must learn to harness the value of good thinking.

CREATING YOUR SUCCESS BLUEPRINT

Success is waking up in the morning, whoever you are,
wherever you are, however old or young, and bounding out
of bed because there's something out there that you love to do,
that you believe in, that you are good at – something bigger
than you are and you can hardly wait to get at it again today.
~ Whit Hobbs, Columnist

I want to share with you four simple, practical and transformative **A.C.T.S.** to creating your success blueprint. I teach and have successfully used this model in my life. I want to emphasize that it is not **THE** only model but just **A** model.

1. A — Articulate your WHY

"Nothing great in the world has been accomplished without passion."
~ Georg Wilhelm Friedrich Hegel

It is said that there are two great days in life - the day you are born and the day you discover why. The inquiry of your **WHY** ultimately leads to the discovery of your passion. The discovery of your passion leads to your life's purpose.

People who know their WHY, develop the strength to overcome challenges and temporary setbacks. Achievement is all about the pursuit of WHAT (your goals) but success is all about the pursuit of your WHY. Successful people understand that success is a journey and not a destination. The greater reward from the pursuit of our goals is not their attainment, but who we become in the process.

Here are a few questions to help you articulate your WHY?

- What will my life count for?
- What gives me the greatest joy and excitement?
- What gives me the greatest reward?
- What gives me the greatest return?
- What do I really care about?
- What would I die for?

2. C — Create a PLAN

"The man who is prepared has his battle half fought."
~ Miguel De Cervantes

As simple as this may sound, never start a journey without a road map. This is all about creating a pathway for your dreams. It all starts with goal setting. Intelligent planning is essential for success and the fulfillment of your passion starts with the very important process of writing down your goals. Written down goals allow you to leverage opportunity, develop focus, promote creativity, foster good thinking and prepares you for the expected challenges while in the pursuit of your goals.

Creating a plan is about making the decision to bet on yourself. Every decision we make ultimately determines who we become and what we get. Quality decisions are the foundation for a quality life. Lasting success is not a result of quantum leaps but it is the outcome of small intentional daily action steps. Plan to win, or fail by default, the choice is always yours.

Important steps in setting your goals:

- Decide what you want and write it down.
- Make it clear and compelling. This creates direction, focus, discipline and excitement.
- Create impact-driven goals. How will the fulfillment of your dream benefit others? This is all about significance.

- Set a deadline. This allows you to prioritize your time and focus your efforts. Set a realistic time frame that creates urgency for the fulfillment of your goals. It is said that there are no unrealistic goals; only unrealistic deadlines.

3. T — Take daily intentional ACTION

"Success seems to be connected with action. Successful people keep moving. They make mistakes but they don't quit." ~ Conrad Hilton

This is where the rubber meets the road! Every dream, every passion is personal and has a price that must be paid. Written-down goals have no power if they are not backed by intentional action.

Goal attainment is all about taking actions. This is the process by which you make the invisible into visible. I love what my co-author Brian Tracy says: "All successful people, men and women, are big dreamers. They imagine what their future could be, ideal in every respect, and then they work every day toward their distant vision, that goal or purpose."

Develop the daily discipline of taking action towards the fulfillment of your goals. Embrace failure because it is a necessity on your way to success. Failure is a great teacher and it only becomes final with your permission.

Four ways to taking intentional action:

- Create your top 5 things to-do list for your top three must-dos. This helps you stay focused and moves you closer to the fulfillment of your goals.
- Create a "Do Not Do List" – this helps you to know your distractions.
- Manage your life by scheduling your day, week and month.
- Reflect and adjust daily. Keep what is working and drop what is not. Never confuse activity with accomplishment.

4. S — Seek and develop empowering RELATIONSHIPS

"It marks a big step in your development when you come to realize that other people can help you do a better job than you can do alone."
~ Andrew Carnegie

I am a strong believer in MENTORSHIP. If you are going to achieve great results in your life, then you need to surround yourself with people who have been where you want to go. Mentors help you to adjust your limiting beliefs, encourage you, push you and hold you accountable. Mentors open doors for you, lend you their credibility and influence until you can develop your own.

I make it a habit to seek mentors in every area that I am determined to grow and achieve results. One such relationship I have is with my friend and mentor John C Maxwell. Through him and his international teaching team, I have been able to pursue my passion to inspire people so that they can live lives that inspire them. This relationship has opened doors for me to learn, speak and teach in places I would never have believed possible. As a founding member of the JOHN C MAXWELL TEAM - I am highly trained and resourced to teach transformational leadership globally. This is the value of seeking and developing empowering relationships.

Four Ways to Finding a Mentor:

- Do a self-assessment: - Know what you want to accomplish. Identify your strengths and weaknesses. Identify your barriers.
- Know your purpose: What are you seeking from the relationship? Are you seeking advice, insight or to learn a specific skill.
- Identify a mentor: Determine who is best to help you. They don't have to necessarily belong to your industry but they have a proven record for achieving results. Identify if they would be best suited to mentor you at your current level of awareness. For example, if you are a manager you may not be best suited to be mentored by the chairman at this moment, but best suited for someone who is 2 to 3 levels above you.
- Seek to connect: - When getting into a mentoring relationship, it is your responsibility to make the choice as easy and flexible for your mentor as possible. Be upfront; share your goals and express your gratitude for their willingness to invest in you.

So there you have the Four (4) **A.C.T.S.** to creating your blueprint for success. My goal was to share with you a simple, practical and actionable model that you can start working with today. Opportunity is all around you. Now is the time to bet on yourself, decide what you want, create a plan and put the plan into action.

With profound gratitude, I want to say thank you for your time and the opportunity to share my passion with you. Thank you very much.

TO YOUR CONTINUED SUCCESS, MY FRIEND!

About Njeru

Njeru Nthigah is President of THE LEADERS UNIVERSITY, a company that specializes in transformational leadership development, personal leadership training, communication and professional coaching.

He works with organizations to improve their top and bottom line results through customized leadership development workshops, seminars, lunch-n-learns and masterminds.

Njeru is a dedicated student of success, human potential and personal leadership. His learning journey has exposed him to countless leadership training conferences with the world's finest and brightest experts. He is a Founder Member, Speaker, Coach and Trainer of THE JOHN C MAXWELL TEAM, where he also serves on the President's Advisory Council.

Njeru is passionate about empowering people to find their passion and purpose in life. He helps individuals to set clear and compelling goals that empower them to take immediate decisive action, so that they can maximize their potential and achieve greater personal and professional success.

For more information and a deeper dive exploring the Four (4) A.C.T.S., please visit: www.njerunthigah.com/changeagents.

To connect with Njeru:

Website: www.njerunthigah.com

LinkedIn: www.linkedin.com/in/njerunthigah

FaceBook: www.facebook.com/njerunthigahspeaker

Twitter: www.twitter.com/njerunthigah

YouTube: www.youtube.com/user/njerunthigah

CHAPTER 44

HOW TO BE LUCKY!

BY SIMON ATKINSON

"It's hard to detect good luck – it looks so much like something you've earned" ~ Frank A Clarke

September 15th 2008, ...the day the world stood still. You might not remember this exact date, but I do. This day was long in the making. Years of corruption and greed at the highest levels had been leading us to this very moment, and like me, most Americans and Europeans simply weren't paying attention. Well we were awake now.

Lehman Brothers, the 4th largest investment bank in the US filed for Chapter 11 bankruptcy, leaving in its wake the largest bankruptcy filing in U.S. history, holding over $600 billion in assets. Banks around the world froze. The financial meltdown was underway, the Government was in turmoil and focusing on damage control. And all I knew was that mass unemployment was inevitable.

The shockwaves immediately hit Houston. Home to petrochemical giants and engineering companies alike. Projects were instantly put on hold, and designers, engineers, surveyors and construction crews laid off by the thousand.

Limping along, my coworkers and I kept our heads down with an "Out of Sight, Out of Mind" philosophy and trying desperately to be invisible. The game lasted until November 27th 2008, when we received "The Call" to head up to the department manager's office for a "Meeting." We expected and received the usual routine. "...We're sorry. Times are hard. We'll hire you back when things pick up....etc, etc." My whole department was axed.

As usual and like many layoffs, it happened just after Thanksgiving and just before Christmas. Just the time when people are winding down, hiring is at a standstill, and Frosty has more chance selling ice in Antarctica, than the average Joe has in finding a job before February, and that's the rule in a good economy. The outlook was bleak. The festive season was upon us and my son was eager to write his letter to Santa. The pressure was on!

Now people say I've been lucky. I've heard it all my life from good friends, overhearing neighbors talking between themselves, and from coworkers with envious remarks disguised as a joke. The answer is: Yes! I'll agree I've been very fortunate. But as any successful business owner / entrepreneur will tell you. It's not luck as you know it.

Now I wish I could claim the following line, but the honor goes to Randy Pausch (1960 – 2008), a Computer Science Professor at Carnegie Mellon University, who in 2007 delivered "The Last Lecture: Really Achieving Your Childhood Dreams" – which went on to be a New York Times Best Seller. In this lecture he delivered one of my favorite quotes:

"Luck is where Preparation meets Opportunity"

It's as simple as that. The more you prepare, the more opportunities present themselves, the more in tune you become at identifying opportunities, and therefore the more chances you have for success.

Christmas 2008, this was the time I needed Lady Luck on my side. I contacted everyone I knew and after just 4 weeks of mass emails and cold calls, there was a light at the end of the tunnel. Not just one job offer, but potentially three. The choices soon narrowed to one firm offer. Wow. Mass unemployment, a pending depression, and I had a good job offer.

So why didn't I feel happy, something just didn't feel right. Yeh! The contract I was sent did have a non-compete clause, but isn't that standard? After a while I realized the problem I was having. I'd worked in my circle for 15 years. It was my industry, and I wasn't prepared to give it away. The other problem I had was I was fed up with the Cubicle World...Dilbert had it pegged. So I turned the job down.

In January 2009, I decided to work for myself. My wife first planted the seed by asking if I could do small jobs on the side, and encouraged me to think BIG. Everyone else said it was reckless, and the worst possible time to go it alone. But with my wife's encouragement and support, that was the positive push I needed. I made the decision and I've never looked back. Having a strong person behind you is a huge benefit. Not having someone second guess your abilities and decisions will allow clarity of thought and focus. Basically, surround yourself with people who make you stronger. In my case, my wife is my strength.

If you've ever thought about starting a business or working for yourself, it never seems the right time. Always the wrong time of year, the economy, bills to pay, competition too strong, etc., the list of excuses is endless. So why did I decide to brave the elements under these daunting conditions? The simple answer is: I was prepared. And unbeknown to me, I'd actually been preparing all my life.

The following is a breakdown of my life preparations, most of which I was unaware of at the time, only able to identify the pivotal points, by looking back and connecting the dots. I hope by identifying the elements that helped me, you can see and follow a similar path.

STEP 1: LIVE A LIFE OF INTEGRITY AND RELIABILITY

Born in Huddersfield in 1965, I was raised by my mother and two sisters. My father had passed away when I was 5, so the 4 of us soldiered on alone. My mother was a strong woman who instilled in me the importance of INTEGRITY. And this has been the foundation for my success. Don't lie. Don't cheat. Don't Steal. You're only as good as your word. Don't be Wishy-Washy. And if you say you're going to do something, DO IT! Don't stab anyone in the back. Don't burn bridges. Don't hold grudges. Always be nice to people on your way up, as you'll surely meet them on your way down. Lead by example. And don't be tight with cash. "There's nothing worse than having deep pockets and short fingers (aka: Don't be a skinflint).

These were the principles my mother instilled in me as a child, and they have stuck with me to this day. Following the same moral code is the first step in preparation to spot and chase life's opportunities. People genuinely want to work, and do business with people they Know, Like and Trust. Exhibiting these attributes throughout every aspect of your life builds a strong reputation, which is essential for long-term success. To quote Will Rogers "It takes a lifetime to build a good reputation, but you can lose it in a minute"...What needs to be added to that is, "...it's more precious than gold, so don't give anyone a chance to take it from you."

STEP 2: ADOPT A FINANCIAL PLAN TO LIVE WITHIN YOUR MEANS

Prior to the meltdown most people lived well beyond their means, and some still do. If you can resist the temptation to keep up with your Facebook friends (who are making most of their Crazy Life up anyway) then that's great. Keep up the good work. For me, being able to reject that precious job offer was not as difficult as it could have been for many. Yes it would have paid the bills and paid for Christmas. But that would have been a short-term gain and long-term misery.

In 2000, we had moved into a modest house, valued at less than half of what the bank was offering to loan me. I also got rid of the flashy car, which had a flashy payment. Having no car note and a reasonable mortgage is a great stress reliever. To complete the process of becoming debt-free, we decided to follow the Dave Ramsey program. The plan worked and I'd highly recommend it. So by December 2008, when I turned the job down, I knew I had 6 months of bills covered in my savings, and was free to follow my dreams (well, for the next 6 months anyway). I've since learned that if you're struggling with debt, a good place to seek guidance is: www.wssic.com. Commercial Redemption: I really wish I'd known this knowledge sooner.

STEP 3: DEVELOP A SOLID NETWORK OF BUSINESS FRIENDS

I guess Facebook and LinkedIn, etc. help with this to some extent. But the network I would recommend is a personal one. A network where you actually keep in touch, talk and meet people. If possible, go to trade conferences and focus groups in your chosen industry. Yes! These can be expensive, but my philosophy is "if you don't ask you don't get." So ask if there's a reduced rate for "job hunters." And if you're a STEP# 1 person, people will want to help. Don't let pride get in your way. This isn't charity, because you are the sort of person who will pay it forward x2 and people will know that.

I always have to force myself to go to the pre and post-conference parties. But afterwards I'm always glad I did. Building a solid network is essential. I've made so many good friends through business, all of whom are rock solid Step #1 people. To such an extent that all my current key business agreements are sealed with nothing more than a handshake. That's the power of Know, Like and Trust.

Now I'm not suggesting you shouldn't have a written contract in place for the most important of plans; especially where potentially Big Money is involved. Big Money is relative, and that's when a person's true character is exposed, and that's when a solid contract is required. This is not only to protect your business agreement, but it also protects your friendship. Without one, avarice can creep in, and when it does, be prepared for the House of Cards to tumble.

So always start with STEP#1 and cover yourself with STEP #2.

STEP 4: EDUCATE YOURSELF

By this I don't mean head to University and get yourself into debt with student loans. I mean pick up a book and dive in. "As a Man Thinketh" by James Allen is free on the Internet and inspired me greatly. "Outliers" by Malcom Gladwell is fascinating and "How Rich People Think" by Steve Siebold is spot-on accurate.

Also question what you see, hear and read. Don't believe everything you hear on the news. Most of what the networks tell you are cherry-picked sound bites intended to shock and scare. So don't waste your time. Investigate on the Internet while it's still free and unregulated. There is a wealth of information if you're willing to look. A good place to start, especially if you're struggling with debt, are the lectures by Winston Shrout at: www.wssic.com.

Now the term "Conspiracy Theory" has been hijacked by the politicians and media who have redefined it as: "This is a Fairy Story! And if you believe it, we'll make sure everyone will laugh at you, …etc., …etc." My Philosophy is to listen to both sides and then search for the truth. If you find 100's or 1000's of experts, scientists and professionals saying one thing; and the politicians and media with some cherry-picked "professionals" saying another… Guess what? I'm going with the facts that don't defy the laws of physics / nature. I then try and find out why the other side is lying, and what the implications are.

I know at the time of writing this that the information is time sensitive. I just hope this information is still out there when you go and look for it. Search YouTube or similar for **"20 Lies Every American Should Know!"** the clip invites viewers to research for themselves topics you won't see on mainstream news. Including the following which have been thoroughly investigated and chronicled by scientists and industry professionals:

"Chemtrails vs. Contrail", "Fluoride in Water", "Strawman Illusion", "Architects and Engineers Truth" and interviews with Dr. Steven Greer, Randy Kelton, Guy Taylor and Bill Thornton.

Also, try not to be too distracted by FOX, NBC, CBN, ESPN and 24/7 NFL, MLB, NBA, NHL … It's a dumbing-down technique that's getting worse. The Romans used this tactic 2000 years ago, by using the Coliseum and Gladiators to distract and entertain the angry mobs, while the senate increased taxes to seal crooked deals. Don't fall for it.

"Self-education is, I firmly believe, the only kind of education there is."
~ Isaac Asimov

STEP 5: BE PROACTIVE – CARPE DIEM

Go out and take chances. Look for holes in the market you can fill. Focus on a niche / specialized market if possible.

Example: 2008, I saw a hole in the market. My previous clients were now left without a service provider. My previous company had panicked and laid off the whole department over the Christmas period expecting there to be no work. They were wrong. I contacted my old clients independently and they were pleased I was still available. I contacted friends in the industry who lent me equipment, and software. I used my expertise on a number of small jobs and minimized my financial risk exposure to travel expenses only. I took on one project at a time, and the rest is history. My Company Texas Surveys is now a world leader in laser scanning industrial power station turbines and the building of engineering quality as-is 3D models. The process is quick, accurate and extremely valuable to the customer. The focus of Texas Surveys has always been to Exceed Expectation on Quality, Accuracy and Customer

Service. Our Clients know that we will exceed to succeed to deliver what they need.

So go for it. What's stopping you?

"The greatest discovery of my generation is that human beings can alter their lives by altering their attitude of mind.... If you change your mind, you can change your life." ~ William James 1842 – 1910

IN CONCLUSION

I'm guessing what's stopping you are the two biggest excuses I always hear:

"It's not the right time." And it never will be if you choose to think so. I made a decision to change my life in the worst economic meltdown in recent global history. The reason I could was because I was prepared.

"What if I fail?" The truth is you will fail… That sounds really bad but bear with me. The more you prepare the less likely you are to fail big. Yes! You'll make mistakes and trip now and again, because you're human. But sensible planning and following the previous 4 Steps will help you get back on track quickly. The most valuable lessons you learn are from your own mistakes. Just don't make the same mistake twice, and don't set yourself up to fail big. Always plan to have a safety net to break your fall. Fine tune your backup plan(s). And always have an exit strategy ready to go.

PREPARATION IS THE KEY!!!

"If we are to achieve results never before accomplished, we must expect to employ methods never before attempted."
~ Sir Francis Bacon 1561 - 1626

About Simon

Simon Atkinson's career in surveying, "as-is" data collection and 3D modeling started in 1994. Still active in fieldwork operations and new procedures development, Simon is one of the most experienced Laser Scanning Professionals in the world.

Born in Huddersfield, England, Simon graduated from Anglia Ruskin University with a B.Sc. in Construction Management in addition to a Post Grad. Diploma in Building Studies.

In Jan 1994, Simon joined Kvaerner Surveys in Warrington, UK as part of a pilot project to build a specialized photogrammetry survey team targeted at offshore engineering. Tasked with capturing "as is" or "as built" data safely, quickly and efficiently, by using a combination of traditional survey with HD stereo photography, to build highly detailed and accurate 3D digital models.

1996 Simon Transferred to Fluor Daniel as Houston Office Manager for the Applied Computer Solutions group. The group was tasked with co-developing procedures with Fluor Daniel California, to combine photogrammetry with a new technology called Laser Scanning. So successful were the results, that these same procedures are widely used throughout the industry to the present day.

In 1998 Simon joined Cyra Technology (now Leica Geosystems), to assist in developing software and procedures for the developing Cyrax 2400 & 2500 Laser Scanning units before moving to INOVx Solutions.

1999 - Simon was asked to help setup and launch a startup company called INOVx Solutions. As one of the original 8 members from Fluor Daniel, Simon headed the Houston Office to promote laser scanning services in the Mexican Gulf region.

In 2005, Simon was asked to develop a new "Business Vertical" for CDI Houston. The new discipline introduced was HDDS (High Definition Digital Surveying). Working closely with the Piping Dept., new procedures were developed and exceptional results were achieved. Based on these developments, he introduced the same concept and procedures to General Electric and their Energy Services Division.

The economic crash of 2008 caused mass unemployment throughout the engineering spectrum across Houston and the engineering world globally. Like every company at the time, CDI needed to downsize immediately to weather the pending storm. The HDDS department was put on hold and all personnel laid off. In this harsh economic environment, Simon moved forward and founded Texas

Surveys, developing a trusted network of colleagues and associates around the world. Texas Surveys focused on supporting companies left without the trusted laser scanning services of CDI. Working closely with General Electric and Axiem International, Texas Surveys has become the world leader in the scanning and surveying of large industrial turbine power systems. With over 100 turbines scanned globally since Jan 2009, G.E. has been able to significantly reduce rework and develop new and improved shutdown schedules, in addition to offering their clients additional enhanced services. Laser Scanning is now a standard operation for all G.E. turbine upgrades.

To find out more about Laser Scanning please visit: www.Texas-Surveys.com

CHAPTER 45

BROKEN ROADS CAN LEAD TO SUCCESS

BY MICHAEL HARPER

Life isn't for the faint of heart! From your own life experiences and the accompanying wounds and battle scars, I'm sure you are well aware of how difficult life circumstances can become. It takes a great deal of patience, courage and tenacity to fight your way back to the top when you feel like the proverbial rug has been pulled out from under you. I'm sure many of us could tell our share of horror stories that may rattle the emotional fiber of some that have not experienced such tragedy. However, whether your life circumstances have been outrageously heartbreaking or subtly benign, each of us has the opportunity to learn from them, and often they have a place in changing the course of our entire existence.

My wife and I have declared "our song" to be "Bless the Broken Road" by Rascal Flatts. The words to the song play out a scenario of two individuals that started out on one road only to have it "broken" by untold circumstances. Yet, the broken roads each of us wandered were on a trajectory that eventually led to each other. Interestingly, if it weren't for the broken roads we would never have met.

Without exception, all of us have experienced broken roads to some extent. Some have experienced more brokenness than others. But, none of us are exempt. I am convinced that the broken roads in our lives can lead us to places of prosperity if we respond to life's twists and turns in a positive way. We cannot afford to allow our circumstances to defeat us. Never did I imagine my life would turn out the way it has, but I'm extremely thankful for my life today. I can honestly say the broken roads of my life have been blessed. Today I want to be able to encourage others that may be going through difficult times in their life or business. I want them to know that their current circumstances are temporary and they have the opportunity to use these interruptions as stepping stones to much better things.

I am part of a small group of agents that have dedicated ourselves to bring about change and to help others experience change in their business as well as in their personal lives. We refer to ourselves as the Ambassadors of Change. We are committed to making changes which result in business growth, and to show others how they can do the same. Our motto is "No Agent Left Behind." Today, my goal is to help others become successful and avoid some of the pitfalls I encountered.

THE "BROKEN ROAD" OF MY LIFE

There have been numerous things that have taken place within my life that have been pivotal points for me. I am a deeply-rooted family man with a loving wife, five of the greatest kids you could ever imagine, eight beautiful grandchildren and a strong faith in God. Without hesitation I can say, "Life is great!" But, it hasn't been an easy road to be able to get to this place. Allow me to give you a brief synopsis of the "Broken Road" of my life that will serve to demonstrate some principles that I would like to share with you.

I was married two weeks out of high school at the age of 18. Never being afraid of hard work and long hours, I worked for my in-laws who owned a glass company during my senior year of high school and at the beginning of college. I was in class from 8 a.m. to 1 p.m., and then worked in the glass shop after classes. Study time came after my work schedule was completed.

Shortly after starting college, a local bank was looking for a night operator for their computer systems. Because of my work ethic and dedication, my college instructor recommended me for the position. I continued with my daytime college classes and worked at the bank, usually until 10 or 11 p.m. After a year, the bank then offered me a position in computer programming which was an 8-5 position. I dropped out of college and began my career in computer programming.

After a couple of years I was offered a job as a Computer Programmer at First City National Bank in Midland, Texas. There I continued to excel and wrote the software for the first ATM's the bank used in that area. At the age of 25, I was the head of the Data Processing Department and became the youngest Vice President in the bank.

An oil company located in the bank building offered me a position with their company, which I accepted. I was responsible for researching and purchasing computer equipment, software, revising software and writing new software. The atmosphere at the oil company was very laid-back and they paid me very well. I had a country club membership and all the perks a young man of 30 could desire, but I was bored to death. I began contemplating a strategy that would lead to something more challenging and entertained the thought of going back to college to finish my degree in Computer Science.

About this same time, another opportunity came my way. My uncle was a district manager with Allstate Insurance in Houston and suggested I consider Allstate as a career path. Sales were a very foreign area to me and I couldn't imagine myself getting in front of people and talking to them. I had a horrible stutter in my younger years and although it had gotten better as I got older, I was still very uncomfortable talking in front of people. However, I was unable to talk myself out of the opportunity, so in 1987 I began working with Allstate Insurance. In the first year I qualified for all sales incentives, won trips and various other awards.

In the late 80's I went through a marriage separation, which culminated in divorce in 1992. This took a toll on me in many ways, including financially. I started with Farmers Insurance on April 1, 1992, April Fool's Day. I wondered if anything good could come out of an April Fool's Day beginning. I was a life insurance specialist with Farmers Insurance and was paid solely on commission. Divorce is never easy, but add to it the financial turmoil divorce can cause and a new commission-only job, and you have a recipe for hardship.

By July of 1992, my family was homeless; after being evicted from our apartment my children were staying with family out of town. Being very stubborn, prideful and not wanting others to know my situation, I found myself sleeping at night in the back seat of my 1989 Toyota Corolla.

Fortunately, I still had a gym membership so I would go to the gym early in the morning to work out and shower, change clothes, and then go to the office. I would then work until 8 or 9 o'clock at night because the office was much cooler than the hot Texas summer. My daily meal consisted of going through the Taco Bell drive-thru and feasting on the five-pack of tacos for $1.99. I had an ice chest in my trunk and I would stop by a motel that had an ice machine out back and I would fill my ice chest. I lived off water, soft drinks and fast food for several weeks. I did find a house to lease, but had to wait to make enough money for the down payment and the first month's rent.

Every night I tried to find a street where I could park my car to sleep and go unnoticed by the police or anyone else. As soon as I earned enough commissions, I was able to lease a house and was rejoined with my children. That experience taught me that there probably wasn't much that was going to keep me down. Somehow, no matter the circumstances, I would find my way through and survive.

Lying in the back seat of that Corolla in the July Houston heat, living on fast food and soft drinks was a far cry from the great pay I was used to, not to mention the membership at a country club and a house with a swimming pool that was just a fleeting memory by that time.

After a short period of time with Farmers, I began to see significant success. Fortunately, my homeless situation only lasted about one month, and I have been the number 1 or 2 life insurance producer in my district for the past 21 years.

A LIFE ENHANCING EVENT

I refer to this as a life-enhancing event because, while I already had a deep appreciation for my family, my business, and life in general, this recent incident enhanced my gratitude for these things. One day in October of 2010 I was driving back to Houston from Dallas where I was visiting my Mom in the hospital. I was driving a brand new Toyota Sequoia, a seven-passenger SUV. I grew up in West Texas where tornados were common but had never personally seen one until that day. Not only did I see this tornado, but also I was right in its path and there was absolutely nowhere for me to go. I felt things slamming against my SUV, and then I felt a huge crash and finally felt the tornado go overhead. After it passed I looked around and saw that every seat in my seven-passenger SUV was crushed except for the driver's seat. I climbed out the driver's door window and initially thought there were two vehicles on top of my SUV. I then realized it was an 18-wheeler with an 87,000-pound Caterpillar dump truck on the bed of the trailer that the tornado had picked up and dropped on top of my SUV. I miraculously escaped from that incident with only a small cut on one finger on my left hand from the broken glass. I honestly believe it was divine intervention that spared me that day; God's plan for my life was not complete. I believe God still had work for me to do; it was now my job to determine what that was to be. That's one reason I have such a passion for helping others. Things like this make you stop and assess how precious life really is, and how quickly one's life can possibly be taken or severely altered.

YOU REALLY CAN TEACH AN OLD DOG NEW TRICKS

In my business I've tried hiring people in the past to help on the sales side, but it never seemed to work out. It was always easier for me to just do it myself. However, what I didn't realize was that I was stifling my own business growth and development. In 2012 I sat at a conference listening to an agent who had been in the business about the same length of time. He related the story about the changes in his business. In 2007 he had 4 office people and about 2,500 policies. That same year someone recommended he attend the Staffing for Success class at the University of Farmers. He commented, "I didn't think there was anything new Farmers could teach me, but I went ahead and scheduled to attend." After attending the class, he went back to his office and began to implement the principles he learned. By the end of 2011, he had 12 office staff and over 8,000 policies and has recently opened up a 9,000 square foot office building that is state of the art. He finished his speech that day by saying, "You can stay where you are, doing the same thing day after day, and in a couple of years I'll own your agencies. Or, you can go to the Staffing for Success class, get on the right track and build your agencies."

Knowing I needed to experience that type of change in my own business, I enrolled in the Staffing for Success class and attended in April of 2012. I came back to my office and immediately started implementing what I learned. I interviewed countless people, hired a couple but they didn't work out. Still determined but frustrated, in December of 2012 I put an ad on Craig's list and had someone respond who was licensed and experienced. I hired that person and they referred another person with the same qualifications, I hired the second person as well. I then hired a third person on April 1st and then a fourth. I now have 4 associates working with me and everyone is complementing and supporting each other. Last year at this time I had 1,500 accounts and now I have over 2,500. It's a team effort. I used to work "in the business" instead of "on the business." Now I work on the business instead of in the business. I constantly remind my staff that this is "our" agency, not just mine; they take great pride in that fact. I now have agents from other offices coming to my office to spend the day with me and my staff to see what we are doing to experience such growth. I take great pleasure in helping others achieve the same success.

EIGHT PRINCIPLES TO IMPROVE YOUR LIFE AND BUSINESS

Hopefully the overview I have shared with you about my life and business will serve as an inspiration so you know that you can make it through the tough times and that broken roads can have positive results. Life has a way of teaching us things. Below are the principles I have found to be very true. I hope they are helpful to you as you journey through life and business.

1. It is highly probable that Plan A will not work out as you intended. That means that you have to be prepared for, and sometimes even plan for, a Plan B. Often, life also requires a Plan C, D, and E.

2. Don't let circumstances define you or destroy you, instead use them as learning experiences to improve your life and develop wisdom.

3. Don't live in stagnation. If what you are doing is not giving you the results you desire, search until you find out what you can do differently that will give you the results you desire.

4. Always listen to those wiser than you; surround yourself with successful people.

5. Don't resist change, but become an agent of change. Change is inevitable and must be embraced.

6. Don't work in your business, work on your business. You will find this to be transforming.
7. Be exceedingly grateful and appreciative for each day you have and for the people in your life.
8. Broken Roads can be blessed. It all depends on how we respond to the various twists and turns of those roads.

About Michael

Michael G Harper is a Property & Casualty and Life Insurance agent who has served the Greater Houston, TX area for over 27 years. Twenty-one of those years have been with Farmers Insurance Group of Companies. Farmers Insurance Group of Companies is a leading U.S. insurer of automobiles, homes and small businesses and also provides a wide range of other insurance and financial services products. Farmers Insurance is proud to serve more than 10 million households with more than 20 million individual policies across all 50 states through the efforts of over 50,000 exclusive and independent agents and nearly 24,000 employees.

Michael is among the best of the best at Farmers who have achieved a high sales volume for auto, home, life and business policies, while maintaining a high client retention and profitability. Through his agency's excellent customer service, Farmers continues to be his customers' first choice for their insurance needs.

Michael has been a 12-time "Toppers Club" and 4-time "Championship" qualifying agent, which represents the top 1% of over 15,000 exclusive Farmers agents. Year after year he is consistently among the top agents with Farmers Insurance. For the past 21 years with Farmers, he has been among the top Life Insurance agents in his district, which proves his dedication to insure that his clients' family's futures are protected. His customer loyalty and dedication to excellent customer service is second to none.

Michael is a married father of five, grandfather of eight, and is very devoted to his family; he also has an unwavering faith in God to whom he attributes his success in life and business.

To learn more about Michael Harper
please visit: www.farmersagent.com/mharper
and: www.facebook.com/michael.g.harper.farmers.insurance
or contact his agency at: 1-888-240-3139.

CHAPTER 46

6 STEPS TO SECURING MORE CUSTOMERS

BY NEIL TRICKETT, PT

As a physical therapist, I thought that when I opened the doors of my physical therapy practice, just putting my name on the door would drive a flood of new customers through it. Oh boy, was I wrong! After struggling for a few years and doing such crazy things as having my amazing wife (who was my physical therapy partner) put flyers on doors of local houses, I finally smartened up. I realized that I needed to learn more about one of the most critical subjects in business, MARKETING! In the following years, I committed to studying many different marketing systems, trying what worked and what didn't in my business. From this simple action of learning more about marketing, the results for my business were awesome! I finally had control of the volume of customers and much more stability in my business.

You see, without good marketing your business will choke, sputter along and eventually close. One of the positive aspects of marketing is that the more you learn, the better your business will do. However, realize that marketing is a dynamic and changing subject that you have to stay on top of.

With the right marketing your business will have a never-ending supply of customers to build on and will allow you to dream even bigger dreams. I know, four years later, I quadrupled my business, had 20 employees, took long vacations and worked less than 40 hours a week.

I then decided to play a bigger game and help many others learn the basics of marketing to apply in their business and be wildly successful. I'm now sharing my top 6 steps to having 'way' more customers than you can handle!

STEP 1 – STANDING OUT FROM THE CROWD

Do you know that the average person has at least 3000 marketing messages a day smashed in their faces? Whether you market to other businesses or directly to consumers, realize that people are drowning in a sea of marketing. Therefore, what are you doing to make your business stand out from your competitors?

How do you stand out from the crowd? How do you leverage your past customers to spread word of mouth and come back in for repeat business? If you understand these two basic principles, you will have a fighting chance of getting your business well-known and liked:

(i). Marketing is simply the techniques by which you create want, and get someone to think newly or differently about what you do.

(ii). The biggest barrier to getting more customers is an understanding of what you do to solve their problems!

Whether you are a small or large business, the goal is to differentiate yourself from your competitors. First you have to identify who your competitors are, and I'm not just talking about the business down the street. Your real competitors are all the other companies trying to attract the eyeballs of your customers.

A good portion of the way you communicate to other professionals, potential customers and past customers is with your marketing promotions. If they are sloppy, look boring and don't push the right buttons, you are not only throwing your money down the drain, but you are hurting your company image, your brand. If you don't send out a multitude of marketing promotions, then how are you expecting to get more business in your door? Remember that:

Low Quality or No Promotion = Poor Perception of Your Business.

STEP 2 – MAKE YOUR MARKETING MONEY WORK FOR YOU

We all know that we have to market to get more business and more customers. However, if you don't spend enough on marketing, you strangle the endless possibilities of your business. The question is on what do you spend your precious money, so that it will generate you much more business in return? The key is to understand what marketing is. Marketing is getting your customers, referral sources and the public to think about your products and services first when they need help for their problem. That's it.

Is marketing an expense?

You have to look at your marketing like an investment, because that is what it really is. You are investing in your business so that you can get much more income out of it than you put in. Marketing is really an investment. You are investing money into your business with the expectation that you will make more money out of it.

When you invest in the stock market you just don't throw your money at a stock and hope it will make you a lot of money. That is a 'sure fire' way to lose a lot of your hard earned money. You research and seek the help of a financial professional, like Christopher Music and Econologics Financial Advisors.

Look at your marketing the same way. Survey your customers, referral sources and different people you want to target. Then, invest wisely and use marketing professionals so that you will get the most return on your investment. Most business owners are hesitant to spend money on marketing because they see it as an expense and not for what it really is, an investment in their business.

You should expect a good return on your marketing dollar. It should be producing you 3, 5, even 10 times your investment into it. If it is not, ditch it! How do you get these kinds of returns you ask? You track the number of new customers you are getting and where they are coming from of course! You track when your marketing hits, and correlate that to the number of customers you are seeing. You track, you track, you track!!!

How much should you be spending on your marketing?

This really depends on the time you have already spent marketing, whether you are new or have been established for awhile. Many expert business owners know a good rule of thumb is to be spending between 10-15% of your gross income on marketing. However, this may be more, or even as much as 25% if you are just jump-starting your business. This may sound like a lot, but what if you were making 5 times the amount of money that you were putting into your marketing? That is a pretty sweet investment. No stock market can give you those returns.

STEP 3 – GETTING THE MOST PROFESSIONAL REFERRALS

Why should a professional such as an attorney, doctor or industry leader refer others to your business? It is a valid question and one that you should be able to answer quite easily. However, wouldn't it be nice to walk into the potential referring person's office and have them say to you, "yes, I know who you are and I have heard the great things that you do, what's the best way to refer to you?" It's not science fiction, it can be done.

The secret lies in how you are promoting yourself and generating a "buzz" in the community. Here are a few things you can do to make yourself better known and get more "buzz":

- Make sure that you are always asking your customers for testimonials. Promote them frequently to different referral sources, your current and past customers, online and more.

- Train your staff to ask the customer when they may be returning to the person who referred them or using their product or service again. They should then remind the customer to let the referring person know how happy they are and to thank the referring person for sending them to you.

- Make sure the referring person is constantly receiving interesting promotional information from you, like a newsletter. Realize that most referral sources have little understanding of what you truly offer and when to send a referral your way. Don't assume that they know this. Most customers who need you will never be referred to you, simply by lack of know-how.

- Help the different people of the referral source know what are the best types of problems your services or products solve with good promotional handouts. Don't kill them with trying to say everything at once. Make yourself known for what you are best at and how you can help solve common problems their customers have. Then focus on one topic per month and get them to be interested in the types of problems and solutions you provide for them.

- Make sure you have good-looking promotional materials for your office. A good brochure, newsletter, handouts, stationary and other materials make your business look professional and a trustworthy place to refer to. Remember, the person who is referring the customer to you is sticking his / her neck out on the line by referring their customer to you, so you better look and act like a place that is truly professional.

- Practice good manners. Make sure the referring person is thanked for their referral even if it is just a handwritten note.

Poor promotion of your business with little or poorly designed brochures, flyers, websites, newsletters, etc. can drag your business image down and kill your buzz. In fact, it can downright sink you. However, with the right kind of marketing and amazing looking promotion, you will get many more referrals and a lot more customers in your door

STEP 4 – HAVING PAST CUSTOMERS COME BACK FOR SERVICES AND PRODUCTS

If you are like most businesses, you have seen quite a few customers over the years. In most businesses, you should be able to see 40% or more of your past customers back each year. How much would that increase your income? Now there's your gold mine! How often are you keeping in contact with all of your past customers? You should be reaching out to your past customers at least every month!

There are so many variables as to what is going on with your customer's lives and when they could potentially use your products or services again, you can't possibly imagine. However, if you are not on the mind of your customers, your business will easily be forgotten, unless you keep in constant communication with them. What your patients receive from you makes or breaks your relationship with them. You want them to continually perceive you as the expert to go to for their problems. You build this with informative and educational marketing promotion that stimulates their interest. Then you need to provide them with offers to entice them to use your business again or refer a friend.

Send out frequent emails, online and print promotions, interact on social media and much more, to help your past customers understand how your products or services help solve their problems. Make sure that your staff call, email and send out personal letters to follow up with your customers.

If you are a service professional, promote to your customers a free seminar or webinar on common issues they encounter. Give to get, so give free information and get referrals. If you keep in constant communication with your past customers, you will see a large increase in your business volume.

STEP 5 – GETTING CUSTOMERS TO REFER OTHERS

You worked hard with your customers to make them happy and get them the results they wanted. It took a lot of coaxing, customer service and perseverance. Your customer is very thankful for you helping them and is very happy with your product or service, but that doesn't mean they are going to send anyone to you.

You have to ask the customer to spread the good word of your business, product or service. Word of mouth advertising does take work and the best way to do it is with a high level of communication with the customer and something to give to them.

Get your customers to help you spread the word about your business with word of mouth. Give them the tools they need to tell others about you. This takes a little bit of training with your staff and customers. Train your staff on how to ask for referrals. "Who do you know that needs our help, product or service?" is a great way to get the conversation rolling. Let the customer know that you want to help more people and this depends on them telling others about your service or product. Ask them to tell a friend or family member, and talk to any local associations, etc., that they belong to. In fact, ask if you can give a referral card with the persons name right on it, so they can hand deliver it to that potential customer. Make it a game and give rewards to customers for their referrals.

Give your customers the ammunition they need!

Customers sometimes feel shy approaching friends or family with a problem, who could use your help. If they have a brochure, referral business card, or some other promotion they can give to a friend, it makes the conversation much easier to get started for the customer. Do you have different brochures on your services or products that you can give to your customers, not only for educational purposes, but also for distribution to friends and family?

Do you have a referral business card, which customers can give to their friends and family? This is a great tool to offer a free consultation or other offer to get someone to call your office or visit your website.

Can you imagine if every customer replaced themselves with another person? It sure would be a lot easier to get new customers. Supercharge your customer referral system with professional referral materials and watch your business take off!

STEP 6 – ONLINE MARKETING STRATEGIES

What is the first thing you do when you are interested in a certain product, service or business? You Google, Bing or Yahoo them! Your customers do the exact thing for your business, so you better have a stellar website that captivates customers, generates leads and gets customers taking that next step to contact you or buy directly online.

Key online strategies you need to get more patients:

- Interactive website with email / name capture for lead generation with free give away
- Email newsletters
- Google adwords
- Google places
- Writing articles for e-zines and generating outside links to your website

• Facebook / Twitter/ LinkedIn, Yelp, blogs and more

Marketing is an integrated approach and needs to use all kinds of media to get the results you want. When you combine print marketing, social media, online marketing and word of mouth, you have a powerful combination to draw the most customers into your business. Use your print media to funnel patients to your website to sign up for free downloads and useful information, which shows you as the expert to go to. You also get to capture the identities that are most interested in your products and services. Then you have a warm list to go after and bring them to the point of a sale.

Use online advertising services to get people interested to go to your website for a free download and ask for their email or address on a web form. Offer them free education with an e-newsletter, social media posts and print materials. Do realize that it takes 7 – 8 times of contacting someone for them to actually do something. The more you market to an individual or business, the more chances are that the person you are contacting will get interested enough to contact you.

More and more people use the web to research whatever problem they have and who to go to. Your website should contain a lot of useful information that your potential customers can download and review to learn more about their condition. Don't just have a website that focuses on your business and how great it is. Keep your focus on educating your customer and ease of contacting your office. There are also great ways to integrate online shopping of your products, appointments online, automatic texting and so much more to remind customers of how important your products or services are to them.

By applying these simple, yet powerful 6 steps you will be guaranteed to ramp up your customer base and expand your business. Remember to always invest in your own learning about marketing; test and don't be afraid to go big.

Dream big dreams, develop big goals and execute big plans.

Here's to your success!

About Neil

Neil Trickett, PT is a healthcare marketing expert and also a physical therapist. Having had a successful physical therapy practice with his wife for eight years, he is now helping healthcare practices across the world grow their businesses with sound marketing principles that work.

His company Practice Promotions has skyrocketed to become a leading expert in healthcare marketing, highly sought after by the rehabilitation industry. In just two years, his company is now producing over 2.5 million customized marketing promotions a year for private practices internationally.

To learn more about Neil Trickett, visit: www.practice-promotions.com
Or call Toll-Free 800-594-7656.
www.practice-promotions.com

CHAPTER 47

THE SPIRIT OF AN ENTREPRENEUR

LESLEY SULLIVAN

"You can have it if you really want it!"

Those words are first words I remember hearing the most when I first came to America. My name is Lesley Sullivan and I am The Pawkeeper.

I never heard those words when I was growing up in England. As a young lady, I was not given many choices and being an entrepreneur certainly wasn't on the list presented to me. The choices I was given were, I could be a wife, a hairdresser or a telephone operator. Those three choices gave me the shivers they didn't fit in with what I planned on doing with my life I wanted to be like James Herriot, the author of *All Creatures Great and Small.* I would drive around in an old car and visit dogs and dog people. I wanted to be a writer, an artist. My own individual person! Be very careful what you wish for because it can come true.

"Young ladies do not attract attention to themselves".

"Women are not supposed to be leaders!"

"No one likes a bossy woman".

These negative statements would constantly be ringing in my ears. We, as female entrepreneurs, have so few role models. I will always have a tremendous gratitude for the incredibly strong women that has given so much to lead the way. Margaret Thatcher, Oprah Winfrey, Ellen DeGeneres, Anita Hill, Louise Hay, and Princess Dianna have all paid the price of helping carve our futures.

I do believe that you can have what you really want but you have got to really want it. There will be many obstacles and tests to find out if you really truly have a heart's desire to be something that makes you so proud and happy that it doesn't really feel like working.

I say that I am a product of the UK, but I was made in America. I smile at the past and see my growth and hope that some of these words will help a young entrepreneur, or a female entrepreneur, or somebody who just really wants something different in their life and needs to see a way to get there. It is time for women to become leaders and entrepreneurs. It is our duty to encourage others, to know that it is OK to be strong and making your own money is a good thing.

Seventeen years ago, I had the most devastating news that turned out to be the most wonderful experience in my life. I have been told in the past that I couldn't have children and when I turned forty, I got this amazing surprise that I was pregnant. Waiting for my husband to come home I was so excited. As he walked through the door looking pale and distraught, he said that he been downsized and lost his job. I told him I was pregnant.

We lost our health insurance and a good salary. Things got worse from that point on. My husband couldn't get another job and we ended up being evicted from our townhouse. We managed to get an apartment in a not-too-comfortable area, but nonetheless, there were a lot of professionals going to work each day. Every morning they would catch the shuttle bus and arrive home very late at night. I knew some of them had dogs and I wondered if those dogs would have to wait all day for the owner to come home. I knew I could make a difference in the lives of the dogs and their owners. I began walking one dog at a time, one step at a time, with a little baby in a stroller.

There were many huge obstacles. My husband, prior to our marriage had a small business as a graphic artist and textile printer. He couldn't pay his sales tax. He had incurred a lot of credit card debt. Somehow, I needed to resolve these problems and start over. No income, no vehicle and a ton of debt are a daunting task for a mother with a newborn.

THE SECRET WAS TO FOCUS ON THE SOLUTION AND NOT THE PROBLEM.

After my son was born, I decided I was not going to put him into daycare, he was a beautiful miracle that needed his Mum. I wanted to spend every moment I could with him. He was my son and the thought of putting him day care was not an option.

I put up a little flyer in each apartment building advertising that I would walk dogs at lunchtime. I had decided that $25 a day would make a major difference in my life. I put each notice in the buildings and business cards under the door and went to schmooze the office staff and told them that I was a dog walker and would be available to assist the maintenance crew with any of my clients should they need to do repairs in the apartments. The rental office was overjoyed as this solved a huge problem for them. My husband said nobody is going to want to let you walk their dogs! That was enough encouragement for me to make him eat his words.

FOCUSING ON THE SOLUTION BECAME MY DAILY MANTRA.

I was charging the huge sum of five dollars a dog walk and life began to change very quickly. My confidence started to improve and pretty soon I was making $50 a day. I raised my goals and my creative entrepreneurial juices started to roll. I was going against everything that I had been taught as a child.

The questions that I got us the most by my clients was,

- "Where can I take my dog when I have to go away on business, vacations, and family emergencies?"
- "Where do you recommend boarding my dog?"

LISTEN TO YOUR CLIENTS AND FOCUS ON A SOLUTION!

We were living in a two-bedroom apartment and sometimes I was taking their dogs to stay with me. My clients were thrilled and the dogs were so happy. I went to look at the boarding kennels and veterinarians in our area. I was shocked at the poor conditions. …Crates stacked one on top of another with small dogs at the top and the large dogs in the bottom crate. …Concrete runs with no raised beds. There were sad-looking confused dogs that had no idea what they had done to be away from their homes.

I started to formulate The Pawkeepers, a Bed and Biscuit Inn for dogs. I did not have a computer or Google or YouTube to guide me through this venture; and as I type these words, I hope you the reader will understand that words do not teach. It is your life experiences that give you knowledge. Your time, effort and mistakes make you the expert in your chosen field.

NETWORK, LISTEN AND RESEARCH ARE THE FOUNDATIONS OF A SUCCESSFUL STARTUP.

The solution was for me to have a house to turn into a Bed and Biscuit Inn. With poor credit history, no capitol to invest, I knew it was going to a long, hard, road. I refused to focus on the problem.

Enter another client in my life. They owned four houses and she was getting divorced from her husband. They divided the properties and she approached me on renting-to-own one of her properties.

I told her I needed a property and a landlady that would allow me to invite furry guests to the house. She laughed and said,

"As long as there's always a permanent reservation for my dogs, then we have a deal!"

LISTEN TO THE CLIENT. FOCUS ON THE SOLUTION!

From a two-bedroom apartment in a horrible neighborhood to a beautiful four-bedroom house with a fenced yard, my income started to rise to $200 a day. Sometimes it was up to $400 a day, depending on public holidays and I started to build a reputation on Yahoo and Google.

I began working on the debt problem. I started to pay off one credit card at a time. Filing Chapter 7 for the sales tax, a payment plan was in effect to eliminate this debt.

I was trying to make the next major move and buy a house of my own. The house we were renting was wonderful but not my dream home. I found a wonderful Cape Cod, with a half-acre of land in a cul-de-sac and knew that this was The Pawkeepers Inn. In our County, the law is only four dogs per house. This is a great law, because if you have 12 or 16 dogs in your house, there is no peace. To be constantly cleaning carpets – it's hard work with little joy.

I was turning away many wonderful dogs and owners.

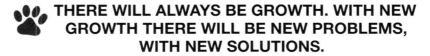

THERE WILL ALWAYS BE GROWTH. WITH NEW GROWTH THERE WILL BE NEW PROBLEMS, WITH NEW SOLUTIONS.

I turned to a church community and spoke to the congregation. I asked if anybody would want to learn how to be a Pawkeeper. I would train them and evaluate which dogs would be happiest in their home. I created jobs for others and developed many wonderful caregivers. For example, a little Bichon or Yorkshire Terrier has different needs than a Labrador or German Shepherd.

The smaller breeds are lapdogs that want to sit and be loved, watch TV, to be adored and petted. I really didn't have time to give them that special attention. A few active seniors stepped forward; they loved dogs but could not afford the vet and grooming bills. Who better to just love and care for these bundles of joy? They did such wonderful work and it also bought joy to their lives. It was a joy for me to visit them and it was a joy to see their happiness. To have a dog in their life for short periods also helped a lot with the medication and daily living expenses. When I would show up with a furry bundle of joy, it became a win for everyone.

I also have some stay-at-home moms with children. Some dogs are used to children, and missed them. I have some houses with cats. Yes, cats and dogs can get along! I had the houses that have no dogs for the older dogs that cannot run around the garden. Their needs are for peace and naptime, not play and noise.

My position had changed with growth of The Pawkeepers. I evaluate the personality and the character of the dog, and then I choose the caregiver appropriate for the booking.

In the years that I have been working with dogs and running a Bed and Biscuit Inn, the dogs have taught me so much about life I would like to share some of those lessons with you. These are guidelines on how to survive as an entrepreneur.

- NUMBER ONE - Recognize who is top dog! This means you! You are the top dog. You call the shots; you choose clients, your rules. You are the leader of your pack. Do not blame others.

- NUMBER TWO - Must play well with others! What you choose to achieve has nothing to do with what other people think of you.

- NUMBER THREE - There will always be another race to run. You will not take first place every time, you are not supposed too! You can position yourself to be the lead dog!

- NUMBER FOUR - Work for joy and treats not money!

- NUMBER FIVE - If you are feeling too much negativity, go to the bathroom. Flush, wash your paws and move on!

- NUMBER SIX - It does not matter if you are a mutt or a purebred. Age, size or breed is never a factor and every dog gets its day!

- NUMBER SEVEN - You will not catch every ball. Sometimes the curve balls can cause you to turn in another direction. Who knows where that direction will lead?

- NUMBER EIGHT - Step out of your crate! Staying in your comfort zone will make you stagnant and grouchy.

- NUMBER NINE - Go to the groomers regularly. A bit of spit and polish will work wonders for your spirit.

- NUMBER TEN - When you're in the race there is to be NO butt sniffing, comparing or pouting. Your goal is to move forward at a pace that helps you grow and win your personal race.

When I started, there wasn't Facebook, webinars, coaches and mentors. Now the playing field has become so much larger. There is always help and advice. With these many business tools, the life of an entrepreneur has just opened up for everyone to start a business with just a computer you can do amazing marketing on Yahoo, Google, Facebook, and so many other places.

At the tender age of 58, I am just starting to branch out into different areas although I have noticed some physical limitations as I grow into my prime. The mind and the spirit are still as strong. My next goal is to start The Pawkeepers Academy. This will be an online training course to teach other people how to run a Bed of Biscuit Inn from their home and how to work with dogs and make a great living.

I look at my past journey and marvel that it had nothing to do with money. There was no money! It had everything to do with an attitude and a mindset. We are all creators and we all are capable of developing a mindset. Remember what I said at the beginning; be careful what you wish for!

Today I am driving around in my old car, visiting dogs and dog people. I am a wonderful Mum, The Pawkeeper, a writer and an artist with so much more to accomplish!

Life is not about finding you; life is about building and creating yourself!

About Lesley

To say that Lesley Sullivan is a dog-enthusiast is an understatement. Her passion, knowledge and love for dogs started at a very early age. Her goal in life was to always be in the company of dogs.

Born in Bedfordshire, England, Lesley is no stranger to dog behavior, having spent many years as a kennel maid for racing greyhounds, service dog trainer, shelter assistant and veterinarian technician.

Her passion for advising and helping people and to encourage a healthy lifestyle for dogs and owners has developed into a thriving business for Lesley Sullivan. She has decades of experience working with dogs and studying dog behavior, and is now focused on socialization of dogs. Lesley lectures nationally sharing her knowledge and passion on the art of dog social behavior with an emphasis on successful social situations and pack integration.

Prior to starting her pet-sitting business, Lesley Sullivan followed her passion for art. She attended the Hammersmith School of Arts and then travelled to America to attend the Art Institute of Pittsburgh.

A wonderful job opportunity with the Columbus Symphony Orchestra allowed Lesley to enjoy her love for classical music, giving her time to reflect on her future. On a trip to Virginia, Lesley met her husband and decided to settle down and raise their son.

Since 1998, Lesley has become a national leader in the pet-sitting industry, combining her love of dogs with running a Bed and Biscuit Inn, teaching group classes for pet owners and writing books about dog behavior.

Lesley Sullivan's high-spirited, outgoing personality and knowledge of dogs now looks to explore online classes for those who wish to own and operate their own in-home boarding facility. Her mission is to teach the importance of cage free boarding for the health and wellbeing of all dogs, allowing the owners stress-free travels for when they cannot be with their dogs.

If you wish to be notified of upcoming online courses on how to run your own Bed & Biscuit Inn, please email: thepawkeepersacademy@yahoo.com

For information on booking The Pawkeepers for speaking engagements and consultations please email: www.thepawkeepers.com

Become a fan and join the fun pack on Facebook: https://www.facebook.com/thepawkeepers

CHAPTER 48

FOUR PILLARS: Foundation For Success In Business And Life

BY KAPIL SAHNI

Each individual has infinite potential to succeed, but more often than not majority of people report that they struggle in life; they achieve some level of success, but seldom use their entire potential, and hence aren't able to manifest great levels of success. Why? The answer is simply: people are seldom aware or have ever been formally taught about laws and core principles that serve as a foundation for success in any endeavor, be it business, relationships or life.

Having studied some of the most successful business and thought leaders around the world, a ton of already available self development books on the subject and my own experience using some of the indisputable universals laws of success - I've personally distilled four key ingredients that serve as the core foundation for success in business and life. I call these the Four Pillars of Success. Each of these individual pillars are absolutely critical to build a strong foundation for success.

I'm so glad you picked up this book since the content I'll share in the next few sections can truly change your life if you apply it diligently. If you stay engaged through the end of this chapter, I promise you'll walk away with a blueprint to succeed and attain the levels of success that you truly deserve in every aspect of your life.

1. DEVELOP A COMPELLING VISION

"I can teach anybody how to get what they want out of life. The problem is that I can't find anybody who can tell me what they want."
~ Mark Twain

The foremost requirement to any achievement in life is to get crystal clear about **what it is that you desire and why you desire it**. Everything else is secondary. It's often noticed that when an individual takes inventory of his core values and aligns them with their vision, something magical happens. An individual experiences a deep sense of resonance with their core being and their vision seems to come to life.

When developing a vision, it's always best to start with the aspect of life that matters to you most, and the one which would contribute most to the quality of your life. I'd recommend you block some time frequently to diligently craft your vision. This is not a one-time activity; it needs to be worked on continually for both your short-term and long-term goals.

One of the most reputed and highly respected authors, Steven Covey, describes one of the core habits most effective people have is of "beginning with the end in mind." You may consider developing a compelling vision in the same light such that you're thinking and projecting an ideal outcome in the future. By doing so, you'll get in touch with your thoughts, desires, emotions, your core values, and bring to life all your active as well as your dormant faculties, such as creativity, imagination, etc. The clearer you are about your destination, the easier it is to plan the next set of steps to get there.

A vision serves as a guideline to ensure all choices and decisions you're making going through life are in alignment with your vision, so that you stay the course and don't drift away. Nonetheless, if you do drift away, it assists in course-correction, reminding you that you've gone astray and need to make changes in your life that align with your vision.

Let's talk briefly about something very specific about a vision. You may have noticed the first pillar of success is to not just develop a vision but a compelling vision. It's not a mere hope or wish, it's an irresistible, overpowering desire that moves you. It's something that you can sense and very often brings forth a lot of strong emotions. More often than not, it's something that's on your mind constantly.

Is this something you can perhaps relate to in your life? If not, I dare you to find yourself a compelling vision of something extremely important to you - something that you wish to accomplish in your life (long-term or short-term). It could be anything from losing a few pounds, to regaining your lost self confidence, to solving a problem in society that makes your heart cry, to winning the Ms. Universe pageant, to being a special needs teacher, to qualifying for the Olympics, to being a CEO of the company you currently work for, to being an absolute role model to your kids or perhaps getting out of your comfort zone and finally starting your own company. Once you've developed your compelling vision, whatever it may be – you need to commit to achieving it by a non-negotiable date.

The next most important thing you need to do is: develop a detailed plan of how you're going to get there and get to work.

When you have a definite goal with an associated deadline and you commit to it with all your being, you miraculously summon incredible amounts of energy, enthusiasm, integrity, will power, and motivation. You make monumental progress and little by little, you begin to conquer the milestones you've set for yourself. It's as if the goal has this almost unbelievable magnetic effect of drawing you towards it with a pull that grows in magnitude with each passing day. It's extremely exhilarating and very frequently it's observed that you develop a great amount of endurance within yourself, and in turn develop hidden creativity and resourcefulness to overcome any obstacle that comes in your path towards your goal.

When you lack vision for your life, you're simply reacting to the circumstances of life rather than having the reigns in your hand and marching confidently towards your vision, regardless of the obstacles on your path which you recognize as temporary set backs, and don't let them overpower you.

One of the most widely-read Bible verses, Proverbs 29:18 states, ***"Where there is no vision, the people perish."***

This is as true for any organization as it is for your personal life. A separate distinct vision must be developed for each aspect of your life. When you lack vision for each important aspect of your life, namely your career, health, relationships etc., you'll fail to achieve your desired level of success in your career, your health will be far from ideal and your relationships will be strained. As a result, you'll be resigned and lack meaning in your life. You'll go through the motions of life uninspired and demotivated and have a rather disappointing experience of life.

Visions have a profound affect on every aspect of our lives and the sooner you understand the gravity of this key ingredient for success and put it to use as recommended, you'll well be on your way to creating an extraordinary life for yourself and manifesting any level of success you desire.

2. MASTER YOUR PSYCHOLOGY

"Success is 80% Psychology and 20% Mechanics."
~ Tony Robbins

Let's consider a quick example. When it comes to having good health, majority of people already know the basic steps to follow, such as:

1. Eat a balanced diet daily with a good mix of greens, fruits and vegetables.
2. Drink 8-10 glasses of water daily.
3. Get at least 7-8 hours of sleep daily.
4. Exercise at least for 30 minutes 4 to 6 times a week.

In the example above, as you can see, the know-how, i.e., mechanics, is no rocket science; it's a set of four simple steps accounting for 20% of your success, but the psychology one needs to stay disciplined and consistent is the hard part and accounts for 80% of your final results.

Knowing and implementing the mechanics amounts to only 20% of what contributes to anyone's success regardless of the endeavor. The bulk of what dictates an individual's success in life is one's psychology. This is an undisputed fact. Psychology of a person encompasses many attributes – some of the most prominent ones are one's mindset, thoughts, inner dialogue or self talk, core beliefs, perception, attitude, self-confidence, self-esteem, will power, motivation and ability to be self-disciplined and self-reliant.

Have you ever had the experience of doing everything in your capacity to accomplish your goals, but you just don't seem to be able to make it happen? There could be many different reasons for not being able to manifest what you desire most in life despite all your efforts, but one of the most common causes that often goes unnoticed is an unresolved inner conflict. Inner conflicts are best described as opposing intentions or beliefs. You may desire a better, a high paying job, but internally you may have a strong core belief that you're not good enough and lack adequate skills to get such a job. In this example, the latter is an inner conflict and unless that inner conflict is resolved, you will struggle with manifesting your desired job into reality. Inner conflicts by nature are difficult to identify on your own and hence often go unnoticed.

I'd like to take a moment and share with you briefly how I personally coach my clients around inner conflicts. While working with clients, I'll often ask them thought-provoking direct questions that encourage them to explore their fixed considerations about a situation or circumstance. This approach often brings to light their underlying assumptions and core-beliefs which do not serve them, instead work entirely against them. I shed more light on such things to help them fully understand for themselves how certain fixed considerations, assumptions and core beliefs they have are holding them back and directly impeding their forward movement to accomplish their goals. Identifying such inner conflicts is only half the story; then I work with them closely and encourage them to try on a new consideration - sometimes involving a paradigm shift in the way they think and perceive a situation and their capabilities. Doing so helps them understand how to resolve their inner conflict and change their psychology which accounts for 80% of their success and this in turn leads them to have incredible breakthroughs in their lives.

The sooner you develop more self-awareness about your true psychology and get a deeper understanding of why you think the way you think, why you feel the way you feel and why you do what you do and map that way of being to the outcomes you're getting in life – you'll begin to unravel the mystery of how your psychology is shaping all your reality. Once you comprehend and understand the true power of this insight, you can literally hardwire your brain and subconscious mind with a new set of programs, thoughts and way of doing things which will lead to a different set of results.

I absolutely love the following quote by T. Harv Eker, which further drills down the significance of mastering your psychology and programing your subconscious mind:

"It all comes down to this: If your subconscious 'financial blueprint' is not set for success, nothing you learn, nothing you do will make much of a difference."

Our subconscious mind can be best described as a storehouse of everything we experience going through our daily lives right from our birth. It doesn't have an ability to filter between real or unreal, good or bad; its job is simply to record everything we see, hear, feel, interpret, (i.e., attach a meaning, etc.) and it does this seamlessly without our conscious knowing. The information it records is commonly referred to as programs similar to computer programs that are downloaded in our subconscious minds. Substantial research has been done in this area and it's been proven that our overall psychology is invariably a sum-total of the programs that have been downloaded in our subconscious minds over the years based on the conversations we've had, repetitive ideas we've been exposed to from our childhood to adulthood, and our personal life experiences to date.

The key is to understand how our subconscious mind works and learn ways and means to program our subconscious mind deliberately towards the ends we desire. I cannot emphasize enough how critical it is to master this aspect of your psychology and the role it plays in your success.

3. TAKE PERSISTENT ACTION

"Nothing in the world can take the place of Persistence. Talent will not; nothing is more common than unsuccessful men with talent. Genius will not; unrewarded genius is almost a proverb. Education will not; the world is full of education derelicts. Persistence and determination alone are omnipotent. The slogan 'Press On' has solved and always will solve the problems of the human race."
~ Calvin Coolidge

The quote above, emphasizing the importance of persistence has been one of the cornerstones that has contributed significantly to all the successes in my life. This is undoubtedly a non-negotiable ingredient that dictates whether or not you'll be successful in life, be it your career/business, relationships or health, regardless of any external circumstance.

There are umpteen examples of movers and shakers in business as well as political leaders across the world such as Mahatma Gandhi, Martin Luther King and Nelson Mandela who've brought about everlasting change and changed the fate of an entire country by stepping up to the plate and demonstrating the power of perseverance when faced with continuous defeat or obstacles. It's easy to be motivated and really excited at the beginning when pursuing any goal; but it's the ability to persevere and take persistent action by being resourceful and creative when faced with obstacles or defeat that leads one to success.

It's unfortunate, but most people tend to throw in the towel at the first sign of defeat or loss, as opposed to staying inside the ring long enough to enjoy the benefits of their labor. Your desire to succeed is directly proportional to your achievements in business and life. The stronger your desire and will power, the greater your motivation to overcome any obstacle in your path towards achieving your goals. A burning desire, combined with a positive mental attitude and persistent action, always results in success.

Lack of persistence is one of the major causes of failure in business and life. Nobody is born with persistence per se. It's a habit and like any other habit, it can be developed over time. It is truly one of the core foundations for success in business and life.

4. DEVELOP A MASTERMIND ALLIANCE

Napoleon Hill, author of *'Think and Grow Rich'* defines mastermind as a "coordination of knowledge and effort, in a spirit of harmony, between two or more people, for the attainment of a definite purpose." An alliance in the context of our discussion can be simply defined as a partnership, an agreement based on some form of kinship or a formal/informal relationship (coaching, mentorship etc.) between two or more people who have a vested interest in your success.

Do you want to know one of the best-kept secrets that can literally impact your results in business and life by over 10x? It's the ability to tap into the shared, infinite knowledge base, experience, intelligence, skills and resources of a mastermind group as if it were your own.

Success often leaves clues. Think about this phrase for a moment. This is a very powerful concept and it emphasizes the idea of duplicating success. It encourages you to learn the steps used by someone else to succeed and then modeling it. Its always good to be creative and have your own unique way of doing things, but often if you're not mindful – it can come with a great cost of time, money and resources. Instead of re-inventing the wheel, if you simply become a student and develop a mastermind alliance with someone you admire, respect and would like to model – you'll be setting yourself up for success.

"You are the average of the five people you spend most time with."
~ Jim Rohn

I find the above quote by Jim Rohn extremely thought provoking. I want to extend the invitation to you right now to do some introspection. Think of five people you spend most time with and keep the following questions in mind:

- Are they always excited, on top of their game and thriving in their respective businesses and careers or are they demotivated and going through life resigned, focused on just punching the clock and paying their bills?

- Are they dreamers who take action and make things happen or are they nay sayers who're always pessimistic and blaming the economy or perhaps have an excuse ready for why things can't be done?

- Are they health conscious and make time for working out despite their busy lives or do they have poor eating habits and are least concerned about their health?

- Are they enjoying passionate and loving relationships or are their relationships constantly strained with a lot of pain and hurt?

Your environment, the people you interact with and the kind of conversations you have on a daily basis directly influence your thoughts, and as a result influence your potential to earn, your outlook on life, your daily habits, your overall well-being and your relationships. Chose the people you spend most time with well; it will alter your life entirely for the good. It's absolutely vital that you associate regularly with people with common goals, dreams and aspirations who may have either already achieved the levels of success you desire or are in pursuit of the same. When you do so, your vision inevitably expands; you get multiple perspectives on the possible options that lie ahead of you, and last but not the least, you learn new actionable strategies and tools to overcome any obstacle that may be impeding your progress.

I hope you've enjoyed reviewing the content above. My objective was to share the "Four Pillars of Success" with you in an easily understandable manner so that you can very quickly make them your own personal mantra for success. Now that you know the mechanics for manifesting success in business, relationships and life, the million-dollar question is whether you'll take action by putting what you've learnt into practice or simply let life pass by. I urge you to take action – it's the only way you'll be able to achieve your goals.

I wish you all the very best and hope that you live an extraordinary life that inspires and motivates you to be your very best. If you have any major goals related to any aspect of your life, that you're currently struggling with or haven't been able to make much progress, please contact me via my website: www.kapilsahni.com. I'd love the opportunity to work with you and empower you to accomplish all your goals.

About Kapil

Kapil Sahni has an outstanding decade-long software quality management background in the high tech industry. He has held multiple positions as a Senior Consultant with top Fortune 500 companies in Silicon Valley, California such as Microsoft, Google, Apple, etc. and supported multiple global launches during his career. His expertise also includes leadership, strategic planning and tactical execution, process improvement, business analysis, project management and web analytics. He has been mentoring and coaching his team in all his leadership roles. He has a Bachelors Degree in Mechanical Engineering from Pune University, India and has attended San Diego State University, California for a Masters Program in Computer Science. He is also a globally-certified Project Management Professional (PMP).

He has lived briefly in New York in the past, but has been based out of California since 2002. He made San Jose his home since he was smitten by California's picturesque landscape and incredible weather. He loves the rich and diverse community that Silicon Valley offers which keeps him both grounded and inspired being in touch with visionaries who are constantly working on ideas to change the world. He's an avid reader, deep intellectual thinker who's very compassionate and genuinely cares for people. He has a high zest for life, is fascinated by the capabilities of the human mind and is a personal development enthusiast. He supports many humanitarian causes and volunteers at community events.

He's currently training to be an Internationally Certified Success Coach through the Certified Coaches Alliance. He has an innate ability to lead, motivate and inspire, and is passionate about peak performance, leadership, coaching and training and development. He is also actively working on developing programs to impart life skills to children and youth in their formative years, helping adults find more meaningful and fulfilling careers that they absolutely love, and elevating human consciousness.

Besides his corporate career, Kapil coaches people from all walks of life on myriad different aspects that contribute to their quality of life. He assists people in getting un-blocked and making positive changes in their lives. He's committed to people winning in all areas of their life (personal, professional, relationships, health, and spiritual) and living a life that they absolutely love. He helps people get crystal-clear about their goals and what's holding them back to live the best version of their lives yet. Using his unique coaching style, he then assists them unravel solutions to overcome each obstacle and map out a step-by-step plan to manifest their dreams into reality.

His message to the world is:

DREAM BIG. BE YOURSELF. LIVE PASSIONATELY.

To learn more about Kapil Sahni and the services he offers, kindly visit: www.kapilsahni.com

Kapil Sahni
City: San Jose, CA, USA

CHAPTER 49

"YOU COULD BE EXERCISING, *RIGHT NOW!*"

BY DR. JULIA PEWITT-KINDER

I don't have time to exercise. Between working full-time and taking care of my three children and a home (plus a cocker-spaniel puppy), I barely have time to catch my breath. Why would I want to spend my precious time on a treadmill, making myself completely out of breath? If I have a spare moment, I would rather read or play a game with my kids. Besides, by the end of the day, *I am too tired to exercise*.

But eight years ago, I found out the hard way I would have to find the time and energy to exercise – that exercise is vital to health. Without health, a successful and happy life is not possible. I had just finished my medical residency, stepped into a new career, and delivered my first child - a child with special needs. Besides being a doctor, wife, and mother, I had to become a teacher and therapist to help my daughter thrive. With so much to accomplish each day, I reduced my sleep and increased my caffeine. I often forgot to eat, or did so hurriedly while driving or folding laundry. I was running on fumes, with stress driving me forward regardless of how exhausted I was. I never exercised; there wasn't time. Even though as a doctor I knew the importance of taking care of myself, I didn't. I thought I was invincible, that sheer willpower would get me through each day.

One evening, after the simple movement of opening a window, I developed severe shoulder, neck, and back pain. I was unable to turn my head, lift my arm, or even lie down. An MRI revealed torn muscle fibers that had become thin and weak because of my lack of physical strengthening. I honestly wasn't concerned; it was only a few torn muscles, which I expected would quickly heal. It wasn't as if I broke a bone or herniated a disk. I would simply get the proper treatment and move on. But over the next year, I tried numerous conventional and alternative treatments. Anti-inflammatories, muscle-relaxers, physical therapy, massage, steroid injections, and reflexology all failed to quickly relieve my pain. The years I had allowed my muscles to wither away from lack of exercise meant my recovery would be slow and difficult.

Pain is a thief, stealing energy and endurance and robbing us of time, money, and sleep. Pain makes our bodies work harder than normal. My pain kept me from sleeping, so I became chronically tired. Regardless of my exhaustion, I had no choice but to drag myself out of bed each morning and face the day; work, kids, cooking, and home-care couldn't be neglected. Each activity was made difficult by my arm weakness. I became irritable and downright grumpy from a combination of fatigue, pain, and lack of energy to do anything fun. I was furious that this injury was slowing me down. I knew I had only myself to blame because I hadn't cared for my health.

I vowed that once I got "caught up" I would start strength training to overcome this injury and prevent future ones. I ignored a developing sore throat, blaming my hoarseness on over-using my voice at work. But in fact, I was a sitting target for infection because I was completely run-down from a vicious cycle of pain, lack of sleep, excess work and stress, over-caffeinating, and under-hydrating. Awakening one night with a high fever and chills, I ended up in the hospital for an emergent tonsillectomy. I now had no choice but to slow down and recover.

Forced to rest in a hospital bed while watching reruns of "Little House on the Prairie," I had time for reflecting upon my life. Something was wrong. Even though I had a great family and career, I painfully admitted to myself I wasn't happy. I didn't have any fun because by the time I got through work and daily responsibilities, I was frazzled and wanted to just sit down rather than engage in any activity. When had I last taken Ella on a stroller ride? Or gone for a bike ride? Or simply been awake enough to stay up late to watch a movie? Because I was so tired all the time, I moved at a snail's pace through daily chores, which left no extra time or energy to do things I loved. What about bigger goals I once had, like canoeing the entire Current River? Because of my lack of strength, that dream wasn't even a possibility. My health – or rather my lack of – was getting in the way of living my life. Aches, pains, injuries, illness, and fatigue were barriers to being happy each day, placing limits on what I could accomplish.

I now understood that if I had my health as a foundation to stand upon – if I had strength, energy, endurance, and mental clarity – I could then build the life I wanted. If I felt great I could tackle tasks in less time, with free time and energy left over for dreams and goals I had forgotten. I had to find time to exercise.

After recovering from surgery and back home, I paced in my office, staring at my complicated weekly schedule. Where could I pencil in "exercise?" Back and forth I paced for 20 minutes, until tired, I sat to rest. Wondering briefly why I was tired, I realized that whenever I am deep in thought, I briskly walk around my office. Out of habit, I alternate walking on my tiptoes. My tired calf muscles confirmed I had been exercising while I was working. And it was easy; I didn't even know I was working-out. Excited at the concept of getting in shape while I worked, I plopped down on the floor and did sit-ups with my calendar at my side. I was "Exercising, *Right Now*."

I hadn't exercised routinely in the past because I didn't have time, I was too tired, I wanted to do something else, or I forgot. I now had the solution for all my excuses to not exercise. I could fit in bits of exercise while I worked and during other routine activities. No extra time would be needed! I didn't have to find huge blocks of time for exercise. Small bursts of exercise would give me more energy, rather than wearing me out. If I exercised during the workday, I could spend my free time doing something fun. And by pairing exercise with habits like brewing my tea, I would never forget to exercise.

With my training as a fitness instructor, I immediately thought of exercises that could be done anywhere, anytime, and without any equipment. I developed exercises to do while watching TV, folding clothes, or even driving. I knew my concept of "Exercise, *Right Now*" would be effective because it was backed by science: Exercise is cumulative - <u>*every little bit counts*</u>. Huge blocks of time to exercise aren't needed.

Within days of starting my Exercise, *Right Now* program, I experienced improvement in my energy level. I quickly developed toned and defined muscles and slept better, my chronic fatigue vanishing. My pain also went away. Each day, I was able to accomplish more in less time because I had eliminated the barriers of poor health. Those closest to me noticed my improved mood and appearance, asking how I juggled career, family, exercise, and time for me.

My friends, family, and patients began sharing with me similar experiences. They, too, had experienced fatigue that prevented them from pursuing favorite pastimes. Many had tried unsuccessfully to lose weight. All complained of not having enough time or being too tired to exercise. I shared the exercises I had developed, which could be done by anyone of any age or fitness level. Everyone loved that the program was easy to learn and didn't take extra time. Plus, they didn't have to spend money on expensive gym memberships, equipment, and diet programs. The results were exciting: weight loss, decreased blood pressure and cholesterol, fewer illnesses, and increased stamina were all commonly experienced. Along with physical health came a more important benefit – happiness.

I believe we all seek to improve our lives, wanting to make changes which lead to our daily satisfaction and sense of well-being. We wish to be happier and to look and feel great each day. Some want more time with family. Others strive for financial security. Whatever it is that you desire, you are responsible for achieving it. You are your own Change Agent. But you must stand on a foundation of health to reach your goals. You must exercise every day if you want to eliminate barriers to your success.

Take a moment to think about what it is you most value in your life. What are your dreams and goals - have you taken the time lately to remember? What would you enjoy doing every day if given the energy? How much more productive could you be with crystal-clear mental clarity and creativity? Would you like to improve the way you look? Are you ready to get rid of aches and pains? Are you tired of being tired? Exercise is the solution to feeling great so you can enjoy each day. Why not get started, *Right Now*?

To help you begin building a foundation of health, strength, and energy, I have compiled my favorite **Top 7 Times to Exercise** and the **Top 7 Exercises** to target those **Top 7 Body Parts**!

THERE ARE ONLY THREE RULES:

1. Don't count the number of repetitions.
Exercise until you are tired or out of time. The number of repetitions isn't important. It is important to tire the muscle and to exercise as often as possible during each day. *Exercise Right Now* is designed to make exercise easy and fun. If I count repetitions, I worry about keeping track of numbers in logs or notes, which is extra and unnecessary work. Without focusing on counting, your mind is free to wander or simply relax.

2. Maintain proper posture during each exercise.
Each exercise, standing or sitting, starts with the same Set Position (see instructions below). This Set Position is maintained throughout the exercise. Simply holding this Set Position will burn calories because muscles are engaged.

3. Focus on the working muscle.
Mentally focus on the muscle you are exercising, holding other muscles still. Isolating a muscle gets quicker results.

BEGIN ALL EXERCISES IN SET POSITION:

1. Stand/Sit up tall, straightening and lengthening spine.
2. Lift chest and chin.
3. Roll shoulders forward, up, and back, which will further push your chest forward.
4. Pull abdominal muscles in hard towards spine.
5. Relax arms, bending slightly at the elbow.
6. If standing, squeeze bottom and thigh muscles, with knees softly bent.

START EXERCISING, *RIGHT NOW!*

1. Brush your teeth: Lift and tone your backside.

Do you brush your teeth every day? If so, you could be exercising every day. An added bonus is fewer trips to the dentist!

- While brushing teeth with right hand, place left hand lightly on vanity for stability.
- Face vanity straight-on.
- Straighten right leg behind you, with toes pointed and resting lightly on floor.
- Slowly raise leg as high as possible, tightening all muscles.
- Hold until muscles tire.
- Repeat other leg.

2. Stand in a line: Sculpt your calves.

Irritated while waiting at the bank, post-office, or grocery store? Don't waste time; get fit! Exercise can be done discreetly, without anyone knowing.

- Place feet hips-width apart, toes pointing forward, knees slightly bent.
- Raise heels slightly off floor; hover.
- Raise higher, pretending to look over the person in front of you.
- Lower without allowing heels to touch floor.
- Continue to slowly lift and lower your body in a controlled manner.
- Squeeze your rear for added benefit.
- Feeling wobbly as you try to balance? The wobble is good, as it indicates you are exercising your abdominal and back muscles, too.

3. Drive the car: Get six-pack abs.

- Crank up your favorite upbeat music.
- Pull abs in tight toward your spine, release, and repeat, while keeping beat with the music.

4. Microwave leftovers: Build your biceps.

How long do you stand in front of the microwave waiting for leftovers to warm? One minute? Why not complete 60 bicep curls! Store hand weights in your kitchen or office break room. These are affordable and come in many sizes.

- Place a weight in each hand.
- Bending your arm at the elbow, lift the weight towards your shoulder. Weights can be lifted at the same time, or by alternating hands.

5. Clean the house and your arteries: Cardio-Cleaning.

Every moment is precious. Yes, we have to clean, but why waste an hour when you could get the job done in half the time AND complete your cardio workout?

- Blast some high-energy music.
- Jog in place as you vacuum.
- RUN from room to room as you put away toys or laundry.
- Dust fast and furiously: Your arms will notice the burn.
- Pretend your mother is coming to visit in an hour for extra motivation to finish chores quickly.

6. Sit at a desk: Get sexy legs.

- Extend right leg straight out in front of you, toes pointed.
- Raise leg as high as you can, hold until tired, lower slightly without touching ground, then lift leg again.
- Repeat until tired.
- Switch legs.

7. Gas up the car: Define and tone triceps.

Keep a set of hand weights in your car.

- Hold weight with both hands, right in front of your chest.
- Lift weight above head.
- Bending arms at the elbow, lower weight behind your head.
- Lift weight back up over your head.
- Repeat until your tank is full.

Here's a **Bonus Exercise for sculpting legs and buttocks. Try this *Right Now!***

1. Stand in Set Position with feet hips-width apart and toes pointing forward.
2. Place hands on hips.
3. Pull abs in tight and hold during entire exercise.
4. Bend knees slightly.
5. HOLD this posture while you begin to gently and slowly jump up and down in place.
   - Land softly, rolling through your feet with toes touching first and heels last.
   - Keep knees soft – always slightly bent.
   - Jump higher each time. Point your toes as you jump into the air.

**Note: Even those with knee or back problems can do this carefully and gently.*

In the past few minutes, you have burned calories, increased energy, and strengthened muscles: You are more fit than before you read this chapter. Congratulations! You have started ***Exercising, Right Now, moving forward to the change you desire in your life!***

About Dr. Julia

Dr. Julia Pewitt-Kinder is a practicing physician, national speaker, fitness consultant, best-selling author, and busy mom of three.

Dr. Kinder is Board Certified in Family Practice and maintains a private practice in Jackson, Missouri, with her brother. For over 10 years, she has counseled thousands of patients, helping them find time during their day to exercise and showing them easy ways to improve their health.

As a nationally-recognized speaker since 2007, Dr. Kinder is an established authority on health and fitness. She has shared her life-changing techniques with audiences that include corporations, local community groups, universities, national organizations, the media, and various conferences. Leading keynote presentations and workshops, her high-energy and down-to-earth presence inspires participants to begin making change during her presentation by showing them how to exercise while listening to the lecture. Combining her medical background and passion for making fitness easy, she gives participants the tools to establish a foundation of health by incorporating nutrition, exercise, and soul-nurturing activities into their daily routine. Dr. Kinder encourages the audience to achieve their life's goals by giving them the tools to implement change *Right Now.*

Continuing on her mission to simplify getting fit, Dr. Kinder also offers personal consultations and has developed a line of effective and affordable fitness products. By working one-on-one with clients, she tailors exercise and eating-healthy programs that fit any schedule and fitness level. Her clients range in age from teenagers to over 80; anyone who desires more energy, less brain-fog, improved mood, and weight loss will immediately achieve results.

Dr. Kinder understands from personal experience the importance of maintaining her health so she has the energy to care for her family. Ella, age eight, may have Down syndrome, but she is otherwise a healthy and typical child who loves reading and swimming. Twins Dexter and Paxton are lively three-year-old boys. Paxton has Crohn's Disease and requires a restricted diet. With Dr. Kinder leading by example, all of her children also exercise daily.

If you'd like to learn more about how Dr. Kinder manages to look and feel great and also make time for herself - all while juggling her career and family, contact her today! She can show you how to incorporate fitness into your normal, daily routine without spending extra hours at the gym. Here are easy ways for you to get started, *Right Now*!

Website: www.juliakinder.com
Golden Rules to Fitness: www.juliakinder.com/ExerciseRightNow/
Facebook: https://www.facebook.com/ExerciseRightNow
Twitter: twitter.com/juliakinder

For Speaking Engagements or Personal Consultations, email Dr. Kinder: julia@juliakinder.com

Shop the *Right Now* store for affordable products to get you in shape, fast! http://store.juliakinder.com/exercise-right-now-fitness-program-products/

CHAPTER 50

HOW TO GET OUT OF YOUR OWN WAY AND PURSUE YOUR ULTIMATE DREAMS

BY AJ ROBERTS

The biggest thing in your life that you can control is what goes on between your ears. We can have all these tactics, we can have all these tools, we can have secrets, and tricks and strategies, but none of that matters unless we can control our own brain. You see the biggest challenge you're going to face is Resistance. Resistance against your true calling, your higher power, the very thing you've been put on this earth to do.

Just a few years back, I was literally the strongest man in the world and held the All-Time World Record total in powerlifting. **This was after ten years of training my heart out every single day, pushing through boundaries and barriers, going beyond what anyone else would do in order to achieve, what I thought, was the ultimate success.** However, along this journey I knew I was heading in the wrong direction but never did anything to correct this, and one day woke up and had had enough. My health was diabolical, I hated my job and I was in an unhappy marriage and I just couldn't take it anymore.

But I had lived feeling this way for years, why?

I was…

- scared of losing my identity.
- scared of being broke.
- scared of being alone.
- scared of what others would say about me.
- scared I'd have to go back to working fourteen plus hours a day and give up the five bedroom house with two master bathrooms, swimming pool, pool house, huge basement bar, and the luxury life I was living.
- scared I'd fail and embarrass myself. What if I got things wrong and wanted to go back to my previous life?
- scared I was simply being selfish and that I'd be letting my family, my friends and my business associates down.

So I just stayed where I was for years. Letting resistance win time and time again.

But, I was not living the life I was supposed to be living, and it was slowly eating away at me. The voices in my head got louder and louder.

I tried a few times to address the thing, but then I started to think, what if I actually do succeed?

What if my vision is possible? What would that mean? What new responsibilities would I have?

And I'd become terrified of the potential of success. How will I handle it? I'm sure you may have similar fears.

I started to get angrier at myself and asked why I was so scared and so terrified to step into my true calling? …The thing that was eating away at me, the thing that I dream about. Why was I procrastinating? Why was I waiting around? Why wasn't I taking action? Why was I continually putting food into my body that I knew was not good for me? Why was I continually avoiding opportunities I had that would push me in the direction I wanted to go?

And then I discovered I wasn't alone and that the reason I was living this way was because any time we have a higher purpose, any time our true calling is there, resistance creeps in and wants to prevent us from reaching our destiny.

"Resistance is a bitch. And it does not like us."
~ AJ Roberts

The more you begin to understand what your higher purpose is, the more you begin to tune into what it is you were meant to do, the bigger the resistance and the bigger the barriers you'll put in place. As I began to move closer to what I felt called to do, and as I began to I deconstruct my life and move away from those things that I had been clinging to, I was constantly attacked by Resistance and would question what I was doing – doubting whether or not I was making the right choices, or doing the right thing.

What's crazy is the universe supports you in these decisions in such a magnetic way that if you can fight through all this, unbelievable things will begin to happen. But this doesn't come without a struggle and it seems the closer you get to where you're supposed to be, the harder Resistance attacks.

The thing is, Resistance isn't always so obvious to spot. It's covert. You can't see it as it's internal, it's centralized inside each of us and hidden from the world. It's cunningly clever. It'll sneak up on you when you least expect it. It's cruel. It wants to hurt you and take you down. It's cold-blooded. It doesn't matter who you are, it doesn't matter how much success you have, it's coming to get you.

Every single person at some point will face this. You may have already faced this and guess what, you will continue to face this as Resistance never quits. There is no escaping the Resistance that we face. There is no running away from it. It doesn't care if you're a beginner, if you're intermediate or if you're advanced. It doesn't care if you're just starting out or if you've already living a successful life. It has no remorse.

It's consistent. It comes back time and time and time again, and when you think you've got it under control, guess what: there it is again.

Lastly, it can be crucifying. It's out to kill you. It's out to destroy your entire world. You have to be prepared to go to war again and again with it.

So how do you prepare?

STEP 1 IS TO BE CONSCIOUSLY AWARE OF RESISTANCE.

Be aware that no matter what, Resistance is going to rear its ugly head at some point. We need to be aware that it is a cosmic force we are going to be battling against, and the only way you will get through it is if you've prepared for battle.

You are going to be battling your utmost inner demons that are telling you to do something else. They are going to be screaming at you to not face Resistance and to run the other way. So, you have to be aware of it. Once we're aware, when it creeps up on you, you'll be ready for the way. You'll be ready to stand your ground and you'll be ready to do whatever it takes to win.

STEP 2 IS TO KNOW YOUR WHY.

Why are you doing this?

I grew up in a family that literally had no money. To get to school, which was over two miles away, I used to walk every day regardless of the weather. And if you've ever visited England, then you know we're not famous for good weather.

It was 20 pence to catch the bus. I'd ask my mother for the money and she'd always tell me that she didn't have any to give. I remember going into my mother's purse to look thinking that she was lying to me, and it was completely empty – no cash, no change, nothing!

My friends would go to movies, I couldn't go. I remember as a kid not having the nice clothes, not having the nice things, and I remember thinking to myself - I'm going to do whatever it takes when I grow up so I never have to go without again.

Once I figured that out, I decided I wanted to teach others the same thing, as I never wanted them to have to tell their kids what my mother told me. That's why I choose to be a leader. That's why I choose to try to inspire, to help build others build successful businesses.

So, know your why.

STEP 3 IS TO UNDERSTAND THAT D x V x FS > R

D is the dissatisfaction. Most of us are in this state, dissatisfied with where we currently are. Unhappy with what we've achieved. We haven't reached where we want to get to. If you're truly completely happy with where you are and living your dream life, then I congratulate you. But I believe most of you are somewhat dissatisfied with where you are.

V is for vision. You've got to know what your vision is. If you haven't figured this out yet then my advice is to sit in silence and listen to yourself. Allow your head to bounce off the walls. Understand your thoughts may get a little crazy, but if you wait, and you listen, and you wait some more, everything begins to come clear.

And then we have to take D x V and we multiply that with FS.

FS is for those *First Steps*. You have to take those first steps if you ever want to reach your destination.

Think about Michael Jordan. MJ didn't make the cut his first try, and instead of giving up, he took the first step to move forward: he practiced. He didn't know he was going to end up playing in the NBA for the Chicago Bulls, winning six Championships and becoming arguably the best basketball player to ever live. He didn't know that. He may have wanted to be that, but he didn't know that's how things would end up. He just never waited to find out. He started going to work. You have to go to work. Do that, and you'll beat Resistance.

STEP 4 IS TO HAVE CLEAR AND COMPLETE FOCUS.

In marketing, they call it *shiny object syndrome*, but in real life, everything's a shiny object. A new relationship, a new car, a new house, the Facebook message from a long lost friend, or that hilarious tweet from your buddy, and the list goes on and on. All of these things can distract us, but if you're completely focused day in and day out on the tasks that will take you where you want to go and don't allow yourself to be distracted, you'll get there.

STEP 5 IS TO SIMPLY REMOVE DISTRACTIONS.

Use tools that help you stay on task and block out any websites that simply waste your time. Put your phone in the other room while you sleep, so that when you get up in the morning, you don't lie in bed for an hour checking social media sites and your email when you should be getting ready for the day.

STEP 6 IS TO FIND THAT SPECIFIC TIME WHEN YOU'RE MOST PRODUCTIVE.

Make these hours sacred. Protect them with all your might. Don't let anyone or anything take this from you. You'll find you get 10x the amount of work done that you do any other time. Time is the most precious thing you own, and once it's gone, there's no getting it back.

STEP 7 IS JUMP IN.

You have to jump. Take those first steps. Most people will do these first six things, but then they'll never jump in. They'll continue to plan and look for the best strategy or the best technique, but it's amazing how very few actually dive in.

That's where it's going to come together, and that's when things are going to start to move forward fast. People are going to show up, opportunities are going to show up that you never thought possible.

It won't be easy at first and this brings me to step 8.

STEP 8 IS TO PRACTICE DAILY.

It takes three weeks of daily practice for something to become a habit, and once it's a habit, it's hard to break. **If you haven't read the book *Power of Habits - Why we do what we do* by Charles Duhigg, buy it and read it.** You'll understand your habits a lot better and you'll start to identify all the bad habits. Once you're aware of them, you can begin to replace them with good habits, and quickly we can get to where we want to go.

STEP 9 - HIRE A MENTOR.

People say you have to fail and you have to fail fast. I don't believe in that. I believe in finding successful people who have had the monumental failures, then learning from them and not making those same mistakes, but instead modeling their success.

But there's another reason to hire a mentor and it's something that has changed my life. You see, when you doubt yourself, when you're questioning everything you are doing, a mentor will remind you of the greatness within and then push you in the right direction. They will not allow you to give in to Resistance. Often times, when we are buried in our own crap we've surrounded ourselves with, we can't really see what it is we're meant to do, to really see our true calling, or to see the beauty that we possess inside.

The reason I say hire a mentor is not to simply find a mentor, because unless you have some skin in the game, you're not going to respect or listen to the person who is talking to you. If you have a partner, a wife or a husband, then I'm sure you've had the experience where you told them something and yet they didn't listen. Then someone else comes along and tells them the exact same thing and without question they follow that advice. You're left standing there thinking to yourself, what the heck is going on?

It happens all the time, because the closer you are to someone, the less you'll listen to them. When they challenge you and tell you to step your game up, you don't listen to them because you see it as an attack. But when you hire someone and you've paid that person to get you results, you'll listen to them because you believe they're there to support your success. That's why you hired them.

It's time to stop living in fear. Follow these steps, put on your armor every day and start living the life you were destined to lead.

About AJ

Marketing Expert, Best Selling Author and Seminar Leader - AJ Roberts is widely considered one of the 'go to' guys for all things digital marketing. His unique ability to understand what consumers are thinking better than most of them understand themselves, has allowed him to master the process of turning online prospects into paying customers.

AJ manages some of the marketing industry's top brands and events - drawing hundreds of attendees from all around the world, paying thousands of dollars to hear his message and that of his clients. Roberts has shared the stage with Yanik Silver, Brendon Burchard, Cameron Herold, Rohit Bhargava, Catherine Cook, Noah Kagan, Lewis Howes and many more.

To learn more about how you can work with AJ, visit: www.AJRoberts.com

CHAPTER 51

FIVE STEPS TO SKYROCKET YOUR PRODUCTIVITY AND ENJOY YOUR LIFE

BY TJ OOSTERKAMP

You're riding on a dirt road through the Colorado Rocky Mountains at 100 mph. You don't even have your hands on the steering wheel as you are lying on top of the car, frantically struggling to keep your grip on the roof. Does this describe how you feel at work sometimes?

Many entrepreneurs that I meet, train, and coach feel oppressed by all the urgent demands being made on their time. No wonder they're tired. (Though I mainly work with entrepreneurs, you can substitute "manager," "doctor," or "teacher," and many of the same principles apply.)

There was a time when I, too, worked long hours without seeing many results. All my efforts didn't bring me closer to the things I really wanted from life—growth, change, and the feeling of satisfaction.

To fast forward a couple of years, I'm sitting on the beach sipping white wine and writing this chapter, while my team is running the company. The year before last, I enjoyed a nine-month sabbatical, and we're still growing 20 percent year-on-year even in this depressed economic climate.

What changed?

How can an ordinary business owner like me figure out a better way to live and work? How can I claim that if you follow my suggestions, you'll free up two hours every single day for strategy, innovation, and growth?

I call it "Extreme Productivity." And it will probably be different than anything you've previously read about or heard. Most books on the subject promise that if you do what the author has done, you will get the exact same results.

I believe life is much more complex, more interesting, more exhilarating than that—and just copy-pasting someone else's approach isn't the answer. The only way to become extremely productive is to start with—yourself.

I. SPEND YOUR TIME ON THE MOST VALUABLE ACTIVITIES YOU CAN THINK OF

Productivity is essentially a boring concept. It conjures up images of drudgery, working long hours, and tracking how often you go to the bathroom. Creative people like entrepreneurs loathe the idea of too much structure in their spontaneous lives.

And let's be honest, just improving your typing speed 20 times is not going to do the job (though I'll reveal that secret later in this chapter). The secret to becoming extremely productive is much more profound than that.

So, what is it? Productive people make things happen with a minimum of effort. They don't try to outwork the world—they outsmart it. And extreme productivity is even better: adding much more value in the absolute minimal amount of time.

There are many reasons why entrepreneurs find it hard to work more productively: their team isn't functioning well; they have no thought-out strategy (even though they think they have), and most importantly, they have no clear idea of where they personally add the most value to their business.

Extreme productivity means that you put way too much into the things you do, and you need to cut back. There are five ways to do this:

1. Stop doing it
2. Lower the frequency
3. Delegate it
4. Outsource it
5. Optimize it

Once you apply the Pareto principle to everything you do, you'll save loads of time. The principle says that you can change just 20 percent of what you do and get 80 percent of the improvement! So the main work of an entrepreneur is not, in fact, the work itself, but rather thinking about the work. For instance: What are the best tasks for you to just stop doing? And which tasks will you do less frequently in the future—by delegating or outsourcing?

Any activity that has low-added value and can easily be done by somebody else is a no-brainer. So why are you still doing it? Fixing that can easily save you many hours a week.

II. YOU YOURSELF ARE AT THE CORE OF YOUR PRODUCTIVITY

You should feel energized when you are working. If you are not inspired by most of your daily activities, you could be headed towards serious long-term problems. How clear are you on the criteria for deciding what you should or shouldn't be doing?

How would your life be if you knew exactly the people to surround yourself with? Would you enjoy asking a premium rate for your services and having customers line up to pay that price?

If you are clear about who you are as a person, it is much easier to get all of these things done, allowing you to build a business model that fits you like a glove and is more profitable at the same time.

It all starts with knowledge.

It amazes me that business owners spend weeks or months researching their next office building or car but spend zero time researching their most important asset: themselves. And nobody else will do it for you.

There is no way around it—if you want to become extremely productive, you have to study your own personality, your experiences, and your natural talents and gifts.

In another chapter in this book my colleague, Marlene Scott, describes how to do this in the right way. I won't duplicate it, but I do want to stress that you are probably the biggest influence on the success of your company. Investing time, money, and energy on figuring yourself out is a great way to leverage everything you are and have.

A client of ours realized that he shouldn't teach and train himself, but should spend his time figuring out better ways to market his training courses, and then hire others to do the actual delivery. Can you imagine how much bigger his business can get? And he will have a lot more fun and job satisfaction, because figuring out stuff is more interesting for him than delivering training courses. Leverage!

III. DOES WHAT YOU ARE DOING MAKE ANY SENSE TO YOU?

"Results don't determine the worth of people; people determine the worth of results." ~ P.J. Eby

Some days are just boring. You often experience no sense of accomplishment and don't know if you did anything worthwhile. It was just stuff that had to be done. Too many of these days in a row and you'll start suffering from a critical lack of meaning. If anything kills your productivity in the short and long term, this is it.

Life is much more fun if you work on the things that are the most important to you. When you feel that your future is going to be bigger, better, and more beautiful than your past because of the work you did today, life becomes enjoyable.

For that to happen, you need to know exactly what you are trying to achieve in the long term. This is where working hard and working productively can be two very different things. If you are not absolutely clear about those goals, it makes no sense at all to study productivity.

What made you decide to become an entrepreneur? Was it your desire for freedom? And if so, do you now have the freedom you were looking for? Or did you want to make more money? If so—why? Is it purely the number on the screen when you look at your bank account? Or is money a means to something more important for you? If so, does your current business help you achieve that deeper goal?

Instead of focusing on a single goal, in my experience it is a much more interesting creative challenge to figure out everything you want from your business, then create a strategy that satisfies all these goals simultaneously. In the end, it will probably be more lucrative too!

But, at a minimum, you have to decide what those goals are before you can become more productive.

IV. WHAT BOTTLENECKS ARE YOU CONQUERING?

"Plans are useless, but planning is indispensable."
~ Dwight D. Eisenhower

Do you feel you have to work harder than other people to reach your goals? Are your projects struggling? I always enjoy work more when I know I have picked a strategy that has a decent chance of actually working. It's a great way to get you into a winning frame of mind.

If you use the right method to think about a project before you start working on it, that can greatly increase your chances of success. And it makes it much easier to explain or defend your thoughts to your business partner, bank—or spouse.

According to Professor Rummelt, the best way to start building a strategy is to first figure out which obstacles are in the way of reaching your goals. And then find a way to remove them.

We have found that, with our clients, the easiest way to identify these obstacles is to build a special cause-effect diagram to get to the root of the problems. This analysis, based on the Theory of Constraints by Eli Goldratt, helps to focus your thinking and share it with others so they can contribute too.

I will never forget one meeting where we were helping a client analyze why their new company that they had been building for three years was failing. The tree helped them pinpoint one surprising, but very clear bottleneck.

Once you know what the bottlenecks are, I'd advise you to draw up three to ten completely different scenarios to solve these problems. That forces you and your brain to come up with creative approaches.

You can then combine the best aspects from these scenarios into one winning strategy.

V. TWO FAIRLY EXTREME TIPS TO MAKE THE MOST OF YOUR TEAM (AND YOUR TIME).

I could write a separate book about selecting the right people and delegating to them effectively. But there are two measures that I have implemented with a great deal of success to free up my own time. First, I required my team to send only "yes or no" emails. Instead of describing a problem and waiting for my decision, they were to send emails in which they were already suggesting a specific course of action. If I agreed, I would just reply "yes." This has saved me hours and hours of valuable time, and, simultaneously, made my team accept a much higher level of responsibility.

Then I told them that they could not email me any more at all. This scared them initially, but has worked out great! I now schedule weekly meetings where I meet with each one, who directly reports to me for 20 minutes. I put a kitchen timer on my desk, and they bring a list of the items they want to discuss, sorted on priority and urgency. But they still have to propose solutions. Now, all the practical stuff is taken care of in a single Monday afternoon. This frees up so much of my time for more valuable tasks that hardly anyone would believe my schedule now.

Unfortunately, many entrepreneurs never delegate enough because they struggle with perfectionism. This eventually becomes a curse, because you are doomed to do everything perfectly for the rest of your life. The best way to beat this problem is to focus your quest for perfection on the creation of a perfect team that can do all their jobs well.

HOW TO TYPE 20 TIMES FASTER – WITH NO EXTRA TRAINING

Even when you have a great team, optimizing tasks can bring a huge increase in your own productivity, mainly because cutting down on administrative trivia allows you to focus more and improve your flow.

For instance, in my book *Outsmart Outlook*, I explain how to set up Microsoft Outlook® for maximum productivity. It turns out that by making a couple of small changes, you can clear your inbox in half the time. That by itself could save you an hour per day!

Also, tools like Fingertips or Typinator enable you to create acronyms for some often-used phrases. You'll never have to type the 62 characters of the phrase "Please let me know if there is anything else I can do for you" again. Instead, you just enter the three characters "lmk," hit the spacebar, and, magically, the acronym is replaced by the full phrase. This saves you 59 keystrokes! And the slower your current typing speed, the more time you save.

But it is not just technical tips and tricks that may benefit you. Name one action or project that you know you've got to do, but keep procrastinating on, and I'll show you how your emotions are a much bigger driver of productivity than most people realize. Building emotional intelligence and skills may help improve your productivity even more.

WELCOME TO HO'OKIPA BEACH

Life goes by in a blur when you are not productive enough and yet still putting everything into your business. No time to spend with your children, family, or friends. Too much stress in your body and no way to know when it will end.

Personally, I enjoy sitting in the sun, sipping a cafe solo, knowing that everything is running smoothly at the office.

Wouldn't it be great for you to have the luxury to freely discuss new business opportunities with friends? Or just to hang out and enjoy a day of surfing on Maui's Ho'okipa Beach? Or to be able to ponder new challenges like figuring ways to add some more value as entrepreneurs to places where people now live in extreme poverty?

If there were ever reasons to disregard play and relaxation, being extremely productive is definitely not one of them. Your business needs you to have time off, where your subconscious mind can experience some distance to generate new ideas, solve problems, and gain a new perspective on everything.

So force yourself to take a break at least one day each week. No computer, no business books, no strategizing—no excuses.

BE WHO YOU ARE

Becoming an extremely productive entrepreneur or manager is not a task for the faint of heart. It requires a fair amount of soul-searching, thinking, discussions, and experimentation. Anyone who tells you differently is not worth listening to.

You are a unique individual, and there is no way to prescribe from the outside what you should be doing to add the most value to your world in the least amount of time. In the end, you'll need to base your approach on becoming who you already are, instead of trying to imitate the success of others.

This, certainly, is much more fun than just following a textbook approach. And it's worth the investment of your time, money, and energy. After all, being on top of your world certainly beats lying on top of your speeding car!

About TJ

Are you an entrepreneur and do you feel that you are working way too hard? Are the results you see not in line with all the time and effort that you put into your business? Did you envision success in a totally different way than how your work and life have turned out to be right now?

TJ's clients, one after another, have found that in working with him it is possible to work less, have serious fun, and make a lot more money. It all comes down to working based on who you are, instead of working according to somebody else's ideas.

Most business owners start their company with a great deal of enthusiasm, based on an idea, an ability to solve problems for their customers, and a lot of energy to make it all happen.

But as the business grows, it becomes much harder to spend time on important and enjoyable work, such as creativity, strategy, innovation, and growth. Instead, your business starts to feel like a job in which you spend most of your time on stuff that needs to be done, but drains your energy levels. Things like selecting, hiring, and firing employees. Or, having to put up with a lot of red tape and just plain boring administrative stuff. At the end of the day, you drag yourself home, ready for another night of overtime work. And worst of all, there seems to be no way out!

As a long-time entrepreneur, best-selling author, and productivity expert, TJ Oosterkamp loves to help entrepreneurs to optimize their productivity. Together with his friend and colleague, Marlene Scott, he developed a proven system to help business owners free up two hours every day for strategy, innovation, and growth.

It all started when TJ wrote a book about how to process your email in half the time. Together with his team, he inspired and trained professionals in businesses of all sizes, from small companies to multi-billion dollar enterprises like AkzoNobel, Vodafone, BDO, Boston Scientific, Damen Shipyards, Hennes & Mauritz, Heinz, ING Bank, KLM Air France, Toyota, Nestle, Pepsi Co, Philips, Reed Elsevier, Ricoh, and Unilever.

But TJ finds that he enjoys his work most when he trains and coaches business owners who know that they themselves are the bottleneck in the growth and transformation of their business. They are men and women who want to beat the system and figure out better strategies to do things from their own personality. They want to learn better ways to work with employees, freelancers, and suppliers—loving simple tricks to get the most out of everything. They are business owners who don't want to just improve their email, but also want to improve anything that moves!

If that's you,
please surf to: www.FridaysOff.net

www.FridaysOff.net